Life and Health

1st Edition

License Exam Manual

Important: Check for Updates

States sometimes revise their exam content outlines unexpectedly or on short notice. To see whether there is an update for this product because of an exam change, go to **www.kaplanfinancial.com**. Any updated study material for your state insurance exam is located in the Updates/Errata icon on your course dashboard.

At press time, this edition contains the most complete and accurate information currently available. Owing to the nature of license examinations, however, information may have been added recently to the actual test that does not appear in this edition. Please contact the publisher to verify that you have the most current edition.

This publication is designed to provide accurate and authoritative information in regard to the subject matter covered. It is sold with the understanding that the publisher is not engaged in rendering legal, accounting, or other professional services. If legal advice or other expert assistance is required, the services of a competent professional should be sought.

LIFE AND HEALTH LICENSE EXAM MANUAL, 1ST EDITION

©2017 Kaplan, Inc.

The text of this publication, or any part thereof, may not be reproduced in any manner whatsoever without written permission from the publisher.

If you find imperfections or incorrect information in this product, please visit www.kaplanfinancial.com and submit an errata report.

Published in March 2017 by Kaplan Financial Education.

Revised December 2020.

Printed in the United States of America.

10   9   8   7   6   5   4   3   2

ISBN: 978-1-4754-5644-8

Contents

U N I T   1 3   **Affordable Care Act   271**

U N I T   1 4   **Health Insurance Policy Provisions   293**

U N I T   1 5   **Disability Income Insurance   317**

Introduction

Please read this important letter from the Kaplan team before you start your studies!

Thank you for choosing Kaplan Financial Education to assist with your preparation for the state insurance licensing exam. Our goal is provide you with the information needed in order to learn the language of insurance.

We want you to pass your state exam the **FIRST** time.

Here are some important things to know as you start your studies:

Do I need to read this entire book?

Absolutely! This book is designed around the state licensing exam. Each testing provider distributes an exam content outline which lists all testable topics that could appear on the state exam. You can find this outline on your dashboard in your online tools. You may not get questions on every single possible topic; however you need to be prepared in case that you do.

How is this book organized?

In order to make this book flexible and easy to use each unit is organized in the same way. There is an introduction to the unit, learning objectives, detailed text, and summarized text with a graphic that is used in the classroom or for self-study students. There is a cram sheet, quick quizzes, and a unit quiz that will test you for understanding. Answer keys are provided at the end of each unit for the quick quiz and unit quiz.

What is a cram sheet?

Cram sheets focus on very specific details of each unit. The information is presented throughout the unit and put together at the end of the unit in an easy to understand list.

How do I use this book?

This book includes general insurance information and information that is specific to life and health insurance. Depending on the exam that you are taking you may only need to study a portion of the book. Here is the breakdown by units:

LH Units	Life	Health
1—General Insurance	X	X
2—Life/Health Insurance Underwriting	X	X
3—Basics of Life Insurance	X	
4—Types of Life Insurance Policies	X	
5—Life Insurance Policy Riders	X	
6—Life Insurance Policy Options	X	
7—Life Insurance Policy Provisions	X	
8—Group Life Insurance	X	
9—Annuities	X	
10—Taxation of Life Insurance and Annuities	X	
11—Retirement Plans	X	
12—Introduction to Health Insurance		X
13—Affordable Care Act		X
14—Health Insurance Policy Provisions		X
15—Disability Income Insurance		X
16—Medical Expense Plans		X
17—Other Health Plans		X
18—Group Health Insurance		X
19—Dental Insurance		X
20—Medicare and Medicaid		X
21—Long-Term Care		X
22—Taxation of Health Insurance		X

Does this book include state specific laws and regulations?

No. This book includes general information that is applicable is most states. All state and some federal information can be found in the Law Supplement.

How long do I need to study?

Depending on the state that you are in, you may be required to study for a certain number of hours. In most cases we recommend 40 hours of focused study time. Before you start your studies, build a customized study calendar based on the number of days that you have to study before you plan to sit for your state exam. This calendar can be found in your dashboard in your online tools.

What if I have content related questions during my studies?

If you purchased a package that includes online tools, you have access to our InstructorLink™*. These online instructional resources provide important direction, references, and answers to questions, helping you to prepare fully for the state exam. You also have access to insurance licensing content specialists directly via email for content related advice. Emails are typically answered within one business day.

IMPORTANT: Check for Updates

States sometimes revise their exam content outlines unexpectedly or on short notice. We suggest that you check for updates when you first receive the course, again during your study period, upon completion of your studies, and one last time just before you take your insurance license exam. Updates are located in your online tools on the dashboard.

This book was written by industry professionals, and contains topics included in the multiple-choice questions presented on the state exam. By following the learning format presented in this text and utilizing the additional Kaplan study tools found online, you will enhance and reinforce the knowledge required for state exam success.

Good Luck!

UNIT 1) General Insurance

1.1 INTRODUCTION

When you enter the insurance industry, regardless of your role, you will need to know many things including the purpose of each policy, the claims settlement process, and the language of insurance including important terms, definitions, and concepts. Understanding insurance is like putting a puzzle together piece by piece.

Unit One introduces you to terms and insurance concepts; the border of the puzzle. The definitions in this unit represent the framework for the remainder of the course and are highly tested on the state exam. Important words and content are bolded in the text and a glossary is located in the back of this book to assist you with the learning process.

Throughout this course you will study the pieces of the insurance puzzle and they will build a solid foundation for passing your insurance licensing exam. When you begin studying you might struggle with the content and the language, but like a puzzle, completing all the units will form the entire picture.

⌖ 1.2   LEARNING OBJECTIVES

After successfully completing this lesson, you should be able to:

- define insurance, loss, and exposure;
- identify two types of risk;
- identify three types of hazards;
- give examples of a peril;
- identify the five ways of managing risk;
- describe the parties to an insurance contract;
- define the law of large numbers, adverse selection, reinsurance;
- identify the six elements of an insurable risk;
- identify the eight types of insurers;
- compare private versus government insurers;
- identify domestic, foreign, and alien insurers;
- identify authorized (admitted) versus unauthorized (non-admitted) insurers;
- explain surplus lines insurers;
- explain financial ratings of insurers;
- identify the four agency systems of insurance marketing and distribution;
- identify the direct response system of insurance marketing and distribution;
- define the law of agency, agent, and principal;
- identify the three types of producer authority;
- identify a producer's fiduciary responsibility to applicants/insureds;
- describe the four elements of a legal insurance contract and how those elements apply in an insurance transaction; and
- identify examples of the thirteen distinct characteristics of insurance contracts.

1.3   DEFINITIONS

An insurance policy is a legal contract and the terminology can be confusing. This unit will address common insurance terms and provide realistic examples to help you understand the definitions.

Insurance is a contract that <u>transfers the risk</u> of financial loss from an individual or business to an insurer. In return the insurer agrees to cover the individual or business for certain losses if they occur.

Risk is uncertainty about whether a loss will occur. If a loss is certain to occur, it does not involve risk. Insurance is designed to cover only losses that involve risk. In regard to life insurance, although death is certain to occur to everyone, the timing of that loss is uncertain.

Insurance = transfer of risk

Risk = uncertainty

There are two types of risk: *speculative risk* and *pure risk*. **Speculative** risks have a possibility of a loss and also hold the possibility of making a gain. Insurance companies will not insure gambling losses or investments because someone could win money or you could lose money, these are examples of **speculative risks.**

Pure risks, on the other hand, only involve the possibility of experiencing a loss and they can be covered by insurance. The chance of being in a car accident is an example of a pure risk.

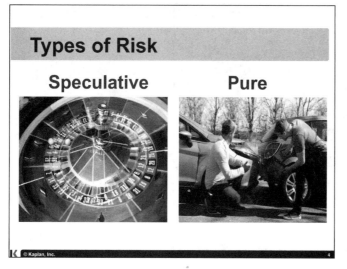

Types of Risk

- Speculative risk–loss or gain can occur–loss is NOT INSURABLE
- Pure risk–only loss can occur– loss IS INSURABLE

Loss is a reduction in the value of an asset. To determine the amount of a loss, the value of the asset is measured before and after the loss.

Loss

Value Before Loss
— Value After Loss
_____
Total amount of loss

© Kaplan, Inc.

Loss–reduction in value of an asset

Exposure is the risk assumed by an insurer and the amount that the insurer is responsible to pay out at any given time. Exposure is expressed in units. For example, the unit for life insurance exposure is $1,000 of death benefit and premium rates apply per unit of exposure.

The calculation for insurance premiums is the rate multiplied by the number of exposure units. For example: if the life insurance rate is $32 per $1,000 of death benefit, the premium for a $100,000 policy would be $32 x $100 = $3,200.

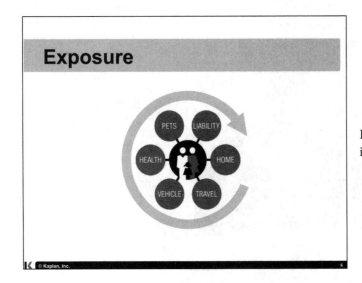

Exposure

PETS LIABILITY
HEALTH HOME
VEHICLE TRAVEL

© Kaplan, Inc.

Exposure–risks for which the insurance company would be liable

A **peril** is a cause of loss. The insurer agrees to cover losses caused by a specified peril. For life insurance, the peril is death. For health insurance, the perils are accidents or illness. For example, if a house burns down, the peril (cause of loss) is the fire. If electronics in a home are destroyed because of lightning, the cause of loss (peril) is lightning. If you drive your car through a hailstorm and the car's body is damaged, the peril is hail. A peril is simply what caused the loss.

A **hazard** is anything that increases the chance that a loss will occur. Hazards do not cause the loss. When you think of the term hazard, think of something that becomes more dangerous and can make a loss more likely to happen. Think of hazards in the same way you parent a child. When the parent says to their child, "Get down before you get hurt!" the parent recognizes a higher chance of the child getting hurt based on what they are doing and, for that reason, the chance of getting hurt is increased.

Hazards do not cause losses, but they make a loss more likely.

There are three types of hazards: *physical, moral,* and *morale.* As their name implies, physical hazards are physically identifiable factors that increase the chance of loss.

In life and health insurance, a heart condition is a **physical hazard** because it is physically identifiable using lab equipment that produces tangible evidence of its existence.

Moral hazards arise from an individual's character. Dishonesty is a moral hazard because it increases the chance that an individual might lie on an insurance application or fake a loss.

Morale hazards are a state of mind or careless attitude. In common usage, a morale hazard is an unconscious change in a person's actions or behaviors, versus a deliberate change with the intent to cheat or benefit from such circumstances. An example of a morale hazard is the insured carelessly leaving the doors and windows unlocked when not at home.

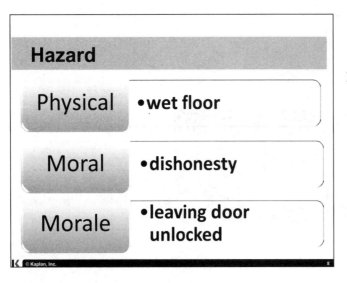

Hazard

- An increase in the chance of loss
  - Physical hazard–can be seen or determined
  - Moral hazard–intentionally causing a loss
  - Morale hazard–carelessness

1.4   METHODS OF HANDLING RISK

There are a number of methods for handling risk. It is easy to remember them by thinking of the acronym STARR.

Sharing—In risk sharing, two or more individuals agree to pay a portion of any loss incurred by any member in the group. Stockholders in a corporation share the risk of profit or loss.

Transfer—Transfer of risk is what happens with insurance. The insurer agrees to pay if an individual or business has a loss. The individual or business has a cost in the form of a premium payment. However, in contrast to the loss, which is large and uncertain, the premium is a much smaller certainty.

Insurance companies use the risk management method of transfer to spread a risk of loss among thousands if not millions of insureds. Not everyone will experience an accident while they own an insurance policy. The large number of insureds who do not have an accident will be paying for the losses of the few who do have an accident. This is the only way that insurance can work and make the premiums affordable.

Avoidance—Risk avoidance means eliminating a particular risk by not engaging in a certain activity. For example, an individual who does not drive avoids the risk of injuring someone in a collision and being held liable for those damages (e.g., work from home if the roads are covered in ice).

Reduction—Risk reduction may refer to lessening the chance that a loss will occur, or to lessening the extent of a loss that does occur. For example, wearing seatbelts reduces the severity of a car accident; installing a smoke alarm will not prevent a fire, but it may keep individuals from serious harm.

Retention—Risk retention means the individual will pay for the loss if it occurs. Without health insurance a person will have to pay the bill if they need hospitalization. This is an example of intentionally retaining a risk.

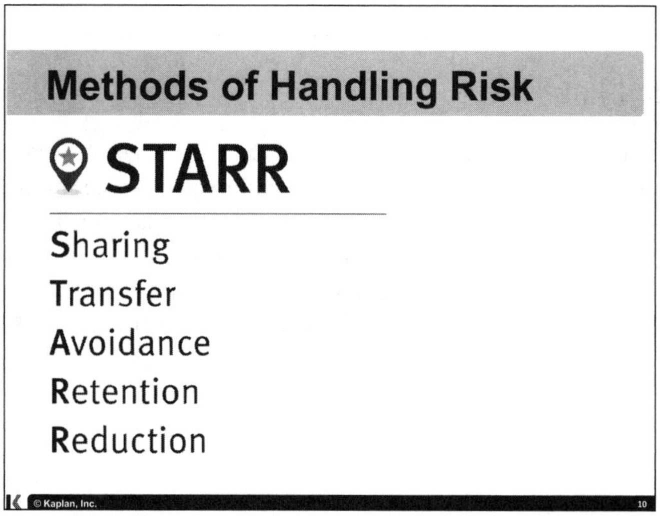

Methods of Handling Risk

⊙ **STARR**

Sharing
Transfer
Avoidance
Retention
Reduction

© Kaplan, Inc.   10

STARR!

- <u>S</u>haring
- <u>T</u>ransfer
- <u>A</u>voidance
- <u>R</u>etention
- <u>R</u>eduction

QUICK QUIZ 1.A

1. If a fire causes damage to a building, the fire is a
   A. hazard
   B. peril
   C. risk
   D. exposure

2. Wearing a seat belt in a car is an example of which method of managing risk?
   A. Retain
   B. Avoid
   C. Reduce
   D. Transfer

3. Tiffany leaves her car unlocked when she goes shopping. She figures her car and the contents are insured so there is no reason to worry. Which type of hazard is this an example of?
   A. Physical
   B. Morale
   C. Careless
   D. Moral

Answers can be found at the end of Unit 1.

1.5 OTHER INSURANCE CONCEPTS

1.5.1 The Law of Large Numbers

The Law of Large Numbers is the principle that makes insurance possible. The larger the group, the more accurately losses can be predicted. Insurance companies cover millions of people and businesses. It is impossible to guess specifically who will suffer a loss in the future, but thanks to the law of large numbers, they can be fairly certain how many losses will occur in the group as a whole. While insurance companies cannot specifically name which individuals will have a loss each year; they can predict fairly accurately how many dollars in claims they will have to pay out each year based on the actual losses they experienced in the past. This prediction allows them to charge each insured a premium that, pooled together, will cover all claims and operating costs.

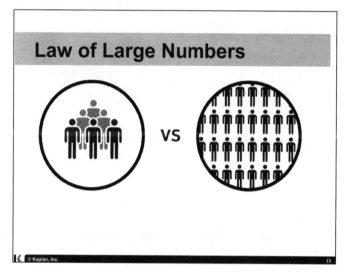

Law of Large Numbers

The larger the group—the more accurate losses can be predicted

1.5.2 Elements of Insurable Risk

Not all risks are insurable. Risks that can be insured have the following characteristics. It is easy to remember them by thinking of the acronym CANHAM.

1. **Calculable**—Premiums must be calculable based upon prior loss statistics for that particular risk in order to predict future losses.

2. **Affordable**—The premium for transferring the risk should be affordable for the average consumer.

3. **Non-catastrophic**—Insurance cannot insure events that cause widespread losses to large numbers of insureds at the same time. That is why the peril of war is excluded from most policies because the risk is much too large for the insurance company to pay.

4. **Homogeneous**—The individual risks that the insurer covers must all be similar, or homogeneous, in regard to factors that affect the chance of loss.

5. **Accidental**—Insurance is a method of handling risk. If a loss is certain to occur, there is no risk.

6. **Measurable**—It must be possible to estimate the loss as a dollar amount. Insurance covers the financial loss of unexpected death or medical bills from sickness.

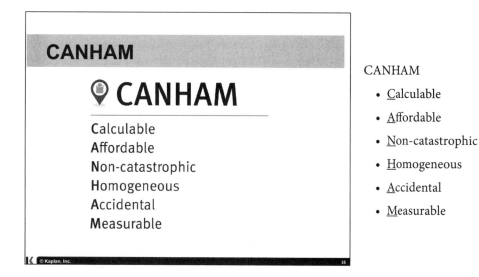

CANHAM

- <u>C</u>alculable
- <u>A</u>ffordable
- <u>N</u>on-catastrophic
- <u>H</u>omogeneous
- <u>A</u>ccidental
- <u>M</u>easurable

1.5.3   Adverse Selection

Adverse selection is the tendency for higher-risk individuals to get and keep insurance more than individuals who represent an average level of risk. The statistics insurers use to predict their losses are based on average risks. Adverse selection could cause the insurance company to experience more losses than predicted. It increases the chance that they have not collected enough premiums to pay for their losses.

To avoid adverse selection, insurers make an extensive evaluation of information related to a particular risk—a process called *underwriting*. If an underwriter determines that a risk is higher than average, the insurer may charge a higher rate to insure the risk, limit the amount of coverage it will issue on the risk, or refuse the application for insurance altogether.

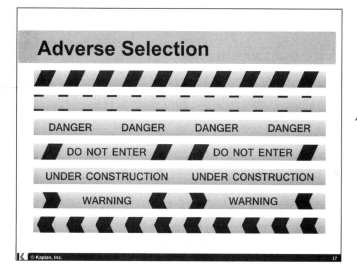

Adverse Selection

- Risks that have a greater than average chance of loss

1.5.4   Reinsurance

Reinsurance is like insurance for insurers. It transfers risk from one insurer to another insurer. To reduce the total amount of loss it is liable for, one insurer may pay the other insurer a premium to assume a portion of its risk. The company reducing its risk is called the *ceding* insurer. The company assuming the risk is called the *reinsurer*.

Example: Insuring risks in certain geographical areas may expose the insurer to the potential of having to pay for a large number of losses at one time. This may happen due to such things as earthquake or hurricane. To protect the company from these catastrophic losses, the insurer pays a premium to another insurer to transfer some or all of its risks in these areas. The company accepting the risk is called the reinsurer. There are two ways this process can work.

1. The reinsurer considers each risk before allowing the transfer to be made from the ceding company. This is called **facultative** reinsurance.

2. The reinsurer accepts all risks of a certain type from the ceding company. This is called **treaty** reinsurance

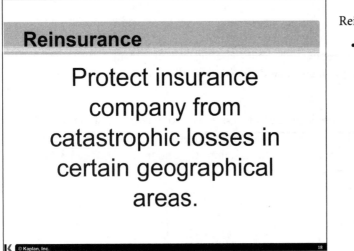

Reinsurance

- An insurance company (the ceding company) paying another insurance company (reinsurer) to take some of the companies risk of catastrophic loss

  - Facultative–the reinsurer evaluates each risk before allowing the transfer

  - Treaty–the reinsurer accepts the transfer according to an agreement called a treaty

1.6   TYPES OF INSURERS

1.6.1   Stock Insurers

A **stock insurer** is a business formed as a public or private corporation and owned by its stockholders, also known as shareholders. The board of directors that oversees the operation of the company is chosen by the stockholders/shareholders. Profits from the insurance operation may be distributed to the stockholders as dividends. The policies issued by stock insurers are called *non-participating*, or *non-par*, policies to distinguish them from the participating policies issued by mutual insurers (covered next).

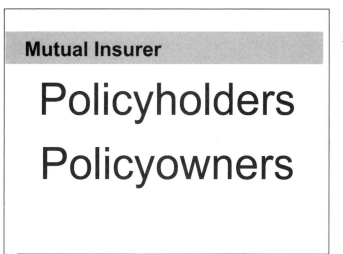

Stock Insurer

- Owned by stockholders/ shareholders
- Board of directors chosen by the stockholders/shareholders
- If the company makes money, a taxable dividend from the profits may be paid to the stockholders/ shareholders
- Issues non-par policies

1.6.2 Mutual Insurers

A **mutual insurer** does not have stock or stockholders. It is owned by its policyholders, also known as policyowners. They elect a board of directors that in turn appoints the officers who operate the company. Funds that remain after paying claims and operating costs may be distributed to the policyowners as policy dividends. Mutual policy dividends are considered to be a non-taxable return of excess premium. Mutual policies are referred to as *participating*, or *par*, policies because the policyowners participate in the operating results of the company.

Mutual Insurer

- Owned by the policyholders (customers)
- Board of directors chosen by the policyholders
- If the company is profitable, excess premiums can be returned to its policyholders– nontaxable dividend
- Issues participating (par) policies

1.6.3 Fraternal Benefit Societies

Fraternal benefit societies exist for the benefit of its members and offer life insurance as one of the benefits of membership. Fraternals also provide social activities and usually engage in charitable and benevolent causes. Fraternals are organized under a lodge system and receive some income tax advantages. They operate their insurance programs under a special section of the state insurance code. Fraternal policies are called *certificates*, and members who own life insurance are called *certificate holders*. A distinctive feature of fraternal life insurance is that certificate holders may be assessed additional charges if premiums are not sufficient to pay claims during a given period. Policies with this feature are referred to as *open contracts*. By comparison, mutual and stock insurers are not assessable and are sometimes referred to as *legal reserve* companies.

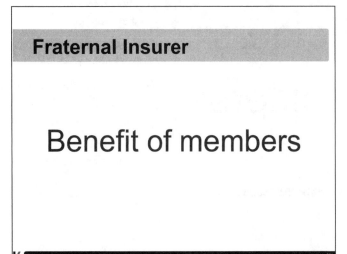

Fraternal Insurer

- Provides insurance and other benefits
- Must be a member of the society to get the benefits

1.6.4   Reciprocal Insurers

Reciprocal insurers are unincorporated groups of people that agree to insure each other's losses under a contract. The members of the reciprocal groups are known as *subscribers*. Each subscriber has an account through which premiums are paid and earned interest is tracked. If any subscriber suffers a loss covered by the reciprocal insurance agreement, each subscriber account is assessed an equal amount to pay the claim. Administration, underwriting, sales promotion, and claims handling for the reciprocal insurance are handled by an *attorney-in-fact*. The attorney-in-fact is often controlled and overseen by an advisory committee of subscribers.

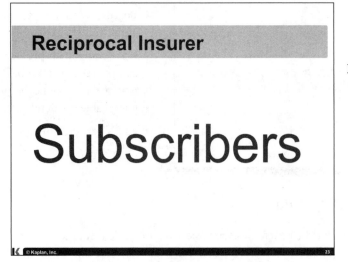

Reciprocal Insurer

- Unincorporated
- Members are assessed the amount they have to pay if a loss to any member of the group occurs
- Run by an attorney-in-fact

1.6.5   Risk Retention Groups

A **risk retention group (called a RRG)** is an insurer formed for the sole purpose of providing liability insurance to its policyholders. An RRG is owned by the insureds or members. The policyholders must all be members of the same type of business. They are regulated by the state where they are headquartered; however, they can operate in other states as well.

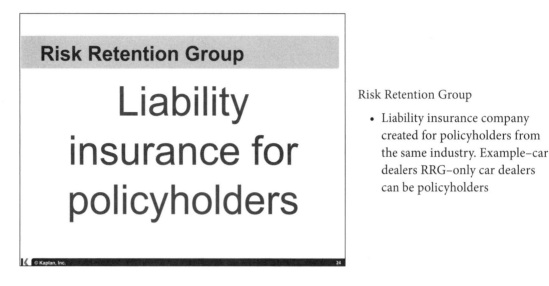

Risk Retention Group

- Liability insurance company created for policyholders from the same industry. Example–car dealers RRG–only car dealers can be policyholders

1.6.6   Lloyd's Associations

Lloyd's Associations, named in reference to the famous underwriting group Lloyd's of London, are not insurance companies. Rather, they provide a hub for the exchange of information among member underwriters who actually transact the business of insurance. Members are individually liable and responsible for the contracts of insurance into which they enter.

Over the years, Lloyd's Associations have insured unusual risks such as hole-in-one contests, the hair of athletes, and the body parts of celebrities. Most Lloyd Association insurance needs to be sold by surplus lines intermediaries because they are only licensed in a few states.

Lloyd's Association

- Insurance provided by individual underwriters, not insurance companies

1.6.7   Self-Insurers

Self-insurance is a means of retaining, rather than transferring, risk. Businesses may develop a formal program for self-insuring all or a portion of certain risks. They set aside savings to cover losses in advance and may even have a claim system like an insurance company. They often contract with an insurance company to manage the day-to-day operation of the business.

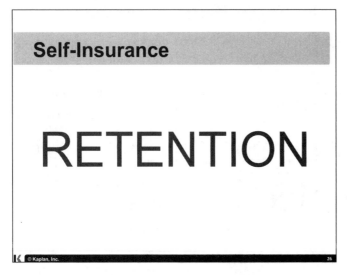

Self-Insurance

- A business that pays its own claims

1.7   CLASSIFICATION OF INSURERS

1.7.1   Private vs. Government Insurers

The types of insurers we have described so far are all insurers that operate in the private sector. In addition to private sector insurers, various government entities may also provide insurance to the public or to certain government employees.

The federal government provides a wide variety of insurance benefits through a number of programs. These include Social Security benefits, military life insurance benefits, federal employee compensation benefits, and various retirement benefit programs. It also provides, supports, or subsidizes a number of insurance programs designed to cover catastrophic risks, including insurance for war risks, flood, and crop losses.

At the state level, governments are involved in providing unemployment insurance, workers' compensation insurance, disability insurance, and medical insurance for the needy. Local governments also participate in providing medical, disability, and retirement benefits.

Residual Market

State or federal?

© Kaplan, Inc.   28

Residual Market

- Insurance from the state or federal government

1.7.2   Domestic, Foreign, and Alien Insurers

Depending on where an insurer is incorporated, it is classified as being **domestic**, **foreign**, or **alien**.

- In its home state–that is, the state in which the insurer was formed (chartered or incorporated) and is headquartered–an insurer is referred to as *domestic* insurer. An insurer's home state is also called its state of *domicile*.

- An insurer that writes business in states other than where it is domiciled is referred to as a foreign insurer. For example, an insurer that is located in Texas, but is selling insurance in Wisconsin, is considered foreign.

- An insurer formed under the laws of any country other than the United States and its territories is considered an *alien* insurer. To citizens of the United States or any U.S. territory such as Puerto Rico, an insurer based in any other country is an alien insurer.

The following illustration provides a visual treatment of these classifications.

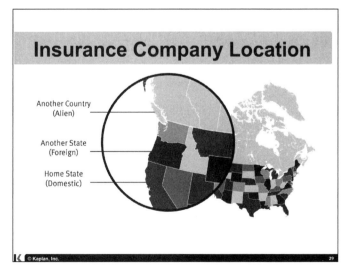

Insurance Company Location

Another Country (Alien)

Another State (Foreign)

Home State (Domestic)

© Kaplan, Inc.   29

Insurance Company Location

- Domestic–the state where a company is incorporated

- Foreign–any state or U.S. territory other than the state where incorporated

- Alien–incorporated in any country other than USA

1.7.3   Authorized vs. Unauthorized Insurers

States usually require companies to have a license to sell insurance in the state. The license is called a Certificate of Authority. When a company is licensed it is called admitted or authorized.

Some states allow companies to sell insurance to certain types of risks (called surplus) without having to have a license. These companies are then called nonadmitted, unauthorized, or nonapproved.

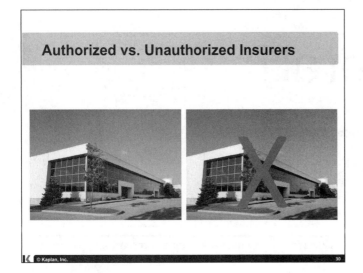

- Certificate of Authority–state license for an insurance company
- Admitted, authorized, or approved–state requires the insurance company to have a Certificate of Authority
- Non-admitted, unauthorized, nonapproved–insurance company not required to have a Certificate of Authority from the state

1.7.4   Surplus Lines Insurers

Sometimes an individual or a business will have an exceptionally large or specialized risk that no authorized insurer can or will cover. In such cases, insurance may be obtained from an unauthorized/ non-admitted insurer on a **surplus lines** basis. Surplus lines insurance is placed with a non-admitted carrier by a surplus lines agent or broker.

Surplus lines insurance can only be transacted according to certain rules governing that type of business. For example, states keep lists of acceptable surplus lines insurers and the insurer through which surplus lines coverage is obtained. There are also rules that do not allow surplus lines insurance to be purchased only to get a cheaper rate when the insurance is available from an authorized insurer.

Surplus lines insurance is also called *excess and surplus lines* because in some cases a limited amount of coverage is available from an authorized insurer, and only the excess is obtained through the surplus lines insurer.

Gaming, casinos and entertainment, mining, and skyscrapers are all examples of exposures that might require surplus lines insurance.

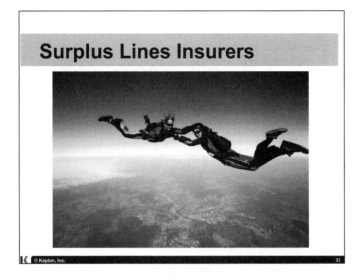

Surplus Lines

- Insurance sold by unauthorized/non-admitted insurers– if on the states approved list of surplus insurers
- Can only be sold to certain high risk insureds
- Can't be sold just for a cheaper rate than licensed/admitted insurers

1.7.5   Financial Ratings of Insurers

Insurers may also be classified according to their financial strength. There are several independent rating agencies that evaluate various factors such as an insurer's loss experience, reserves, investment performance, management, and operating expenses. They then assign an insurer a rating based on that analysis.

The organizations that rate insurers include AM Best, Inc., Standard & Poor's Insurance Rating Services, Moody's Investors Service, Duff & Phelps Credit Rating Company, and Weiss Ratings. These firms do not all rate every company, and each firm has different criteria on which companies are evaluated. Each firm also uses a different rating scale.

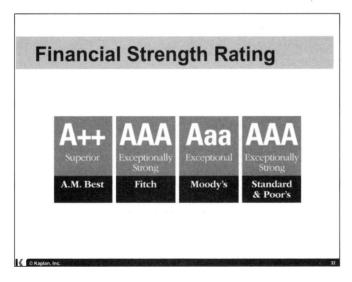

Financial strength rating–a report card of the company

QUICK QUIZ 1.B

1. An insurance company incorporated in Wisconsin and conducting business in Wisconsin is known as a domestic company. What kind of company are they considered if they do business in Minnesota?

   A. Alien

   B. Domestic

   C. Foreign

   D. Nonadmitted

2. All of the following statements about a stock insurance company are true EXCEPT

   A. a stock company sells stock to stockholders

   B. a stock company is a participating company

   C. a stock company is a nonparticipating company

   D. a stock company has shareholders

3. What do insurance companies use to help predict how many losses will occur in a group or class of individuals?

   A. The law of large numbers

   B. Standard and Poor's insurance rating service

   C. Risk retention groups

   D. Adverse selection

4. States require companies to have a license to sell insurance in the state. The license is called

   A. a certificate of authority

   B. a reinsurance license

   C. a producer's license

   D. an admittance license

Answers can be found at the end of Unit 1.

1.8   INSURANCE MARKETING OR DISTRIBUTION SYSTEMS

The following are descriptions of several different systems insurers use to market or distribute their products to the public.

1.8.1   Agency Systems

Most insurers sell their product through insurance producers, or *agents*. There are four different types of agents.

Independent insurance agents sell the insurance products of several companies and work for themselves or other agents. Independent agents own the expirations of the policies they sell, meaning the agent may place that business with another insurer upon renewal if it is in the best interest of the client to do so. These agents represent the insured (client).

Exclusive or captive agents represent only one company. These agents are sometimes referred to as career agents working from career agencies. Most often, these captive or career agents are compensated by commissions. The agents represent the insurer (insurance company).

General agents (GAs) or managing general agents (MGAs) hire, train, and supervise other agents within a specific geographical area. GAs and MGAs receive overriding commissions (overrides) on the business produced by the agents they manage.

Direct-writing companies usually pay salaries to employees whose job function is to sell the company's insurance products from a company office. This type of producer is not usually paid a commission and the insurer owns all of the business produced.

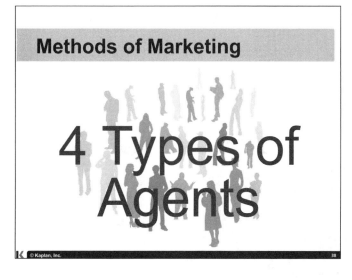

Methods of Marketing

- Independent agents–sales are made by agents/producers who represent more than one company.

- Exclusive or captive agents–sell for one company

- General agent/ managing general agent–recruits other agents in a certain area who actually sell the insurance to the customer.

- Direct writing–the company sells the insurance through salaried employees of the company

1.8.2 Direct Response

In **direct response** marketing, there is no producer/agent. Policies are sold directly to the public by the insurer. Direct response marketing is conducted through the mail, by advertisements in newspapers and magazines, on television and radio or through the internet.

Direct Response

- No agent/producer involved

1.9   LAW OF AGENCY

Agency is a relationship in which one person is authorized to represent and act for another person or for a corporation. The person authorized to act on behalf of the other is called an **agent.** The person on whose behalf the agent acts is called the **principal**. In insurance, the insurer is the principal and the sales representative or producer is the agent. An agency relationship is created by the consent of both the agent and the principal.

Under the law of agency, contracts made by the agent are considered to be contracts of the principal. When the employer/principal provides specific directions and exerts more control over an individual/agents' job duties, then an agency relationship may exist. Payments made to an agent, within the scope of the agent's authority, are considered to be received by the principal. The knowledge of the agent is assumed to be the knowledge of the principal. Therefore, the principal is liable for the statements and actions of their agents.

Agency

- Insurance agent acts on behalf of the principal (insurance company)

1.9.1   Agent Authority

Under the law of agency, there are three types of authority: **express**, **implied**, and **apparent**.

Express authority is the authority made explicit in a producer's *written* agency agreement with the insurer. Express authority is the wording in the contract that specifically tells the producer what they can and cannot do. For example, if the producer is given express authority to write a $100,000 life insurance policy, he cannot write a $105,000 policy.

Implied authority is not written in the agency contract, but it is assumed to be granted to an agent in accordance with general business practices. For example, an agent's contract may not say in writing that the agent has the right to print business cards with the insurer's logo on them, but this authority is implied by allowing the agent to act on the insurer's behalf. Implied authority is power that the *agent believes he or she has* because it is necessary for the agent to conduct the business of the insurer.

Apparent authority is authority that *others believe the agent has.* If the insurer's name is on the sign at the agent's place of business, and the agent takes applications for the insurer's policies, then the agent apparently has the insurer's authority to conduct its business as far as the public is concerned. Sometimes, agents may act with apparent authority that the insurer did not intend the agent to have. But the insurer may still be bound by those actions if the agent's apparent authority creates a *presumption of agency* in the mind of the insured. For example, if an agent sends an insured an email stating their policy covers flooding but in reality the policy excludes flooding from coverage, the company could be made to pay the claim because of the actions of its agent. For example, a company hires an agent to sell its insurance policies. To perform this act the agent must conduct appointments, make sales presentations, assist the customer with the application, and collect premiums. These powers, since they are a necessary part of the express duties of the agent, are implied powers. When the agent performs any or all of these duties, whether express or implied, it is as if the principal has done so.

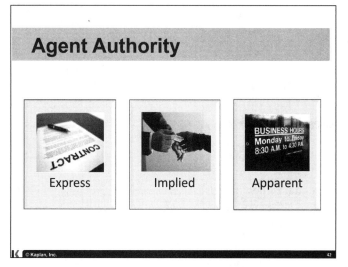

Agent Authority

- Express–what the agents written contract with the company states
- Implied–not written but are the actions agents normally do to sell insurance
- Apparent–actions the agent does that a reasonable person would assume as authority, based on the agents' actions and statements

1.9.2 Responsibility to Applicants/Insureds

Agents have a fiduciary responsibility to applicants and insureds. A **fiduciary** is a person in a position of financial trust. As a fiduciary, the agent has an obligation to act in the best interest of the insured. The following are examples of an agent's fiduciary responsibility.

All premiums received by an agent are funds received and held in trust. The agent must account for and pay the correct amount to the insured, insurer, or other agent entitled to the money. The insured's premiums must be kept separate from the agent's personal funds.

Failure to do this can result in **commingling**—mixing personal funds with the insured's or insurer's funds.

Any agent who takes funds held in trust for personal use is guilty of theft and will be punished as provided by law.

The agent must be knowledgeable about the features and provisions of various insurance policies and be able to explain important features to the insured.

Suitability considerations—An agent has a responsibility to make purchase recommendations that are appropriate, or *suitable,* in light of a client's particular needs, objectives, and circumstances. Suitable recommendations can only be made if an agent obtains information about an applicant's needs, objectives, and circumstances, and then gives thought to how a product's features and benefits will address the applicant's situation.

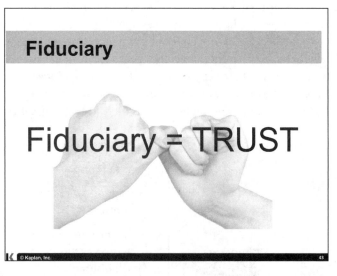

Fiduciary-Trust

- Promptly send premiums to insurer
- Knowledge of products
- Comply with laws and regulations
- No commingling

 QUICK QUIZ 1.C

1. Carl accepts the initial premium when he sells an insurance policy and he sends this to the insurance company along with the application. Which authority represents what others believe his power is by actions taken?
   A. Express authority
   B. Implied authority
   C. Apparent authority
   D. Agent authority

2. Agency is a relationship in which one person is authorized to represent and act for another person or for a corporation. In insurance, the insurance agent acts on behalf of the
   A. principal
   B. insured
   C. claimant
   D. adjuster

3. Which of the following types of advertising does not involve an agent and is conducted through the mail, by advertisements in newspapers and magazines, on television and radio or through the internet?
   A. Direct writing
   B. Captive agency system
   C. Direct response
   D. Cold calling

4. Which of the following individuals represent only one insurance company?
   A. An independent agent
   B. A general agent
   C. A captive agent
   D. A managing general agent

   Answers can be found at the end of Unit 1.

1.10 INSURANCE AND CONTRACT LAW

1.10.1 Elements of a Legal Contract (CLOAC)

Insurance policies are legal contracts and are subject to the general law of contracts. To form a valid contract, five elements must be present.

- Consideration
- Legal purpose
- Offer
- Acceptance
- Competent parties

1.10.1.1 Legal Purpose

To be valid, a contract must be for a legal purpose and not contrary to public policy. For example, an agreement to purchase stolen goods would not be a valid contract because it lacks legal purpose.

1.10.1.2 Agreement (Offer and Acceptance)

There cannot be a contract without the agreement of the parties. The parties to an insurance contract are the insurance company and the applicant. An agreement is reached when one party accepts the offer made by the other party with no conditions.

An **offer** is a proposal made by one of the potential parties to the contract. An applicant who submits a completed application to an insurer along with a payment for the first premium is making an offer to become insured by the insurer. If the policy is issued as applied for, the insurer has accepted the offer.

There is no offer if the applicant sends the application to the insurance company without payment of the premium. Such an application is merely an invitation to the company to make an offer. The insurance company makes an offer by issuing the policy. The applicant accepts it by paying the first premium.

Acceptance of an offer must be unconditional and unqualified. If acceptance is qualified or conditional, no agreement has been reached. A qualified acceptance is actually a rejection of the offer and is called a counter offer.

1.10.1.3 Consideration

Consideration refers to an exchange of value. When you see the word consideration think MONEY! Each party to the contract must give something valuable to the other. In an insurance contract, the applicant provides consideration in the form of the information (representations) in the application and the premium payment, and the insurer provides consideration in the form of a promise to pay if certain loss occurs.

1.10.1.4 Competent Parties

For a contract to be binding, both parties must have the legal capacity to make a contract. The insured or applicant must be of legal age (usually 18) and be mentally competent to make an insurance contract. Applications of minors usually must be signed by an adult parent or guardian.

CLOAC

Consideration
Legal Purpose
Offer
Acceptance
Competent Parties

© Kaplan, Inc.   49

Legal Contract (CLOAC)

- <u>C</u>onsideration—giving something of value
  - Insured gives information and money (premium) to the insurance company
  - Insurance company gives a promise to pay (policy) to the insured
- <u>L</u>egal purpose
  - Risk transfer doesn't violate the law
- <u>O</u>ffer (made by insured)
  - Insured submits application and first month's premium to insurer
  - Counteroffer (made by insurer)
    - Agrees to issue policy but with higher premium or restrictions/exclusions
    - Insured either accepts the conditions or withdraws her application
- <u>A</u>cceptance—insurer accepts risk as presented
- <u>C</u>ompetent parties—insured age 18 and sane

QUICK QUIZ 1.D

1. Which of the following terms describes a legal agreement between two competent parties that promises a certain performance in exchange for a certain consideration?
   A. An offer
   B. An acceptance
   C. A contract
   D. A consideration

2. Which one of the following is not 1 of the 4 elements of a legal contract?
   A. Offer
   B. Acceptance
   C. Legal Purpose
   D. Unilateral

Answers can be found at the end of Unit 1.

1.10.2 Characteristics of Insurance Contracts

Insurance policies possess a number of special legal characteristics. This unique combination of features reflects the distinctive nature of the insurance contract.

1.10.2.1 Adhesion

Insurance policies are contracts of **adhesion**—that is, their provisions are written by only one party to the contract, and the other party is required to *adhere*, or stick, to them. In the case of insurance, it is the insurer who writes the contract's terms and the insured that must adhere.

If there is any ambiguity (doubt) in the wording of a contract of adhesion, courts will interpret the wording in favor of the adhering party. That is, parties that have no input into the wording of a contract and no power to change it cannot be held responsible for any unclear contract language. This puts the insurer at a disadvantage in any legal dispute arising from a lack of clarity in a provision's wording, and gives the advantage to the policyowner, insured, or beneficiary.

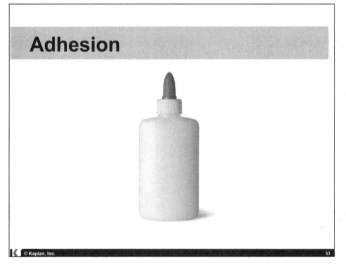

Adhesion

- Policy written by the insurance company
- If ambiguous (not clear)—court will take the side of the insured

1.10.2.2 Aleatory

Insurance policies are **aleatory** contracts, meaning that the value received from the contract by each party may be unequal. Ordinarily, each party to a contract is expected to receive benefits from the contract that are at least roughly equivalent. In the case of insurance, the receipt of unequal value arises because the insurer's performance under the contract depends upon an uncertain event—that is, the occurrence of a loss which may or may not happen. The insured may pay premiums for many years and receive no monetary value in return if the loss does not occur. On the other hand, the insured may pay only one relatively small premium and receive thousands of dollars in return if a covered loss occurs shortly after the policy goes into effect. Such unequal receipt of value is the defining feature of an aleatory contract.

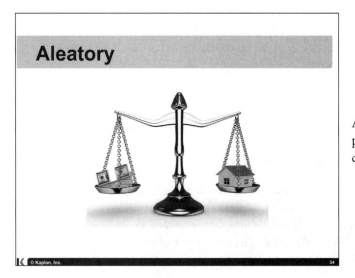

Aleatory–not equal value–small premium for a large amount of coverage

1.10.2.3 Utmost Good Faith, Reasonable Expectation

Insurance is a contract of **utmost good faith.** This means that each party is entitled to a **reasonable expectation** that the other party will not try to conceal pertinent information or otherwise act deceptively. Violation of that reasonable expectation can void the claims of the offending party under a contract of utmost good faith.

Utmost Good Faith–the insured and insurance company have a right to expect honesty from each other

1.10.2.4 Unilateral

Insurance policies are **unilateral**, or one-sided, contracts because only one party is legally bound to perform under the contract. The insured has the right to stop paying premiums at any time. However, as long as the insured keeps the contract in force by paying the premiums, the insurer is required by law to pay for any covered losses that occur.

Unilateral–only ONE promise made

- Insurance company PROMISES to pay for a covered loss
- Insured does NOT promise to pay the premium

1.10.2.5 Personal

Property-casualty insurance policies (such as auto and homeowners insurance) are **personal** contracts, but *life and health* insurance policies are not.

A personal contract is one made with a particular person and no one else. The contract cannot be transferred to a different person.

With a homeowners policy, for example, the insurer evaluates not only the condition of the property, but also whether the insured will take reasonably good care of the property. A different person would represent a different risk, so the contract does not allow a change of parties.

With life insurance, the insurer contracts not with the insured, but with the *policyowner*. The insured and the policyowner are often the same person, but they do not have to be. For example, a wife can apply for a policy on her spouse, in which case the wife applying for the insurance is the policyowner and the spouse is the insured.

In addition, owners have rights, one of which is to transfer their ownership to another party. For example, if the woman wished, she could transfer ownership of the policy on her husband to a trust. (Other examples of ownership rights and policyowners other than insureds will be covered later in this course.)

Such a transfer does not affect a life insurance policy's status as a contract because it is not a personal contract. The insurer has a contract not with a particular person, but with whatever party is the policyowner.

Personal contracts can't be assigned to someone else. NOTE: Auto and homeowner insurance policies are personal contracts. However, assignment can take place with life insurance policies pledged as a security for a bank loan.

1.10.2.6 Conditional

Insurance policies are conditional contracts because they require certain conditions to be fulfilled in order for performance under the contract to be enforced. For example, the contract may require certain documents to be submitted to prove that a loss has occurred. In the case of life insurance, a death certificate must be filed.

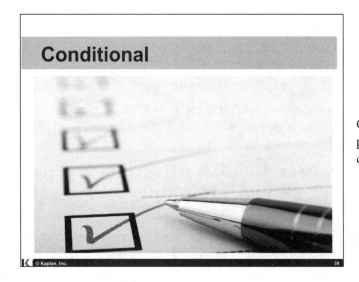

Conditional–insured must pay the premium for coverage and file a claim if a loss occurs

1.10.2.7 Indemnity

Insurance policies are contracts of indemnity, meaning that the contract is intended to restore the insured to the financial state he or she enjoyed prior to the occurrence of a loss–no more and no less. The principle of restoring an insured to his or her pre-loss financial state is known as *indemnification*. This principle applies to health insurance but not life insurance. It is not possible to restore the insured in a life insurance policy because payment occurs upon death.

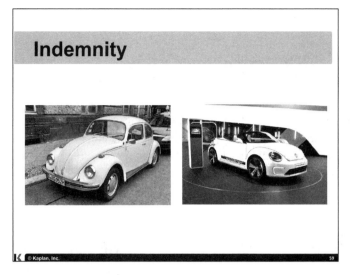

Indemnity–restore to the insured's original pre-loss condition, no better, no worse!

1.10.2.8 Representations, Misrepresentations, and Warranties

A **representation** is a statement that is believed to be true, to the best of one's knowledge at the time it is given. A **misrepresentation** is a representation that is actually false. For example, suppose Adam signs an insurance application as "Adam L. Jones" even though his birth certificate shows no middle name–he just adopted the "L" because he thinks it sounds good. Adam represents himself as Adam L. Jones, but the "L" is a misrepresentation.

Misrepresentations do not necessarily void insurance contracts. To do so, they must be *material* misrepresentations—that is, the false information must have been a determining (or material) factor in the insurer's acceptance of the risk. If the insurer would have rejected the application or written the coverage on a different basis had the correct facts been known, the information is material.

For example, Adam's harmless adoption of middle initial does not affect him as a risk, so it is not a material misrepresentation and would not void his policy. If Adam said he was not being treated for a heart condition when in fact he was, that would be a material misrepresentation.

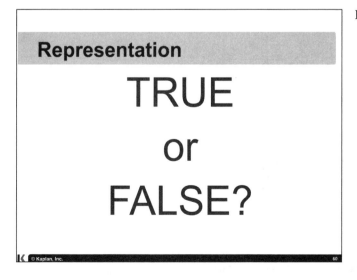

Representation–believed to be true

- Misrepresentation–information given that is not true–however, the correct information would not affect the insurance companies decision–insured mistakenly gives one number of their address wrong–doesn't void coverage

- Material misrepresentation–information given that is not true–this information DOES affect the insurers decision–insured has a conviction for driving while intoxicated–could void coverage

A **warranty** is a statement that is guaranteed to be true. If a warranty is not kept, there is a *breach of warranty* that voids the contract.

Applicants for property-casualty insurance sometimes make warranties to an insurer. For example, a business may guarantee that it will hire a security guard. If it does not, its property insurance policy will be void.

However, for life and health insurance, most state laws say that statements or responses to questions on an application are representations and not warranties. That is, an untrue statement on a life or health insurance application is not a breach of warranty. To be grounds for voiding the contract, it must be material to the insurer's acceptance of the risk.

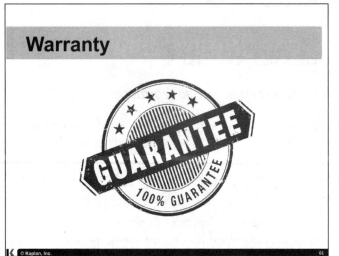

Warranty–promise

- Always made by the insurance company—if promise to pay is broken—company could be sued by the insured.
- May be made by the insured—if promise is broken—insured may have no coverage
- Guaranteed to be true

1.10.2.9 Concealment

Concealment is the intentional failure to disclose known facts. An insurer may be able to void the insurance contract if it can prove that an applicant or insured intentionally concealed a material fact (a previous heart attack).

Concealment–failure to disclose

- If intentional, and the information is material(important)–coverage could be voided
- If NOT intentional–coverage cannot be voided

1.10.2.10 Fraud

Fraud is an intentional act designed to deceive and induce another party to part with something of value.

Fraud may involve misrepresentation, concealment, or both, but not all acts of misrepresentation or concealment are acts of fraud. If someone intentionally lies to obtain coverage or to collect on a false claim, it would be a matter of fraud. If someone misrepresents something on an application (perhaps a medical treatment the person is embarrassed to talk about) without intent to obtain something of value, no fraud has occurred.

Fraud

- Intentional act to cheat another
- Voids the policy

1.10.3 Fraud and False Statements (18 USC Sections 1033 and 1034)

1. A person who transacts insurance in interstate commerce and who intentionally makes false material statements in connection with financial reports or documents presented to insurance regulators appointed to investigate the person and to influence the actions of such officials is subject to:

   - a fine;

   - imprisonment for up to 10 years; or

   - both.

2. Imprisonment may be ordered for up to 15 years if the false statements jeopardized the safety and soundness of an insurer and were a significant cause of the insurer being placed in conservation, rehabilitation, or liquidation by the courts.

3. Officers, directors, agents, and employees of an insurance company who willfully embezzle or misappropriate funds are subject to the same consequence described above.

Fraud and False Statements

- Fine and/or imprisonment (10-15 years)
- Embezzlement included

1.10.3.1 Waiver and Estoppel

Waiver is defined as the intentional and voluntary giving up of a known right.

Estoppel is a legal doctrine that prevents a party from denying an action if it had been accepted previously.

For example, by repeatedly accepting late premium payments, an insurance company may have waived its right to cancel a policy for nonpayment or late payment of premium. In the future, the insurer may be legally estopped from making any prompt cancellation for nonpayment because the policyholder has begun to rely on the prior acceptance of late payments.

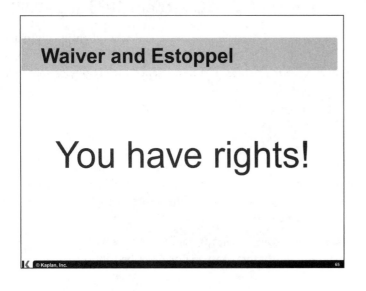

- Waiver—voluntarily giving up a right
- Estoppel—actions reasonably relied on by one party can't be denied by the party that accepted same previously

QUICK QUIZ 1.E

1. Jill is filling out an insurance application with information that she believes to be true. This information that she is providing is considered a
   A. representation
   B. misrepresentation
   C. material misrepresentation
   D. warranty

2. A guarantee that something is true is a
   A. representation
   B. misrepresentation
   C. material misrepresentation
   D. warranty

3. All of the following statements regarding fraud and false statements are correct EXCEPT
   A. a person who commits fraud is subject to a fine
   B. a person who commits fraud is subject imprisonment for up to 10 years
   C. a person who commits fraud is subject to both a fine and imprisonment for up to 10 years
   D. a person who commits fraud is subject to imprisonment for up to 25 years

Answers can be found at the end of the Unit 1.

UNIT 1 CRAM SHEET

Insurance = transfer of risk.

Risk = uncertainty / possibility of a loss

Types of Risk:

- Speculative risk—chance of loss or gain. Not insurable.
- Pure risk chance of loss only. Insurance companies will insure.

Exposure—risks for which the insurance company would be liable.

Peril—a cause of loss

Hazard—something that causes an increase in the chance of loss

- Physical hazard—the hazard can be seen.
- Moral hazard—a belief that intentionally causing a loss is acceptable
- Morale hazard—carelessness

STARR!—methods of handling risk.

- $\underline{S}$haring
- $\underline{T}$ransfer
- $\underline{A}$voidance
- $\underline{R}$etention.
- $\underline{R}$eduction

Insurance—risk transfer

Contract (policy)—an agreement between the insured and the insurer

- 1st Party —insured (customer)
- 2nd Party—insurer (insurance company)

Law of Large Numbers—larger the group; the more accurate losses can be predicted

CANHAM Risks that can be insured have the following characteristics

- $\underline{C}$alculable
- $\underline{A}$ffordable
- $\underline{N}$on-catastrophic
- $\underline{H}$omogeneous
- $\underline{A}$ccidental
- $\underline{M}$easurable

Adverse selection—risks that have a greater than average chance of loss

Reinsurance—an insurance company (the ceding company) paying another insurance company (reinsurer) to take some of the companies risk of catastrophic loss

- Facultative—the reinsurer evaluates each risk before allowing the transfer
- Treaty—the reinsurer accepts the transfer according to an agreement called a treaty

Stock Insurer

- Publically owned by stockholders/shareholders
- If the company makes money, a taxable dividend from the profits may be paid to the stockholders/shareholders
- Issues non-par policies

Mutual Insurer

- Owned by the policyholders (customers)
- If the company is profitable, can return excess premium to its policyholders—nontaxable dividend
- Issues participating policies

Fraternal Insurer

- Provides insurance and other benefits
- Must be a member of the society to get the benefits

Reciprocal Insurer

- Unincorporated
- Members are assessed the amount they have to pay if a loss to any member of the group occurs
- Run by an attorney-in-fact

Lloyd's Association—insurance provided by individual underwriters not companies

Risk Retention Group

- Liability insurance company created for and owned by policyholders from the same industry. Example—car dealers RRG—only car dealers can be policyholders

Risk Purchasing Group

- A group of businesses from the same industry joining together to buy liability insurance from an insurance company
- The RPG is NOT the insurance company

Self-Insurance—a business that pays its own claims

Residual market—insurance from the state or federal government

Insurance company location

- Domestic—state where company is incorporated
- Foreign—any state or U.S. territory other than the state where incorporated
- Alien—incorporated in any country other than USA

Certificate of Authority—state license for an insurance company

Admitted or Authorized—state requires the insurance company to have a Certificate of Authority

Non-admitted—unauthorized—insurance company not required to have a Certificate of Authority from the state

Surplus Lines

- Insurance sold by unauthorized/non-admitted insurers—if on the states approved list of surplus insurers
- Can only be sold to certain high risk insureds
- Cannot be sold just for a cheaper rate than licensed/admitted insurers

Financial strength rating—a report card of the company

Methods of Marketing

- Independent
- Exclusive or Captive
- General Agents or Managing General Agents
- Direct-writing companies
- Direct Response—no agent/producer involved

Agency—the insurance agent acts on behalf of the principal (insurance company)

Agent authority

- **Express**—what the agents written contract with the company says
- **Implied**—not written but are the things agents normally do to sell insurance.
- **Apparent**—things the agent does that a reasonable person would assume as authority, based on the agents' actions and statements.

Fiduciary-Trust

- Promptly send premiums to insurer
- Knowledge of products
- Comply with laws and regulations
- No commingling

Legal Contract (CLOAC)

- Consideration—giving something of value
    - Insured gives information and money(premium) to the insurance company
    - Insurance company gives a promise to pay(policy) to the insured
- Legal purpose—risk transfer doesn't violate the law
- Offer (made by insured)
    - Insured submits application and first month's premium to insurer
    - Counteroffer (made by insurer)
        - Agrees to issue policy but with higher premium or restrictions/exclusions
        - Insured either accepts the conditions or withdraws her application
- Acceptance—insurer accepts risk as presented
- Competent parties—insured age 18 and sane

Adhesion

- Policy written by the insurance company
- If ambiguous(not clear)—court will take the side of the insured

Aleatory—not equal value—small premium for a large amount of coverage

Utmost Good Faith—the insured and insurance company have a right to expect honesty from each other

Unilateral—only ONE promise made

- Insurance company PROMISES to pay for a covered loss
- Insured does NOT promise to pay the premium

Personal—contract between the insurance company and the insured—cannot be changed to someone else

Conditional— insured must pay the premium for coverage and file a claim if a loss occurs

Indemnity—pay for the loss but with no gain

Representation—believed to be true

- Misrepresentation—information given that is not true—however, the correct information would not affect the insurance companies decision – insured mistakenly gives one number of their address wrong—doesn't void coverage
- Material misrepresentation— information give that is not true—this information DOES affect the insurers decision—insured has a conviction for driving while intoxicated—could void coverage

Warranty—promise

- Always made by the insurance company—if promise to pay is broken—company could be sued by the insured.
- May be made by the insured—if promise is broken—insured may have no coverage
- Guaranteed to be true

Concealment—failure to disclose

- If intentional, and the information is material (important)—coverage could be voided
- If NOT intentional—coverage cannot be voided

Fraud—intentional act to cheat another

Waiver—voluntarily giving up a right

Estoppel—actions reasonably relied on by one party can't be denied by the party that accepted same previously

Fraud and False Statements

- Fine and/or imprisonment (10-15 years)
- Embezzlement included

UNIT 1 QUIZ

In order to measure your success, we recommend that you answer the following 10 questions correctly. For more Unit 1 practice questions, please refer to the InsurancePro QBank in your online tools.

1. What is a contract or device for transferring risk from a person, business, or organization to an insurance company?
    A. Insurance
    B. Law of large numbers
    C. Adhesion
    D. Agency

2. Which of the following represents a pure risk?
    A. A poker game
    B. Gambling in the stock market
    C. Investing in a new business
    D. The chance your house may burn down

3. Suzanne regularly leaves her side door unlocked when she leaves for work. One afternoon a thief entered her apartment and stole all of her jewelry. What was the type of hazard in this example?
    A. Physical
    B. Moral
    C. Morale
    D. The neighborhood

4. Since he lives in a good neighborhood and across the street from the fire station, Jeff decides to cancel his fire insurance policy. This is an example of which risk management method?
    A. Retention
    B. Avoidance
    C. Transfer
    D. Control

5. Sometimes an individual or business has an exceptionally large or specialized risk that no authorized insurer can or will cover. In this case they may call
    A. a surplus lines insurance company
    B. an admitted insurance company
    C. an independent agent
    D. a fraternal insurance company

6. Insurance companies often purchase insurance to cover their own exposure to loss. This is called
    A. self-insurance
    B. loss control insurance
    C. surplus lines insurance
    D. reinsurance

7. A type of insurance owned by the federal government that is not typically available from other private insurers' is called
    A. residual market insurance
    B. surplus lines insurance
    C. private insurance
    D. government funded insurance

8. A person in a position of financial trust is called
    A. a commingler
    B. a fiduciary
    C. an actuary
    D. an underwriter

9. The failure to disclose known facts is
    A. material misrepresentation
    B. waiver
    C. concealment
    D. fraud

10. The ABC Insurance Company is incorporated in Mexico. While doing business in Texas, it is
    A. a domestic insurer
    B. a foreign insurer
    C. an alien insurer
    D. an export insurer

ANSWER KEY

QUICK QUIZZES

QUICK QUIZ I.A

1. **B.** peril
2. **C.** Reduce
3. **B.** Morale

QUICK QUIZ I.B

1. **C.** Foreign
2. **B.** a stock company is a participating company
3. **A.** The law of large numbers
4. **A.** a certificate of authority

QUICK QUIZ I.C

1. **C.** Apparent authority
2. **A.** principal
3. **C.** Direct response
4. **C.** A captive agent

QUICK QUIZ I.D

1. **C.** A contract
2. **D.** Unilateral

QUICK QUIZ I.E

1. **A.** representation
2. **D.** warranty
3. **D.** a person who commits fraud is subject to imprisonment for up to 25 years

UNIT QUIZ

1. **A.** Insurance is the transfer of risk.

2. **D.** Pure risk involves the possibility of loss. Speculative risks involve the possibility of loss and gain.

3. **C.** Leaving the door unlocked is a morale hazard.

4. **A.** By not carrying fire insurance, Jeff is retaining the risk of financial loss from an unexpected fire.

5. **A.** Excess or Surplus lines are highly specialized insurance coverages.

6. **D.** Reinsurance helps protect insurance companies from catastrophic losses and from wild fluctuations in underwriting results.

7. **A.** Some examples of residual market insurance are war risk insurance, flood insurance, nuclear insurance, federal crop insurance, and nuclear energy liability insurance.

8. **B.** Agents have a fiduciary responsibility to applicants/insureds and the insurance company.

9. **C.** Generally an insurer can void a contract if it can prove the insured intentionally concealed a material fact.

10. **C.** The insurance company is an alien insurer since Mexico is not a part of the U.S.

UNIT 2) Life/Health Insurance Underwriting

2.1 INTRODUCTION

Underwriting is a critical part of the insurance application process. The information that is gathered enables insurance companies to properly classify and determine premiums for prospective insureds.

Insurance company underwriters are able to determine the amount of risk an applicant poses for the company and whether the company wants to accept or decline that risk. Underwriters work closely with actuaries, risk managers, and claims managers to protect the company from potential claims. Simultaneously, they determine which new risks are going to be profitable and which existing clients are worth retaining.

This unit discusses how insurance agents assist insurers to identify appropriate prospects and describes the steps involved to provide a comprehensive and suitable insurance policy.

🎯 2.2   LEARNING OBJECTIVES

After completing this unit, you will be able to:

- explain the importance of the underwriting process;
- identify the producers responsibilities in completing the insurance application including, confidentiality, accuracy, changes in the application, completeness, backdating, required signatures, producer's report, and information practices;
- describe the collection of the first premium and the two types of receipts that can be issued: conditional and binding;
- explain the underwriter's responsibility once the insurer receives the application;
- list the details that are found in the General (Part I) and Health (Part II) sections of the application;
- describe the following concepts that are related to the underwriting process: attending physician's statement, medical examinations and testing, AIDS considerations, HIPAA disclosures, Medical Information Bureau, Consumer reports, and Investigative consumer reports;
- identify the four classifications of insurance risk: standard, preferred, substandard, and declined;
- explain selection criteria and unfair discrimination;
- explain the producer's responsibility in delivering and servicing the insurance policy: policy review, statement of good health, and effective date of coverage; and
- describe the purpose of the Fair Credit Reporting Act, Stranger Oriented Life Insurance (STOLI/IOLI), the U.S Patriot Act, and the Employee Retirement Income Security Act (ERISA).

2.3   UNDERWRITING

Underwriting is the process of evaluating a risk to determine if it is acceptable based on established insurance company guidelines. Everything begins with the producer/agent when a decision to buy is made and the agent completes the application for insurance and submits it to the company underwriter. The agent/producer is frequently referred to as the field underwriter.

2.4   COMPLETING THE APPLICATION

Completing the application is an important responsibility for the producer/agent. The information in the application is the basis for issuing the policy, which in turn provides the client with valuable benefits. Producers must approach the completion of the application with an eye toward confidentiality, accuracy, and completeness.

2.4.1   Confidentiality

Highly personal information about an applicant is acquired during the application process. Agents need to inform applicants that the information they share will be kept in the strictest confidence and producers must never violate that confidence. Completed applications must be kept out of others' sight except for company representatives and the information gathered should never be the subject of idle talk.

2.4.2 Accuracy

In the interest of both the applicant and the insurer, producers must be conscientious about getting and recording the correct answer to every question on the application. The company underwriter is relying upon application accuracy to correctly assess and rate this business.

2.4.2.1 Changes in the Application

A correction can be made if a producer finds they have mistakenly recorded applicant information. The applicant must certify that an error occurred and *place their initials* next to the correction. Some insurers also require the producer to initial any change.

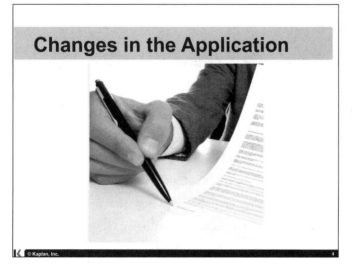

Changes in the Application

- Must be initialed by the applicant

2.4.3 Completeness

Incomplete applications cause a delay in the underwriting process because they must be returned to the agent for completion. This means the applicant will wait longer without needed insurance protection. All the required information must be available for review by the underwriting department before a policy can be approved and issued.

If a policy is issued and the application was incomplete, the underwriter on behalf of the company waives its right to that information. If a claim arises, the company cannot deny it based on the fact that information was missing from the application.

2.4.4 Backdating

Some insurers allow an application to be backdated so the premium can be based on an applicant's earlier age and lower the cost of the premium. *Backdating* would permit a 41-year old applicant to purchase a life insurance policy using the age of 40. Most state laws allow life insurance applications to be backdated up to six months.

If an application is backdated, the policy becomes effective as of the date requested on the application. To receive a less expensive premium, the applicant must pay any additional premiums that would have been paid from the backdate.

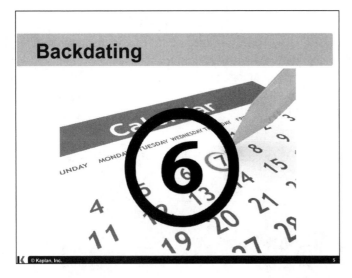

Backdating

- Up to six months

2.4.5 Required Signatures

Several documents must be signed to complete the application process.

- *The application form* – signed by the **applicant** and the **producer/agent**.
  - The **proposed insured** must sign if the applicant is not the insured.
  - A **company officer** must sign a corporation owned policy.
  - A **parent or legal guardian** signs a juvenile policy for the minor.

Required Signatures

- Insured
- Producer/agent
- Applicant, owner (if not the insured)

2.4.5.1 Producer's Report

Part III of a life insurance application is the **Producer/Agents Report**, or *Producer's Statement.* The producer records information that pertains to the proposed insured including the producer's relationship to the proposed insured and anything the producer knows about the proposed insured's:

- financial status,
- habits, and
- character.

The proposed insured does not see the Producer's Report. It is not attached to the policy and the application when it's issued. *The producer's report* will be signed only by the producer.

Producers Report

- Completed by the producer/agent
- Not attached to policy at issue

2.4.6   Information Practices

The life insurance producer must comply with the requirements for notifying applicants about the insurer's privacy policy as it relates to the personal information collected during the application process and how it will be used.

2.4.6.1 Disclosure Notification

State laws require that applicants be given advance written notice stating who is authorized to disclose personal information, the kind of information that may be disclosed, and the reason it is being collected. By signing the disclosure form, the applicant is giving the insurer consent to gather and disseminate information as described in the notice.

2.4.7   Collecting the Premium

An "offer to buy" insurance exists when the first premium is submitted with the life insurance application. If no premium is submitted with the application *coverage is delayed until the premium is paid* for the issued policy. If the insured becomes uninsurable or dies between the time when the application is submitted and the first premium is collected, the policy will pay no benefit.

2.4.8   Receipts

When the first premium is collected at the time of application, the producer must provide the applicant with a receipt. The effective date of coverage will depend on the type of receipt issued.

2.4.8.1 Conditional Receipt

The date of the application is the effective date of a **conditional receipt**, *as long as the applicant is found to be insurable under the company's standard underwriting rules.* Most conditional receipts are effective on the date of the application, or the date of a required medical examination, whichever is later of these two events.

With conditional receipts, if the proposed insured dies before a policy is issued, the application continues through the normal underwriting process and one of the following will occur:

- If the deceased insured meets the company's standard underwriting requirements and a policy would have been issued had they lived, the policy is in force and the death benefit will be paid to the beneficiary.

- If the insured is found to be uninsurable or a substandard risk, no coverage would be in force. The premium that was collected with the application will be returned to the policyowner or beneficiary (in the case of death).

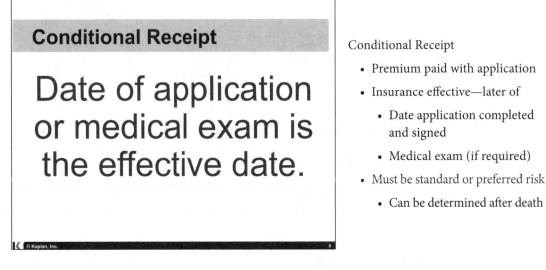

Conditional Receipt

Date of application or medical exam is the effective date.

Conditional Receipt

- Premium paid with application
- Insurance effective—later of
  - Date application completed and signed
  - Medical exam (if required)
- Must be standard or preferred risk
  - Can be determined after death

2.4.8.2 Binding Receipt

Binding receipts are effective for 30 to 60 days from the date of application even if the applicant is found to be uninsurable. Binders are most often used with auto or homeowners insurance and rarely with life insurance. Life insurance binders are called *temporary insurance agreements*. The insurer can either issue a policy or cancel the binder before the end of the stated period.

Binding Receipt—Temporary

30–60 days

Binding Receipt—Temporary
- Not common in life insurance.

QUICK QUIZ 2.A

1. A part of the application that requires the agent to provide information regarding the proposed insured, such as habits, character, and relationship with the insured is known as a

    A. binding receipt

    B. conditional receipt

    C. producer's report

    D. confidentiality report

2. Which of the following individuals is NOT required to sign the application form?

    A. The insured

    B. The producer/agent

    C. The applicant (if not the insured)

    D. The beneficiary

3. The process of evaluating a risk to determine if the risk is one that the insurance company wishes to insure is also known as the

    A. underwriting process

    B. application process

    C. decision making process

    D. insurance process

Answers can be found at the end of Unit 2.

2.5   COMPANY UNDERWRITING

Each insurance company has its own set of underwriting guidelines to help the underwriter determine whether or not the company should accept the risk. The information used to evaluate the risk of an applicant for insurance will depend on the type of coverage involved.

2.5.1   Sources of Information

The factors that insurers use to classify risks should be objective, clearly related to the likely cost of providing coverage, practical to administer, consistent with applicable law, and designed to protect the long-term viability of the insurer. The application is an underwriter's primary source of information.

2.5.1.1   The Application

The application used to purchase life insurance asks the applicant for basic information. There are three parts to an application.

- Part 1—General Information
- Part 2—Health Information
- Part 3—Producer's Report

2.5.1.1.1 General Information

The first part (Part 1) of the application asks for general or personal data regarding the insured. For example:

- Name
- Address
- Date of birth
- Gender
- Social Security number
- Driver's license number
- Marital status
- Income
- Occupation and business address
- Type of policy and face amount being applied for
- Beneficiary
- Other insurance owned

In addition, if the applicant is someone other than the insured, the applicant's name and address will also be requested.

2.5.1.1.2 Health Information

The second part (Part II) of the application is designed to obtain information about the insured's physical condition and habits:

- Height and weight
- Tobacco usage
- Drug usage
- International travel
- Current medical treatments (details of most recent office visit)
- Medications being taken
- Conditions the insured has sought treatment for or been diagnosed with in the past
- History of disability claims
- Health conditions prevalent in the insured's family
- High-risk hobbies (aviation, skydiving, scuba diving, auto/boat/motorcycle racing, mountain climbing)
- Name and address of current physician

2.5.1.2 Attending Physician's Statement (APS)

An underwriter may ask the proposed insured's regular doctor for an **Attending Physician's Statement (APS)** to find out about the applicant's current condition and medical history with the physician. The underwriter may also ask for copies of medical records.

2.5.1.3 Medical Examinations and Testing

Insurers will underwrite some applications on a *non-medical* basis when the death benefit applied for is below a certain level. These applications are evaluated on health information on the application. The insurer usually requires the proposed insured to take a medical examination for larger death benefit amounts. These exams can be conducted by a registered nurse, paramedic, and some applicants are required to have a doctor's examination with stress testing, scans, EKG's, MRI's, etc. The amount of death benefit determines the type of examination and testing required by the insurer.

The ***insurer pays*** for medical exams and tests that are requested during the underwriting process.

2.5.1.3.1 AIDS Considerations

The applicant's sexual orientation cannot be used in the underwriting process or to determine insurability. However, specific questions about being diagnosed with AIDS (Acquired Immune Deficiency Syndrome) or ARC (AIDS-related complex) to determine a medical condition can be asked.

AIDS testing can be required with the applicant's written consent. They must be informed about the purpose of the test and that the results are reported to the insurer.

If the results are positive, a report is sent to the Medical Information Bureau (MIB) that an individual has abnormal blood test results.

The presence of aids is never revealed, reported, or shared and can only be released to persons designated by the applicant, such as a particular physician. If the applicant does not designate a medical provider, state law may require the results to be forwarded to the state's Department of Health. Similar to other required health examinations, AIDS tests are also ***paid by the insurer***.

2.5.1.3.2 HIPAA Disclosures

The Health Insurance Portability and Accountability Act (HIPAA) imposes specific requirements on the disclosure of insureds' health information by medical providers, insurers, and producers. Health information must remain confidential to protect an applicant's privacy. If any health information will be shared, applicants must be given full notice of:

- the insurer's information-sharing practices;
- their right to maintain privacy; and
- an opportunity to refuse to have their information released.

2.5.1.4 Medical Information Bureau

The **Medical Information Bureau** is a non-profit insurance trade association that maintains underwriting information on applicants. According to the Federal Trade Commission, member MIB companies account for 99% of individual life insurance policies and 80% of health and disability policies issued in the U.S. and Canada. When member companies discover unfavorable information about an applicant during their underwriting process, they report it to the MIB using codes signifying certain conditions. If the applicant applies for insurance elsewhere, other members companies will have access to this information. The types of information maintained in MIB files include medical history, hazardous jobs or hobbies, and poor driving records.

The purpose of the MIB is to reduce instances of misrepresentation and fraud. It is important to note:

- Insurers may not make an adverse underwriting decision (such as rejecting the applicant) solely on the basis of information from the MIB. Insurers may only use this information to further their investigation.

- Insurers do *not* report underwriting decisions to the MIB. This prevents other member insurers to accept or reject an applicant based on what other insurance companies have done.

- An applicant must be given written notice that information may be reported to and obtained from the MIB, and insurers must get an applicant's written authorization to do so.

- Applicants must also be notified that applying for insurance or filing a claim with another company may trigger the release of MIB information.

2.5.1.5 Consumer Reports

Consumer reports are used to determine a consumer's eligibility for personal credit (credit report) or insurance or for employment. They may be issued only to persons who have a legitimate business need for the information.

Underwriters use an applicant's credit report to determine if they are reliable when paying their monthly bills. Issuers count on policyholders to pay their premium to defer the high initial costs to issue a life insurance policy. It can take several years for certain policies to become profitable for a life insurer.

2.5.1.6 Investigative Consumer Reports

Investigative consumer reports are reports containing information obtained by interviewing individuals who know something about the consumer such as associates, friends, and neighbors. Consumers must be notified and give their consent to having such reports done. In the insurance industry, investigative consumer reports are also called *inspection reports*.

Underwriting Sources of Information

Application—primary source

Medical exams and testing

Attending physician statement (APS)

AIDS testing

Medical Information Bureau

Consumer reports

Investigative reports

© Kaplan, Inc.   14

Underwriting Sources of Information

- Application—primary source
- Medical exams & testing
- Attending physician statement (APS)
- AIDS testing
  - Applications may not ask about sexual orientation
  - Testing not based on geographical location
  - Requires insured's written consent
- Medical Information Bureau
  - Application cannot be denied solely on MIB information
  - Insured must be informed of MIB
  - MIB gets its information from insurance companies
- Consumer reports
  - Insured must be informed
- Investigative reports
  - Insured must give consent

QUICK QUIZ 2.B

1. Which of the following is NOT included in the general form of the insurance application?

   A. Type of policy and face amount being applied for

   B. Height and weight

   C. Occupation and business address

   D. Beneficiary

2. Which of the following is a non-profit insurance trade association that maintains underwriting information on applicants from hundreds of insurers?

   A. HIPPA

   B. Consumer reports

   C. Medical Information Bureau

   D. Investigative consumer reports

3. During the underwriting process, medical exams and testing are paid for by the

    A. insurer

    B. agent/producer

    C. underwriter

    D. applicant

Answers can be found at the end of Unit 2

2.5.2 Classification of Risks

Every life insurance company has different underwriting guidelines that determine what risk class an individual qualifies for. The company will look at an applicant's personal medical history, smoker status, height/weight profile, medical exam results, family history, motor vehicle record, and any hazardous activities.

After applicants are evaluated, they are sorted into groups, or **classified**, according to the level of risk each represents. There are generally four classifications.

2.5.2.1 Standard

Standard risks mean average health and normal life expectancy and fall into the normal range anticipated by the company when it established its premiums. These risks can be insured for standard rates.

2.5.2.2 Preferred

Preferred risks represent excellent health. A risk of loss that is *below* average and therefore favorable to the company. Favorable risk factors include such things as healthy lifestyle, clean medical history, or low-risk occupation. These risks may be insured at *preferred* or discounted rates.

2.5.2.3 Substandard

Substandard risks represent below average life expectancy, high-risk life insurance. A risk of loss that is *above* average and therefore unfavorable to the company. Unfavorable risk factors include poor health, dangerous occupation, or risky habits. Substandard risks can only be accepted by charging them higher rates. Substandard risks are sometimes referred to as being *rated up* (sometimes shortened to just *rated*). Methods of charging a relatively higher rate for substandard risks include adding a flat additional charge, charging applicants the standard premium for a higher attained age, or reducing the benefits provided by the policy.

2.5.2.4 Declined

An insurer's underwriting guidelines indicate that an applicant is not insurable at any price. In such cases, the application or risk is **declined.**

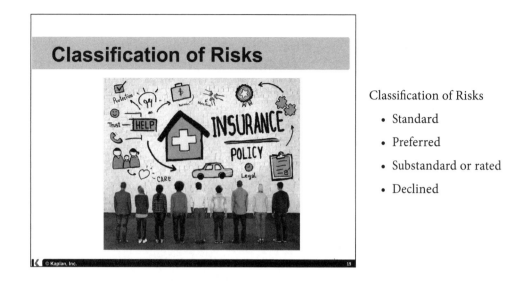

Classification of Risks

- Standard
- Preferred
- Substandard or rated
- Declined

2.5.3   Selection Criteria and Unfair Discrimination

Insurers must not unfairly discriminate between individuals who are in the same risk class. Specifically, use of any of the following is considered unfair discrimination:

- Race
- Religion
- National origin
- Place of residence (the area where someone lives)

In addition, most states prohibit unfair discrimination against individuals who are blind, or victims of domestic violence.

2.6   DELIVERING AND SERVICING THE POLICY

2.6.1   Personal Delivery

When a policy is issued, it must be delivered to the policyowner. It can be mailed, but in most companies it is the producer's responsibility to deliver it in person. In some states, producers must obtain a receipt from the policyowner acknowledging that the policy was delivered and the date.

Agent Delivery

- Will usually get a signed receipt on delivery to the policyowner

2.6.2   Policy Review

During the delivery appointment, the producer will review with the policyowner the policy, riders, exclusions, and other details to make sure they understand it. The producer should also answer any pertinent questions the policyowner has about the policy they purchased.

2.6.3   Statement of Good Health

During the delivery appointment, the agent/producer must collect the first premium if it was not paid at the time of application, Additionally, the policyowner must sign a **statement of good health** attesting that their health is the same as when they applied for the policy.

Statement of Good Health

- Required if no premium with application
- If health changed—agent can't deliver policy

2.6.4   Effective Date of Coverage

When the first premium is collected at the time of application for a policy, the **effective date** of coverage is the date of application or the date of the medical exam, if it was required.

If the proposed insured is found to be a substandard risk, the policy that is issued will require substandard/higher premiums because the initial application for insurance was forwarded with a standard premium.

- If the applicant declines the substandard policy and does not pay the additional premium, coverage has never been in effect.

- If the applicant accepts the substandard policy and pays the additional premium, the effective date of coverage is the date the policy was delivered.

If an application for insurance is sent to the insurer without the first premium, but it is paid at policy delivery, the effective date of coverage is the date the policy was delivered.

Effective Date of Coverage

Effective Date of Coverage

- Terms of conditional receipt is issued

- Substandard and pays additional premium—date of policy delivery

- No receipt—policy delivery date if premium paid at delivery

 QUICK QUIZ 2.C

1. Which of the following is an above average risk of loss and unfavorable to an insurance company?

   A. Standard

   B. Preferred

   C. Substandard

   D. Declined

2. Which of the following factors is NOT prohibited from use in order to classify a risk?

   A. Race

   B. Religion

   C. Marital status

   D. Place of residence

Answers can be found at the end of Unit 2.

2.7   FEDERAL LAWS AND REGULATIONS APPLIED TO BOTH LIFE AND HEALTH INSURANCE

2.7.1   Fair Credit Reporting Act (FCRA)

1. The federal Fair Credit Reporting Act requires consumer reporting agencies to adopt reasonable procedures for exchanging information on credit, personnel, insurance, and other subjects in a manner that is fair and equitable to the consumer with respect to the confidentiality, accuracy, relevancy, and proper use of this information.

    a. All insurers and their producers must comply with the federal Fair Credit Reporting Act regarding information obtained from a third party concerning the applicant.

    b. Reports on consumers are prohibited unless the consumer is made aware that an investigative consumer report may be made, and that such report may contain information about the person's character, reputation, personal characteristics, and lifestyle.

2. A **Notice to Applicant** must be issued to all applicants for life or health insurance coverage. This notice informs the applicant that a report will be ordered concerning their past credit history and any other life or health insurance for which they have previously applied. The agent must leave this notice with the applicant along with the receipt.

    a. This notice must be given to the consumer no later than three days after a report was requested.

    b. A consumer may make a written request for a complete disclosure of the nature and scope of the investigation underlying the report.

        i. Disclosure must be made in writing within five days after the date on which the consumer's request was received.

3. **Consumer Rights** Consumers who feel that information in their files is inaccurate or incomplete may dispute the information, and the reporting agencies may be required to reinvestigate and correct or delete information. Insurance companies may use consumer reports, or investigative consumer reports, to compile additional information regarding the applicant. If applicants feel that the information compiled by the consumer inspection service is inaccurate, they may send a brief statement to the reporting agency with the correct information.

4. **Penalties** Violators of the Fair Credit Reporting Act may be subject to fines and imprisonment and may be required to pay any actual damages suffered by a consumer, punitive damages awarded by a court, and reasonable attorney's fees. The maximum penalty for obtaining consumer information reports under **false pretenses** is $5,000, imprisonment for one year, or both.

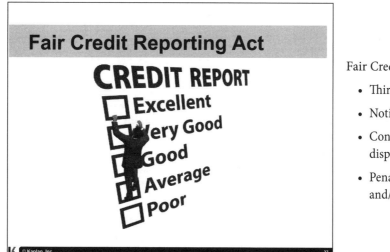

Fair Credit Reporting Act

- Third party information
- Notice to applicant REQUIRED
- Consumers have rights and can dispute information in files
- Penalty: fines (max of $5,000) and/or imprisonment (one year)

2.8   OTHER ERRORS AND OMISSIONS SITUATIONS

Producers are liable for their mistakes, including misstatements and promises of coverage. They must take special care to follow established procedures when:

- taking applications;
- explaining coverages;
- collecting premiums;
- amending policies; and
- submitting claims.

Errors and Omissions

- Producers make mistakes
- May be liable

2.9   STOLI/IOLI

Stranger-Owned Life Insurance (STOLI) or Investor-Owned Life Insurance (IOLI) transactions are life insurance arrangements involve investors who persuade seniors to take out a new life insurance policy, with the investors named as the beneficiary.

The investors often loan money to the insured to pay the premiums for a specific period of time. Often times, that is two years based on the life insurance policy's contestability period. After that period, the insured names the investor as beneficiary of the policy.

Seniors generally receive some financial inducement for this arrangement: an upfront payment, a loan or a small continuing interest in the policy death benefit. Most states are banning STOLI transactions because the investor as a beneficiary does not have insurable interest in the insured and it has become a method of fraud targeted at senior citizens.

STOLI/IOLI

- Banned in most states
- Investors named as beneficiaries

2.10   ANTI-MONEY LAUNDERING PROVISIONS OF THE USA PATRIOT ACT

The overall purpose of the USA PATRIOT Act is to deter terrorist activity, both globally and in the United States in particular. One of the ways it does that is by establishing measures to prevent, detect, and prosecute international money laundering and financing of terrorism. Under the USA PATRIOT Act, companies that issue permanent life insurance, annuities, or other products that have cash value or investment features must adopt procedures and internal controls for recognizing and reporting potential money-laundering activities. An insurer's anti-money laundering program must be headed by a compliance officer responsible for implementing the program, include ongoing training of appropriate individuals within the company, and be independently tested to assure its effectiveness. The types of suspicious activity that insurers must report include:

- receipt of any cash payment in excess of $10,000;
- purchase of insurance that is not consistent with the customer's needs;
- requests to have refund or surrender proceeds or other benefits paid to a party not clearly related to the purchaser;

- greater interest in the early termination features of a product rather than its potential performance; and

- fictitious identification or reluctance to provide identification; and maximum borrowing against a product's value soon after it is purchased.

USA PATRIOT Act

- Designed to prevent and detect money laundering and financing of terrorism

- Report suspicious activity

2.11 EMPLOYEE RETIREMENT INCOME SECURITY ACT (ERISA)

ERISA was enacted to protect the interests of participants in employee benefit plans as well as the interests of the participants' beneficiaries. Much of the law deals with qualified pension plans, but some sections also apply to group insurance plans.

2.11.1 Fiduciary Responsibility

ERISA mandates very detailed standards for fiduciaries and other parties-in-interest of employee welfare benefit plans, including group insurance plans. This means that anyone with control over plan management or plan assets of any kind must discharge that fiduciary duty solely in the interests of the plan participants and their beneficiaries. Strict penalties are imposed on those who do not fulfill this responsibility.

Reporting and Disclosure ERISA requires that certain information concerning any employee welfare benefit plan, including group insurance plans, be made available to plan participants, their beneficiaries, the Department of Labor (DOL), and the IRS. Examples of the types of information that must be distributed include:

- a summary plan description to each plan participant and the Department of Labor;

- a summary of material modifications that details changes in any plan description to each plan participant and the Department of Labor;

- an annual return or report (Form 5500 or one of its variations) submitted to the DOL;

- a summary annual report to each plan participant; and

- any terminal report to the DOL.

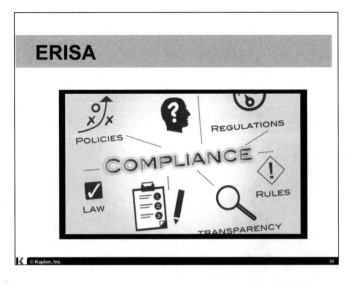

ERISA

- Protects participants in employee benefit plans
- Qualified pension plans & group insurance
- Reporting and disclosure information for plan participants

QUICK QUIZ 2.D

1. The Fair Credit Reporting Act requires which of the following to be issued to all applications for life or health insurance?

   A. A notice to the applicant

   B. A financial disclosure statement

   C. A free credit check

   D. All of these must be issued to applicants

Answers can be found at the end of Unit 2.

UNIT 2 CRAM SHEET

Changes in the Application—must be initialed by the applicant

Backdating—Usually no more than 6 months

Required Signatures

- Insured
- Producer/agent
- Applicant (if not the insured)

Producers Report

- Completed by the producer/agent
- Not attached to policy if issued

Conditional Receipt

- Premium paid with application
- Insurance effective—later of
    - Date application completed and signed
    - Medical exam (if required)
- Must be standard or preferred risk
    - Can be determined after death

Binding receipt—Temporary. Not common in Life Insurance.

Underwriting Sources of Information

- Application—primary source
- Medical exams & testing
- Attending Physician Statement (APS)
- AIDS testing
    - Applications may not ask about sexual orientation
    - Testing not based on geographical location
    - Requires insured's written consent
- Medical Information Bureau
    - Application cannot be denied solely on MIB information
    - Insured must be informed of MIB
    - MIB gets its information from insurance companies
- Consumer reports
    - Insured must be informed
- Investigative reports
    - Insured must give consent

Classification of Risks

- Standard
- Preferred
- Substandard
- Declined

Agent Delivery

- Usually must get signed delivery receipt

Statement of Good Health

- Required if no premium with application
- If health changed—agent can't deliver policy

Effective Date of Coverage

- Terms of conditional receipt is issued
- Substandard and pays additional premium—date of policy delivery
- No receipt—policy delivery date if premium paid at delivery

Fair Credit Reporting Act

- Third party information
- Notice to applicant REQUIRED
- Consumers have rights and can dispute information in files
- Penalty: fines (max of $5,000) and/or imprisonment (one year)

STOLI/IOLI

- Banned in most states.
- Investors named as beneficiaries.

U.S. Patriot Act

- Designed to prevent and detect money laundering and financing of terrorism
- Report suspicious activity

ERISA

- Protects participants in employee benefit plans
- Qualified pension plans & group insurance
- Reporting and disclosure information for plan participants

UNIT 2 QUIZ

In order to measure your success, we recommend that you answer the following 10 questions correctly.

1. A risk that bears the same health, habits, and occupational characteristic as the persons on whose the mortality table was based upon is known as a
    A. standard risk
    B. preferred risk
    C. substandard risk
    D. declined risk

2. A general report in regard to the applicant's finances, health, character, work, hobbies, and other habits that is usually completed by interviewing friends and associates is known as
    A. a consumer report
    B. an investigative consumer report
    C. an attending physicians statement
    D. a Medical information bureau report

3. Most states allow backdating to be done on an insurance application for
    A. up to 2 months
    B. up to 4 months
    C. up to 6 months
    D. up to 9 months

4. All of the following statements about completing the insurance application are correct EXCEPT
    A. any change to an application must be initialed by the applicant
    B. the application form must be signed by both the applicant, proposed insured (if not the applicant) and producer/agent
    C. the producer's report must be signed by both the applicant, proposed insured (if not the applicant) and producer/agent
    D. collecting the first premium with the application is the quickest way to get coverage in force

5. The section of the application that includes information regarding the proposed insured's physical condition, medical history, and alcohol and drug use is known as
    A. first part—general information
    B. second part—health information
    C. the entire application
    D. attending physician's statement

6. Under which of the following receipts is coverage effective as of the date of the application as long as the applicant is found to be insurable under the company's standard underwriting rules?
    A. Conditional receipt
    B. Binding receipt
    C. Standard receipt
    D. Acceptance receipt

7. Which of the following imposes a requirement that the insurer must keep all medical information confidential and protect the applicant's privacy?
   A. Consumer reports
   B. Medical information bureau
   C. HIPAA
   D. Consumer investigative reports

8. A risk that represents a chance of experiencing a loss that is below average and therefore favorable to the company is a
   A. standard risk
   B. preferred risk
   C. substandard risk
   D. declined risk

9. Which of the following is used to determine a consumer's eligibility for personal credit, insurance, or employment?
   A. Consumer reports
   B. Medical information bureau
   C. HIPAA
   D. Consumer investigative reports

10. While delivering the policy, the producer must obtain a signed document that the insured's health is the same as when he or she applied for the insurance policy. This document is called
    A. an inspection report
    B. a delivery receipt
    C. a policy review
    D. a statement of good health

ANSWER KEY

QUICK QUIZZES

QUICK QUIZ 2.A

1. **C.** producer's report

2. **D.** The beneficiary

3. **A.** underwriting process

QUICK QUIZ 2.B

1. **B.** Height and weight

2. **C.** Medical Information Bureau

3. **A.** insurer

QUICK QUIZ 2.C

1. **C.** Substandard

2. **C.** Marital status

QUICK QUIZ 2.D

1. **A.** A notice to the applicant

UNIT QUIZ

1. **A.** Standard risks represent average exposures and fall into the normal range.

2. **B.** An investigative consumer report is also called an inspection report.

3. **C.** Backdating is done so that the premium can be based on an earlier age for the insured. If the application is backdated the policy becomes effective as of that date and the insured must pay back premiums from that date.

4. **C.** The producer's report is only signed by the producer. The proposed insured does not see this report.

5. **B.** Height, weight, tobacco use, drug use, medications, high risk hobbies, family health conditions, international travels, history of disability claims and medical treatments is some of the information included in the second-part of the application.

6. **A.** Some conditional receipts make the coverage effective on the date of application, or the date of the medical examination, whichever is later. A binding receipt is often used with homeowners insurance, not life insurance.

7. **C.** If any health information is going to be shared, applicants must be given notice of the insurer's information-sharing practices, their right to maintain privacy, and an opportunity to refuse to have their information released.

8. **B.** These risks may be insured at preferred or discounted rates.

9. **A.** A credit report is an example of a consumer report. This can tell underwriters if an applicant is likely to be reliable about making premium payments.

10. **D.** This gives the insurer a good basis to contest a claim if it turns out that the insured's health declined before the coverage actually went into effect.

UNIT 3 | Basics of Life Insurance

3.1 INTRODUCTION

The primary reason for buying life insurance is to protect a family when a family member dies. It can also be used to protect a business, transfer wealth from one generation to another, provide retirement income, and serve as a source of financing.

Life insurance is perhaps the most versatile form of insurance and can serve many purposes relating to its value as insurance.

This unit discusses the uses of a life insurance policy, the legal aspects of these policies, ownership considerations, and other fundamental contract provisions.

3.2   LEARNING OBJECTIVES

After successfully completing this unit, you should be able to:

- explain third party ownership;

- identify the relationships that create insurance interest and why and when insurable interest must exist;

- explain the personal uses of life insurance: survivor protection, mortgage payoff, estate creation, estate conservation, liquidity, and cash accumulation;

- identify the different approaches to determining a person's life insurance needs: human life value, needs approach (cash needs, income needs), coordinating with other resources, data gathering;

- identify the business needs of life insurance: buy-sell funding (entity plan and cross purchase plan), key person coverage, executive bonus plan, deferred compensation plan;

- compare and contrasts the different classes of life insurance policies: individual versus group, term versus permanent, participating versus nonparticipating, fixed versus variable;

- explain industrial life insurance and home service life insurance;

- identify the three elements that go into premium calculation: mortality, interest, and expenses;

- differentiate between net premium and gross premium; and

- identify the four common premium payment modes: annual, semi-annual, quarterly, and monthly.

3.3   THIRD-PARTY OWNERSHIP AND INSURABLE INTEREST

When a life insurance policy's applicant and insured are the same, it is a two-party contract between the insurer and the owner/insured. However, as has been previously discussed, the owner of a life insurance policy is not always the insured. In that case, there are three parties to the contract:

- the insurer,

- the insured, and

- the owner/applicant.

Third-party ownership refers to a situation where the owner of a life insurance policy is someone other than the insured.

By allowing a life insurance policy to have third party ownership does not mean people can apply for life insurance on just anyone. To have a policy issued on someone else's life, the applicant must have an **insurable interest** in that person. *Insurable interest* means that the person applying for the policy must be at risk of suffering a significant loss if the insured dies. The loss may be:

- emotional, based on love and affection; or

- economic, based on financial dependency such as the insured's income.

3.3.1   Relationships That Create Insurable Interest

Individuals have an insurable interest in their own life. That is, there is no question of insurable interest in two-party situations where the applicant and the insured are the same person.

In the personal insurance market, insurable interest exists:

- between spouses or domestic partners;
- between parents and children; and
- among other close family members.

In the business insurance market, insurable interest exists:

- among business partners;
- between corporations and their officers and directors; and
- between any type of business and its key employees.

Insurable interest exists between lenders (creditors) and the people that owe them money (debtors).

3.3.2   When Must Insurable Interest Exist?

In property and casualty insurance (auto, homeowners etc.), insurable interest must exist at the time a loss or claim occurs. If someone sells a house and it later burns down, that individual cannot claim a loss even if a policy remained in force.

With life insurance, insurable interest is only required at the time of application. For example, a business buys key person life insurance on the life of the senior vice president of marketing. The business is the owner of the policy and the party designated to receive the money if the insured dies; the beneficiary. If the senior vice president quits working for the company in six months and premiums are paid to keep the policy in force, the company remains the beneficiary because the only requirement for life insurance is that **insurable interest** existed when the policy was purchased.

Must Prove Insurable Interest

- Have financial or emotional loss
  - Only have to prove if owner different than applicant (third-party ownership)
  - Examples: spouse, kids, business partner, key employees
- Assumed you have insurable interest when purchasing policy on yourself
- Insurable interest must be present at time of application only

3.4   PERSONAL USES OF LIFE INSURANCE

Life insurance helps to relieve the financial strain that a person's death may cause for surviving family members. There are other uses and needs that life insurance can help individuals accomplish.

3.4.2.1 Survivor Protection

The risk of death makes surviving family members financially vulnerable. The deceased party's income ends upon their death and for a one-income family, the source of their financial support ends. In a two-income family, the loss of one earner's wage can make it impossible to keep up a standard of living built on a multiple income household.

Survivors can be a spouse and children or other loved ones that depend on the financial support of the income earner. This could include aging parents or a disabled sibling.

Another need for life insurance is the death of a stay-at-home mom or dad who provided daycare or homemaking services. This can put a strain on the widowed working parent's or their children's finances.

In any case, the life insurance death benefit can be used to replace a deceased individual's economic contribution to relieve or eliminate a surviving family's financial distress. While still alive, the insured has the peace of mind of knowing that their **survivors are protected** financially if the worst should happen to them.

3.4.2.2 Mortgage Payoff

The largest lifetime financial obligation for families is their home mortgage. A mortgage life insurance policy will pay off this debt if the insured dies and assures that their surviving family will be able to stay in their home.

3.4.2.3 Estate Creation

An individual's *estate* are the assets they leave behind at death. The source for most family estates is built over years by saving money out of income, by purchasing a home, making sound investments, and other items of value. Dying too young robs an individual of the time needed to accumulate assets. For people in their working years, life insurance can **create an estate** if pre-mature death prevents them from doing so themselves.

3.4.2.4 Estate Conservation

Death poses a different problem for people who have accumulated an estate. Dying comes with debt that must be paid from an individual's estate. This includes estate (death) taxes and probate expenses— the size of the estate determines the amount of taxes due. What starts out as a large estate may be much smaller by the time the money gets to the heirs and they are not able to enjoy the standard of living that the deceased wanted them to have.

Estate planning is also important with life insurance so that it can be used to pay the expenses incurred at someone's death. Life insurance can ensure the **estate is conserved** and kept intact for the heirs as the individual intended.

3.4.2.5 Liquidity

Liquidity can be a problem when an individual dies because the costs incurred at death must generally be paid in cash. If the estate does not have enough cash, other assets must be *liquidated* to get it. If those assets are illiquid or if the stock market happens to be down when securities must be sold, those assets cannot be liquidated for their full value.

Liquidity refers to how easily an asset can be turned into cash without loss of value. Examples of *liquid assets* are:

- bank savings or checking accounts—the most liquid assets after cash itself; and

- life insurance proceeds—are paid in cash.

Examples of *illiquid assets* include:

- precious metals (gold, silver, etc.), precious gems, or stamps;

- real estate;

- farms and farming equipment; and

- small or privately held business interests.

A life insurance policy is a good solution to estate liquidity problems. When the insured dies, it turns into cash to pay the estate's expenses, avoiding the possibility that other estate assets will have to be sold at a loss.

3.4.2.6 Cash Accumulation

Another personal use of life insurance is to **accumulate cash**. Permanent life insurance policies have a cash value component that grows over time. The life insurance cash value is called the policies *living benefits*. This money can be used for a number of purposes, such as:

- emergencies; to fix a heating system or repair a leaking roof;

- opportunities; starting up a new business;

- an education fund for children or grandchildren; and

- a supplementary retirement income.

Personal Uses of Life Insurance

- Survivor protection
- Mortgage payoff
- Estate creation
- Estate conservation
- Liquidity
- Cash accumulation

QUICK QUIZ 3.A

1. In life insurance contracts, when must insurable interest exist?
   A. Only at the time the policy is purchased
   B. At the time the policy is purchased and at the time the loss occurs
   C. Only at the time that the loss occurs
   D. It does not need to exist in life insurance contracts

2. Which of the following is NOT a personal use of life insurance?
   A. Estate creation
   B. Cash accumulation
   C. Mortgage payoff
   D. Third party ownership

3. The assets left behind after an individual's death is known as
   A. liquidity
   B. an estate
   C. debt
   D. financial obligations

Answers can be found at the end of Unit 3.

3.5   DETERMINING AMOUNT OF PERSONAL LIFE INSURANCE

3.5.1   Human Life Value

According to the principle of *human life value*, the purpose of life insurance is to replace an individual's economic value and this begins with a straightforward calculation:

the amount of the individual's annual income × the number of years until retirement

Example: Dan is 35 years old, earns $50,000 yearly, and plans to retire in 30 years at age 65. Calculation: $50,000 × 30 = $1,500,000 is the amount of money Dan will earn by the end of his working years.

3.5.2   The Needs Approach

The *needs approach* is similar to the human life value and is used to find the amount of insurance coverage an individual should buy. But instead of focusing on income, the needs approach looks at the financial situation the survivors will face if the individual dies. The needs approach is much more detailed than the human life value approach, and it results in a more accurate number. The needs approach is also more commonly used than the human life value approach.

Survivors' financial needs fall into two categories:

- cash needs; and
- income needs.

3.5.2.1 Cash Needs

Cash needs are those that can be met with a lump of money. This includes:

- final expenses—funeral/burial costs and final medical bills;
- debt payoff—home mortgage, credit cards, car loans, other installment loans;
- children's education—a fund to pay the future cost of college or trade school; and
- emergency fund—unexpected expenses that can cause a hardship for the surviving family.

3.5.2.2 Income Needs

Income needs are those created by ongoing living expenses such as food, clothing, utilities, and a mortgage. There are three distinct income need periods.

- *Family Dependency*—during this period the surviving children are too young to support themselves and depend on the surviving parent for their needs.
- *Preretirement*—at this point the children have grown up and become self-supporting, but the surviving spouse has not yet reached retirement age.
- *Retirement*—now the surviving spouse is no longer earning an income.

Social Security pays survivor benefits during the family dependency and retirement periods. However during the preretirement period, often called the *blackout* period, payments are suspended.

Blackout period—The Social Security Administration provides benefits for surviving spouses with children under age 16. When the youngest child turns 16, benefits stop and do not resume until the surviving spouse turns 60. Example: A widowed spouse is 40 years old with two children, ages 12 and 14. Social security would stop paying a benefit to the spouse at age 44, and resume/begin paying a benefit at age 60.

3.5.2.3 Coordinating with Other Resources

After determining the income needs of the survivors, those amounts are reduced by any financial resources that will be available to the survivors when the income earner dies. Those resources may come from three places:

- existing assets such as bank savings accounts and investment accounts or Individual Retirement Accounts (IRAs);
- employer life insurance or retirement benefits payable to a surviving spouse; and
- Social Security that can pay benefits to the surviving dependents.

3.5.2.4 Data Gathering

The insurance agent must conduct a ***data gathering*** or ***fact-finding*** interview to acquire information required for the needs approach. This includes:

- names and birthdates of every member of the family to determine the length of the three income periods;
- sources and amounts of income available upon the death of the individual;
- debt, like home mortgages, that must be eliminated upon the death of an individual;
- existing assets that can be used to offset survivors' cash needs upon individual's death;

- amounts of life insurance already owned, including group life insurance obtained through an employee benefit plan; and

- financial objectives such as the education level desired for the children and retirement income goals.

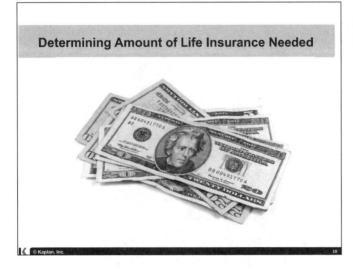

Determining Amount of Life Insurance Needed

- Human life value – income replacement – annual income × # of years until retirement

- Needs approach—more detailed approach

  - Cash needs (final expenses, debt, children's education, emergency fund)

  - Income needs (ongoing living expenses)

3.5.3   Business Uses of Life Insurance

Life insurance has long been a valuable tool that business owners use to reduce risk and to provide the basic financial foundation for continued success. Most business owners recognize the importance of life insurance and use it to solve many of the problems associated with maintaining and growing a successful company.

3.5.3.1 Buy-Sell Funding

Buy-sell agreements provide for the sale of a business interest at the death or disability of an owner. They are often referred to as *business continuation plans*.

To make sure that purchasers have the money needed to buy a business interest when an owner dies, buy-sell agreements can be funded with life insurance. The policy is on the business owner's life, and the buyer of the business is the beneficiary. The amount of the death benefit is the purchase price of the business interest as stated in the buy-sell agreement.

There are two types of buy-sell agreements: entity and cross-purchase plans.

- Under an *entity plan*, the purchaser of a deceased owner's business interest is the business entity itself. When funded by life insurance, the business entity owns a policy on the life of each business owner. If the business is a corporation, entity plans are often called *stock redemption plans* because the corporation is actually redeeming the deceased owner's stock. The term entity plan is usually used with non-incorporated businesses such as partnerships.

- Under a *cross-purchase plan*, the surviving owner(s) purchase the deceased owner's interest in the business. When funded by life insurance, each partner (or shareholder, if the business is a corporation) owns a policy on the lives of each of the other partners. If there are more than two partners or shareholders, many more policies are needed for a cross-purchase plan than an entity plan.

3.5.3.2 Key Person Coverage

Just as a family depends on the financial contribution of an income-earner, a business may depend on a particular employee whose contribution is key to its success. Businesses can protect themselves against the financial harm that would result from the death of such an employee with **key person coverage**.

The business owns, pays for, and is the beneficiary of the policy on the key person's life. If the key person dies, the insurance proceeds can be used to offset direct financial losses such as a drop in sales as well as to help pay the costs of finding and training a replacement.

3.5.3.3 Executive Bonus Plans

Rather than giving a yearly bonus to an employee in cash, companies can use the money to buy a life insurance policy for the employee. Under an **executive bonus plan**, a business pays the premiums on a life insurance policy which the employee owns. During life, the employee has full access to the policy's living benefits, and at death the proceeds are paid to the beneficiary named by the employee.

3.5.3.4 Deferred Compensation Plans

Under a **deferred compensation plan**, an employer agrees to pay an employee a stated amount of income beginning at retirement rather than paying the money now. This benefits the employee because the money is not taxable until the employee actually receives it. If the money were paid now, it would be included with the employee's current earnings and probably taxed at a higher rate. After retirement, the employee may be in a lower tax bracket.

In return, the employee agrees to work for the employer until a specified future date—typically at retirement. The deferred compensation benefits are forfeited if the employee leaves the company before then. This benefits the employer by helping to assure that a valuable employee continues to contribute to the company's success and does not leave to work for a competitor or start a competing business of his or her own.

If the employee dies before retirement, the deferred compensation benefits become payable immediately to the employee's surviving spouse or other beneficiary. Companies often buy a life insurance policy to make sure they will have the money to pay those benefits if that happens. If the policy is permanent insurance, the cash values can be used to help pay the deferred compensation benefits to the employee if he or she lives to retirement.

Under the life insurance policy that funds a deferred compensation plan:

- the company is owner, premium payer, and beneficiary; and
- the employee is the insured.

Business Uses of Life Insurance

- Buy sell funding
    - Cross purchase
    - Entity purchase
- Key person
- Executive bonus
- Deferred compensation

 QUICK QUIZ 3.B

1. The preretirement period, one of the distinct income needs periods, is also known as the
   A. blackout period
   B. family dependency period
   C. cash needs period
   D. expense period

2. Which of the following states the purpose of life insurance is to replace the economic value of an individual?
   A. The needs approach
   B. The human life value principle
   C. The income needs principle
   D. The business needs approach

3. In a buy-sell agreement, the life insurance policy is written on the
   A. business
   B. person who will buy the business in the event that the owner dies
   C. business owner's life
   D. family of the business owner

Answers can be found at the end of Unit 3.

3.6   CLASSES OF LIFE INSURANCE POLICIES

Group life insurance is a single contract that covers an entire group of people. Typically, the policyowner is an employer and the policy covers the employees or members of the group. Group life insurance is often provided as part of a complete employee benefit package. In most cases, the cost of group coverage is far less than what the employees or members would pay for an *individual policy* with similar coverage.

Individual	vs.	Group
Cost based upon individual insured		Cost based upon the group
Individual policy issued		Policy issued to employer or group sponsor
Policyowner chooses amount of insurance		Employer determines amount of insurance
Term	**vs.**	**Permanent**
Death benefit only		Living and death benefits
Increasing premiums		Level premiums
Temporary coverage; expires at end of term		Lifetime coverage; no expiration
Cannot be renewed (extended) after a certain age		Protection continues through advanced ages
Participating	**vs.**	**Nonparticipating**
May pay dividends to policyowner		Does not pay dividends
Somewhat higher premium		Somewhat lower premium
Can be issued by mutual or stock insurers		Issued by stock insurers
Fixed	**vs.**	**Variable**
Guaranteed cash value		No guarantee cash value
Values expressed in dollar amounts		Values expressed in investment units

3.6.1   Industrial Life Insurance

Industrial life insurance was developed as a way for people of limited means to obtain some of the benefits of life insurance. The face amounts are usually small—$2,000 or less—and are often bought simply to help pay burial expenses. A distinctive characteristic of industrial policies is that the premiums come due weekly and are collected in person by producers who go door to door.

3.6.2   Home Service Life Insurance

A variation on industrial life insurance is known as **home service life insurance**. Home service policies are sold by industrial or *home service*, producers in the neighborhoods where they collect premiums at the houses of industrial life policyowners. However, the policies are somewhat larger in size, typically ranging from $10,000 to $25,000 in face value. Policyowners are encouraged to pay the premiums through an automatic bank draft (often called a *monthly debit plan*) or by mail, so that producers do not have to collect them personally.

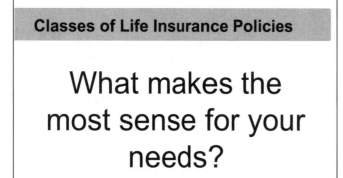

Classes of Life Insurance Policies

- Individual vs. group
- Term vs. permanent
- Participating vs. non-participating
- Fixed vs. variable
- Industrial & home service

3.7 DEVELOPMENT OF LIFE POLICY PREMIUMS

3.7.1 Premium Elements

Three elements go into the calculation of insurance premiums:

Mortality—the relative frequency of deaths in a specific population; death rate.

Interest—earnings on premium dollars between the time they are collected and the time they are paid out as claims.

Expenses—insurer operating costs, referred to as the *expense load*. Adding the expense element to insurance premiums is called *loading*.

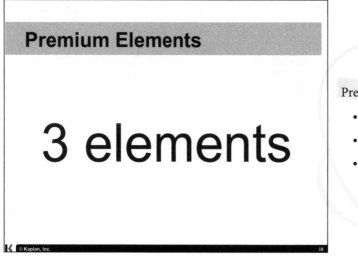

Premium Elements

- Mortality
- Interest
- Expenses

3.7.2 Net Premium, Gross Premium

Net premium is the premium before loading or the mortality element minus the interest element. The *net single premium* will fund a policy's benefit with one premium payment.

Net Premium = Mortality – Interest

Gross premium is the net premium plus the expense element, referred to as the *loaded premium*. The *gross annual premium* is the amount a policyowner pays for a policy.

Gross Premium = Mortality – Interest + Expenses

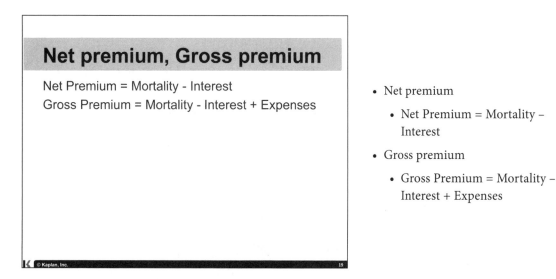

- Net premium
  - Net Premium = Mortality – Interest
- Gross premium
  - Gross Premium = Mortality – Interest + Expenses

3.7.3 Premium Payment Mode

The **premium payment mode** reflects how frequently premiums come due. Premiums may be paid annually, semi-annually, quarterly, or monthly.

Premium calculations are based on the assumption that the policyowner will pay the annual premium mode. Premiums will be higher if not paid annually.

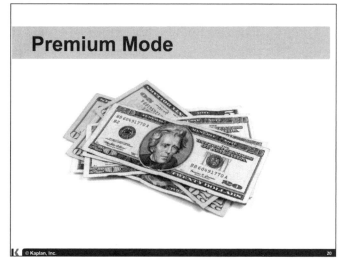

Premium Mode

- Annual, semi-annual, quarterly, monthly
  - Annual is the lowest

QUICK QUIZ 3.C

1. Life insurance premiums are lowest under which premium payment mode?
   - A. Monthly
   - B. Quarterly
   - C. Semi-annual
   - D. Annual

2. The number of individuals who die each year at a given age is also known as
   - A. morbidity
   - B. mortality
   - C. actuaries
   - D. expenses

3. Living and death benefits, level premiums, and lifetime coverage are characteristics of which of the following classes of insurance?
   - A. Term life insurance
   - B. Industrial life insurance
   - C. Permanent life insurance
   - D. Home service life insurance

Answers can be found at the end of Unit 3.

UNIT 3 CRAM SHEET

Insurable Interest

- A risk of loss
  - Assumed in one's self and relationships (spouse, children)
  - No obvious relationship
- Must be proven before policy can be purchased
- The relationship doesn't have to exist at death

Personal Uses of Life Insurance

- Survivor protection
- Mortgage payoff
- Estate creation
- Estate conservation
- Liquidity
- Cash accumulation

Determining Amount of Life Insurance Needed

- Human life value
  - Current income
- Needs approach
  - Money for specific needs

Business Uses of Life Insurance

- Buy sell funding
  - Cross purchase
  - Entity purchase
- Key person
- Executive bonus
- Deferred compensation

Classes of Life Insurance Policies

- Individual vs. group
- Term vs. permanent
- Participating vs. non-participating
- Fixed vs. variable
- Industrial and home service

Premium Elements

- Mortality
- Interest
- Expenses
- Net premium
  - Mortality minus interest
  - Net single

Gross premium

- Net premium plus expenses
- Gross annual

Premium Mode

- Annual, semi-annual, quarterly, monthly
  - Annual is the lowest

UNIT 3 QUIZ

In order to measure your success, we recommend that you answer the following 10 questions correctly.

1. Which of the following factors does NOT have an effect on the insurance premium rates?
   A. Mortality or morbidity
   B. Interest rates
   C. Producer certification
   D. Expenses

2. Which of the following types of insurance has premiums that are due weekly and are collected in person by producers who go door to door?
   A. Term life insurance
   B. Industrial life insurance
   C. Permanent life insurance
   D. Home service life insurance

3. Which of the following describes an employer that agrees to pay an employee a stated amount of income beginning at retirement rather than paying them the money now?
   A. Deferred compensation plan
   B. Executive bonus plan
   C. Buy sell agreement
   D. Key person coverage

4. All of the following are examples of buy-sell agreements EXCEPT
   A. cross-purchase plan
   B. entity plan
   C. stock redemption plan
   D. executive bonus plan

5. All of the following are examples of an insurable interest EXCEPT
   A. Sue would like to buy a life insurance policy on her spouse
   B. Tom would like to buy life insurance on his best friend
   C. Amy would like to buy a life insurance policy on her business partner
   D. Michael and Megan would like to buy a life insurance policy for each of their children

6. Which of the following terms refers to how easily an asset can be turned into cash without loss of value?
   A. Liquidity
   B. Estate conservation
   C. Estate creation
   D. Hard assets

7. When the owner of a life insurance policy is not the insured, there are three parties to the contract. Which of the following is not a party to this type of contract?
   A. Insured
   B. Applicant
   C. Beneficiary
   D. Insurer

8.   Which of the following classes of life insurance has a death benefit only, increasing premiums temporary coverage and expires at end of the term?
   A.   Variable life insurance
   B.   Term life insurance
   C.   Permanent life insurance
   D.   Home service life insurance

9.   Which of the following premiums is the mortality element minus the interest element?
   A.   Loaded premium
   B.   Gross premium
   C.   Net premium
   D.   Fixed premium

10.   All of the following are names of distinct income need periods EXCEPT
   A.   family dependency
   B.   preretirement
   C.   retirement
   D.   social security

ANSWER KEY

QUICK QUIZZES

QUICK QUIZ 3.A

1. **A.** Only at the time the policy is purchased

2. **D.** Third party ownership

3. **B.** an estate

QUICK QUIZ 3.B

1. **A.** blackout period

2. **B.** The human life value principle

3. **C.** business owner's life

QUICK QUIZ 3.C

1. **D.** Annual

2. **B.** mortality

3. **C.** Permanent life insurance

UNIT QUIZ

1. **C.** The producer's certification does not have any effect on premium rates. Mortality, morbidity, interest rates, and expenses do.

2. **B.** With industrial life insurance the face amounts are usually small—$2,000 or less and are often bought simply to help pay burial expenses. This is the only policy that you will learn about that has weekly premiums.

3. **A.** This benefits the employee because the money is not taxable until the employee actually receives it. In return, the employee agrees to work for the employer until retirement so it also benefits the employer.

4. **D.** Rather than giving a yearly bonus to an employee in cash, companies can use the money to buy a life insurance policy for the employee. The other 3 answer choices are buy-sell agreements and provide for the sale of a business at the death of an owner. They are often referred to as business continuation plans.

5. **B.** Spouses, children, close family members, and business partners are all examples in which insurable interest exists. A neighbor or a best friend would not be an example of an insurable interest.

6. **A.** An example of a liquid asset is a bank savings or checking account. Illiquid assets are those that lack liquidity and are also called hard assets)

7. **C.** When a life insurance policy's applicant and insured are the same, it is a two-party contract between the insurer and the owner/insured. When the insured and policyowner are different, it is a three party contract between the insurer, insured, and policyowner.

8. **B.** Term is temporary, permanent is for a lifetime.

9. **C.** Gross premium is the net premium plus the expense element. It may also be referred to as the loaded premium.

10. **D.** Social Security actually pays the survivor benefits during the family dependency and retirement periods, but not during the preretirement period. For this reason, the preretirement period is often called the blackout period.

UNIT 4

Types of Life Insurance Policies

4.1 INTRODUCTION

Life insurance policies have been designed and molded over three centuries.

Life insurance can be divided into two basic classes: term and permanent policies. Policies that are sold today have the same fundamental structure as those created years ago. However, insurers continue to refine their products to meet the demands of a changing society.

This unit explores the basic policies—term, whole life, and universal life—as well as popular hybrids. You will learn how they work, when they are used, and how they can be customized for special situations.

4.2   LEARNING OBJECTIVES

After successfully completing this lesson, you should be able to:

- describe characteristics of term insurance, the types of policies, the advantages, and the disadvantages;
- describe characteristics of whole life insurance, the types of policies, the advantages, and the disadvantages;
- describe characteristics of flexible insurance, the types of policies, the advantages, and the disadvantages;
- describe characteristics of variable insurance, the types of policies, the advantages, and the disadvantages; and
- describe characteristics of specialized insurance, the types of policies, the advantages, and the disadvantages.

4.3   LIFE INSURANCE POLICIES

All life insurance policies pay a benefit upon the death of the insured. The amount of the death benefit is called the *face amount* because it's usually found on the first (face) page of the policy. Depending upon the type policy, the actual death benefit payable after the initial purchase of the policy can be equal to, less than or greater than the face amount.

Certain types of life insurance policies also offer *living benefits* – that is, financial benefits that are available while the insured is still alive. The differences between the types of life insurance policies arise from variations in how living and death benefits are provided.

4.4   TERM INSURANCE

4.4.1   Characteristics of Term Insurance

Term life insurance is the simplest type of life insurance. Term life insurance policies only offer a death benefit and remain in force for a specified period of time, or *term*. No death benefit is payable if the insured dies after the term expires.

4.4.2   Types of Term Policies

4.4.2.1   Level Term

The death benefit of a **level term policy** equals the face amount throughout the term of coverage. The premium also remains level during the term. The policy's term of coverage may be expressed in reference to either:

- a number of years, such as 1-year term, 5-year term, 10-year term; 20 year term and 30 year term; or
- a specified age, such as term to age 65 or term to age 70.

4.4.2.2 Decreasing Term

The death benefit of a **decreasing term policy** declines over the coverage period until it reaches zero at the end of the term. Decreasing term is appropriate coverage for financial obligations that decrease steadily over time, like home mortgages, bank loans, or financial obligations that require regular periodic payments.

4.4.2.3 Increasing Term

The death benefit of an **increasing term policy** begins near zero and grows over the term of coverage. Increasing term insurance is appropriate to cover financial obligations that increase steadily over time. Increasing term coverage also helps keep life insurance death benefits current with inflation and keep pace with rising cost of living expenses.

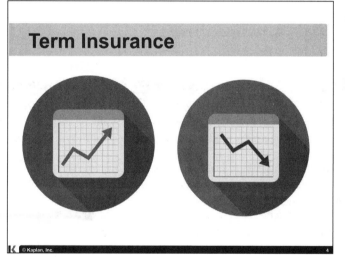

Term Insurance

- Level term
    - Death benefit is level
    - Premium is level for the term
- Decreasing term
    - Death benefit decreases
    - Premium remains level
- Increasing term
    - Death benefit increases
    - Premium increases

4.4.2.4 Return of Premium Term

Return of Premium term policies will return all or a part of the premium paid for the policy if the insured is still alive at the end of the term. The premium for this policy will be higher than a regular term insurance policy, and the premium will also be dependent upon the percentage of premium that will be returned. A 100% return of premium policy would have a higher premium than a 50% return of premium policy, and a return of premium policy would be more expensive than a comparable level term policy.

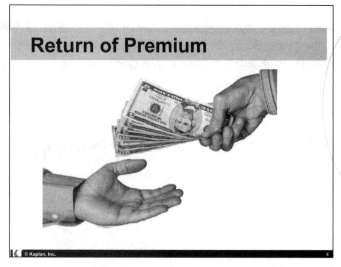

Return of Premium Term

- Premium higher than regular term policy
- Premium paid by insured is paid back if insured alive at the end of the term

4.4.2.5 Renewability

The **renewability** feature, with term life insurance, guarantees that the policy will renew (extend) at the end of its term. The insured does not have to re-apply or qualify medically for the coverage. The new renewal period will be for the same term as originally purchased. For example, at the end of each five-year renewal period, a 5-year renewable term policy automatically renews for another five years.

The renewability feature guarantees the same amount of death benefit, however, the premium for the new renewal period will increase based upon the insured's age at renewal; the insured's *attained age*.

The payment of the higher premium at each renewal results in what is called a *step-rate premium*. The following illustration shows the step-rate premium from age 30 to age 40 for a 1-year renewable term policy or A.R.T. (Annual Renewal Term) contract. The policy automatically renews each year but note that the renewal premium increases each year as the insured ages.

Step-Rate Premiums in Renewable Term

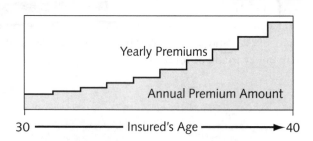

A 5-year renewable term policy would have level coverage and premium for 5 years then increase upon renewal for the next 5 years.

Renewable term policies expire at an age specified in the policy (e.g., age 65 or 70).

4.4.2.6 Convertibility

A **convertibility** feature allows a policyowner to convert a term insurance policy to a permanent type of policy without *evidence of insurability* and without having to submit an application. The conversion must be made before the term insurance policy expires. The premium for the converted policy will be based on one of two options:

- **Attained age:** Insured's age at time of conversion

- **Original age:** Age at the time the original term policy was written. A lump sum amount is required (down payment) that equals what the cash value would have been if a permanent policy was originally purchased instead of the term policy.

4.4.3   Advantages and Disadvantages of Term Insurance

4.4.3.1 Advantages

Because term insurance provides only a death benefit, its premiums are lower than other types of life insurance policies. A term policy is initially the least expensive form of life insurance.

4.4.3.2 Disadvantages

- Term coverage lasts only for the term of the policy; it's like **renting** not owning the policy.

- Term premiums increase as the insured gets older.

- Renewability features expire before the age of average life expectancy. As a result, individuals may not be able to obtain or afford coverage at older ages when their risk of dying is greater.

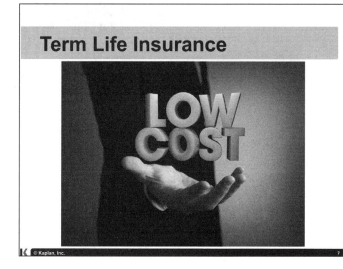

- Term life insurance
  - Renewable
    - No new application required
    - New premium based upon attained age
- Convertible
  - Can be changed to permanent insurance
  - No new application required
- LOW initial cost
- Coverage for a short period of time

QUICK QUIZ 4.A

1. In which type of term policy does the annual premium remain level throughout the policy while the death benefit decreases?
    A. Increasing term
    B. Level term
    C. Decreasing term
    D. Convertible term

2. All of the following statements about term insurance are correct EXCEPT
    A. term coverage lasts only for the term of the policy
    B. term insurance provides only a death benefit
    C. premiums are higher than other types of life insurance policies
    D. no death benefit is payable if the insured dies after the term expires

Answers can be found at the end of Unit 4.

4.5   WHOLE LIFE INSURANCE

4.5.1   Characteristics of Whole Life Insurance

Whole Life is a *permanent insurance* policy which is guaranteed to remain in force for the insured's entire lifetime ("whole life") provided the required premiums are paid, or to the policy maturity date. In contrast to term insurance, which becomes unaffordable or unobtainable at older ages, *whole life insurance* is designed to remain in force for the whole life of the insured and the premiums will never increase.

4.5.1.1 Level Premium

The purpose of a *level premium* with whole life policies is to make lifetime coverage affordable at older ages. The *level premium* system results in overpaying for the risk of dying at younger ages, and underpaying in later years toward the end of life expectancy. As a result the premium amount paid for a whole life policy never increases from its original amount even if the insured lives to a very old age.

4.5.1.2 Fixed Premium Schedule

The policyowner selects the mode of payment for the policy's **level premium** on a **fixed schedule**. This can be a monthly payment schedule or another mode. If a premium is not paid when it is due, the policy will go out of force, or *lapse*.

4.5.1.3 Fixed, Level Death Benefit

Like its premium, the death benefit of a whole life policy is **fixed and level**. For as long as the policy is in force, the face amount remains the same.

4.5.1.4 Cash Value

Cash values are an integral part of a whole life policy, and reflect the reserves necessary to assure payment of the guaranteed death benefit.

4.5.1.5 Guaranteed Interest Crediting

The policy cash value increases steadily over the life of the contract because it is regularly credited with a **guaranteed (level) rate of interest**. The scheduled increases in the cash value are stated in the policy illustration.

4.5.1.6 Policy Surrender

The "cash surrender" value of the whole life policy arises from the policyholder's rights to quit the contract and reclaim a share of the reserve fund attributable to the policy. By cashing in a policy, the policyowner gives up the death benefit.

4.5.1.7 Policy Loans

Life insurance policies with a cash surrender value usually have loan provisions (**policy loan**) that allow the policyholder to borrow up to the cash value of the policy. The policy and its death benefit remain in force when cash is loaned and interest must be paid on the amount borrowed.

If a policy loan has not been paid back and the insured dies, the amount borrowed plus any interest charges are deducted from the policy's death benefit.

4.5.1.8 Death Benefit Components

The whole life policy ***death benefit*** is payable upon the insured's death. The death benefit consists of two components:

1. The cash value, sometimes referred to as the *savings element*; and
2. An insurance protection element that must be paid in addition to the cash value so that the death benefit equals the policy's face amount. This is known as the net amount of risk to the insurance company, which represents the amount of money the insurer must have on hand to pay the death benefit. The death benefit equals the cash value plus the net amount at risk at any given time.

Cash values increase each year; the insurance protection element decreases each year.

Whole life policies mature or endows at some point in the future. A whole life policy usually endows either at age 100 or 120. If the insured is still living when maturity occurs, the cash value in the policy will equal the policy face amount and is paid to the policyowner. At endowment, the policyowner will pay income tax on any taxable gain.

Traditional Whole Life

- Fixed premium
- Fixed & level death benefit
- Cash values
  - Guaranteed interest
  - May be surrendered
  - May be borrowed
  - Endows at age 100
- Death benefit
  - Amount at risk to the company
  - Plus cash values

4.5.2   Types of Whole Life Policies

4.5.2.1 Continuous Premium Whole Life

The premiums for this whole life policy are the same each year for the duration of the contract. It is also referred to as **straight life** or **ordinary life**. If the policyowner discontinues making premium payments, they will receive the cash value of the policy.

4.5.2.2 Limited-Payment Whole Life

Limited-payment whole life policies allow for a lifetime of premiums to be paid in a shorter period of time. Common forms of limited payment whole life are:

- 10-pay or 20-pay whole life; the premiums are payable in 10 or 20 level annual installments, and
- life paid-up at age 65; premiums are payable in level annual installments from the date of purchase to the year the insured turns 65.

Annual premiums for limited payment policies will be higher than continuous payment policies. The premium payments are compressed into a shorter time frame resulting in a higher premium. As with all whole life policies, coverage is for the insured's entire life.

The cash value of a limited payment policy accumulates faster than a continuous premium policy. The cash value of a limited payment policy will continue to earn interest at the guaranteed rate at the end of the premium-paying period, and the policy still endows at age 100 (or 120).

This illustration compares the cash value accumulation of a limited payment whole life policy (policy B) to a continuous premium whole life policy (policy A). Both policies have a $50,000 face amount.

Comparison of Whole Life and Limited Pay Life

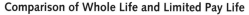

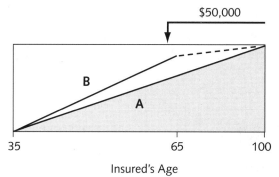

Insured's Age

4.5.2.3 Single Premium Whole Life

A **single premium whole life policy** has one payment made at the time of purchase. The amount of this single premium, along with interest earnings, will cover all future costs of maintaining the policy. Single premium policies create immediate cash value.

4.5.2.4 Modified Premium Whole Life

Modified premium whole life policies, sometimes called *modified whole life policies*, have lower premiums during the first three to five years. Compared to a continuous premium whole life policy, in those early years, modified whole life policies have a lower cost similar to term insurance. However, after the initial period, premiums increase to a certain amount and then are level for the life of the policy, making them higher in cost than a continuous premium whole life policy.

4.5.2.5 Graded Premium Life Insurance

Graded premium whole life policies have an even lower initial premium than modified whole life policies. The graded premium starts out lower than other types of whole life policies and increases every year for five to ten years until leveling off for as long as the policy remains in force.

4.5.2.6 Indeterminate Premium

An **indeterminate premium whole life policy** is similar to a nonparticipating whole life policy except that it provides for adjustable premiums. The company will charge a current premium based on its current estimate of investment earnings, mortality, and expense costs. If these estimates change in later years, the company will adjust the premium accordingly but never above the maximum guaranteed premium stated in the policy.

4.5.2.7 Interest-Sensitive or Current Assumption Whole Life

Interest-sensitive whole life, also known as *current assumption whole life* is a type of whole life insurance where the cash value can increase beyond the stated guarantee if economic conditions warrant. The interest-sensitive policy has:

- a fixed, level death benefit, and
- a premium schedule fixed in regard to the timing of payments.

With interest sensitive whole life, the insurer will make investments with a percentage of each premium payment. Excess or current interest from those investments may be credited to the policy to make the cash value rise. The interest rate is not fixed for the life of the policy and can fluctuate depending on current economic conditions.

Not only can the cash value increase more quickly, but the death benefits can also grow. The primary indicator for any increase is the current economic conditions. The policyowner will be protected from a drop in value below a stated minimum.

Types of Whole Life Policies

- Continuous premium
- Limited payment
- Single premium
    - Immediate cash values
- Modified premium
    - Lower premium first three to five years
    - Premium jumps once then levels off
- Graded premium
    - Lowest initial premium of all whole life policies
    - Premium increases for 5 to 10 years then levels off
- Indeterminate premium
    - Premiums adjusted by the company
    - Has a guaranteed maximum premium
- Interest sensitive
    - Has a current interest rate
    - Guaranteed interest rate

4.5.3   Advantages and Disadvantages of Whole Life Insurance

4.5.3.1 Advantages

Whole life insurance is permanent coverage with guaranteed level premiums and it does not expire after a specified term. Cash values in whole life insurance policies accumulate tax deferred. By law permanent policies offer certain options in the event the policy lapses after premiums have been paid into the policy. These values include cash surrender value, paid-up insurance, or extended term insurance.

4.5.3.2 Disadvantages

Because the policy is providing lifetime coverage, the initial premium for whole life is higher than term insurance. Unlike other types of permanent insurance, whole life premiums cannot be decreased and are not flexible. The death benefit cannot be increased. Lastly, the policyowner has no control over how the cash value is invested.

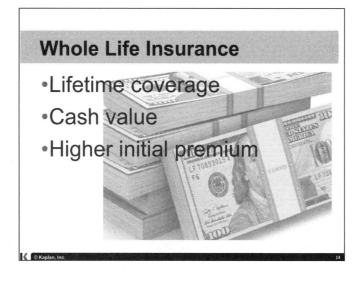

Whole Life Insurance

- Advantages
  - Permanent Coverage
  - Guaranteed Level Premiums
  - Lifetime coverages
- Disadvantages
  - Premium not flexible
  - Higher initial premium

 QUICK QUIZ 4.B

1. Whole life insurance is often referred to as
   A. permanent insurance
   B. level insurance
   C. term insurance
   D. less expensive insurance

2. Which whole life policy allows for a lifetime of premiums to be paid in a shorter period of time such as 10 or 20 years?
   A. Continuous premium whole life
   B. Limited-pay whole life
   C. Single premium whole life
   D. Modified premium whole life

3. The death benefit of a whole life policy is
   A. variable
   B. decreasing
   C. increasing
   D. fixed and level

Answers can be found at the end of Unit 4.

4.6   FLEXIBLE POLICIES

4.6.1   Characteristics of Flexible Policies

Flexible policies give the policyowner numerous options in terms of premiums, face amounts, and investment objectives. These policy components can be adjusted in response to changing needs and circumstances.

4.6.2   Types of Flexible Policies

4.6.2.1 Adjustable Life Insurance

An adjustable life policy gives the policyowner the options to adjust the face value/death benefit, the premium, and the length of coverage without having to change policies. It also offers the ability to have term and whole life coverage in one policy. The amount of premium that the policyowner can afford is used to determine what type of insurance will best meet their needs.

If initially, an individual purchases an adjustable life policy with a large death benefit and low premium, it would operate much like a term insurance. All of the premium would be used to pay the death benefit and nothing would generate cash value. If however the policyowner decided to lower the death benefit, the policy would now accumulate cash value like whole life insurance, assuming no reduction occurred in the premium payment. Increasing the premium without changing the death benefit would accumulate cash value more rapidly, and now the adjustable life policy would perform similar to a whole life policy.

4.6.2.2 Universal Life

Universal life (UL) was designed for people who want flexible premiums and flexible coverage over the course of their lifetime. UL premiums are flexible, not fixed, like whole life. Premiums paid into a universal life policy accumulate as interest in the policy's cash value. Monthly interest credited to the cash value is either the guaranteed rate or current rate, whichever is higher. Every month a term cost of insurance and a monthly administrative fee are taken from the cash value by the insurer. As long as there is enough cash value to cover these monthly expenses, the policy will stay in force.

The policyowner may increase or decrease the death benefit, subject to any insurability requirements. In addition, the policyowner has the flexibility to choose one of two policy death benefit options.

Option A (or *Option 1*) provides for a level death benefit equal to the policy's face value. As a result of this choice, more of the premium is placed in the cash account, making the cash value rise more quickly.

Option B (or *Option 2*) provides for an increasing death benefit equal to the face value of the policy plus the cash account. Cash value does not increase as quickly because more of the premium is applied to the higher cost of the increasing death benefit over the life of the policy.

Withdrawals and loans may be made against the cash value account. The policyowner can also surrender or "cash in" the universal life contract for its current cash value whenever he or she wishes.

These illustrations depict how each death benefit options works. The *corridor* at the right of the Option A illustration shows an automatic increase in the amount of insurance protection required under the tax law when policies accumulate a high proportion of cash value compared to the death benefit.

Option A—Universal Life Level Death Benefit

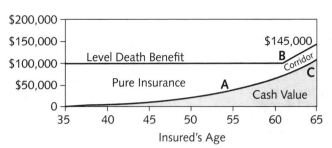

Option B—Universal Life Increasing Death Benefit

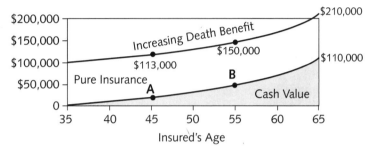

Both whole life and universal life allow policy loans from the cash value. However, only universal life allows withdrawals (partial surrenders) from the cash value. Withdrawals reduce the cash value and the death benefit by the amount of the withdrawal. A withdrawal is federal income tax-free up to the cost basis (i.e., premiums paid). Withdrawals above the cost basis are taxed as ordinary income. Unlike a policy loan, withdrawals do not require repayment.

4.6.2.3 Equity-Indexed Universal Life Insurance

Equity-indexed universal life is a permanent life insurance policy that allows policyholders to tie accumulation values to a stock market index such as the Standard & Poor's 500 Index. Indexed universal life typically contains a minimum guaranteed interest rate component along with the indexed account option. Indexed policies give policyholders the security of fixed universal life insurance with the growth potential of the underlying market index.

Unlike the interest-bearing investments that support most life insurance policies, stocks have no stated rate of return and may even lose value. However, the downside protection of equity-indexed universal life policies guarantee that the interest credited to the cash value will never be below zero.

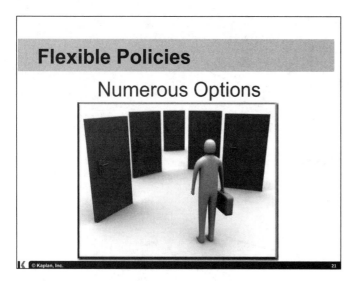

Flexible Policies

- Adjustable life
  - Policyowner
  - Adjusts the death benefit
  - Increase requires proof of insurability
  - Adjusts the premium
- Universal life
  - Flexible premium
  - Cash account
    - Cost of insurance withdrawn monthly
    - Fees withdrawn monthly
    - Current or guaranteed interest
  - Option A—level death benefit (insurance amount only)
  - Option B—increasing death benefit (insurance amount plus cash account)
- Equity indexed universal life
  - Current interest on cash account
    - Up or down based upon a stock market index
    - Account still guaranteed by the company

4.6.3   Advantages and Disadvantages of Flexible Policies

4.6.3.1 Advantages

Adjustable life combines the guarantees of whole life insurance with the affordable premiums of term insurance in one policy. The policyowner is allowed to adjust the mix of whole life and term based on his desire for affordable premiums and cash value growth.

Universal life's flexible premium means that policyowners can skip premiums without losing their coverage when money is tight, as long as there is enough cash value to cover the policy's monthly expenses. The flexible death benefit allows the policyowner to adjust the death benefit as his life changes. Withdrawals allow access to the policy cash values without the requirement to pay it back.

Equity-indexed life insurance provides the upside potential of the underlying index with the downside guarantee that the interest crediting rate to the cash value will never be below zero.

4.6.3.2 Disadvantages

Unlike whole life or term insurance, these policies are more complex. It is important the policyowner understand that premium payment amounts, interest rates, withdrawals, and death benefit changes can significantly impact the policy's long-term benefits.

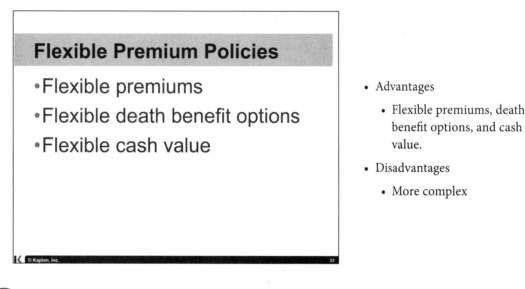

- Advantages
  - Flexible premiums, death benefit options, and cash value.
- Disadvantages
  - More complex

 QUICK QUIZ 4.C

1. Which of the following statements about flexible polices is NOT correct?
   A. Flexible polices are temporary insurance
   B. Policyowners can change their premium or death benefit with an adjustable life insurance policy
   C. A universal life insurance policy is cash-value driven rather than premium-driven
   D. Policyowners cannot know in advance what their flexible policies' values will be

Answers can be found at the end of Unit 4.

4.7   VARIABLE POLICIES

4.7.1   Characteristics of Variable Policies

Variable policies are permanent insurance policies designed to provide lifetime coverage for the insured and have cash value and a death benefit. The major advantage of *variable policies* is that they allow the policyowner to participate in various types of options while not being taxed on the earnings until the policy is surrendered.

4.7.1.1 Separate Account

The **separate account** is a fund held by the life insurance company and maintained separately from the insurer's general assets. This account is established to hold premiums used to purchase funds/investments that the company offers. This account is distinct from the *general account* established to hold insurer assets and premiums for their fixed insurance products.

4.7.1.2 Policyowner Choice of Separate Account Investments

The number and type of investment choices available to the policyowner varies from company to company, and from policy to policy. Most companies have suggested model portfolios to simplify the policyowner's selection for the variable policy.

4.7.1.3 No Guaranteed Rate of Return and Risk of Loss

Separate account investment options usually include a mixture of stocks, bonds, mutual funds, money market instruments, and even commodities. Although investment performance is not guaranteed, it can provide higher rates of return than the guaranteed or current rates paid on other traditional insurance policies.

4.7.1.4 Variable Insurance: Producer/Agent Registration

Variable insurance is an insurance product that contains an investment element. For this reason, both the securities industry and state insurance commissioners regulate these policies.

- Agents selling variable policies must have a valid life insurance license. An additional variable products license is required in some states.

- To sell investment products, agents must register with the Securities and Exchange Commission (SEC) and the Financial Industry Regulatory Association (FINRA). Exams are required to obtain the necessary licenses.

4.7.2   Types of Variable Policies

4.7.2.1 Variable Life

Variable life insurance has a separate account instead of guaranteed cash value. It's also called *variable whole life* or *fixed-premium variable life*.

Variable universal life policies have two death benefit options like the universal life policy. Death benefit Option A (or Option 1) remains level regardless of increases or decreases in the cash value, while death benefit Option B (or Option 2) varies with the fluctuating cash values.

The death benefit of a variable life policy will increase with positive investment results however in the event of negative performance, it cannot decrease below the original face amount. The original face amount is the variable life policy **guaranteed minimum death benefit**.

This illustrates the variable life death benefit.

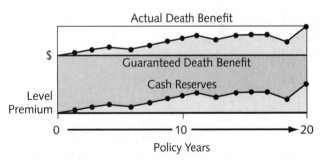

Variable Life Insurance Death Benefit

4.7.2.2 Variable Universal Life

Variable life is whole life with a separate account. **Variable universal life** is universal life with a separate account. Variable universal life is also called *flexible premium variable life.*

Variable universal life is a type of permanent life insurance, because the death benefit will be paid if the insured dies any time as long as there is sufficient cash value to pay the costs of insurance in the policy. A VUL policy can lapse if the cash value falls below the amount needed to cover the monthly insurance premiums this means it does not have a *guaranteed minimum death benefit.*

Variable universal life policies have two death benefit options like the UL policy. Option 1 remains level regardless of increases or decreases in the cash value and the Option 2 death benefit varies with the fluctuating cash value.

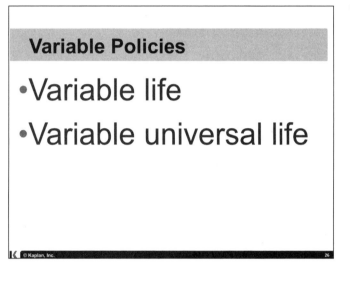

Variable Policies

- Life insurance plus investments
- Must have life insurance license & securities license
- Investments are in the separate account (securities)
  - Owner can lose money
- Types
  - Variable life
    - Death benefit can increase
    - Has guaranteed death benefit
  - Variable universal life
    - No guaranteed death benefit

4.7.3   Advantages and Disadvantages of Variable Policies

4.7.3.1 Advantages

Variable policies offer the potential of higher returns than the guaranteed rates paid on traditional life insurance products. Investment-based returns have the potential to keep pace with inflation and because of the tax-deferred feature they may offer an attractive tax advantage for those in higher income brackets.

4.7.3.2 Disadvantages

Variable policies have no guaranteed rate of return. The policies are complicated and can be difficult to understand. Variable policies are highly regulated by both federal and state agencies.

Variable Policies

- •Potential for higher returns
- •Keep pace with inflation
- •State and Federal regulated

RISKS AHEAD

© Kaplan, Inc.   27

- Advantages
  - Potential for high returns
  - Keep pace with inflation
  - Tax Advantages
- Disadvantages
  - No guaranteed rate of return.
  - Complicated
  - Highly regulated

Let's compare the life insurance policies!

© Kaplan, Inc.   28

Comparison of Life Insurance Policies

	Level Term	Whole Life	Current Assumption Whole Life	Universal Life	Variable Life	Variable Universal Life
Death Benefit	Expires at end of term	Fixed and level	Fixed and leve	Adjustable, level, or increasing options	Varies with investment performance; original face amount is guaranteed minimum	Adjustable; level or increasing options
Premiums	Fixed schedule, increases at each renewal	Fixed schedule, level amount	Fixed schedule; amount may increase or decrease, but may not go above a guaranteed maximum	Flexible schedule, flexible amount	Fixed schedule, level amount	Flexible schedule, flexible amount
Cash Values	None	Fixed and guaranteed	Current interest with guaranteed minimum rate	Current interest with guaranteed minimum rate	Varies with investment performance; no guaranteed minimum and at risk for loss	Varies with investment performance; no guaranteed minimum and at risk for loss

 QUICK QUIZ 4.D

1. The distinguishing feature of a variable policy is that all of the earnings depend on the investment performance of a
    A. general account
    B. separate account
    C. personal account
    D. bank account

2. All of the following statements regarding variable life insurance are true EXCEPT
    A. variable life's cash values will go up and down based on performance of the separate account
    B. variable universal life does not have a guaranteed minimum death benefit
    C. agents who sell variable life must be licensed to sell insurance by the state and also registered as securities representatives
    D. most variable life policies offer a guarantee of a minimum return

Answers can be found at the end of Unit 4.

4.8   SPECIALIZED POLICIES

4.8.1   Joint Life Policies

A *joint life policy* usually covers two or more lives with the death benefit being paid when the first insured dies. For this reason, they are also called *first-to-die* policies. Once the death benefit is paid out, the policy ends.

A first-to-die policy may be the right product for married people who want a surviving spouse to be able to maintain a certain lifestyle but they want to pay ***less than the cost of two individual polices***. Or a retired couple living on income from both of their pension plans would be ideal candidates for this policy. When either spouse dies, the other will only have their own pension benefit to live on and the joint live policy death benefit would now supplement their retirement income.

4.8.2   Survivorship Policies

A *survivorship life policy* insures two individuals and will pay the death benefit when the last insured dies. Survivorship policies are also called *second-to-die or last-to-die* policies. A survivorship policy **costs less than purchasing two individual policies**. This policy can provide money to pay estate settlement costs and related expenses upon the death of a second spouse.

4.8.3   Juvenile Policies

Juvenile life insurance is coverage written on the life of a child or a minor. Juvenile policies are most often permanent life insurance. In addition to the death benefit, juvenile life insurance provides the benefit of locking in the low premium for the child's entire life, and guarantees the child has life insurance in case their health changes in the future.

The death benefit of a juvenile policy may seem too small when the child is grown up. To address this, the face amount of some juvenile policies automatically increases when the child reaches age 18 or 21, with no corresponding increase in premium. These are called *jumping juvenile* policies. In some policies, the face amount of these policies jumps to five times its original amount.

Specialized Policies

- Joint life
  - First to die
  - Second to die (survivorship life)
- Juvenile
  - Death benefit may increase at a future age
- Jumping juvenile
  - Policy automatically increases at age 18 or 21

QUICK QUIZ 4.E

1. When does the face amount of a jumping juvenile policy typically increase?

   A. Age 15

   B. Age 18

   C. Age 35

   D. Age 65

2. Which of the following specialized policies insures two people and pays its benefit when the first one dies?

   A. Joint life policy

   B. Survivorship policy

   C. Juvenile policy

   D. Family policy

Answers can be found at the end of Unit 4.

 UNIT 4 CRAM SHEET

Term Insurance

- Level term
  - Death benefit is level
  - Premium is level for the term
- Decreasing term
  - Death benefit decreases
  - Premium remains level
- Increasing term
  - Death benefit increases
  - Premium increases
- Return of premium term
  - Premium higher than regular term policy
  - Premium paid by insured is paid back if insured alive at the end of the term
- Term features
  - Renewable
    - No new application required
    - New premium based upon attained age
- Convertible
  - Can be changed to permanent insurance
  - No new application required

Traditional Whole Life

- Fixed premium
- Fixed & level death benefit
- Cash values
    - Guaranteed interest
    - May be surrendered
    - May be borrowed
    - Endows at age 100
- Death benefit
    - Amount at risk to the company
    - Plus cash values

Types of Whole Life Policies

- Continuous premium
- Limited payment
- Single premium
    - Immediate cash values
- Modified premium
    - Lower premium first three to five years
    - Premium jumps once then levels off
- Graded premium
    - Initial premium lower than whole life
    - Premium increases for five to ten years then levels off
- Indeterminate premium
    - Premiums adjusted by the company
    - Has a guaranteed maximum premium
- Interest sensitive
    - Has a current interest rate
    - Guaranteed interest rate

Flexible Policies

- Adjustable life
    - Policyowner
        - Adjusts the death benefit
            - Increase requires proof of insurability
                - Adjusts the premium

- Universal life
  - Flexible premium
  - Cash account
    - Cost of insurance withdrawn monthly
    - Fees withdrawn monthly
    - Current or guaranteed interest
  - Option A—level death benefit (insurance amount only)
  - Option B—increasing death benefit (insurance amount plus cash account)
- Equity indexed universal life
  - Current interest on cash account
    - Up or down based upon a stock market index
    - Account still guaranteed by the company

Variable Policies

- Life insurance plus investments
- Must have life insurance license & securities license
- Investments are in the separate account (securities)
  - Owner can lose money
- Types
  - Variable life
    - Death benefit can increase
    - Has guaranteed death benefit
  - Variable universal life
  - No guaranteed death benefit

Specialized Policies

- Joint life
  - First to die
  - Second to die (survivorship life)
- Juvenile
  - Jumping juvenile
    - Policy automatically increases at age 18 or 21

UNIT 4 QUIZ

In order to measure your success, we recommend that you answer the following 10 questions correctly.

1. Pam owns a 1-year term policy. At the end of the year, she may purchase another identical policy without showing proof of insurability. Pam's policy is
   A. convertible term
   B. renewable term
   C. increasing term
   D. decreasing term

2. Zelda agrees to pay premiums on her policy every year for 20 years. After that, she will no longer have to pay premiums, but her insurance protection will continue until she dies. Zelda has
   A. a whole life policy
   B. a limited-pay policy
   C. a single premium policy
   D. a modified premium policy

3. Ashley has a policy that she must pay premiums on until she is 100 years old or until she dies. Ashley has
   A. a continuous premium whole life policy
   B. a limited-pay policy
   C. a single premium policy
   D. a modified premium policy

4. Which of the following is NOT flexible in a universal life policy?
   A. Premium amounts
   B. Premium schedule
   C. Guaranteed interest rate
   D. Death benefits

5. Martha has a universal life policy she purchased several years earlier. At that time, the death benefit in the policy was $100,000. Her cash value is now $50,000, and she has selected death benefit option A. How much is her current death benefit?
   A. $50,000
   B. $80,000
   C. $100,000
   D. $150,000

6. Karen has a universal life policy she purchased several years earlier. At that time, the death benefit in the policy was $100,000. Her cash value is now $20,000, and she has selected death benefit option B. How much is her current death benefit?
   A. $20,000
   B. $80,000
   C. $100,000
   D. $120,000

7. Which of the following is NOT required to be able to sell variable policies?
   A. A state insurance producer license
   B. Registration with FINRA
   C. Registration with the NAIC
   D. A passing score on the appropriate securities exam

8. Which of the following types of insurance is designed to provide life insurance protection for only a limited time?
    A. Whole life insurance
    B. Variable life insurance
    C. Term life insurance
    D. Universal life insurance

9. Which of the following types of insurance requires a level premium and provides lifelong protection?
    A. Whole life insurance
    B. Variable life insurance
    C. Term life insurance
    D. Universal life insurance

10. Christy has a term policy that will allow her to switch over to a whole life policy at any time during the first half of the term without providing evidence of insurability. What type of policy is this?
    A. Level term insurance
    B. Renewable term insurance
    C. Convertible term insurance
    D. Reentry term insurance

ANSWER KEY

QUICK QUIZZES

QUICK QUIZ 4.A

1. **C.** Decreasing term

2. **C.** premiums are higher than other types of life insurance policies

QUICK QUIZ 4.B

1. **A.** permanent insurance

2. **B.** Limited-pay whole life

3. **D.** fixed and level

QUICK QUIZ 4.C

1. **A.** Flexible policies are temporary insurance

QUICK QUIZ 4.D

1. **B.** separate account

2. **D.** most variable life policies offer a guarantee of a minimum return

QUICK QUIZ 4.E.

1. **B.** Age 18

2. **A.** Joint life policy

UNIT QUIZ

1. **B.** Renewable term may be renewed at the end of a specified period without proof of insurability. The renewal is for the same term of the time as originally purchased.

2. **B.** This is a limited-pay policy because Zelda is required to pay premiums for only a limited period.

3. **A.** Ashley's policy is a continuous premium whole life policy because she is required to pay premiums for her whole life or until she is 100.

4. **C.** The guaranteed interest rate is not flexible in a universal life policy.

5. **C.** Option A in a universal life policy provides a level death benefit equal to the policy's face amount. If she would have chosen Option B, the amount of the death benefit would have been $150,000.

6. **D.** Option B provides for an increasing death benefit equal to policy's face amount plus the cash value. If she would have chosen Option A, the amount of the death benefit would have been $100,000.

7. **C.** Registration with the NAIC is not a requirement.

8. **C.** Term life insurance provides insurance protection for a limited time.

9. **A.** Whole life insurance requires a level premium and provides lifelong protection.

10. **C.** A term policy that will allow the insured to switch over to a whole life policy at any time during the first half of the term without providing evidence of insurability is a convertible term insurance policy.

UNIT 5 Life Insurance Riders

5.1 INTRODUCTION

Life insurance is not a one size fits all solution; *life insurance riders* are benefit options to tailor a policy to the owner's needs.

The total price for purchasing a new car will reflect the upgraded tires and fog lights requested by the owner. Adding a rider to a life policy is just like customizing a car, purchasing a rider will increase the premium on the policy.

This unit will discuss the most common insurance policy riders including the waiver of premium, the accidental death benefit—commonly referred to as "double indemnity"—the guaranteed insurability rider.

An agent/producer must follow the "know your customer" rule by understanding the customer's current situation and budget and then recommending the most appropriate policy rider(s).

🎯 5.2   LEARNING OBJECTIVES

After successfully completing this unit, you should be able to:

- define riders;
- identify disability riders including waiver of premium, waiver of monthly deductions, waiver of cost of insurance, disability income rider, and the payor benefit rider;
- explain the accelerated death benefits rider;
- identify the Other Insured Riders and exchange privilege (substitute insured) riders;
- identify the death benefit term insurance rider, return of premium rider, accidental death benefit rider, accidental death and dismemberment rider, guaranteed insurability rider, and cost of living rider; and
- describe the long term care rider.

5.3   LIFE POLICY RIDERS

Riders add benefits to a life insurance policy. They customize coverage to fit the insured's needs. Policyowners are charged an additional premium for certain types of riders.

5.4   DISABILITY RIDERS

5.4.1   Waiver of Premium

This is one of the most common types of life insurance riders. If the policyholder becomes disabled, the **waiver of premium** rider will pay the premiums so the policyholder can continue to have coverage for the duration of the policy. The policy stays in force during the period of disability, and scheduled policy cash values continue to be credited.

The insured must be unable to work for a certain period, called the *waiting period*, before the waiver takes effect. The waiting period is usually 90 to 180 days. If the insured is still disabled at the end of the waiting period, the company *retroactively* refunds any premiums paid during the *waiting period*.

The definition of *disabled* often changes after a period of time to the inability to work at any job that fits with the insured's education, training, or experience.

The waiver of premium rider is available during the insured's working years and expires between ages of 60 and 65. However, if an insured becomes permanently disabled before that age, premiums will continue to be waived for life.

5.4.1.1   Disability Waiver for Flexible Premium Policies

The disability premium waiver for flexible premium policies, such as universal life, suspends the monthly cost of insurance deductions that are made from the cash account instead of waiving the premium payment. For this reason, the disability waiver for flexible premium policies is called **waiver of monthly deductions** or **waiver of cost of insurance**.

A flexible premium policy cannot lapse while the waiver of monthly deductions benefit is in effect and cash values continue to grow with the interest that is credited monthly.

Disability waiver for flexible premium policies also has a three- to six-month waiting period and expires between the ages of 60 and 65.

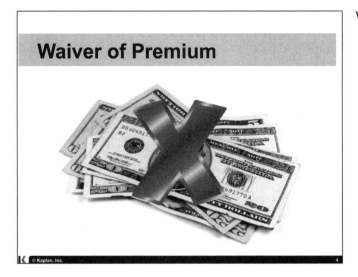

Waiver of Premium

- Insured and owner are the same person
- Waives premiums as long as the insured is disabled
- Insured pays premium during the waiting period
- Company pays premiums after waiting period
- Premiums paid during waiting period reimbursed
- Insured pays premiums when disability ends

Waiver of Cost of Insurance (Universal Life)

- Cash account deductions waived
- Waiting period & standard expiration

5.4.2 Disability Income Rider

The **disability income rider** provides the insured with a monthly benefit check if they become disabled.

The benefit amount is typically based on the life insurance policy death benefit and an industry standard is 1% of the face value. The length of time that income payments will continue depends on the definition of disability in the policy.

During the time that premiums are waived, the life insurance policy stays in force, so that if the insured dies, the beneficiary receives the face value of the policy. Cash values continue to build, and if the policy is participating, dividends continue to be paid.

Disability Income Rider

- Pays monthly income while disabled
- Benefit amount 1% of face amount

5.4.3   Payor Benefit Rider

The *payor benefit rider* is usually found with juvenile policies. This provision states that if the person responsible for the premiums, for example the child's parents, becomes disabled or dies before the child legally becomes an adult, the rest of the premiums are waived until the child reaches a stated age, usually 18 or 21. Since this rider adds insurance on the payor (the adult), medical underwriting may be required.

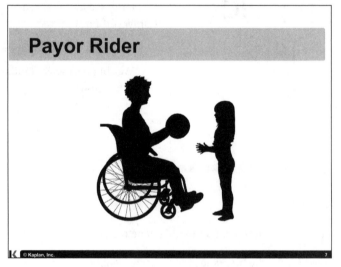

Payor Rider

- Pays premiums if the adult payor
  - Dies
  - Disabled
- Requires evidence of insurability (adult)

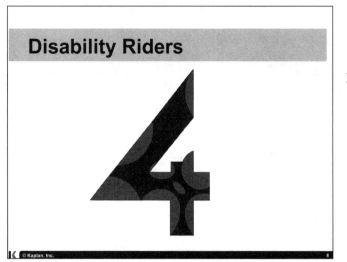

Disability Riders

- Waiver of premium
- Waiver of cost of insurance (universal life)
- Disability income rider
- Payor rider

5.5 ACCELERATED BENEFITS RIDER

An accelerated death benefit rider is an option added to a life insurance policy that enables the policyowner to apply for an advance on the death benefit proceeds during the lifetime of the insured. The insured must have a limited life expectancy or meet certain medical circumstances in order to be eligible for an advanced payment of all or a portion of a life insurance policy's death benefit.

5.5.1 Qualifying Events

An accelerated death benefit payment can be requested when the insured has limited life expectancy or meets certain medical circumstances including:

- terminal illness, with death expected within 24 months;
- serious illness, such as cancer, which would result in a reduced life expectancy;
- long-term care due to the inability to perform a number of the activities of daily living;
- being admitted to hospice or permanent confinement in a nursing home; or
- catastrophic illness requiring extraordinary treatment, such as an organ transplant.

5.5.2 Reduction of Death Benefit

Accelerated death benefit payments range from 25–100% of the death benefit. The payment depends on the policy's face value, the terms of the contract, and the state of residence. The amount of the accelerated payment will be reduced by any outstanding loans against the policy and the death benefit is reduced by the amount of the accelerated benefit payment.

5.5.3 Disclosure

A written disclosure including, but not necessarily limited to, a brief description of the accelerated benefit and definitions of the conditions or occurrences triggering payment of the benefits shall be given to the applicant. The description shall include an explanation of any effect of the payment of a benefit on the policy's cash value, accumulation account, death benefit, premium, policy loans and policy liens.

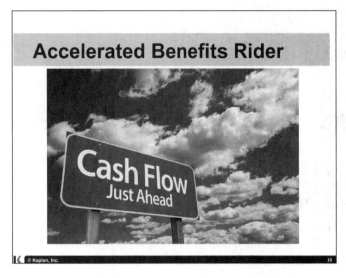

Accelerated Benefits Rider

- Advances part of the death benefit while insured is still alive
  - Death expected within 24 months
  - Permanent confinement in a nursing home due to a chronic illness or catastrophic injury
- Reduces death benefit payable to beneficiary upon death of the insured
- Disclosure by company of effect on death benefits and other benefits (Medicaid etc.)

 QUICK QUIZ 5.A

1. Which of the following terms describes something that is used to add benefits to a life insurance policy and customize the coverage to an insured's particular needs?

   A. A life insurance addition

   B. A rider

   C. A premium

   D. A contract

2. All of the following statements about the waiver of premium rider are true EXCEPT

   A. with the waiver of premium rider, at first, insureds are considered disabled if they are unable to work at their present job

   B. with the waiver of premium rider, if an insured recovers and returns to work after a disability they must begin paying policy premiums again

   C. with the waiver of premium rider, premiums are reduced by 80% during any period that the insured is disabled

   D. with the waiver of premium rider, if the insured becomes permanently disabled before the insured's working years end, premiums will continue to be waived for life

3. Which of the following riders allow insureds who are terminally ill to obtain benefits from insurance policies prior to their death?

   A. Accelerated benefits rider

   B. Payor rider

   C. Disability income rider

   D. Waiver of premium rider

Answers can be found at the end of Unit 5.

5.6   RIDERS FOR OTHER INSUREDS

5.6.1   Other (Additional) Insured Term Riders

Other (additional) insured riders provide convertible term insurance for a spouse or an immediate family member of the primary insured. This rider is called a *spouse rider* or a *children's rider*.

A *family rider* covers both the insured's spouse and children. Other insured riders can also be bought for certain non-family individuals such as business associates. The term insurance coverage provided by the **other (additional) insured rider** is often convertible to permanent coverage during the effective period of the rider.

5.6.2   Exchange Privilege (Substitute Insured) Riders

The **exchange privilege rider** also called the **substitute insured rider** is used to change the insured to a different person. This rider is typically used when a business owns the policy and is also the beneficiary and the insured is a key employee. This rider switches the insured to another employee if the key employee retires or leaves the company. The policy's face amount stays the same and premiums are adjusted based on the new insured's age and other rating factors. The new insured is required to provide proof of insurability (submit to a medical examination).

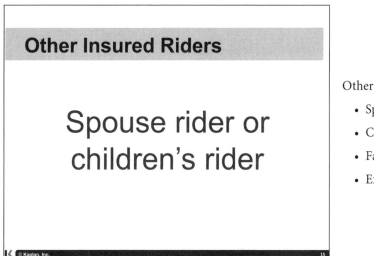

Other Insured Riders

- Spouse
- Children
- Family
- Exchange of insured

5.7   RIDERS AFFECTING THE DEATH BENEFIT

5.7.1   Term Rider on the Insured

The insured can add term insurance to a permanent insurance policy using the **term insurance rider**. It provides coverage similar to a term insurance policy however the premium is lower than purchasing a separate policy.

In the event of insured' death, both the term insurance rider and the underlying permanent insurance policy's death benefit would be paid to the named beneficiary.

There are three term insurance riders available:

1. level,

2. decreasing, and

3. increasing.

The term rider expires at a specified age or after a certain number of years. The premium for the rider is paid while it's in force.

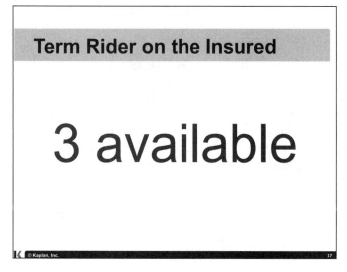

Insured Term Rider

- Added to a permanent policy
- Premium lower than a separate policy
- Limited time for rider
- Expires at a certain age or number of years

5.7.2   Return of Premium

The **return of premium rider** is an increasing term rider; the death benefit always equals the total of premiums paid for the rider and the underlying permanent policy. The rider does not return the actual premiums but pays an additional term insurance death benefit that equals the amount of premiums paid. Term riders have a limited duration and expire at a specified age or after a specified number of years.

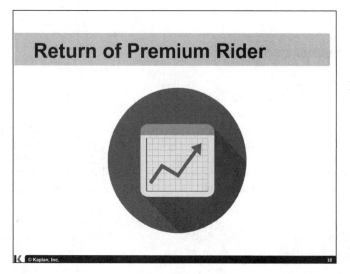

Return of Premium Rider

- Increasing term insurance rider
- Amount of rider equal to all premiums paid
- Death must occur while rider is in force

5.7.3   Accidental Death Benefit (ADB)

The **accidental death benefit (ADB) rider** pays an extra benefit if the insured dies as the result of an accident. This rider is sometimes referred to as *double or triple indemnity* because the death benefit is twice or three times the face amount of the policy.

For the extra benefit to be payable, the insured must die within 90 days of an accident. The extra benefit is only payable if the insured's death was the result of an accident. The ADB rider does not cover other causes of death like:

- illness,
- disability, or
- self-inflicted injury.

Also excluded from coverage is death resulting from:

- war,
- commission of crimes, or
- aviation activities other than on a commercial flight.

This rider usually expires when the insured reaches age 60 or 65.

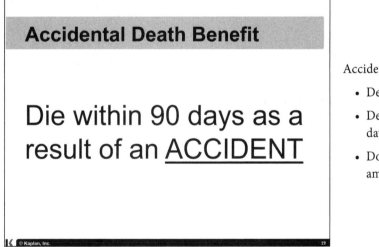

Accidental Death Benefit

- Death due to accident
- Death must occur within 90 days of accident
- Doubles or triples the face amount

5.7.3.1   Accidental Death and Dismemberment (AD&D)

Accidental death and dismemberment insurance, also known as AD&D insurance, is supplementary coverage that can be added to traditional life insurance policies. In addition to paying an extra benefit if the insured dies as the result of an accident, the **accidental death and dismemberment (AD&D) rider** also pays an extra benefit if the insured lives after suffering a severe dismemberment. The AD&D rider has a stated amount of coverage.

If a policyholder dies as a direct result of an accident, a full death benefit will be paid out to the policy's beneficiary. If the policy amount is for $100,000, the benefit will be $100,000. If the policyholder does not die as a result of the accident and instead loses a limb, he/she will receive a 50% benefit payout. Losing two or more limbs would compound for a full benefit payment.

The *principal sum* is the amount of the rider and 100% of the death benefit is paid upon accidental death of the insured

The *capital sum* is the dismemberment benefit and is 50% or ½ of the principal sum. Dismemberment includes:

- Severance of legs, arms, feet or hands
- Loss of sight
- Loss of hearing
- Paralysis

The definition of dismemberment and the benefits payable can vary widely from one policy to another

Accidental Death or Dismemberment Rider

- The principal sum 100% of death benefit
  - Paid if death due to accident
  - Within 90 days of accident date
- Pays benefit if dismemberment occurs
  - Severance of feet, arms legs or hands
  - Loss of sight or hearing
  - Paralysis
- Dismemberment is the capital sum–50% of the principal sum
- For multiple dismemberment claims maximum paid is principal sum

5.7.4 Guaranteed Insurability

The **guaranteed insurability rider (GIR)**—also called a **guaranteed-insurability option (GIO)** or a **guaranteed-insurability benefit (GIB)**—may be attached to a permanent life insurance policy and allows the owner to purchase additional life insurance at specified intervals in the future for certain amounts without having to provide evidence of insurability. Options to purchase may be exercised typically between ages 25 and 40 at 3-year intervals. The insurance is available at standard rates and must be exercised within 90 days of the listed option date.

When this rider is added to a policy, the current age of the insured determines the number of options available to purchase additional insurance. Example: At age 25 the insured would have five options available at ages 28, 31, 34, 37, and 40. A 34-year old insured would only have two options available at ages 37 and 40.

The insured may advance the next option date due to a life event (defined as marriage, birth, or adoption).

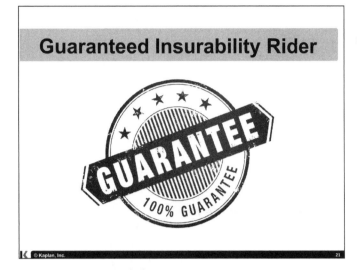

Guaranteed Insurability Rider

- Add life insurance up to a specified amount
  - Certain ages—between 25 and 40
  - Life events—marriage, birth, or adoption of a child
  - No medical questions asked
  - Cost based on the insured's attained age

5.7.5   Cost of Living

The **Cost of Living** rider is based on the Consumer Price Index (CPI). As inflation increases, so does the death benefit of the policy. For example, if an insured had a $100,000 policy and the Consumer Price Index increased by 2%, at the end of the year, the insured's death benefit would increase to $102,000. The premium for the additional coverage would be based on the insured's attained age. If the CPI decreases, the insured's coverage is not reduced.

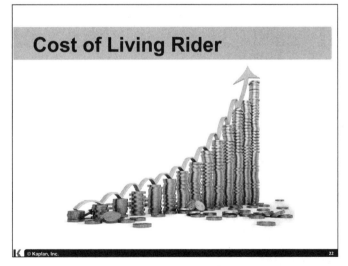

Cost of Living Rider

- Extra coverage to keep up with inflation
- Premium based on attained age
- Without proof of insurability

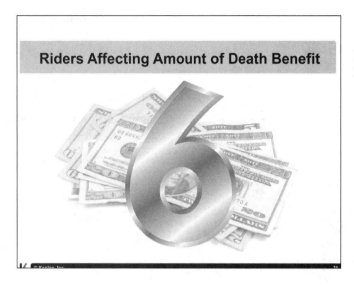

Riders Affecting Amount of Death Benefit

- Insured term rider
- Return of premium rider
- Accidental death rider
- Accidental death or dismemberment rider
- Guaranteed insurability rider
- Cost of living rider

5.8   LONG-TERM CARE RIDER

There are two approaches to the LTC rider concept. The independent approach recognizes the LTC benefit as independent from the life policy because the benefits paid to the insured will not affect the life policy's face amount or cash value. The integrated approach links the LTC benefits paid to the life policy's face amount and/or cash value. Similar to the accelerated benefits rider, the LTC rider may be used to pay for qualified services such as home care, assisted living, or nursing home care.

The long-term care rider may offer benefits consistent with the benefits offered by a stand-alone long-term care policy. Because of this special rider, the insured can elect to use all, some, or none of their life insurance benefit—while they are still living to help pay for long-term care expenses.

While evidence of insurability is necessary for underwriting, some insurance companies may also offer simplified one-page applications.

Long Term Care Rider

- Advance of the death benefits while insured is living
- Percentage of face amount each month
- May pay for home care, assisted living, and nursing home care
- Reduces death benefit payable upon death

QUICK QUIZ 5.B

1. For an accidental death benefit rider to be payable the insured must die (due to injury from the accident) within how many days of the accident?

A. 30

B. 60

C. 90

D. 180

2. Which rider lets insureds buy additional coverage without proof of insurability in order to keep pace with inflation?

A. Guaranteed insurability

B. Accidental death and disability rider

C. Cost of living

D. Payor rider

Answers can be found at the end of Unit 5.

 UNIT 5 CRAM SHEET

Disability Riders

- Waiver of premium

  - Written if the insured and owner are the same person

  - Waives future premium payments as long as the insured is disabled

  - Has a waiting period—insured pays during premium during this time even though disabled

  - Company will pay future premiums after waiting period

  - Will reimburse insured for premiums paid during waiting period

  - Once no longer disabled, insured pays future premiums

- Waiver of cost of insurance (universal life)

  - Deductions from the cash account are waived

  - Has a waiting period

- Disability income rider

  - Pays insured a monthly income while disabled

  - X dollars per month per $1,000 face amount

- Payor Rider

  - Pays the premium of a juvenile policy if the adult premium payor

    - Dies

    - Disabled

  - May require the adult to provide evidence of insurability

Other Insured Riders

- Spouse
- Children
- Family
- Exchange of insured

Riders Affecting Amount of Death Benefit

- Insured term rider
  - Added to a permanent policy
  - Premium lower than if bought as separate policy
  - Rider is for limited time
- Return of premium rider
  - Increasing term insurance rider
  - Amount of rider equal to all premiums paid
  - Death must occur while rider is in force
- Accidental death rider
  - Death due to accident
  - Death must occur within 90 days of accident
  - Doubles or triples the face amount
- Accidental death or dismemberment rider
  - Amount of the rider is the principal sum (100%)
    - Paid in addition to face amount if death due to accident
    - Death must occur within 90 days of accident date
  - Also pays a living benefit if dismemberment occurs
    - Severance of feet, arms, legs, or hands
    - Loss of sight or hearing
    - Paralysis
  - Dismemberment benefit is called the capital sum—usually a percentage of the principal sum (50%)
  - If multiple dismemberment claims while inured is alive, the principal sum is the maximum paid for all claims combined
- Guaranteed insurability rider
  - Allows additional insurance up to the amount of the rider to be added
    - Certain ages—usually no older than 40
    - Life events—marriage, birth of a child, or adoption
    - No medical questions asked
    - Cost of additional insurance based on the insured's attained (current) age

Accelerated Benefits Rider

- Advances part of the death benefit while insured is still alive
  - Death expected within 24 months
  - Permanent confinement in a nursing home due to a chronic illness or catastrophic injury
- Reduces death benefit payable to beneficiary upon death of the insured
- Disclosure by company of affect on death benefits and other benefits (Medicaid etc.)

Long Term Care Rider

- Advance of the death benefits while insured is living
- Stated percentage of the face amount each month
  - Nursing home
  - Nursing/assisted living care
- May pay for
  - Home care
  - Assisted living
  - Nursing home care
- Reduces the death benefit payable upon death

UNIT 5 QUIZ

In order to measure your success, we recommend that you answer the following 10 questions correctly.

1. Tammy has a $100,000 life insurance policy with a double indemnity rider. Tammy is killed in an automobile accident. How much will the policy pay?
   A. $100,000
   B. $180,000
   C. $200,000
   D. $400,000

2. Kumar has a life insurance policy with a rider that will pay him $1,000 per month if he is totally and permanently disabled. Which type of rider does he have?
   A. Waiver of premium rider
   B. Accidental death and disability rider
   C. Disability income rider
   D. Payor rider

3. Paul has a life insurance policy on his son for which he pays all the premiums. A rider to this policy states that if Paul becomes permanently and totally disabled, the premiums will be paid until his son reaches age 21, at which point his son will take over the premium payments. Which type of rider does he have?
   A. Waiver of premium rider
   B. Accidental death and disability rider
   C. Disability income rider
   D. Payor rider

4. Which of the following riders allows for an advance of the death benefit if the insured is confined to a nursing home or cannot perform the activities of daily living?
   A. Guaranteed insurability rider
   B. Accidental death or dismemberment rider
   C. Return of premium rider
   D. Long-term care rider

5. Alberta is concerned that if she became totally and permanently disabled, she would not be able to pay her life insurance premiums and the policy will lapse. Which type of rider should she consider to protect against this possibility?
   A. Waiver of premium rider
   B. Accidental death and disability rider
   C. Disability income rider
   D. Payor rider

6. Which of the following riders is increasing term insurance that always equals the total premiums paid during the time the policy is in effect?
   A. Guaranteed insurability
   B. Return of premium
   C. Accidental death
   D. Waiver of premium

7. Which of the following is waiver of all future premiums in the event of total and permanent disability?
   A. Guaranteed insurability
   B. Return of premium
   C. Accidental death
   D. Waiver of premium

8. Which of the following is a guarantee that at specified ages, dates, or events, the insured may buy additional insurance without a medical exam?
   A. Guaranteed insurability
   B. Return of premium
   C. Accidental death
   D. Waiver of premium

9. The amount of money paid by an accidental death benefit rider if the insured dies in an accident is referred to as the
   A. principal sum
   B. principle sum
   C. capital sum
   D. capitol sum

10. The amount of money paid by an accidental death and dismemberment rider if the insured is disabled in an accident is referred to as the
    A. principal sum
    B. principle sum
    C. capital sum
    D. capitol sum

ANSWER KEY

QUICK QUIZZES

QUICK QUIZ 5.A

1. **B.** A rider

2. **C.** with the waiver of premium rider, premiums are reduced by 80% during any period that the insured is disabled

3. **A.** Accelerated benefits rider

QUICK QUIZ 5.B

1. **C.** 90

2. **C.** Cost of living

UNIT QUIZ

1. **C.** The policy will pay a death benefit of $200,000. The extra benefit is usually the same amount as the policy, so it doubles the death benefit.

2. **C.** Kumar has a disability income rider because it is providing him money to help with bills during the period that he is disabled.

3. **D.** This is a payor rider because it provides for a waiver of premiums on the son's coverage if the payor (Paul) becomes disabled.

4. **D.** The payment advance reduces the death benefit payable upon death.

5. **A.** A waiver of premium rider will waive the premiums on Alberta's policy if she becomes disabled.

6. **B.** A return of premium rider is increasing term insurance that always equals the total premiums paid during the time the policy is in effect.

7. **D.** Waiver of premium is waiver of all future premiums in the event of total and permanent disability.

8. **A.** Guaranteed insurability is a guarantee that at specified ages, dates, or events, the insured may buy additional insurance without a medical exam.

9. **A.** The amount of money paid by an ADB rider if the insured dies in an accident is referred to as the principal sum.

10. **C.** The amount of money paid by an AD&D rider if the insured is disabled in an accident is referred to as the capital sum.

UNIT

6 Life Insurance Policy Options

6.1 INTRODUCTION

Life insurance is the foundation of any financial plan. It protects an individual's goals and can take care of loved ones if the breadwinner dies unexpectedly. But the value of life insurance goes beyond risk protection, it can be an asset and offer other financial benefits at various stages during the life of the insured.

Term and permanent life policies have the primary function of providing a death benefit. Permanent insurance offers additional financial benefits throughout the insured's lifetime, and participating policies may pay dividends to a policyowner.

This unit focuses on "living benefits," how can the cash value and/or dividends be used during the insured's lifetime, and "settlement options," what choices are available to a beneficiary upon the death of the insured.

6.2   LEARNING OBJECTIVES

After successfully completing this lesson, you should be able to:

- explain the seven settlement options: interest only, fixed period, fixed amount, life income, life with period certain, life with refund certain, and joint-and-survivor life;

- describe the insureds access to cash values through policy loans, withdrawals, and partial surrenders;

- explain policy dividends and the six dividend options: cash, reduced premium, accumulation at interest, paid up additions, paid up insurance, and one year term insurance; and

- identify the three nonforfeiture options: cash surrender, reduced paid up insurance, and extended term insurance.

6.3   LIFE INSURANCE POLICY OPTIONS

All life insurance policies have a death benefit and the **settlement options** are used to determine how the proceeds will be distributed to the beneficiary(s).

Permanent life contracts accumulate cash value and policies issued by participating policies may pay dividends to a policyowner. The policyowner can choose how to use these "living benefits."

Nonforeiture options give permanent life insurance policyowners alternatives for using cash value if the policyowner wants to change the existing policy.

This section details the use of these important elements of a life insurance policy.

6.4   SETTLEMENT OPTIONS

The life insurance policyowner may designate a specific settlement option to be paid upon his or her death. If the policyowner does not indicate a specific option, the death benefits are distributed as a **lump sum**. Settlement options include interest income only option, fixed period option, fixed amount option, life income option, life with period certain, life with refund certain, and joint and survivor life. Please see the following sections for explanations of each of these options.

6.4.1   Interest Income (Only) Option

Under the **interest income (only)** settlement option, the insurer retains the death benefit and pays a stated amount of interest on the money. The interest is paid to the beneficiary at regular intervals.

This could be a good choice for those who do not need the life insurance proceeds until a later date, perhaps to be used for a child's future education expenses.

The following illustration depicts the interest only settlement option:

Interest Only Settlement Option

Insurer holds the death benefit
Pays interest to the beneficiary at regular intervals

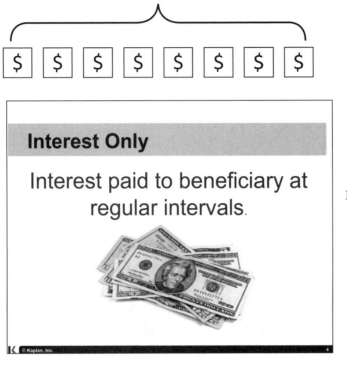

Interest Only

- Interest is paid on the death benefit
- Death benefit paid at a later date

6.4.2 Fixed Period Option

The **fixed period option** will pay both an amount of principal and interest to the beneficiary over a certain stated period of time. Should the policy's primary beneficiary die before all of the proceeds are paid out, the remainder of the money will be paid to the contingent beneficiary that was named in the policy. Three factors are used to calculate each payment:

1. Amount of death benefit;

2. A guaranteed interest rate; and

3. The length of the chosen period.

This illustration depicts the fixed period settlement option:

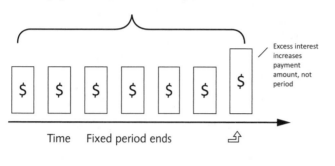

Fixed Period Settlement Option

Proceeds and interest divided into equal
payments over the selected period

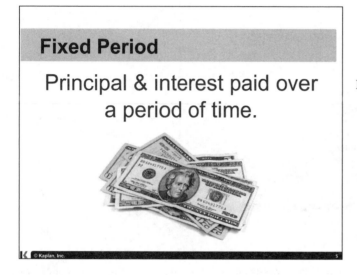

Fixed Period

- Death benefit + guaranteed interest over a set time

- If interest greater than the guaranteed rate, final payment will be larger

6.4.3   Fixed Amount Option

With the **fixed amount** settlement option, the proceeds will be paid out in a fixed amount over time until both the principal and interest have been completely paid to the beneficiary. The recipient of the payments has the ability to either increase or decrease the payment amount and if they choose, they could also even change to a different settlement option altogether. Three factors are used to determine the minimum length of the payment period:

1. Amount of death benefit;

2. A guaranteed interest rate; and

3. The chosen payment amount.

If interest exceeding the guaranteed rate is earned, the money will last longer than expected. It will increase the length of the payment period, not the size of the payment amount. If the beneficiary dies before the money runs out, payments may continue to another person or the remaining funds will be paid into the beneficiary's estate.

This illustration depicts the fixed amount option:

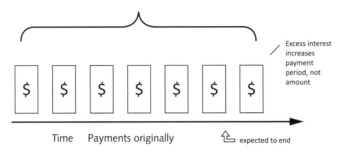

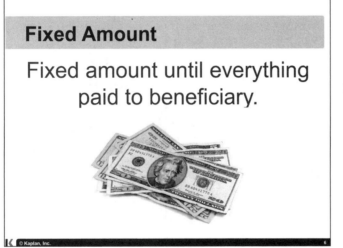

Fixed Amount

- A fixed amount is paid
- Interest earnings will affect the payment period timeframe

6.4.4   Life Income Option

The **life income** option is similar to an annuity; the policy beneficiary will be guaranteed to receive an income for the rest of their life, regardless of how long that may be. The actual amount of the income depends on the policy death benefit and the life expectancy of the beneficiary; their age and gender. The beneficiary can select to receive the entire annuity payout until they die or share it with another individual.

The choices for the annuity are life only option, life with period certain, life with refund, or joint and survivor life.

6.4.5   Life Only Option

The **life only** or *straight life* option will pay the largest amount to the beneficiary for as long as they live, regardless of how long that may be. Upon their death no further payments are made.

This illustration depicts the life only settlement option:

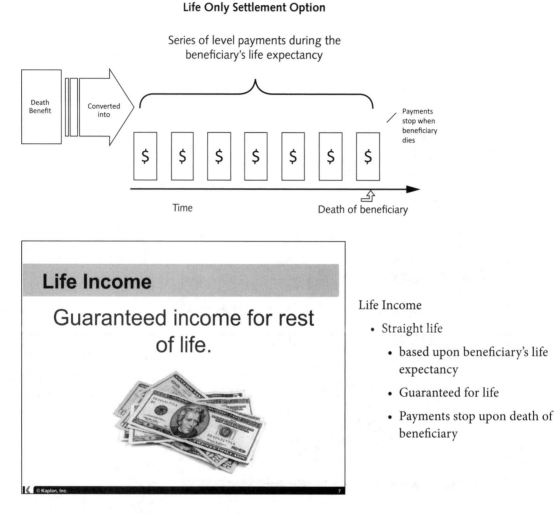

Life Income

- Straight life
  - based upon beneficiary's life expectancy
  - Guaranteed for life
  - Payments stop upon death of beneficiary

6.4.6   Life With Period Certain

Life with period certain also pays an income for as long as the beneficiary is alive. However, the beneficiary selects a payment period, typically 5, 10, or 20 years can be chosen, and payments are guaranteed to be made for at least that number of years. If the beneficiary dies before the end of the selected period, payments continue to another person for the rest of the payment period.

This illustration depicts the life with period certain settlement option:

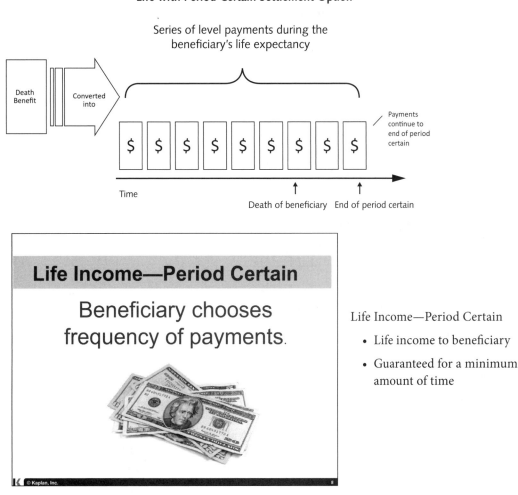

Life with Period Certain Settlement Option

Series of level payments during the beneficiary's life expectancy

Life Income—Period Certain

- Life income to beneficiary
- Guaranteed for a minimum amount of time

6.4.7   Life With Refund

The **life with refund** settlement option pays an income for as long as the beneficiary is alive, but also guarantees total payments will be at least the amount of the death benefit. If the beneficiary dies before the total of payments reaches the death benefit, the balance is paid to another person. The payment to the other person is either the remainder of the death benefit or in installments.

This illustration depicts the life with refund settlement option:

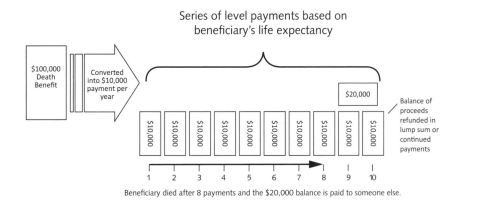

Life with Refund Settlement Option

Series of level payments based on beneficiary's life expectancy

Beneficiary died after 8 payments and the $20,000 balance is paid to someone else.

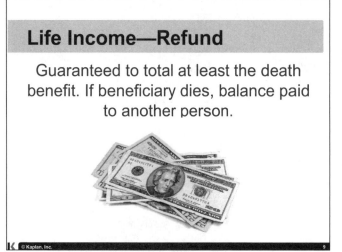

Life Income—Refund

- Pays beneficiary an income for life
- Guarantees payments will at least equal the death benefit
  - Pays someone else balance of death benefit if beneficiary doesn't live long enough

6.4.8   Joint-and-Survivor Life

The **joint-and-survivor life settlement option** continues paying a benefit for as long as either beneficiary lives. This option is often used when a married couple will be receiving the payments.

After the death of the first beneficiary, the same or a reduced payment amount is paid to the survivor. Selecting a reduced payment for the second beneficiary will allow a larger payment while both beneficiaries are alive.

This illustration depicts the joint-and-survivor life settlement option:

Joint-and-Survivor Life Settlement Option

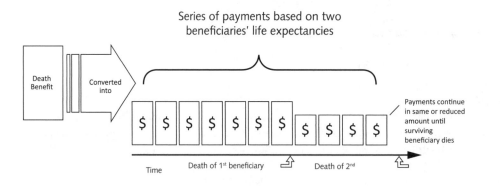

Joint and Survivor

- Pays two beneficiaries an income for life
  - The survivor receive the same or a reduced payment
    - 100%
    - 75%
    - 66 2/3%
    - 50%

 QUICK QUIZ 6.A

1. Which settlement option pays only the earnings on the death benefit to a beneficiary?
   A. Life income
   B. Fixed amount
   C. Fixed period
   D. Interest only

2. Emily has chosen to receive the payout from her husband's life insurance policy so that she will receive an income for the next 15 years. At the end of that time, the entire proceeds from the policy will have been paid out. Emily has selected the
   A. interest-only option
   B. fixed-period option
   C. fixed-amount option
   D. life-income option

Answers can be found at the end of Unit 6.

6.5   ACCESS TO CASH VALUES

6.5.1   Policy Loans

Permanent life insurance policies have two components, the death benefit or face value and cash value – the savings element funded by a portion of the premium. If the policyowner needs cash but does not want to surrender their policy, they can access the cash value that is available using the ***policy loan provision***.

The main advantages of a policy loan over other loans is that there is no credit check; the interest rate is usually much lower; the policyholder can pay back the loan according to virtually any repayment schedule; and, in fact, the policyholder is not even legally obligated to pay back the loan. The value of the life insurance policy is reduced while the loan is outstanding. If death occurs while the loan is outstanding, then the insurance proceeds are reduced by the amount of the loan outstanding plus interest.

When the policy loan and the accumulated interest exceed the cash value of the policy, it lapses.

Some policies have an **automatic premium loan provision.** If the insured fails to pay the policy premium by the end of the grace period, then the insurer will pay the premium with a policy loan and will continue to do so until the cash value of the policy falls below the premium amount, in which case, the policy will lapse.

6.5.2   Withdrawals and Partial Surrenders

A loan is a sum you borrow and use your policy as collateral. Loans are subject to loan interest and any unpaid loan will be deducted from the death benefit upon the insured person's death. Loans may be repaid at any time while the policy is in force. *Withdrawals*, or partial surrenders, are allowed on universal life insurance policies but not whole life policies. A withdrawal will result in a reduction of the cash value and the death benefit amount. A withdrawal may be subject to a pro-rata surrender charge and/or processing fee. A withdrawal cannot be repaid.

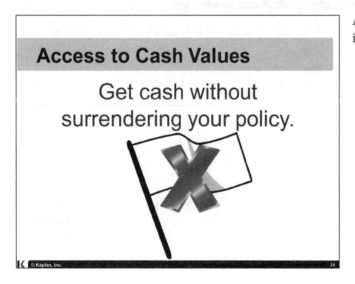

Access to Cash Values While Insured is Living

- Policyowner makes decision
- Loan reduces the death benefit
    - Fixed or variable interest
- If interest not paid
    - Loan taken to pay interest
- Automatic premium loan
    - Prevents lapse
    - Interest is charged
- Insurer must notify policyowner
    - Policy lapse
    - No cash value
- Universal life withdrawals
    - No interest or repayment
    - Fees

6.6   POLICY DIVIDENDS

6.6.1   Source of Policy Dividends

Life insurance policies that pay policy *dividends* are referred to as participating policies. Life policies that do not pay policy dividends are referred to as nonparticipating policies. **Policy dividends** are a refund of a portion of the premium. Dividends are based on the difference between the gross premium charged and the actual experience of the insurer. Dividends are not guaranteed. Because policy dividends are a return of premium, they are not taxable.

6.6.2   Dividend Options

Use the acronym CARPPO to remember the dividend options:

6.6.2.1 Cash

The insurer can send a check to the policyowner in the amount of the dividend.

6.6.2.2 Accumulation at Interest

The dividend can be left with the insurer to earn interest in a savings account. The ***dividend is not taxable***, however the interest credited to the account is ***taxable***.

6.6.2.3 Reduced Premium

The dividend can be applied and reduce the next premium due.

6.6.2.4 Paid Up Additions

The paid-up additions option uses each annual dividend to purchase an additional amount of life insurance. The result of a paid-up addition is a larger amount of life insurance. In turn, each paid-up addition builds its own cash value and also earns dividends. The cash value build-up is tax-deferred under the tax rules for life insurance cash value.

6.6.2.5 Paid Up Insurance

Dividends plus interest on dividends are applied to the annual premium and are enough to pay the entire annual premium. In a high interest rate environment, this may allow the policyowner to not have to pay premiums out-of-pocket. Since dividends are not guaranteed, a producer cannot tell a policyowner the policy is "paid up."

6.6.2.6 One-Year Term Insurance

The dividend may be used to buy one-year term insurance equal to the policy's cash value.

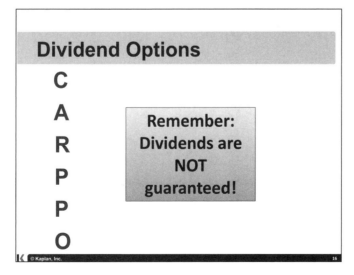

Dividend Options—"CARPPO"

- Cash
- Accumulate interest
- Reduce next premium amount
- Paid Up additions at attained age
- Paid up insurance sooner
- One year term insurance at attained age

6.7   NONFORFEITURE OPTIONS

The *nonforfeiture clause* in an insurance policy allows for the insured to receive all or a portion of the benefits or a partial refund on the premiums paid if the insured misses premium payments, causing the policy to lapse.

There are three **nonforfeiture options**:

- *Cash surrender*—the policy is canceled and the policyowner receives the current cash value.

- *Reduced paid-up insurance*—Under this option, the policyowner obtains a reduced amount of paid-up whole life insurance based the insured's attained age and the amount of guaranteed cash value available to buy a single premium policy. The policy will pay the reduced death benefit whenever the insured dies.

- *Extended term insurance*—The net cash surrender value is used to buy a term insurance policy with a death benefit the same as the original whole life policy and is based on the insured's attained age. The policy will terminate after a stated number of years found in the non-forfeiture table. If the policyowner fails to select one of the nonforfeiture options when premium payments cease, this option generally goes into effect automatically.

$100,000 Whole Life Policy, Male, Age 35, Nonsmoker

End of Policy Year	Cash Surrender or Loan Value	Reduced Paid-Up Insurance	Extended Term Insurance	
			Years	Days
1	$.00	$0	0	0
2	.00	0	0	0
3	641.00	3,658	2	169
4	1,632.00	8,927	5	312
5	2,659.00	13,944	8	246
6	3,727.00	18,741	11	4
7	4,832.00	23,304	12	316
8	5,978.00	27,656	14	116
9	7,165.00	31,803	15	174
10	8,395.00	35,759	16	146
11	9,657.00	39,483	17	40
12	10,965.00	43,042	17	236
13	12,320.00	46,442	18	18
14	13,727.00	49,705	18	123
15	15,183.00	52,822	18	197
16	16,691.00	55,807	18	244
17	18,251.00	58,666	18	268
18	19,860.00	61,397	18	271
19	21,519.00	64,010	18	256
20	23,225.00	66,506	18	222
25	31,461.00	75,080	17	29
27	34,993.00	77,940	16	124
30	40,464.00	81,688	15	59
35	49,800.00	86,687	13	42

Policyowner Non-Forfeiture Options

$100,000 Whole Life Policy, Male, Age 35, Nonsmoker

End of Policy Year	Cash Surrender or Loan Value	Reduced Paid-Up Insurance	Extended Term Insurance Years	Days
1	$ .00	$ 0	0	0
2	.00	0	0	0
3	641.00	3,658	2	169
4	1,632.00	8,927	5	312
5	2,659.00	13,944	8	246
6	3,727.00	18,741	11	4
7	4,832.00	23,304	12	316

© Kaplan, Inc.   18

Policyowner Non-Forfeiture Options
- Surrender policy for cash
- Reduced insurance
  - New single premium policy
  - Premium based upon attained age
  - Less face value than old policy
  - Immediate cash values
- Extended term
  - Single premium term insurance
  - Same face amount as old policy
  - Only for a stated term of time
  - Default option selected by insurer

QUICK QUIZ 6.B

1. Which of the following statements about paid-up additions is TRUE?
   A. The dividends are used to purchase additional insurance protection
   B. The additional protection is almost always restricted to term insurance
   C. The single premium for the added coverage will be based on the insured's original age
   D. The operating expenses of putting this coverage in force are higher than original policy expenses

2. All of the following statements about policy dividends are true EXCEPT
   A. the insurer can send a check to the policyowner in the amount of the dividend
   B. the dividend can be applied against the next premium due, reducing its amount
   C. dividends can be guaranteed to be paid every year
   D. a dividend can be left with the insurer in a savings account to earn interest

3. Cash surrender, reduced paid up insurance, and extended term insurance are all examples of
   A. nonforfeiture options
   B. dividend options
   C. paid up additions
   D. paid up insurance

Answers can be found at the end of Unit 6.

UNIT 6 CRAM SHEET

Settlement Options

- Interest only
  - Interest is paid on the death benefit
  - Death benefit paid at a later date
- Fixed period
  - Death benefit plus guaranteed interest paid over a set amount of time
  - If interest earnings greater than the guaranteed rate
    - Amount of final payment will be larger
- Fixed amount
  - A fixed amount is paid
  - Interest earnings will not change the amount of the payment but will affect how long the payments can be made.
- Life income
  - Straight life
    - Income to beneficiary based upon life expectancy
    - Guaranteed for life
    - Payments stop upon death of beneficiary
- Life income—period certain
  - Life income to beneficiary
  - Guaranteed for a minimum amount of time
    - Paid to someone else if beneficiary dies before end of period certain.
- Life income—refund
  - Pays beneficiary an income for life
  - Guarantees payments will at least equal the death benefit
    - Pays someone else balance of death benefit if beneficiary doesn't live long enough
- Joint and survivor
  - Pays two beneficiaries an income for life
    - If one dies the payment to the survivor stays the same or is reduced.
      - 100%
      - 75%
      - 66⅔%
      - 50%

Access to Cash Values While Insured is Living

- Policyowner makes decision
- Loan reduces the death benefit
  - Interest is charged
  - Fixed or variable
- If interest not paid
  - Loan automatically taken to pay interest
- Automatic premium loan
  - Prevents lapse
  - Interest is charged
- Cash values running out to pay interest on loans
  - Company must notify policyowner
  - Policy may lapse
- Universal life allows withdrawal
  - No interest or repayment
  - Fees

Dividend Options—CARPPO

- Cash
- Accumulate at interest
- Reduce next premium amount
- Paid up additions—attained age
- Paid up policy
- One year term insurance—attained age

Policyowner Non-Forfeiture Options

- Surrender policy for cash
- Reduced paid-up insurance
  - Cash values used to buy new single premium policy
  - Premium based upon insureds current (attained age)
  - New policy has less insurance than the old policy
  - New policy has immediate cash values
- Extended term
  - Cash values buy single premium term insurance
  - Same amount of insurance as old policy
  - Only for a stated term of time
  - Default option selected by the insurer

UNIT 6 QUIZ

In order to measure your success, we recommend that you answer the following 10 questions correctly.

1. Heath has chosen to receive the payout from his wife's life insurance policy in such a way that he will have an income for the remainder of his life, regardless of how long he lives. Heath has selected the
   A. interest-only option
   B. fixed-period option
   C. fixed-amount option
   D. life-income option

2. Jim has selected to receive only the interest from his mother's life insurance policy. When Jim dies, his children will receive the lump-sum benefit in addition to the benefit from his life insurance policy. Jim has selected the
   A. interest-only option
   B. fixed-period option
   C. fixed-amount option
   D. life-income option

3. Walter is the beneficiary of his mother's life insurance policy. He wants to make sure the proceeds will last not only as long as he lives but also as long as his wife is alive. Walter should select the
   A. straight life income option
   B. refund annuity option
   C. life income certain option
   D. joint and survivorship life income option

4. Of all of the life income options, which settlement option has the largest payment?
   A. Life with period certain
   B. Life only
   C. Life with refund certain
   D. Joint-and-survivor life

5. Which of the following is not a factor in determining the amount the beneficiary will receive each time a payment is made under the fixed amount option?
   A. The specified amount of each payment
   B. The principal amount
   C. The interest earned on the principal
   D. The capital amount

6. Carmen has selected to receive $10,000 per month until the principal and interest on her husband's life insurance policy have been paid out. Carmen has selected the
   A. interest-only option
   B. fixed-period option
   C. fixed-amount option
   D. life-income option

7. All of the following statements regarding the life only settlement options are correct EXCEPT
   A. payments are guaranteed to continue for as long as the beneficiary lives
   B. payments continue even if the beneficiary dies shortly after payments begin
   C. life expectancy is a factor used in calculating the size of the payment
   D. life income payments are smaller for younger beneficiaries

8. Thomas has chosen to receive the settlement from his wife's $100,000 life insurance policy according to the life income option. Under the option he chooses, he will receive an income for his life and his daughter will receive payments if he dies before receiving $100,000 in income. Thomas has selected a
    A. straight life income option
    B. refund annuity option
    C. life income certain option
    D. joint and survivorship life income option

9. Which of the following is NOT a factor in determining the amount the beneficiary will receive each time a payment is made under the fixed period option?
    A. The age of the beneficiary
    B. The principal amount
    C. The interest earned on the principal
    D. The length of time payments is to be made

10. Which of the following statements about reduced paid-up insurance option is NOT true?
    A. The new policy will build cash values for the policyowner
    B. No further premiums need to be paid on the reduced policy—it is paid up
    C. The new protection is for the same amount as the original policy
    D. A full share of expense loading is usually not included in the premium on the reduced coverage because the costs of setting up the coverage are greatly reduced

ANSWER KEY

QUICK QUIZZES

QUICK QUIZ 6.A

1. **D.** Interest only

2. **B.** fixed-period option

QUICK QUIZ 6.B

1. **A.** The dividends are used to purchase additional insurance protection

2. **C.** dividends can be guaranteed to be paid every year

3. **A.** nonforfeiture options

UNIT QUIZ

1. **D.** This is an example of the life-income option because the proceeds will be paid over the beneficiary's life, regardless of how long that might be.

2. **A.** Because Jim has elected to receive only the interest, this example represents the interest-only option.

3. **D.** Walter should select the joint and survivorship life income option.

4. **B.** Life only is also known as straight life and has the largest settlement payment.

5. **D.** The capital amount is not a factor in determining the amount the beneficiary will receive each time a payment is made under the fixed amount option.

6. **C.** Carmen has elected to receive a fixed amount per month until all the proceeds have all been paid, so this is an example of the fixed-amount option.

7. **B.** With the life only settlement option payment ends even if the beneficiary dies shortly after payments begin.

8. **B.** Thomas has selected a refund annuity option.

9. **A.** The age of the beneficiary is not a factor in determining the amount the beneficiary will receive each time a payment is made under the fixed period option.

10. **C.** The reduced paid-up amount is simply the amount of paid-up insurance that can be purchased using the existing cash value.

UNIT 7 Life Insurance Policy Provisions

7.1   INTRODUCTION

Provisions were created to protect the interests of one or both parties named in a contract or legal document. A life insurance policy is a legal document, and as such it can be somewhat intimidating.

The life insurance industry is highly regulated and policies contain many standard provisions that explain how the policy works and define the parties involved in the contract and their rights, privileges, and obligations. The common policy provisions provide more details and include the free look clause, grace period, suicide and incontestability clause, policy loans, and others that enhance or limit a policy and impose duties on the owner and beneficiary.

This unit discusses the various provisions, important terms, and conditions in life insurance policies.

7.2   LEARNING OBJECTIVES

After successfully completing this lesson, you should be able to:

▫ explain the 13 life insurance policy provisions: free look, insuring clause, ownership rights, assignment, entire contract, modifications, consideration, payment of premium, grace period, reinstatement, incontestability provision, misstatement of age or sex, and payment of claims;

▫ describe the different types of beneficiaries and their succession in receiving proceeds;

▫ compare per capita and per stirpes;

▫ compare revocable and irrevocable beneficiaries;

▫ explain the facility of payment provision, common disaster provision, and the spendthrift provision;

▫ identify the Uniform Simultaneous Death Act; and

▫ identify the four common exclusions that define when life insurance coverage does not apply.

7.3   LIFE INSURANCE POLICY PROVISIONS

The terms of a life insurance policy are spelled out in its **provisions** or *clauses*. They describe how certain common situations will be handled, as well as the rights and the obligations of the policyowner and the insurer.

Life insurance provisions have been standardized for the most part, so every policy contains these contractual provisions.

7.4   STANDARD PROVISIONS

7.4.1   Free Look

The **free look**, or *right to examine*, provision gives the policyowner a period of time to return a policy for any reason *within ten days of delivery* and receive all premiums paid. The policy will be considered null and void.

Free Look

- Begins when the owner receives the policy
- Usually no fewer than 10 days
- Policy can be returned for a full refund

7.4.2   Insuring Clause

The **insuring clause** or *insuring agreement* sets forth the insurer's promise to pay benefits upon the insured's death. It includes what the company will pay, the death benefit amount, and to whom it will be paid. An authorized officer of the company signs this clause.

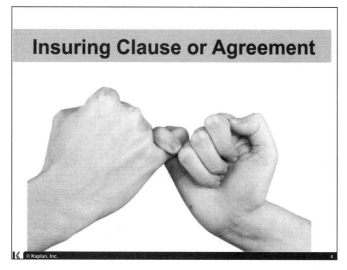

Insuring Clause or Agreement

- Usually found on the first page of the policy
- Insurers promise to pay upon death
- Includes the face amount
- Usually signed by an officer of the company

7.4.3   Ownership Rights

The owner of a policy may exercise all policy rights and privileges without the consent of any beneficiary including the right to:

- choose and subsequently change a *beneficiary* (as long as the beneficiary is not an irrevocable beneficiary);
- select settlement options, conversion options, or any non-forfeiture options;
- receive or borrow any cash values and/or dividends that have accumulated;
- cancel the policy;
- assign or transfer ownership of the policy;
- select or change the premium payment mode; and
- receive policy proceeds upon maturity or endowment.

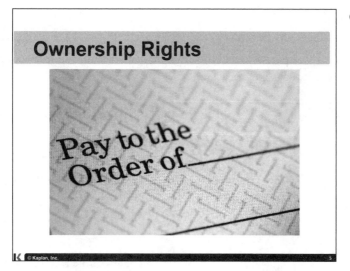

Ownership Rights

- Name or change the beneficiary
- Select settlement options
- Borrow or withdraw policy cash values
- Receive policy dividends (participating policies)
- Surrender or cancel the policy
- Assign or transfer ownership
- Select/change the premium payment mode
- Select a non-forfeiture option

7.4.4 Assignment

Assignment of life insurance is a transfer of the owner's rights, in whole or part, to another individual or entity.

There are two types of assignment.

1. **Collateral assignment** (*temporary* or *conditional* assignment) does not change ownership of the policy. The most common type of partial assignment is to pledge all or part of the death benefit as collateral for a loan.

2. **Absolute or permanent** assignment of a policy transfers all rights of ownership to another person or entity. Example: a parent may transfer policyownership to a daughter when she reaches age 18.

Policy Assignment

Transfer of owner's rights

© Kaplan, Inc.

Policy Assignment

- Collateral—a pledge for a loan
- Absolute—permanent change

7.4.5   Entire Contract

The life insurance policy and a copy of the original application constitute the ***entire contract***.

The provision states "no statement shall void this policy or be used in defense of a claim under it unless contained in the application."

This reinforces the idea that the policy itself constitutes the entire contract along with a copy of the original application. The insurer may not refer to documents other than these when denying or paying a claim.

Entire Contract

- Policy plus
- Copy of the application plus
- Any riders or amendments (if any)

7.4.6   Endorsements (*Modifications*)

Endorsements or any change made to the contract must be made in writing and agreed to by both the insurer and the policyowner. This amendment must be signed by an executive officer of the company and cannot be authorized by an agent/producer.

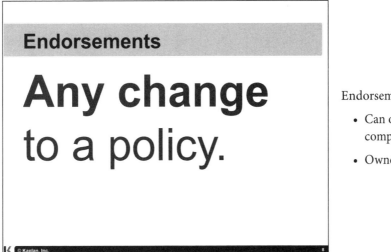

Endorsements (*Modifications*)

- Can only be made by the company
- Owner can request a change

7.4.7 Consideration

Consideration is a legal term meaning something of value. An exchange of value is necessary to form a valid contract. The insured's consideration is the premium paid and the representations made in the application. The insurer's consideration is the promise to pay the face amount of the contract to the named beneficiary upon the death of the insured.

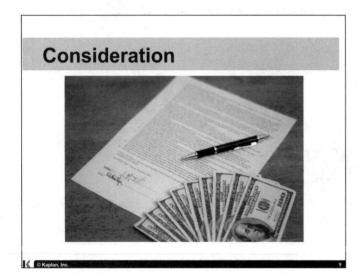

Consideration—think MONEY!

- Insured's consideration— premiums and truthful statements made on the application

- Insurer's consideration—pay benefits at time of claim

7.4.8 Payment of Premium

The **payment of premium** provision states that premiums are due *in advance*—that is, on or before the date on which the next period of coverage begins. The mode of the premium payment is frequency of the payment. Modes of payment are annually, semi-annually, quarterly, and monthly. Premium payment amounts can be either level, single payment, graded, or flexible.

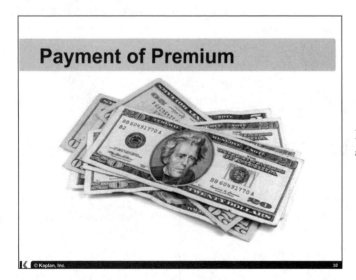

Payment of Premium —due in advance of the coverage period

7.4.9 Grace Period

If the insured does not pay the premium on date when due, the policy will stay in force for a limited time before the coverage actually lapses. This is the policy's **grace period** and lasts for a period of up to 31 days.

If the insured dies during the grace period, the policy will pay the death benefit minus the amount of the past due premium as of the date of death.

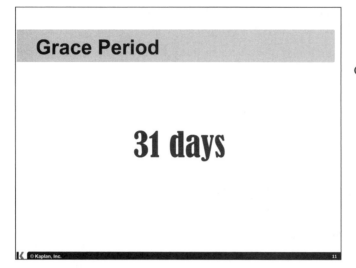

Grace Period

- Premium not paid by due date
- Usually 31 days following due date
- Insurance still in force
- Death benefit paid minus premiums due

7.4.10 Reinstatement

Reinstatement is the restoration of a lapsed policy as originally purchased. Permanent life policies permit reinstatement in nearly all cases. The insured will receive the protection of the original policy, if the policy has not been surrendered for cash, and they do the following:

- submits an application for reinstatement within three years of lapse;
- pay all past due premiums, with interest; and,
- provides satisfactory evidence of insurability (medical examination)

The premium for the reinstated policy will be the same as the original. A reinstated policy usually starts a new contestability period (two years); but it does not require a new suicide period.

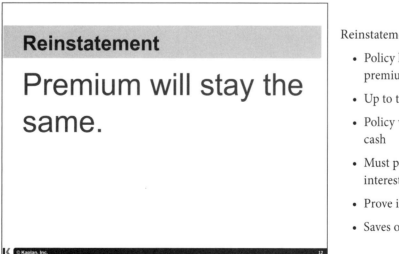

Reinstatement

- Policy lapsed for nonpayment of premiums
- Up to three years to reinstate
- Policy was not surrendered for cash
- Must pay missed premiums + interest
- Prove insurability
- Saves original policy + issue age

7.4.11 Incontestability

The **incontestability provision** is provided to protect the insured. It states that after a life insurance policy has been in effect for two years the company cannot claim that a statement made in the application for insurance was meant to defraud the insurer.

The first two years of a policy are known as the *contestable* period. The insured might be required to substantiate statements in application during this period.

If a policy has been reinstated after lapse, a new contestability period begins but it only applies to information given on the reinstatement application, not the information given when the policy was originally purchased.

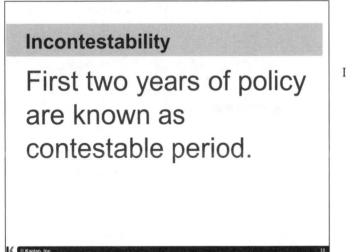

Incontestability

- Usually after two years
- Policy can't be taken away
  - even if material misrepresentation or
  - fraud (concealment)

7.4.12 Suicide Clause

The suicide clause states that if an insured, whether sane or insane, commits suicide during the first two years after a life insurance contract has been issued, the company will pay only the premium paid by the insured, not the face amount of the policy. Once the policy has been in effect for two years, an insured's suicide will result in payment of the full-face amount of the policy. Suicide is excluded from accidental death benefits.

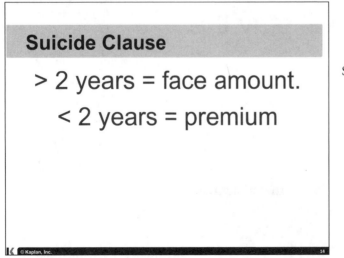

Suicide Clause

- If insured commits suicide prior to having a policy for two years, only the premium will be paid back
- After two years the full face amount will be paid

7.4.13 Misstatement of Age

The incontestability clause previously discussed does not pertain to an insured's ***misstatement regarding age***. If a deceased insured misrepresented their age, the face amount of the policy will be adjusted to an amount the premium would have purchased at the insured's correct age, at the time of purchase of the policy.

For example, if an insured claimed to be 30 years old when in fact they were 40 years old, the $50,000 policy purchased would be adjusted to a lower face amount in the event of his/her death. If the insured claimed to be 30 years old when in fact he/she was 20 years old, the $50,000 policy purchased would be adjusted to a higher face amount.

If a misstatement of age is discovered while the insured is alive, this mistake will be rectified usually at the insured's option.

When a ***misstatement of sex*** occurs the face amount of a policy will be adjusted in a similar way.

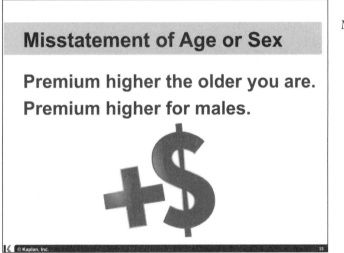

Misstatement of Age (Gender)

- Insured older than application states
  - Death benefit reduced to correct premium amount
- Insured younger than application states
  - Death benefit increased to correct premium amount
- Incontestability provision does not apply

7.4.14 Payment of Claims

The **payment of claims** provision says the insurer will pay the death benefit *promptly*. The insurance company is generally required to pay a death claim within 60 days (two months) after receiving notification of the claim. If the claim payment is made more than 60 days after notification of the claim, interest must be paid.

Time Payment of Claims
- Immediately
- Usually no longer than 60 days

Life Insurance Policy Provisions

Free look

Insuring clause

Ownership rights

Assignment

Entire contract

Modifications

Consideration

Payment of premium

Grace period

Reinstatement

Incontestability provision

Misstatement of age or sex

Payment of claims

QUICK QUIZ 7.A

1. Which clause contains the basic promise of the life insurance company to pay a specified sum of money to a beneficiary upon the death of the insured?

   A. Consideration clause

   B. Insuring clause

   C. Policy loan clause

   D. Payment clause

2. Which clause identifies the components of the contract?

   A. Consideration clause

   B. Insuring clause

   C. Entire contract clause

   D. Payment clause

Answers can be found at the end of Unit 7.

7.5   BENEFICIARIES

The policyowner names the **beneficiary**—the person or entity who will get the death benefit.

7.5.1   Who Can Be a Beneficiary?

Almost any person or other legal entity can be the beneficiary of a life insurance policy. A beneficiary is defined as a "person or interest" to whom payment of life insurance policy proceeds will be made upon the death of the insured.

For each type of beneficiary, certain considerations need to be kept in mind.

7.5.1.1 Individuals

An individual or a class of persons can be named beneficiary. Each type must have an insurable interest in the insured when the policy is originally purchased.

If a specific individual is intended to receive benefits, it is important that he or she be clearly identified by name, preferably including the person's middle name or at least middle initial. For example, a designation of "my spouse" would cause confusion if the policyowner gets divorced and remarried.

If two or more beneficiaries are named, the policyowner needs to define how the benefits are to be shared among them. Any division is acceptable. If no division is given, the beneficiary provisions of most policies say that the benefits will be paid in equal shares.

7.5.1.2 Classes

Life insurance beneficiaries can be designated by *classes*. For example, "my children" or "my siblings" are class designations. Class beneficiaries need not be identified by name.

7.5.1.3 Trusts

A trust is a legal entity which can hold title to property while it is managed for the benefit of others. There are three parties to a trust.

1. The **grantor** is the individual who sets up the trust, transfers property into it, and writes the instructions as to how the trust will operate.

2. The **trustee** is the party that manages the property according to the grantor's instructions. The trustee may be an individual or another legal entity such as a bank.

3. The **beneficiary** is the person who receives the benefits of the trust.

Trusts can be set up for multiple reasons; they are generally designated to receive life insurance proceeds in order to allow someone to enjoy the benefit of those proceeds without giving them ownership. This is commonly done when the beneficiary may not be capable of managing a large sum of money.

7.5.1.4 Minors

A minor is a person under age 18 and is deemed *legally incompetent*, therefore they cannot take ownership of life insurance proceeds. Paying the proceeds to a trustee or guardian who is legally entitled to receive and manage such funds on behalf of the minor is a valid beneficiary arrangement. However, the insurer may be instructed to hold the death proceeds and credit interest until the minor attains legal/majority age.

7.5.1.5 Estates

The insured's **estate** may be designated as beneficiary and used to pay debts and the costs of legally closing the estate. After the estate's debts are paid, the remaining proceeds will be distributed to the insured's heirs along with the estate's other assets.

Life insurance proceeds paid into an estate are counted toward the total value of the estate for estate tax purposes.

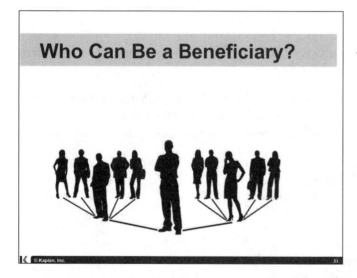

Who Can Be a Beneficiary?

- Individuals
- Classes
- Trusts
- Minors
- Estates
- Charities
- University/Colleges

7.5.2   Per Capita, Per Stirpes

When more than one person in a class is the primary beneficiary it is important to know the difference between **per capita** and **per stirpes** distributions.

Per capita means "by the head," and it divides the policy's death benefit equally among the surviving members of the class. Example; an insured has two adult children designated as primary beneficiaries:

- Both are living when the insured dies, each receives 50% of the policy's death benefit;
- One dies before the insured, the surviving child will receive the entire death benefit.

The *per capita* beneficiary designation does not transfer death proceeds below a generational level. If the deceased child had children they would not receive proceeds upon the death of their grandparent.

Per stirpes means "by the branch," and it signifies that the children of a deceased class beneficiary are entitled to that beneficiary's share of the proceeds. Using the same example as above:

- Both children are living when the insured dies, each gets 50% of the policy's death benefit;
- One child dies before the insured, the surviving child gets 50% of the death benefit and the two children of the deceased child, the insured's grandchildren, receive 25% each of the proceeds.

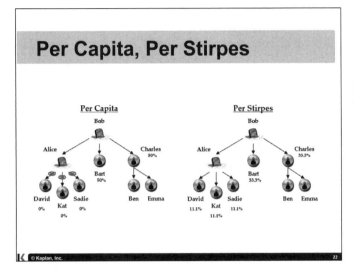

Multiple Beneficiaries in the Same Class

- Per capita—by the head (not inheritable)
- Per stirpes—by branch (inheritable)

7.5.3   Secondary/Contingent Beneficiaries

The ***primary beneficiary*** is the first in line to receive the policy's death benefit.

The ***contingent beneficiary*** is the next in line to receive the policy's death benefit if the primary beneficiary dies before the insured. There can be more than one level of contingent beneficiary.

The *secondary/contingent beneficiary* is next in line if the primary beneficiary has died, and the *tertiary beneficiary* is third in line if the secondary beneficiary has died.

A secondary/contingent beneficiary has no right to benefits if any primary beneficiary is still alive. Contingent beneficiaries get proceeds only if all the beneficiaries on the level above them have died before the insured.

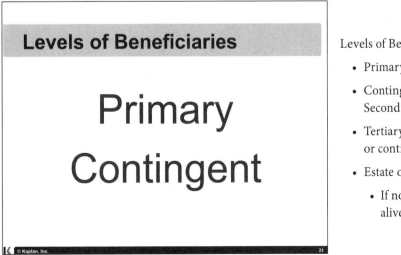

Levels of Beneficiaries

- Primary—First
- Contingent or secondary—Second (if no primary alive)
- Tertiary—Third (if no primary or contingent alive)
- Estate of insured
  - If no beneficiary named or alive

7.5.4   Revocable Versus Irrevocable

Beneficiary designations can be changed, or *revoked* without notice and without their knowledge or consent. Such designations are called **revocable beneficiaries.**

Policyowners can give up their right to change a beneficiary designation. Such designations are called **irrevocable beneficiaries.**

An irrevocable beneficiary designation can only be changed with their written consent. If an irrevocable beneficiary dies before the insured, the policyowner usually has the right to name a new beneficiary.

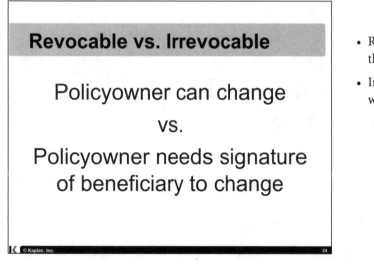

- Revocable—can be changed by the owner at any time
- Irrevocable—can't be changed without beneficiary consent
  - Loan or withdrawal from cash values requires permission of beneficiary
  - Usually becomes revocable upon death of irrevocable beneficiary

7.5.5   Changes

The owner of the policy may designate and change primary and contingent beneficiaries, as often as desired, during the lifetime of the insured. Changes generally take effect as of the date on the written request.

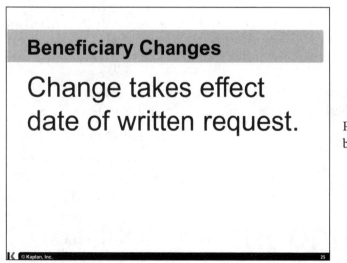

Policyowner can change the beneficiary. Must notify insurer.

7.5.6   Facility of Payment Provision

The **facility of payment provision** allows the insurer to pay all or part of the policy's death benefit to someone other than a designated beneficiary if:

- the beneficiary is a minor, is deceased, or cannot be found; or
- someone other than the beneficiary incurred the insured's final medical or funeral expenses.

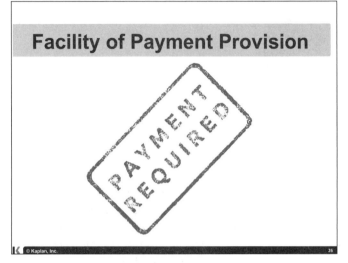

Facility of payment provision— insurer can pay someone other than beneficiary.

7.5.7   Uniform Simultaneous Death Act

Consider the problem that may arise if the insured and the primary beneficiary both die in the same accident. Payment of the policy proceeds differs dramatically depending on who died first. Let's go through some scenarios and discuss how this act affects these situations.

- If the insured dies first, the proceeds should be paid to the primary beneficiary. What happens if the primary beneficiary dies in a common accident along with the insured?
- If the primary beneficiary dies first, the proceeds should be paid to the contingent beneficiary.
- If there is no contingent beneficiary, the proceeds should be paid to the insured's estate.

However, in such accidents, it is sometimes impossible to tell who died first. If so, who gets the proceeds?

The **Uniform Simultaneous Death Act** solves this problem by directing that the primary beneficiary is assumed to have died first. That is, if the insured and the primary beneficiary die as a result of the same accident, the policy proceeds will not be paid to the primary beneficiary since this person just died. Instead, proceeds are paid to the contingent beneficiary or to the insured's estate if no contingent beneficiary is listed.

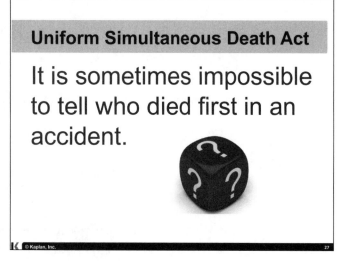

Uniform Simultaneous Death

- Insured and primary beneficiary are in same accident
- Both die in accident
- Assumes primary beneficiary dies first
- Proceeds paid to contingent beneficiary

7.5.8 Common Disaster Provision

This common disaster provision expands on the intent of the Uniform Simultaneous Death Act by providing a more lenient timespan between the death of the insured and the primary beneficiary when by a common accident. Many times, one person could live several hours or days beyond the accident but ultimately die due to the accident. Insurance companies call this the Common Disaster Provision, and this language will appear on the policy. This provision presumes that, for insurance purposes, the primary beneficiary dies first (when death occurs within a few days of the insured after a common accident). Most insurance policies define this timeframe as death within 30 to 90 days of the accident (exact number will be specified in the policy). This prevents the life insurance proceeds to be paid to the estate of the primary beneficiary.

 EXAMPLE

> John is married to Marcy. John has a $500,000 life insurance policy and has named the primary beneficiary as Marcy and the contingent beneficiary as their children. John and Marcy are in the car together and are in a very serious automobile accident. John dies on the scene, and Marcy is rushed to the hospital. Marcy lives for 10 days and then passes away. How are John's life insurance proceeds distributed? Since Marcy died within a few days of John after the accident, the Common Disaster Provision assumes that Marcy died first. Since the primary beneficiary was deceased when proceeds are to be paid, they are paid to the contingent beneficiary (their kids).

If the primary beneficiary lives beyond the period of time stated in the policy, the proceeds would be paid to the primary beneficiary or the primary beneficiary's estate, if deceased.

Common Disaster Provision

Assumed that insured survived beneficiary

© Kaplan, Inc.   28

Common Disaster Provision

- Insured and primary beneficiary are in common accident

- Both die within 30–90 days after accident

- Proceeds paid as if the primary beneficiary died first

- Proceeds paid to contingent beneficiary

7.5.9   Spendthrift Provision

A spendthrift clause may be included in a life insurance policy requiring that the policy proceeds be paid to the beneficiary in installments of a defined amount and at set intervals. The beneficiary has no right to elect a different settlement. Furthermore, the beneficiary is not allowed to borrow from the policy proceeds nor assign any of the proceeds. In this way, the insured is assured that the beneficiary will not spend money foolishly as a "spendthrift" (hence the name) upon the insured's death. This clause acts to prevent creditors from attaching the policy proceeds upon the insured's death.

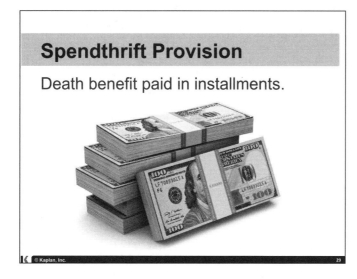

Spendthrift Provision

Death benefit paid in installments.

© Kaplan, Inc.   29

Spendthrift Provision

- May be included in the policy

  - Death benefit cannot be paid in a lump sum

  - Death benefits cannot be claimed by creditors before payment to beneficiary

  - Death benefits cannot be pledged by the beneficiary to a creditor

  - Death benefits cannot be used by the beneficiary as collateral for a loan

QUICK QUIZ 7.B

1. Steve is the beneficiary on his spouse's life insurance policy. When they divorce, his spouse cannot remove him as beneficiary on the policy without his written permission because
    A. most states require the beneficiary's written consent
    B. Steve is a revocable beneficiary
    C. Steve is an assigned beneficiary
    D. Steve is an irrevocable beneficiary

2. Ginny is a revocable primary beneficiary on her mother's life insurance policy. Which of the following statements is TRUE?
    A. Ginny can probably assign her rights in the policy as collateral on a loan
    B. Ginny will receive benefits before any other beneficiary upon her mother's death
    C. Ginny will receive benefits only if another beneficiary has died before her mother dies
    D. Ginny's mother may not change the beneficiary without Ginny's permission

3. An insured and the primary beneficiary died in a car accident. Which of the following states that the primary beneficiary died first unless there is evidence to the contrary?
    A. The facility of payment provision
    B. The Uniform Simultaneous Death Act
    C. The common disaster provision
    D. The spendthrift provision

Answers can be found at the end of Unit 7.

7.6 EXCLUSIONS

Many life insurance policies contain **exclusions**, or exceptions that define when coverage does not apply. A life insurer is not liable for a loss caused by the insured engaging in an illegal activity. In addition to illegal activities, the most common exclusions are as follows.

7.6.1 Suicide

Under the **suicide exclusion**, death by suicide is not covered for a certain period of time after the policy goes into effect. Depending on the policy, the period may be one or two years.

If the insured commits suicide during this initial period, the policy's death benefit is not payable, but all premiums paid for the policy are refunded. After the policy has been in force for the stated period, suicide is covered and the full death benefit is payable.

7.6.2 Aviation

The **aviation exclusion** eliminates coverage only for certain types of aviation activities. It *does not apply* to commercial flight. That is, coverage still exists for insureds who are fare-paying airline passengers or commercial airline pilots or crew. The exclusion applies only to individuals such as private pilots, test pilots, military pilots and crew.

7.6.3   War or Military Service

There are two versions of the **war or military service exclusion**.

Status-type—This version eliminates coverage for the entire period during which the insured is in the military, regardless of how the insured dies. Under the status-type war or military service exclusion, even if the insured were home on leave and died driving to the golf course, no death benefit would be paid.

Results-type—Under this version, coverage is eliminated only if the cause of death was related to military service.

7.6.4   Hazardous Occupation or Hobby

The **hazardous occupation** or **hobby exclusion** may be included if the insured engages in activities such as mountain climbing, auto racing, sky diving, or scuba diving, either for pay or recreation. As an alternative to excluding coverage entirely for death resulting from these activities, the insurer might charge an additional premium or limit the amount of coverage it would issue.

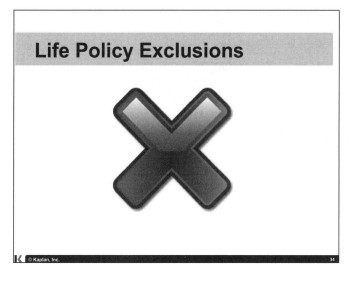

Life Policy Exclusions

- Suicide
  - Death by suicide not covered before two years (time may vary)
- Aviation
  - Death due to an airplane accident
  - Does not apply if a passenger or crew member of a commercial airline
- War or military service
  - Status type—death occurs while in the military—regardless of the reason
  - Results type—death occurs related to the military

 QUICK QUIZ 7.C

1. The aviation exclusion eliminates coverage for all of the following EXCEPT
   A. a commercial flight
   B. a private flight
   C. military pilots and crew
   D. test pilots

Answers can be found at the end of Unit 7.

🧠 UNIT 7 CRAM SHEET

Free look

- Begins when the owner receives the policy
- Usually 10 days
- Policy can be returned for a full refund

Insuring clause or agreement

- Usually found on the first page of the policy
- Insurers promise to pay upon death
- Includes the face amount
- Usually signed by an officer of the company

Ownership rights

- Name or change the beneficiary
- Select how the death benefits will be paid (lump sum or over time)
- Borrow or withdraw from the policy cash values (if any)
- Receive policy dividends if a participating policy
- Surrender or cancel the policy
- Decide what to do with the policy cash values (if any)
- Assign the policy values or ownership
- Decide the premium payment mode

Assignment by policyowner

- Collateral—pledging the policy as collateral for a loan
- Absolute—complete change of ownership

Entire contract

- Policy plus
- Copy of the application plus
- Any riders or amendments (if any)

Modifications

- Can only be made by the company
- Owner can request a change

Consideration—value given by policyowner

- Information in the application
- Premium

Payment of Premium—Premiums are due in advance

Grace period

- Premium not paid by due date
- Usually 31 days following due date
- Insurance still in force
- Death benefit paid minus premiums due

Reinstatement

- Policy has lapsed for nonpayment of premiums
- Up to three years following lapse
- Policy was not surrendered
    - Pay all missed premiums plus interest
    - Prove insured still insurable
    - Done to save terms of original policy (issue age)
- Incontestability
- Usually after two years
- Policy can't be taken away
    - Due to material misrepresentation
    - Fraud

Misstatement of age or gender

- If insured is older than application states (under payment)
    - Death benefit amount reduced to correct amount premium would have purchased
- If insured is younger than application states (over payment)
    - Death benefit amount increased to correct amount premium would have purchased
- Incontestability provision does not apply

Time payment of claims

- Immediately
- Usually no longer than 60 days

Life Insurance Policy Provisions

- Free look
- Insuring clause
- Ownership rights
- Assignment
- Entire contract
- Modifications
- Consideration
- Payment of premium

- Grace period
- Reinstatement
- Incontestability provision
- Misstatement of age or sex
- Payment of claims

Who can be a beneficiary?

- Individuals
- Classes
- Trusts
- Minors
- Estates

Multiple beneficiaries in the same class

- Per capita—by the head (not inheritable)
- Per stirpes—by branch (inheritable)

Levels of beneficiaries

- Primary—first
- Contingent or secondary—second (if no primary alive)
- Tertiary—third (if no primary or contingent alive)
- Estate of insured
    - If no beneficiary named or alive

Revocable—can be changed by the owner at any time

Irrevocable—can't be changed without beneficiary consent

- Loan or withdrawal from cash values requires permission of beneficiary
- Usually becomes revocable upon death of irrevocable beneficiary

Changes to Beneficiary must be requested in writing.

Facility of payment provision—insurer can pay someone other than beneficiary.

Common Disaster Provision

- Insured and primary beneficiary are in common accident
- Both die within 30–90 days after accident
- Proceeds paid as if the primary beneficiary died first
- Proceeds paid to contingent beneficiary

Uniform Simultaneous Death

- Insured and primary beneficiary are in same accident
- Both die in accident
- Assumes primary beneficiary dies first
- Proceeds paid to contingent beneficiary

Spendthrift provision

- May be included in the policy
- Death benefit cannot be paid in a lump sum
- Death benefits cannot be claimed by creditors before payment to beneficiary
- Death benefits cannot be pledged by the beneficiary to a creditor
- Death benefits cannot be used by the beneficiary as collateral for a loan

Life Policy Exclusions

Suicide

- Death by suicide not covered before 2 years (time may vary)

Aviation

- Death due to an airplane accident
- Does not apply if a passenger or crew member of a commercial airline

War or military service

- Status type—death occurs while in the military—regardless of the reason
- Results type—death occurs related to the military

UNIT 7 QUIZ

In order to measure your success, we recommend that you answer the following 10 questions correctly.

1. Which clause identifies the fact that the policyowner must pay something of value for the insurer's promise to pay benefits?
   A. Consideration clause
   B. Insuring clause
   C. Entire contract clause
   D. Payment clause

2. All of the following are designations of beneficiaries EXCEPT
   A. secondary beneficiary
   B. primary beneficiary
   C. tertiary beneficiary
   D. final beneficiary

3. Which of the following is allowed when policy proceeds are being paid through a spendthrift clause?
   A. The proceeds are paid directly to the beneficiary in monthly installments
   B. The proceeds may be transferred directly to a creditor by the beneficiary
   C. The proceeds may be commuted by the beneficiary to receive the present value of future payments in a lump sum
   D. The beneficiary may borrow against the strength of the proceeds

4. Carl purchased a life insurance policy when he was 44. The insurer accidentally recorded his age as 42. When the accident is discovered in a review of the files 5 years later
   A. the policy will be canceled because of misrepresentation
   B. the policy will not change because the incontestable period will have passed
   C. the coverage will be reduced because the premium is lower than it should have been
   D. the coverage will be raised because the premium is higher than it should have been

5. All of the following can be named beneficiaries in a life insurance contract EXCEPT
   A. the insured's estate
   B. a trust
   C. the insured
   D. a minor

6. If the named beneficiaries cannot be found, under the facility of payment provision the insurer may
   A. select a beneficiary
   B. retain the proceeds
   C. pay a mortgage company directly
   D. pay proceeds directly to a minor

7. The incontestability provision is usually in effect after
    A. 1 year
    B. 2 years
    C. 4 years
    D. 5 years

8. John leaves his $300,000 estate to his 3 children to split equally according to a per capita distribution. One of his children dies before John does. Upon John's death, which of the following statements is TRUE?
    A. The proceeds are split 3 ways between the remaining children and John's estate
    B. The proceeds are split 2 ways between the remaining children only
    C. The proceeds are split 3 ways between the remaining children and the beneficiary of the deceased child's estate
    D. The proceeds are split 4 ways between the remaining children, John's estate, and the deceased child's estate

9. When Tom dies, Rosemary receives the death benefit. If Rosemary had died before Tom, George would have received the benefit. Which of the following statements is TRUE?
    A. Rosemary is the primary beneficiary, and George is the contingent beneficiary
    B. Tom is the primary beneficiary, and Rosemary is the contingent beneficiary
    C. Rosemary is the contingent beneficiary, and George is the primary beneficiary
    D. George is the contingent beneficiary, and Rosemary is the tertiary beneficiary

10. John leaves his $300,000 estate to his 3 children to split equally according to a per stirpes distribution. One of his children dies before John does. Upon John's death, which of the following is TRUE?
    A. The proceeds are split 3 ways between the remaining children and John's estate
    B. The proceeds are split 2 ways between the remaining children only
    C. The proceeds are split 3 ways between the remaining children and the beneficiary of the deceased child's estate
    D. The proceeds are split 4 ways between the remaining children, John's estate, and the deceased child's estate

ANSWER KEY

QUICK QUIZZES

QUICK QUIZ 7.A

1. **B.** Insuring clause

2. **C.** Entire contract clause

QUICK QUIZ 7.B

1. **D.** Steve is an irrevocable beneficiary

2. **B.** Ginny will receive benefits before any other beneficiary upon her mother's death

3. **B.** The Uniform Simultaneous Death Act

QUICK QUIZ 7.C

1. **A.** a commercial flight

UNIT QUIZ

1. **A.** The consideration clause identifies the fact that the policyowner must pay something of value for the insurer's promise to pay benefits.

2. **D.** Contingent beneficiaries get all proceeds only if all the beneficiaries on a level above them die first.

3. **A.** The spendthrift provision is designed to prevent a beneficiary whom the policyowner believes cannot control their money from squandering all policy proceeds.

4. **C.** If the insurer would have recorded his age as older than he is, the coverage would be increased.

5. **C.** There are a number of options for designating a beneficiary; the insured is not one of these.

6. **A.** Under the facility of payment provision, the insurer may select a beneficiary if the named beneficiaries cannot be found.

7. **B.** This gives the insurer a certain period of time in which to question the truth of any statement contained in the application. Misstatement of age does is excluded from this provision.

8. **B.** Per capita means "by the head" so it is divided equally between surviving members of the family.

9. **A.** George would have received the benefits if Rosemary was no longer alive.

10. **C.** Per stirpes means "by the branch" and it means that children of a deceased beneficiary are entitled to that beneficiary's share of the proceeds.

UNIT 8

Group Life Insurance

8.1   INTRODUCTION

In the middle ages, guilds were formed for the mutual aid, protection, and the furtherance of the professional interests of craftsmen. Most craftsmen were trained through this system and the wealthier guilds had large coffers that acted as a type of insurance fund.

If a business burned down, the guild would rebuild it using money from its coffers. If a master were robbed, the guild would cover his obligations and if a master were disabled or killed, the guild would support him or his widow and family.

This style of insurance is still around today in the form of group insurance. This unit introduces you to *Group Life Insurance*, a group coverage frequently offered by companies to their employees and by unions to their members.

🎯 8.2   LEARNING OBJECTIVES

After successfully completing this unit, you should be able to:

▫ identify the groups that are eligible for group insurance: employer group plans, multiple employer trusts (METs), labor union, association group plans, and group credit life insurance;

▫ explain master policy and certificates of insurance;

▫ explain the difference between contributory and noncontributory polices and the group insurance policies;

▫ explain the underwriting process in group insurance including eligibility requirements, probationary period, and enrollment period;

▫ describe how the insurance coverage amount for the employee is decided in group insurance;

▫ identify group insurance coverage for dependents of the employee;

▫ explain the conversion privilege; and

▫ compare and contrast the characteristics of individual and group credit insurance.

8.3   GROUP LIFE INSURANCE

An individual life insurance policy provides coverage for one person; group life insurance however, provides coverage for many lives using one contract. For this reason, group life insurance premiums are less expensive than an individual policy.

The distinctive and unique characteristics of group life insurance and the regulatory and underwriting requirements are the subject of this unit.

8.4   TYPES OF ELIGIBLE GROUPS

The general rule for eligibility to sponsor a group insurance plan is the group must have been formed for a purpose other than for obtaining group insurance for its members.

Group insurance eligibility is limited to the following types of groups.

- **Employer Group Plans**: A group insurance plan sponsored for employees is sometimes referred to as *employee group plans.*

- **Multiple Employer Trusts (METs)**: A trust made up of multiple small employers in the same or similar industries that form to provide life insurance or other benefits for their employees while gaining tax benefits.

- **Labor Unions**: Two or more labor unions may join together to provide group insurance for their collective members. Labor union plans are sponsored under a *Taft-Hartley Trust.*

- **Association Group Plans**: A trade, professional, or other type of association may sponsor a group plan for its members.

- **Group Credit Life Insurance**: A lender, or creditor, may sponsor a group life insurance plan for its group of debtors. Two features that separate group credit insurance from other plans:
  - group credit insurance can be made payable to the sponsoring group, and
  - the amount of coverage is limited to the amount of the each insured's individual debt.

Types of Eligible Groups

The group must have been formed for purpose other than obtaining insurance for its members

© Kaplan, Inc.   4

Types of Groups

- Single Employer sponsored
- Multiple Employer Trust (MET)
  - Trust formed by group of small employers in same or similar industries
- Labor union
  - Taft Hartley Trust
- Professional or trade association
- Group credit life
  - Lender automatically the beneficiary
  - Insurance cannot exceed the debt
- Employer Sponsored Group Life
  - Employer is the policyowner
  - Employee receives a certificate of insurance and also names the beneficiary

8.5   MASTER POLICY VS. CERTIFICATES OF INSURANCE

One ***master policy*** is issued to the sponsoring group and the applicant is policyowner or *policyholder*. This could be an employer or the labor union.

The individual employee or member is not a party to the group insurance contract. Instead of getting a copy of the master policy, they receive a ***certificate of insurance*** as evidence of their coverage under the master policy. The certificate contains a summary of the insured's benefits under the plan, the individual's certificate number, and their beneficiary's name.

The employee, a certificate holder, has the right to name their beneficiary.

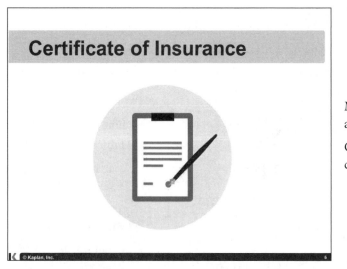

Master Policy—Policyholder or applicant

Certificate of insurance—evidence of coverage

8.6 CONTRIBUTORY VS. NONCONTRIBUTORY

With a *contributory* employer group plan, the employee pays part of the premium. If the employer pays the entire premium on behalf of the employees, the plan is *noncontributory.*

- *At least 75% of eligible employees must participate in a contributory plan.* If an employer had 200 eligible employees under a group insurance plan, at least 150 must enroll and pay their part of the premium for the employer to sponsor the plan.

- *100% of eligible employees must participate in a noncontributory plan,* The employer can sponsor the plan if they pay 100% of the premium and 100% of the eligible employees enroll.

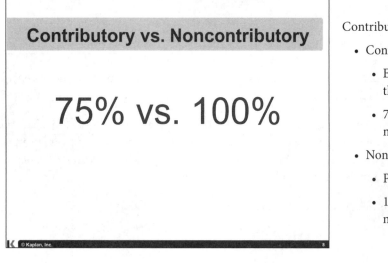

Contributory vs. Noncontributory
- Contributory
  - Employee pays part or all of the premium
  - 75% of eligible employees must enroll
- Noncontributory
  - Premium paid by employer
  - 100% of eligible employees must enroll

🎯 QUICK QUIZ 8.A

1. For group insurance policies, the covered individual receives proof of coverage in the form of
    A. an insurance policy
    B. an insurance contract
    C. a certificate of policy
    D. a certificate of insurance

2. If a group insurance policy is contributory, what percentage of employees must participate?
    A. 50%
    B. 75%
    C. 90%
    D. 100%

Answers can be found at the end of Unit 8.

8.7   GROUP UNDERWRITING

The insurance underwriter focuses on the group as a whole, rather than its singular members. Each group participant is required to complete a short form that usually consists of the individual's name, address, Social Security number, dependent information and beneficiary designation. There are typically no medical questions; thus, no actual medical underwriting takes place. It's therefore possible for individuals with poor health to receive group insurance benefits.

Once the group plan is in force, premiums are based on the experience of the group. Group life insurance usually renews annually, and premiums can fluctuate from year to year.

Some underwriting considerations may include:

- Stability of the group—group does not have excessive employee turnover;
- Persistency of the group—groups that change insurers every year may not represent a good risk; and
- Existence of the group—insurance purchase must be incidental to the group's formation.

Group Underwriting

- Underwriter underwrites the group not individual insureds
- Usually no medical questions or exams.

8.8   ELIGIBILITY REQUIREMENTS

Employers need not include every employee in the plan, but they cannot choose which individuals will be covered and which will not. They are allowed to determine which *classes* of employees will be eligible for the plan.

Employers may classify employees using almost any standard. The two most common are:

- full-time versus part-time, and
- years of service.

For example, an employer could decide to make the group life insurance plan available to employees who have been working for the employer on a full-time basis for at least one year.

Another common requirement is that employees be on active status at the time they enroll in the plan—that is, not on a disability leave of absence or other inactive status.

8.8.1   Probationary Period

A ***probationary period*** requires new employees to wait for a certain period of time before they can enroll in the plan. During this period they **are not** covered by the group insurance plan. Probationary periods typically range from one to twelve months. The time period is chosen by the employer and must apply to all eligible employees without discrimination.

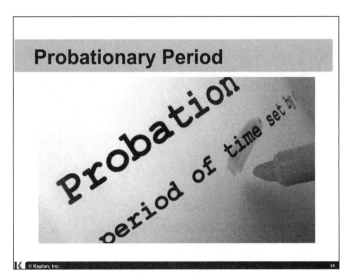

Probationary Period

- Waiting period before eligibility for insurance

8.8.2   Enrollment Period

Individuals (employees/union members/etc.) become covered by the plan automatically after fulfilling the probationary period. In a contributory plan, employees decide whether they want to participate, in a noncontributory plan, all eligible employees must be included.

To avoid adverse selection, eligible employees must sign up within 31 days after the probationary period ends, called the **enrollment period**. The employee can enroll without providing evidence of insurability; no medical questions or exams will be needed. If the employee declines coverage during the enrollment period and then decides later to enroll, the insurer may ask medical questions and require a medical exam. Many plans do not allow "late enrollees" to enroll until the annual open enrollment period.

Enrollment Period

- Follows probationary period— usually 31 days
- No medical questions

8.9 COVERAGE AMOUNT

Employers and unions determine the amount of coverage their employees and members will receive from the group life insurance plan. The actual amount of coverage does not have to be the same. However, coverage must be based on a formula that applies uniformly to all plan participants. Some common formulas are:

- a *percentage or multiple of earnings*. Example: participating employees receive coverage equal to their earnings, or half of their earnings, or some other multiplier; an amount of coverage based on years of service. Example: participants receive $5,000 of coverage for each year of employment, i.e. a two-year employee receives $10,000, a 10-year employee would receive $50,000; and

- a coverage limit for different classes of employees. Example: employees receive $20,000, supervisors $50,000, and corporate officers $100,000 of coverage.

Coverage for dependents is usually a lesser amount than the limits established for employees.

Group Eligibility
- Employer determines class
  - Full time vs. part time
- Probationary period
  - Waiting period before eligibility for insurance
- Enrollment period
  - Follows probationary period – usually 31 days
    - No medical questions
- Late enrollment
  - If allowed—may require underwriting

8.10 COVERAGE FOR DEPENDENTS

In addition to eligible employees, their dependents may be provided with coverage under a group life insurance plan. Eligible dependents typically includes:

- the insured's spouse;
- the insured's children;
- the insured's dependent parents; or
- other individuals financial dependent on the insured.

Typically, dependent coverage is a smaller amount than the employee.

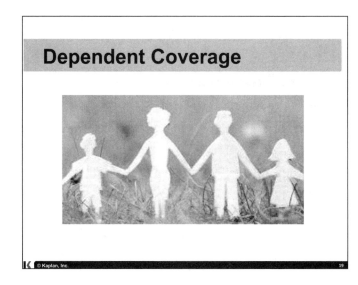

Dependent Coverage

© Kaplan, Inc.   19

Dependent Coverage

- Typically less coverage than the employee

 QUICK QUIZ 8.B

1. Kathleen is hired to work at a restaurant. She is not eligible to join the group insurance plan for 30 days. This is an example of

    A. an introductory period

    B. a weeding-out period

    C. a probationary period

    D. an eligibility period

2. Group insurance generally does NOT require

    A. stringent medical underwriting

    B. a short application form

    C. a minimum level of participation among eligible insureds

    D. a master policyowner to hold the policy

Answers can be found at the end of Unit 8.

8.11   CONVERSION PRIVILEGE

A drawback of group life insurance is that certificate holders and dependents lose their coverage if:

- the certificate holder leaves the employer;
- the employer discontinues the plan; or
- the insurer does not renew the policy.

Dependents also lose their coverage if:

- the certificate holder dies; or
- they are legally divorced from the certificate holder.

As a remedy, certificate holders and dependents must have the right to convert their group coverage to an individual policy if any of those events occur. While this varies from state to state, the following rules apply:

- the conversion must be done within 31 days from the date coverage is lost;
- the converted policy must be permanent insurance, not term;
- the converted policy must provide the same coverage amount as the individual had under the group policy;
- the premium will be based on the insured's attained age at the time of conversion; and
- no proof of insurability is required.

Coverage continues through the conversion period (the 31 days following the loss of group coverage). If the insured dies during that period, the death benefit is paid as if the insured had decided to convert the group coverage to an individual policy.

<table>
<tr><td>

Conversion

31 day conversion period.

© Kaplan, Inc.   23

</td><td>

Conversion

- Termination of employment
- Employer stops plan
- 31 days
  - Convert to individual permanent policy
  - Cost based upon attained (current) age
  - No medical questions
  - Death during conversion is covered

</td></tr>
</table>

8.12   CREDIT LIFE INSURANCE – INDIVIDUAL VS. GROUP

Creditors sponsor *group credit life insurance plans* for their borrowers as part of the loan transaction. The amount of insurance is equal to the debt owed. Example: an individual, during the financing process, may be offered credit life insurance in the amount of a car loan and the cost will be included in the monthly car note. If the borrower dies, the lender, the beneficiary, will receive the amount of life insurance to pay off the outstanding debt.

The same borrower could choose to purchase an *individual policy* and assign the death benefit to the lender.

Advantages for an individual policy:

- the policyowner controls the individual policy, the lender controls/owns the group policy, and
- the policy can continue even after the debt/loan has been paid off.

Disadvantages for an individual policy:

- individual policy premiums can be higher than group coverage, and
- evidence of insurability is required for individual coverage, not usually for group coverage.

Credit Life

- Group
  - Sponsored by lender
  - Lender is beneficiary
  - Usually no medical questions
  - Cheaper than individual policy
  - Insurance no greater than debt owed
  - Stops if debt is paid
- Individual
  - Insured is usually policyowner
  - Assigned to lender
  - Death benefit can exceed the debt
  - Doesn't stop when debt is paid
  - Can be more expensive than group
  - Usually requires medical questions

 QUICK QUIZ 8.C

1. All of the following statements regarding the conversion privilege are true EXCEPT
   A. the conversion must be done within 31 days from the date coverage is lost
   B. the converted policy must be permanent insurance, not term
   C. the converted policy must provide the same coverage amount as the individual had under the group policy
   D. proof of insurability is required

2. Which of the following characteristics about group credit life insurance is NOT correct?
   A. The lender is the beneficiary
   B. It is more expensive than individual credit life insurance
   C. If debt is paid, the policy is canceled
   D. Coverage can be included as part of the loan transaction

Answers can be found at the end of Unit 8.

UNIT 8 CRAM SHEET

Types of Groups

- Employer sponsored
- Multiple Employer Trust (MET)
    - Trust formed by group of small employers in same or similar industries
- Labor union
    - Taft Hartley Trust
- Professional or trade association
- Group credit life
    - Lender automatically the beneficiary
    - Insurance cannot exceed the debt

Employer Sponsored Group Life

- Employer is the policyowner
- Employee receives a certificate of coverage
- Employee names the beneficiary

Contributory vs. Noncontributory

- Contributory
    - Employee pays part or all of the premium
    - 75% of eligible employees must enroll
- Noncontributory
    - Premium paid by employer
    - 100% of eligible employees must enroll

Group Underwriting

- Underwriter underwrites the group not individual insureds
- Usually no medical questions

Group Eligibility

- Determined by the employer
    - Classes not individuals
- Probationary period
    - Waiting period before eligibility for insurance
- Enrollment period
    - Follows probationary period—usually 31 days
    - No medical questions
- Late enrollment
    - Usually requires medical questions

Dependent Coverage

- Less insurance than the employee

Conversion

- Termination of employment
- Employer stops plan
- 31 days
    - Convert to individual permanent policy
    - Cost based upon attained (current) age
    - No medical questions
    - Death during conversion is covered

Credit Life

- Group
    - Sponsored by lender
    - Lender is beneficiary
    - Usually no medical questions
    - Cheaper than individual policy
    - Insurance no greater than debt owed
    - Stops if debt is paid
- Individual
    - Insured is usually policyowner
    - Assigned to lender
    - Insurance can be greater than the debt
    - Doesn't stop when debt is paid
    - More expensive than group
    - May require medical questions

UNIT 8 QUIZ

In order to measure your success, we recommend that you answer the following 10 questions correctly.

1. Gianna starts work at a new job on March 1. She is not eligible for insurance coverage until July 1. The period between start date and her eligibility date is
    A. the probationary period
    B. the eligibility period
    C. the selection period
    D. the waiting period

2. Adam is eligible for coverage on July 1. He enrolls on July 15. He does not need to show evidence of insurability because he enrolled within
    A. the probationary period
    B. the enrollment period
    C. the selection period
    D. the waiting period

3. The baker's union and the butcher's union worked together to form a trust to provide insurance to their employees. This type of group is sponsored by
    A. an employee group
    B. a multiple employer trust
    C. a Taft-Hartley Trust
    D. a labor group

4. Jimmy's Print Shop and Emily's Boutique join together to form a trust to provide insurance to their employees. This type of group is called
    A. an employee group
    B. a multiple employer trust
    C. a Taft-Hartley Trust
    D. a labor group

5. General Electricians offers insurance to its employees. About 80% of its eligible employees are currently covered under the plan. This plan is
    A. contributory
    B. noncontributory
    C. inclusive
    D. noninclusive

6. All of the following are correct regarding group insurance EXCEPT
    A. the employer is the policyowner
    B. a group cannot be formed only for the purposes of purchasing insurance
    C. an individual policy will be provided to all members of the group
    D. the employer cannot discriminate when determining eligibility of its members

7. If the employer pays the entire group insurance premium for 100% of its employees, the plan is
    A. contributory
    B. noncontributory
    C. inclusive
    D. noninclusive

8. A typical enrollment period is how many days after the probationary period?
    A. 30
    B. 31
    C. 45
    D. 60

9. In group insurance, the sponsoring group is issued
    A. a master policy
    B. a certificate of insurance
    C. a certificate of authority
    D. a policyholder policy

10. All of the following group insurance eligibility requirements are true EXCEPT
    A. employers can determine which classes of employees will be eligible for the plan
    B. employers can choose which individuals will be covered and which will not be covered
    C. the 2 most common classifications for employees are full time versus part time and years of service
    D. probationary periods usually range from 1 to 6 months

ANSWER KEY

QUICK QUIZZES

QUICK QUIZ 8.A

1. **D.** a certificate of insurance

2. **B.** 75%

QUICK QUIZ 8.B

1. **C.** a probationary period

2. **A.** stringent medical underwriting

QUICK QUIZ 8.C

1. **D.** proof of insurability is required

2. **B.** It is more expensive than individual credit life insurance

UNIT QUIZ

1. **A.** The probationary period is the time period from the hire date to when the employee is eligible to enroll in the group plan. There is no coverage during the probationary period.

2. **B.** Adam does not need to prove evidence of insurability because he enrolled within the enrollment period.

3. **C.** The Taft-Hartley Trust is a group that is made up of 1 or more unions to form a group.

4. **B.** A multiple employer trust (MET) is when 2 or more employers form together to sponsor a group plan for their employees.

5. **A.** It is most likely that this plan requires employees to contribute toward the premiums.

6. **C.** Individuals in a group policy receive a certificate of insurance.

7. **B.** 100% of eligible employees must participate in order for a plan to be noncontributory.

8. **B.** If an employee enrolls during the enrollment period, no medical questions are asked. If they wait and enroll after the enrollment period has ended, the insurance company may require evidence of insurability.

9. **A.** One master policy is issued to the sponsoring group as policyholder. The individuals in the group receive certificates of insurance.

10. **B.** Employers do not have to include every employee in the plan, but they cannot exclude specific individuals. They can determine which classes are eligible and which are not eligible.

UNIT 9 Annuities

9.1   INTRODUCTION

Medical science is keeping people alive longer and that's a good thing. On the other hand, people are living beyond their life expectancy and outliving their money.

Annuities were designed to provide a steady cash flow for an individual during their retirement years and to alleviate fears of outliving one's assets; referred to as longevity risk.

An annuity is a financial product sold by financial institutions like insurance companies. This unit discusses the different types of annuity contracts, the unique provisions, and the tax implications of the distributions made to annuitants.

⊙ 9.2   LEARNING OBJECTIVES

After successfully completing this unit, you should be able to:

- ▢ explain the purpose of an annuity;
- ▢ identify accumulation period and annuitization period;
- ▢ identify the parties involved in an annuity contract: owner, annuitant, and beneficiary;
- ▢ describe the insurance aspect of annuities;
- ▢ identify the different types of annuities, immediate and deferred;
- ▢ explain premium payment options, surrender withdrawal charges, and death benefit of a deferred annuity;
- ▢ identify the differences between life annuities and temporary annuities;
- ▢ identify the five annuitization payout options for life annuities: life only, life with refund, life with period certain, joint-life-and-survivor, and joint life;
- ▢ explain the four factors used to determine the amount of a life annuity payout: annuitant's age, gender, payment guarantee, and assumed interest rate;
- ▢ identify the payout options for temporary annuities: fixed period and fixed amount;
- ▢ describe the four types of annuity products: fixed, variable, equity indexed, and market value adjusted; and
- ▢ identify the personal uses of annuities.

9.3   BASIC ANNUITY CONCEPTS

When an individual purchases life insurance, the insurance company that issued the policy promises to pay the death benefit to the named beneficiary when the named insured dies, regardless of when that occurs. The insurance company that issues an annuity also makes a promise but, in this case, it is to an annuity contract owner. The promise is that if the contract is annuitized, it will pay an income to the annuitant, regardless of how long they live. Life insurance protects people from dying too soon, while annuities protect people from living too long.

As a financial product, annuities can be used to:

- accumulate funds over a period of time;
- evenly distribute a fund over a period of time; or
- both accumulate a fund and then evenly distribute it over a period of time.

An annuity contract has two phases; "Pay-In" and "Pay-Out."

9.3.1   Annuity Phases

An annuity can have two phases or periods. The "Pay-In" phase called the accumulation period when principal and periodic deposits grow with credited interest. The "Pay-Out" or distribution phase is called the annuitization period. Now the contract generates an income stream from its accumulated value.

An annuity cannot be used for both phases at the same time and once the contract is annuitized, no more contributions can be made.

9.3.1.1 Accumulation Period

The *Accumulation Period* is when an annuity is being funded, before a payout begins. Life insurance companies issue these contracts and the money paid into the annuity is called a *premium*.

Interest is credited on the accumulated value in the contract and the accumulated contract value grows beyond the contract owner's deposits.

During the accumulation period, the owner can generally:

- make additional premium payments or deposits;
- take withdrawals from the accumulated value;
- surrender the annuity for its cash value; and
- make other changes to the contract.

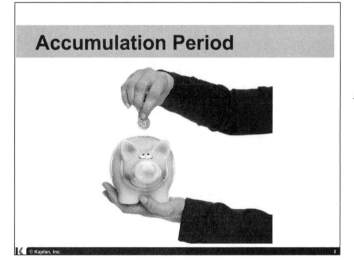

Accumulation Period
- "Paying-in" money
- Interest grows tax deferred
- Annuity value belongs to owner

9.3.1.2 Annuitization Period

The *Annuitization Period* is the "Pay-Out" phase of the contract. Money in the contract is converted into a series of regular income payments that can continue for life or for a stated period of time.

When the annuitization period starts, the accumulated value no longer belongs to the annuity owner:

- no additional premium payments can be made;
- no withdrawals can be taken;
- the annuity cannot be surrendered; and
- the owner can't change the contract.

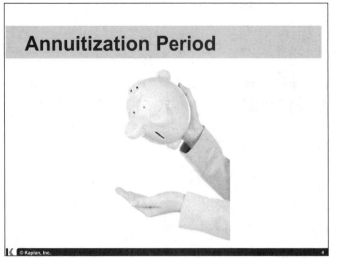

Annuitization Period

- Income generated from accumulated money
- Money from the accumulation period or from inheritance, lottery winnings, or court settlements
- Money belongs to the insurance company

9.3.2   Parties Involved in the Annuity Contract

There are four parties involved in an annuity contract:

- contract owner,
- annuitant,
- beneficiary, and
- insurer.

9.3.2.1 Contract Owner

The contract owner is the person or the couple who buy the annuity and has certain rights. The contract owner has the right to:

- name or change the annuitant;
- name or change the beneficiary;
- choose the payout option;
- add more money or take withdrawals; and
- surrender or terminate the agreement.

9.3.2.2 Annuitant

The **annuitant (insured)** is similar to the insured in a life insurance policy. They are chosen by the owner to receive the income payments during the annuitization period. The annuitant's life expectancy is used to determine the amount of the guaranteed payments. The annuitant must be an individual—a natural person—and cannot be a corporation or a trust.

The annuitant does not have the power to make withdrawals, deposits, change the names of the parties to the agreement, or terminate the contract. They must also sign the annuity contract.

The **contract owner** and the **annuitant** are frequently the same person.

9.3.2.3 Beneficiary

The beneficiary has no voice in the control or management of the annuity and only benefits upon the death of the contract owner. The beneficiary can be a natural person or an entity like a trust or corporation.

9.3.2.4 Insurer

The insurer is the party who issues the annuity contract. Representing the insurer may be a local bank, a financial planner, a brokerage firm, or an agent/producer.

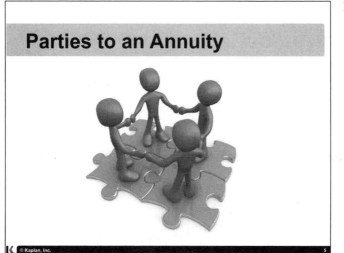

Parties to an Annuity

- Contract owner
  - Names the annuitant
  - Names the beneficiary
  - Can withdraw money
  - Can end the contract
- Annuitant (insured)
  - Receives the income
  - Can be more than one person
- Beneficiary
  - Receives the accumulation value if owner dies
  - May receive income payments if annuitant (insured) dies sooner than expected
- Insurer

9.3.3   Annuities vs. Life Insurance

Insurance companies create both annuities and life insurance. While both have features that resemble each other, their purpose is very different. Life insurance provides money when you die to pay for any remaining bills, cover the cost of the funeral, give money to loved ones or for any other financial obligation or desire you wish to fulfill even in death. Annuities provide tax-deferred savings for retirement.

Annuities are often called upside down life insurance; both offer a death benefit to a named beneficiary. However, that's where the comparison stops.

Life Insurance	vs.	Annuities
Can be used to create an estate		Can be used to liquidate an estate
Protects against dying too soon		Protects against living too long
Uses a series of payments to guarantee a lump sum of money upon death		Uses a lump sum of accumulated money to guarantee a series of income payments while living

Both life insurance and annuities have tax benefits. No matter what kind of life insurance you select, the beneficiary receives the funds tax-free when the insured dies. However, if you leave money in an annuity to a beneficiary, they will have to pay taxes on any growth (interest) on the money that was put into the contract.

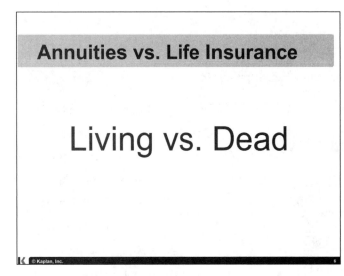

Annuities versus Life Insurance

- Life insurance—death
  - Premium buys a death benefit
- Annuities—living
  - Premium used to
    - Accumulate money or
    - Provide an income while living

9.4   IMMEDIATE AND DEFERRED ANNUITIES

An immediate annuity is structured to provide current income and a deferred contract's payout is a specific date in the future.

9.4.1   Immediate Annuities

After paying a lump-sum premium, an **immediate annuity** or single premium immediate annuity (SPIA) provides an individual with an income that may begin as soon as a month after purchase or may be delayed for up to one year. The funds in the contract accumulate on a tax-deferred basis. When payments begin, the portion of each payment that is attributed to interest is subject to taxes; the rest is treated as a return of principal and, therefore, is tax free.

A *single premium immediate annuity (SPIA)* pays a monthly income immediately. The first payment would be made after a delay of one payment interval or period. The earliest an income payment could be paid is one month. The latest payments can start in one year.

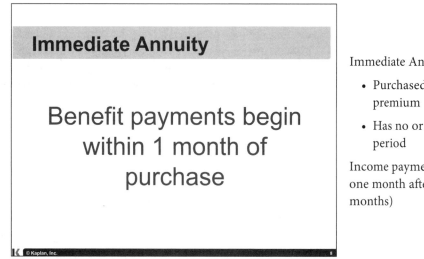

Immediate Annuity

- Purchased with a single premium (SPIA)
- Has no or short accumulation period

Income payments begin within one month after purchase (up to 12 months)

9.4.2   Deferred Annuities

Unlike immediate annuities, **deferred annuities** do not start an income stream immediately. With deferred annuities, the annuity owner chooses the premium amount and the frequency of premium payments. Accumulated funds may be withdrawn at any time, subject to a possible surrender charge. Lastly, the deferred annuity owner is not required to annuitize the contract.

9.4.2.1   Premium Payment Options

Deferred annuities can be purchased with a single premium [single premium deferred annuity (SPDA)], or ongoing premium payments [periodic or flexible premium deferred annuities (PPDA or FPDA)]. The premium payment options are similar to life insurance: monthly, quarterly, and so forth. With all deferred annuities, the emphasis is on the accumulation of money for future use.

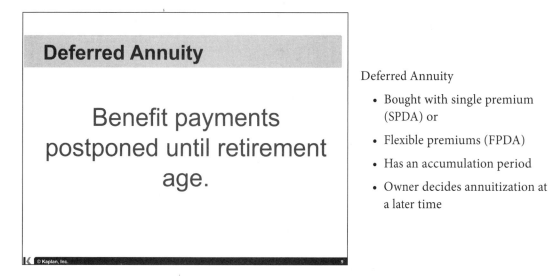

Deferred Annuity

- Bought with single premium (SPDA) or
- Flexible premiums (FPDA)
- Has an accumulation period
- Owner decides annuitization at a later time

9.4.2.2 Withdrawal Penalties and Surrender Charges

A withdrawal from an annuity is taxed different than annuitized payments. When a withdrawal is taken from an annuity, the earnings, or the growth portion, is taxed as ordinary income. Funds continue to be taxed at ordinary income tax rates until the account value is reduced to the original investment amount. For example, if you purchased a $20,000 annuity and it has grown to $45,000, the first $25,000 withdrawn will be fully taxable. Additionally, if a withdrawal is made prior to age 59½, there is an additional 10% penalty on taxable earnings.

In order for the annuitant to avoid additional fees from the insurance company for early withdrawal, there is a waiting period called the surrender period. Surrender periods may be as short as two years up to 12 or more years. If funds are withdrawn during that time, a surrender charge may apply. Surrender charges are stated in the contract and commonly start at 10%, declining each year. For example, if the surrender period is 10 years, then funds withdrawn in Year 1 will be charged a 10% fee, in Year 2 a 9% fee, in Year 3 an 8% fee, and so on.

For example, a $10,000 annuity contract has a schedule of surrender charges beginning with 7% in the first year and declining by 1% each year thereafter. 10% of the contract value can be withdrawn each year free of surrender charges. If the contract owner decides to withdraw $5,000, 10% of the $10,000 contract value, $1,000 is free of surrender charges. A 7% surrender charge, or $280, would apply on the other $4,000 withdrawn.

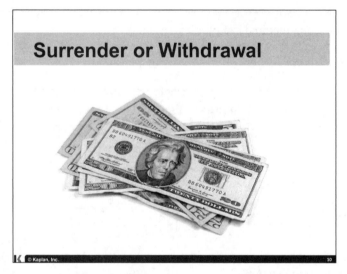

Surrender or Withdrawal

- 10% tax if withdrawn before 59½
- Surrender period—waiting period
- Surrender fee—penalty for early withdrawal

9.4.2.3 Death Benefit

The deferred annuity death benefit does not provide a surviving family a life insurance policy. Rather, the accumulated contract value is paid to a selected beneficiary if the annuity owner dies during the accumulation period. The amount paid as a death benefit is the greater of:

- the accumulated value of the annuity; or
- the total premiums paid to that point, minus any withdrawals.

If the owner has not named a beneficiary for the death benefit, it will be paid to the owner's estate.

Death Benefit

NOT life insurance

Death Benefit
- Accumulated value paid if owner dies

© Kaplan, Inc. 11

QUICK QUIZ 9.A

1. The period during which a person receives the annuity benefits is called the
   A. accumulation period
   B. annuitization period
   C. payout period
   D. putting in period

2. Under which annuity do the benefit payments begin within 12 months of the purchase?
   A. An immediate annuity
   B. A deferred annuity
   C. A retirement annuity
   D. An accumulated annuity

3. All of the following statements about annuities benefits vs. life insurance benefits are correct EXCEPT
   A. annuities can be used to liquidate an estate
   B. annuities protect against living too long
   C. annuities protect against dying too soon
   D. annuities use a lump sum of accumulated money to guarantee income payments while living

Answers can be found at the end of Unit 9.

9.5   ANNUITIZATION PAYOUT OPTIONS

Annuity payout options are similar to life insurance settlement options. They fall into two categories:

- *life annuities*, which have a payment that is guaranteed to last for at least as long as the annuitant lives; and

- *temporary annuities*, which do not.

9.5.1   Life Annuities

9.5.1.1 Life Only

Under the **life only** option, sometimes called a pure life income, payments stop when the annuitant dies, regardless of when that occurs; one month or 20 years.

The advantage of the life only option is that *it pays the highest monthly income amount* because there are no other *contingencies* and only the annuitant's life expectancy was considered to determine the amount of the monthly pay out.

The disadvantage of this selection is that the annuitant may die before their life expectancy and the total payout they received was much less than the total amount paid into the contract.

The life only annuity payout option is also referred to as:

- straight life,

- pure life, or

- life—no refund.

Life

Also referred to as:
–straight life,
–pure life, or
–life—no refund.

© Kaplan, Inc.   16

Life

- Guarantees income for life— regardless of how long

- Death stops payments (even if after one payment)

- Largest monthly check from life options

9.5.1.2 Life with Refund

Under the **Life with Refund** option, if the annuitant dies and the total payments received are less than the amount paid for the annuity, the difference is paid to the beneficiary. The money may be paid either as a:

- lump sum, called a cash refund; or

- continuation of payments in the same amount as was being paid to the annuitant, called an installment refund.

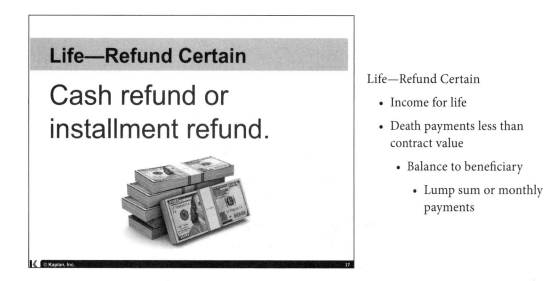

Life—Refund Certain

- Income for life
- Death payments less than contract value
  - Balance to beneficiary
    - Lump sum or monthly payments

9.5.1.3 Life with Period Certain

The **life with period certain** option also pays an income for as long as the annuitant is alive. In addition, the annuitant selects a payment period, typically 5, 10, or 20 years, and payments are guaranteed to be made for at least that number of years. If the annuitant dies before the end of the selected period, payments continue to the beneficiary for the rest of the period certain. No payments are made to the beneficiary if the annuitants lives past the period certain.

Life—Period Certain

- Income for life they live
- Choose period such as 10 or 20 years
  - Annuity will pay beneficiary if annuitant dies within that period

9.5.1.4 Joint-Life-and-Survivor

With the **joint-life-and-survivor** option, the insurer promises to make payments until the last survivor of two annuitants dies. For example, if the two annuitants were a married couple and the husband died first, payments would continue to the spouse for the rest of her life.

The owner can choose for continued payments in the same amount for the survivor, or in a lesser amount such as two-thirds or one-half of their monthly pay out.

Joint Life and Survivor

- One dies
  - Payments to survivor until their death
    - Same or reduced

9.5.1.5 Joint Life

The **joint life** annuity option pays income until the death of the first of two or more annuitants. While the monthly payment is greater than other joint annuities, it is not considered suitable as a joint annuity because the survivor is left without an income.

Joint Life

- Payments stop when first of two annuitants dies.

9.5.1.6 Factors in Determining a Life Annuity Payment Amount

Several factors are used to determine the payout of an annuity.

- **Annuitant's age**   Age is used to determine life expectancy, which indicates how long payments will have to be made. The younger the annuitant, the lower the payment amount.
- **Annuitant's gender**   Life expectancy statistics show that as a group, women live longer than men. Women generally receive lower payments than men of the same age.
- **Payment guarantee**   A refund option will lower the payment. With a period certain option, the longer the period, the lower the payment.
- **Assumed interest rate**   The insurer assumes that it will earn some rate of interest on the funds used to buy the annuity. The lower the assumed interest rate, the lower the payment.

Factors Affecting Payment Amount

- Annuitants age
- Annuitants gender
- Length of payment guarantee
- Assumed interest rate

 QUICK QUIZ 9.B

1. All of the following are factors in determining a life annuity payout amount EXCEPT the
   A. annuitant's age
   B. beneficiary's age
   C. annuitant's gender
   D. payment guarantee

2. Fixed period and fixed amount are types of
   A. life annuities
   B. temporary annuities
   C. life-period certain annuities
   D. joint life annuities

3. Under which of the following life annuity payout options do the payments stop when the first of two annuitants die and not continue on to the survivor?
   A. Joint life
   B. Joint life and survivor
   C. Life only
   D. Life with period certain

Answers can be found at the end of Unit 9.

9.6   ANNUITY PRODUCTS

There are literally hundreds of different annuity types—enough to boggle the mind of anyone at first glance. Furthermore, the companies that issue annuities are busy creating new types of annuities every day to meet the changing needs of consumers. However, when all the different types of annuities are clustered together, it is easy to see that most differ on just a few important variables.

There are four basic types of annuities:

- fixed,
- variable,
- equity-indexed, and
- market value adjusted.

9.6.1 Fixed Annuities

Fixed annuity values are guaranteed against loss. Aside from surrender charges that may apply, the value of a fixed annuity will never be less than the amount paid into the contract.

9.6.1.1 General Account Assets

Fixed annuities are supported by the insurer's **general account**; the investment risk is borne by the insurer. The assets in the general account are conservatively invested typically in debt securities and other fixed-rate investments that provide a steady return for many years.

9.6.1.2 Interest Rate Guarantees

During a fixed annuity's accumulation period, accumulated values earn a current rate of interest that is competitive with prevailing rates on other interest-bearing investments. The current rate is generally declared at the beginning of the year and guaranteed for the year. The current rate may rise or fall from year to year, but it will never be less than a guaranteed minimum rate that is stated in the contract.

9.6.1.3 Level Benefit Payment Amount

During the annuity period, fixed annuities provide a level payment amount. Annuitants can count on getting a specified dollar amount of income on a regular basis.

Fixed payment can lose purchasing power during periods of inflation and over a number of years, the fixed benefit may become inadequate to live on even though the dollar amount is the same.

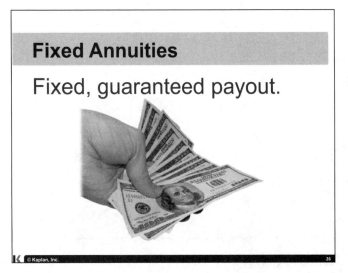

Fixed Annuities

- General account
- Long term low risk investments
- If annuitized—fixed income payments
- Money guaranteed by company

9.6.2   Variable Annuities

Variable annuities have the potential to keep pace with inflation because they are supported by investments (stocks and bonds). Historically stocks have tended to rise faster than the cost of living; however, there is no guarantee that they will always do so. Variable annuities have investment risk because values are not guaranteed against loss.

9.6.2.1 Separate Account Assets

Insurers are not allowed to bear the risk of variable annuities. Investment losses could impair the insurer's ability to maintain the value of their fixed annuities and other guaranteed products.

The assets that support variable annuities are kept in a **separate account** where the investment risk is borne by the annuity owner. The owner makes the various investment choices called *sub-accounts*, which resemble mutual funds.

9.6.2.2 Accumulation Units

The accumulated values of variable annuities are expressed as **accumulation units**, similar to shares purchased in a mutual fund. The value of an accumulation unit is found by dividing the total value of the separate account by the number of existing accumulation units.

9.6.2.3 Annuity Units

When the annuity period begins, the accumulation units are converted to ***annuity units***. From that point on, the number of annuity units stays the same throughout the annuity period; however, the value of an annuity unit varies with the value of the investments in the separate account. If the value of the separate account goes up, the amount of the annuity payment increases. If the value of the separate account goes down, the annuity payment decreases.

9.6.2.4 Regulation as Securities

Variable annuities are regulated as insurance products and are also regulated as securities. This is called *dual regulation*.

To sell variable annuities, a producer must have a life insurance license, a special variable annuities certification (in certain states), and both a federal and state securities registration.

Under federal securities law, insurers must register their separate accounts with the Securities and Exchange Commission and comply with certain requirements for selling securities. One important provision of those laws requires producers to provide customers with a *prospectus* – a document containing a detailed description of the product being offered – before beginning a sales presentation.

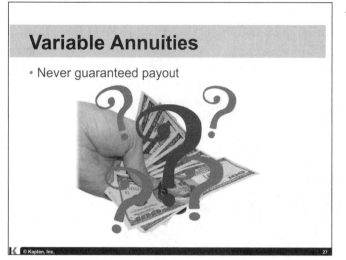

Variable Annuities

- Separate account
- No guarantees by company-owner assumes risk
- Premium buys accumulation units
- If annuitized, accumulated money buys annuity units
- Value can go up or down
- Must be licensed by the state and security regulators (SEC & FINRA)

9.6.3 Equity-Indexed Annuities

Equity-indexed annuity (**EIAs**) is a type of tax-deferred annuity whose credited interest is linked to an equity index—typically the S&P 500. It guarantees a minimum interest rate, typically between 1% and 3%, if held to the end of the surrender term and protects against a loss of principal.

EIA returns may be higher than fixed annuities. However, because of the costs of providing the minimum guarantees, the returns will not be as high as a variable annuity. EIAs are a form of fixed annuities and, therefore, the guarantees in the contract are backed by the insurer's general account (not a separate account).

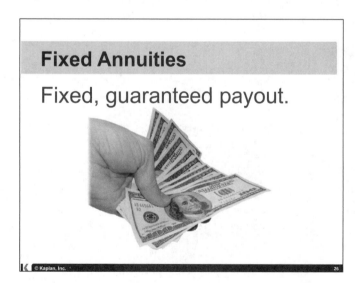

Equity Indexed Annuities

- Are fixed annuities
- Value is guaranteed by company
- Interest earned can go up or down like the stock market
- Interest tied to stock market index (S&P 500)
- No securities license required

9.6.4 Market Value Adjusted Annuities

A fixed annuity with a market value adjustment feature, also referred to as a modified guaranteed annuity, offers the flexibility of various guarantee terms combined with the potential for higher interest rates than traditional fixed investments. The guarantee terms range from shorter term to longer term and typically credit higher interest rates for longer-term commitments. A guaranteed fixed rate is declared for the length of each guarantee term.

The guaranteed rate is valid only if the investment is held until maturity. Investments may be split amongst several guarantee terms to match various time horizons when funds may need to be accessed. Withdrawals made before maturity of the guarantee term may be subject to a contingent deferred sales charge (CDSC) and/or a market value adjustment (MVA). Typically, the length of the CDSC schedule matches the duration of the guarantee term.

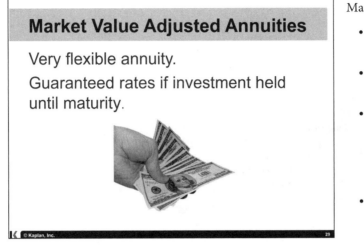

Market Value Adjusted Annuities

Very flexible annuity.
Guaranteed rates if investment held until maturity.

© Kaplan, Inc.   29

Market Value Adjusted Annuities

- Single premium deferred annuities
- Interest rate for a fixed number of years
- Early surrender
  - Withdrawal penalty
  - Interest penalty—maybe be higher or lower
- Not a variable product—no securities license required

 QUICK QUIZ 9.C

1. Which of the following is NOT a type of annuity product?
   A. Fixed
   B. Variable
   C. Retirement
   D. Equity-indexed

2. Which of the following types of annuities is guaranteed against loss and not tied directly to the stock market?
   A. Fixed
   B. Variable
   C. Market value adjusted
   D. Equity-indexed annuity

3. Fixed annuities are supported by insurers
   A. personal account
   B. separate account
   C. general account
   D. high risk investment accounts

Answers can be found at the end of Unit 9.

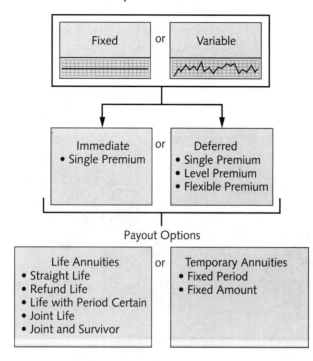

Comparison of Annuities

9.7   USES OF ANNUITIES

The common uses for annuities are as follows.

9.7.1   Personal Uses

9.7.1.1   Lifetime Income at Retirement

The most common annuity contract is one that has tax deferred investment gains with the promise that the investment savings and gains will provide income in the future in the form of regular distributions. These days, human life expectancy can go well beyond the minimum retirement age, so retirees are looking for guaranteed lifetime income that is consistent, safe and secure.

9.7.1.2   Accumulating Funds Prior to Retirement

Earnings on accumulated values are tax deferred until distributions begin. The recipient must pay the ordinary income rate on any interest or investment earnings.

9.7.1.3   Funding Individual Retirement Accounts (IRAs)

Flexible premium annuities are designed to be used for funding **Individual Retirement Accounts**; a tax-favored retirement savings plans set up through a bank, securities firm, or insurance company.

9.7.1.4   Accumulating Education Funds

Annuities can be used for a long-term funding need like the accumulation of money that will be needed to pay for a college education.

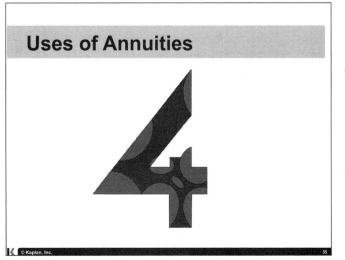

Uses of Annuities

- Life income

- Tax favored savings

- Funding individual retirement accounts (IRA)

- Education funds

9.7.2   Employer-Sponsored Retirement Plans

Annuities are designed to accept employer contributions made to the retirement plans set up for their employees. The annuity's payout options can provide a lifetime income for the employee and their spouses.

9.7.2.1 Group vs. Individual Annuities

Annuities can be used for both individual and group applications. Employer-sponsored retirement plans may be funded with **group annuities**. The retirement plan owns the group annuity, and the retirement plan document describes the benefits to which employees are entitled.

Group Annuities

- Funded by employer contributions

- Distributions determined by employer

QUICK QUIZ 9.D

1. A tax favored retirement savings plan that people can set up themselves through a bank, securities firm, or insurance company is known as

    A. an individual retirement account (IRA)

    B. a savings account

    C. a term insurance policy

    D. a whole life insurance policy

Answers can be found at the end of Unit 9.

UNIT 9 CRAM SHEET

Annuity Periods

- Accumulation period
    - Money is being deposited
    - Will be allowed to grow with interest tax deferred
    - Annuity value belongs to the contract owner
- Annuitization period
    - Income is generated from accumulated money
    - Money may come from the accumulation period or
    - Other source (inheritance, winning the lottery or a car accident)
    - Money belongs to the insurance company.

Parties to an Annuity

- Owner
    - Names the annuitant (insured)
    - Names the beneficiary
    - Can withdraw money
    - Can surrender the contract during accumulation for value
- Annuitant
    - Receives the income if contract is annuitized
    - May be more than one person
- Beneficiary
    - Receives the accumulation value if owner dies
    - May receive income payments if annuitant dies sooner than expected

Annuities vs. Life Insurance

- Life insurance—Death
    - Premium buys a death benefit

- Annuities—Living
  - Premium used to
    - Accumulate money or
    - Buy an income while living

Immediate or Deferred Annuities

- Immediate annuity
  - Purchased with a single premium (SPIA)
  - Has no accumulation period
  - Income payments begin within 12 months
- Deferred annuity
  - Bought with single premium (SPDA) or
  - Flexible premiums (FPDA)
  - Has an accumulation period
  - Owner will decide later if annuitization is desired

Surrender or Withdrawal

- 10% tax if withdrawn before 59½
- Surrender period—waiting period
- Surrender fee—penalty for early withdrawal

Death Benefit

- Not life insurance
- Pay out of accumulated money if owner dies
- Pay out of money if annuitant dies too soon

Annuitization Options

- Life
  - Guarantees income for life—regardless of how long
  - Death stops payments (even if after one payment)
  - Larges monthly check from life options
- Life—refund
  - Income for life—regardless of how long
  - Death before payments equal accumulation money
    - Balance to beneficiary
  - Lump sum or monthly payments
- Life—period certain (X number of years)
  - Income for life—regardless of how long
  - Death occurs before end of period
    - Remaining payments to beneficiary

- Joint life and survivorship
    - Payment continues until death of survivor
- Joint life and survivor
    - Payment may decrease to ⅔ or ½
- Joint life
    - Payment ends with first annuitant

Factors Affecting Payment Amount

- Annuitants age
- Annuitants gender
- Length of payment guarantee
- Assumed interest rate

Temporary Annuities

- No payment for life
    - Fixed period
    - Fixed amount

Annuity Products

- Fixed annuities
    - General account
    - Long term low risk investments
    - If annuitized—fixed income payments
    - Money guaranteed by company
- Variable annuities
    - Separate account
    - No guarantees by company-owner assumes risk
    - Premium buys accumulation units
    - If annuitized, accumulated money buys annuity units
    - Value can go up or down
    - Must be licensed by the state and security regulators (SEC & FINRA)
- Equity indexed annuities
    - Are fixed annuities
    - Value is guaranteed by company
    - Interest earned can go up or down like the stock market
    - Interest tied to stock market index (S&P 500)
    - Not a variable product – no securities license required

- Market value adjusted annuities
  - Single premium deferred annuities
  - Interest rate for a fixed number of years
  - Early surrender
    - Withdrawal penalty
    - Interest penalty—maybe be higher or lower

Not a variable product—no securities license required

Uses of Annuities

- Life income
- Tax favored savings
- Funding individual retirement accounts (IRA)
- Education funds

Group annuities

- Funded by employer contributions
- Distributions determined by employer

UNIT 9 QUIZ

In order to measure your success, we recommend that you answer the following 10 questions correctly.

1. Annuities exist to
   A. accumulate a sum of money
   B. distribute a lifetime income
   C. both accumulate a sum of money and distribute a lifetime income
   D. neither accumulate a sum of money nor distribute a lifetime income

2. Tracey is paying money into an annuity she hopes will support her in her retirement years. Her contract currently is in which of the following periods?
   A. Accumulation period
   B. Nonforfeiture period
   C. Payout period
   D. Annuity period

3. Liz purchases an immediate annuity. The annuity contract must be a
   A. fixed annuity
   B. variable annuity
   C. deferred annuity
   D. single premium annuity

4. Which type of annuity is most likely to provide death benefits if the insured dies during the accumulation period?
   A. Fixed annuity
   B. Variable annuity
   C. Deferred annuity
   D. Immediate annuity

5. Which of the following factors is NOT used to determine annuity premiums?
   A. Annuitant's retirement date
   B. Assumed interest rate
   C. Income amount and payment guarantee
   D. Applicant's sex

6. Which of the following types of annuities are regulated as securities?
   A. Fixed annuities
   B. Flexible annuities
   C. Variable annuities
   D. Structured annuities

7. An annuity that guarantees a minimum rate of return is
   A. an immediate annuity
   B. a deferred annuity
   C. a variable annuity
   D. a fixed annuity

8. Devon purchases an annuity that will pay a monthly income for the remainder of his life and then stop making payments. Devon has purchased
   A. a fixed annuity
   B. a straight-life annuity
   C. a variable annuity
   D. a temporary annuity certain

9. Albert has purchased an annuity that will pay
    him a monthly income for the rest of his life. If
    Albert dies before the annuity has paid back as
    much as he put into it, the insurance company
    has agreed to pay the difference to Albert's
    daughter. Albert has purchased a

    A. straight-life annuity

    B. life annuity with period certain

    C. life with refund annuity

    D. temporary annuity

10. Michelle purchases an annuity that offers
    a guaranteed minimum interest rate and a
    guarantee against loss of principal if the contract
    is held to term. However, if the S&P 500 moves
    upward, Michelle's annuity might end up
    accruing more than the guaranteed minimum
    interest rate. Michelle has purchased

    A. an equity-indexed annuity

    B. a market value-adjusted annuity

    C. a market value-indexed annuity

    D. an equity-adjusted annuity

ANSWER KEY

QUICK QUIZZES

QUICK QUIZ 9.A

1. **B.** annuitization period

2. **A.** An immediate annuity

3. **C.** annuities protect against dying too soon

QUICK QUIZ 9.B

1. **B.** beneficiary's age

2. **B.** temporary annuities

3. **A.** Joint life

QUICK QUIZ 9.C

1. **C.** Retirement

2. **A.** Fixed

3. **C.** general account

QUICK QUIZ 9.D

1. **A.** an individual retirement account (IRA)

UNIT QUIZ

1. **C.** Annuities address the risk of living too long while life insurance addresses the risk of dying too young.

2. **A.** This annuity is still in the accumulation phase or the "putting in" phase.

3. **D.** An immediate annuity is purchased with a single premium, and annuity payments begin one payout interval later.

4. **C.** A death benefit is paid if the annuitant dies before the annuity payments begin. This is more likely to occur with a deferred annuity.

5. **A.** All of these factors, except the annuitant's retirement date, are used to determine annuity premiums.

6. **C.** Variable annuities are regulated as securities because the contract owner bears the investment risk.

7. **D.** A fixed annuity guarantees a minimum rate of return.

8. **B.** A straight-life annuity will pay a monthly income for the remainder of Devon's life and then stop making payments.

9. **C.** Albert has purchased a life with refund annuity. The money will be paid either as a lump sum or a continuation of benefits.

10. **A.** Michelle has purchased an equity-indexed annuity. The distinctive feature is that the interest rate credited to accumulated values is tied to stock.

UNIT 10

Taxation of Life Insurance and Annuities

10.1 INTRODUCTION

The life insurance and annuity contracts are purchased for specific reasons and needs. Through the fact-finding process, agents/producers assist customers in determining the type of policies they should buy and the affordability of those products.

During the financial planning process, financial advisors consult with consumers regarding the tax rules that apply to these products. They explain the exclusion of the life insurance death benefit from gross income, the taxation of annuity payments, and deductions related to the purchase of life insurance and annuity contracts.

It is very important for agents/producers to understand how the tax rules apply to insurance company products.

10.2   LEARNING OBJECTIVES

After successfully completing this unit, you should be able to:

◻ explain income tax treatment of individual life insurance on premiums, cash value accumulations, full surrenders, withdrawals or partial surrenders, policy loans, dividends, death benefits, and accelerated death benefits;

◻ explain tax treatment on business insurance;

◻ explain tax treatment on group life insurance;

◻ explain tax treatment on Modified Endowment Contracts (MEC);

◻ identify tax treatment on annuities, premiums, accumulations, withdrawals, annuity payments, and distributions at death;

◻ describe tax treatment of section 1035 exchanges; and

◻ explain estate tax treatment on life insurance proceeds and annuities.

10.3   INCOME TAX TREATMENT

Income tax treatment of life insurance and annuities comes down to two questions.

1. Is the premium tax-deductible or not?

2. Are distributions from insurance products taxable or not?

10.3.1 Individual Life Insurance

10.3.1.1 Premiums

Premiums paid for individual life insurance are **NOT** tax-deductible.

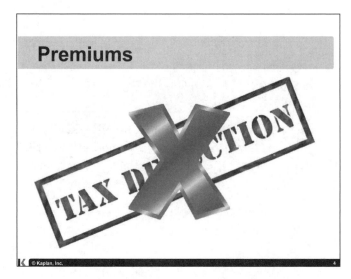

Premiums are not tax deductible

10.3.1.2 Cash Value Accumulations

Interest earnings credited to life insurance **cash values** are *tax-deferred – not* taxable as long as they remain inside the policy.

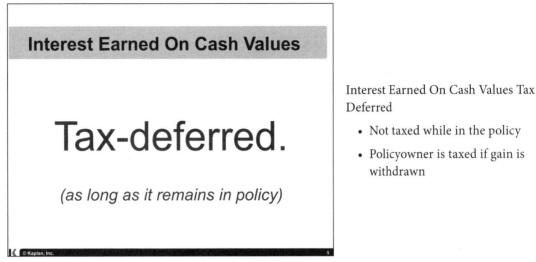

Interest Earned On Cash Values Tax Deferred

- Not taxed while in the policy
- Policyowner is taxed if gain is withdrawn

10.3.1.3 Full Surrenders

When a life insurance policy is surrendered, any *gain* in the cash value is taxable. The gain is the cash value minus the policy's *cost basis*; the sum of all premiums paid. So cash value accumulations are tax-deferred, but *not necessarily* tax-free.

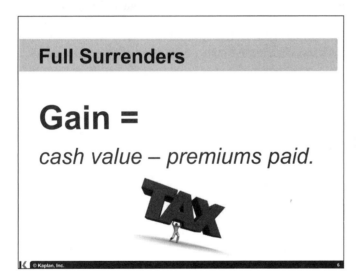

Full surrenders—any gain is taxable.

10.3.1.4 Withdrawals or Partial Surrenders

Withdrawals (partial surrenders) are taxable to the extent of any gain. Withdrawals are taxed on a *first-in-first-out* (FIFO) basis; money withdrawn is considered to come from the premiums paid (cost basis) FIRST and cost basis withdrawals are *not* taxable. The death benefit is reduced by a withdrawal of cash value.

When a withdrawal exceeds the cost basis, the excess *is* taxable. If the cost basis is $10,000 and a withdrawal is $12,000, $2,000 is considered excess and taxable.

Any money received from a policy, other than as a death benefit, reduces the policy's cost basis.

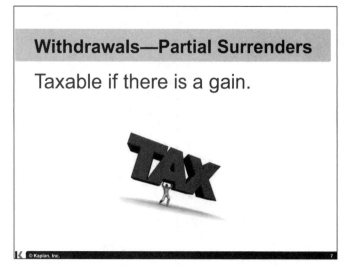

10.3.1.5 Policy Loans

Policy loans reduce the cash value of the policy and can be used as collateral for the loan. Policy loans reduce the death benefit; however, loans can be repaid at any time, which restores the cash value and death benefit. Loans are *not* taxable to the policyowner, even if the amount of the loan exceeds the policy's cost basis. The amount of the loan never becomes taxable even when the insured dies.

If a policy is surrendered or it lapses, under the tax rules for full surrenders, any portion of the loan amount that exceeds the policy's cost basis is a taxable gain.

The interest paid on policy loans is *not* tax-deductible.

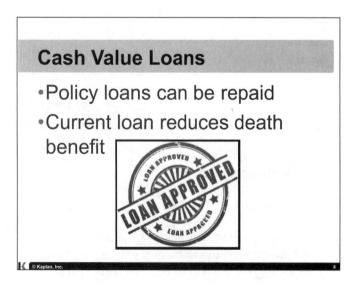

10.3.1.6 Dividends

Dividends are *not* taxable. For tax purposes, dividends are considered to be a return of a portion of the premium paid for the policy. Since premiums are paid with after-tax dollars, they are not taxed again when they are returned in the form of dividends. However, as a return of premium, dividends also reduce the policy's cost basis.

While dividends are not taxable, if they are left to accumulate at interest, the interest *is* taxable.

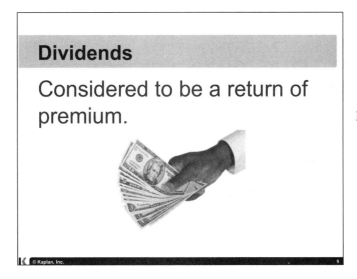

10.3.1.7 Death Benefits

When the entire death benefit amount—"lump sum"—is paid to a named beneficiary it is *not* taxable as income whether the policy is owned by an individual or a business.

If the death benefit payment is made under other settlement options—not a "lump sum"—the original death benefit is not taxable, any interest earned on the proceeds are taxable as ordinary income when paid to the beneficiary.

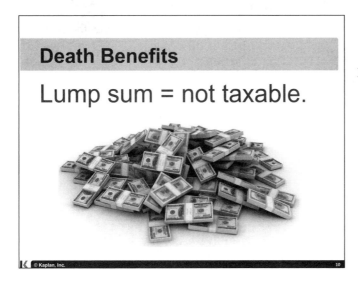

10.3.1.8 Accelerated Death Benefits

Accelerated death benefits are an advance of death benefits. Written certification from a physician is required, diagnosing a qualifying event that will substantially decrease the insured's life span. Qualified events include terminal illnesses expecting to end in death within 24 months, acute illness, emergency organ transplants, permanent confinement to nursing homes, and long-term care (if activities of daily living can no longer be performed). Part or all of the death benefit may be used; the amount reduces the benefit the beneficiaries will receive. Accelerated death benefits are tax exempt.

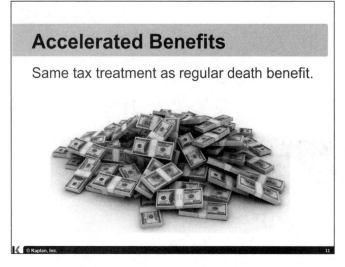

Accelerated Death Benefits
- Critically ill
- Terminally ill
- Death
- Not taxed

 QUICK QUIZ 10.A

1. All of the following statements regarding tax treatment of individual life insurance policies are correct EXCEPT
   A. policy loans are not taxable
   B. premiums are tax deductible
   C. cash value is not taxable as long as it stays in the policy
   D. when a life insurance policy is surrendered for its cash value, only the gain is taxable

2. For tax purposes, which of the following are considered to be a return of a portion of the premium paid for the policy?
   A. Dividends
   B. Death benefits
   C. Cash value
   D. Policy loan

Answers can be found at the end of Unit 10.

10.3.2 Business Insurance

Business life insurance premiums for the following purposes are not tax deductible to the business:

- Key person life insurance policies
- Life insurance policies funding buy-sell agreements
- Life insurance policies that will reimburse the company for benefits paid under deferred compensation arrangements

These are not considered to be approved business expenses because the business receives financial benefits from owning these policies.

Premiums paid for executive bonus plans are tax deductible to the business as employee compensation. As such, the amount of the premium paid is also considered taxable income to the employee.

Taxation of Business Life Policies

- Premiums not tax deductible except for executive bonus
- Death benefits not taxable
- Premiums for executive bonus policies are taxable income to the employee

10.3.3 Group Life Insurance

Group life insurance premiums paid by the employer *are* tax-deductible as a business expense provided under an employer group benefit plan. The premium for the first $50,000 of coverage is *not* taxable to the employee. The premium for any additional coverage above $50,000 *is* taxable as income to the employee.

With contributory plans, the employee portion of the group life insurance premium is *not* tax-deductible.

Taxation of Group Life Insurance

Employer paid =
tax deductible by employer.

Employee paid =
NOT tax deductible by anyone.

© Kaplan, Inc.

Taxation of Group Life Insurance

- Premiums paid by employer are tax deductible
- Premiums paid by employee are NOT tax deductible
- Death benefits to a named beneficiary are not taxable
- Premiums paid by employer for insurance above $50,000 is taxable income to the employee

10.3.4 Modified Endowment Contracts (MECs)

A *Modified Endowment Contract*, or a *MEC*, is a special type of life insurance under federal income tax law. Specifically, the law prescribes a test that is intended to differentiate between policies that are purchased primarily for certain tax advantages, versus policies that are purchased primarily for death protection.

MECs are still life insurance and offer tax-free death benefits and tax-deferred cash value accumulation. If a policy becomes a *MEC* and no distributions are taken from that policy during the insured's lifetime, they will not experience any adverse tax implications due to the contract's MEC status.

To determine if a contract is a *MEC*, a premium limit is set and is referred to as a seven-pay limit or *MEC* limit. It is based on the annual premium that would pay up the policy after the payment of seven level annual premiums. This limit is based upon rules established by the Internal Revenue Code, and sets the maximum amount of premium that can be paid into the contract during the first seven years from the date of issue to avoid *MEC* status.

Under what is known as the *MEC* test, the cumulative amount paid at any time in the first seven years cannot exceed the cumulative *MEC* limit applicable in that policy year.

Example: a $50,000 flexible premium policy and the *MEC* limit is $1,000 each year for the first seven years of the contract. $1,000 premium each year can be paid without triggering *MEC* status. If in the fourth policy year a $2,000 payment is made, the total cumulative premium payments ($5,000) would exceed the cumulative MECpremium limit of $4,000, and the policy would be classified as a *MEC*. The insurer may refund excess premiums within 60 days to avoid having a policy become a *MEC*.

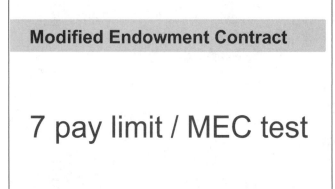

Modified Endowment Contract (MEC)

- Too much premium paid in first seven years of the policy

    - Flexible premium universal life

    - Single premium whole life

- Interest on cash values not taxed while in the policy

- Withdrawals or loans are taxed

    - Interest out first

    - 10% penalty on interest if withdrawn before age 59 ½ unless insured is disabled

- Once a MEC always a MEC

10.3.5 Annuities

10.3.5.1 Premiums

Annuity premiums are *not* tax-deductible, unless the contract is held in a qualified retirement plan.

Premiums not tax deductible.

10.3.5.2 Accumulations

Similar to life insurance, interest earnings credited to individual annuities are tax-deferred. They become taxable when they are paid out.

Earnings on annuities owned by corporations are taxable when they are credited.

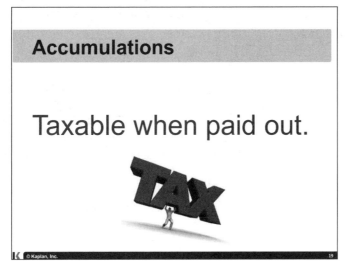

Interest during accumulation not taxed in the contract.

10.3.5.3 Withdrawals

Distributions received from an annuity during the accumulation period receive the same tax treatment as a modified endowment contract.

- Last-in-first-out (LIFO) taxation—the entire taxable gain is received before any non-taxable cost basis.
- If the contract owner is under age 59½, a 10% penalty tax must be paid in addition to the regular tax due on any taxable amount received. The penalty does not apply if the owner is disabled.

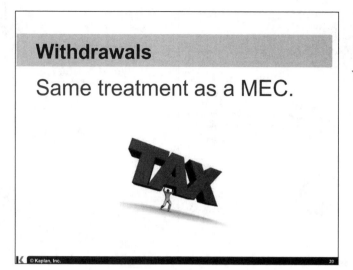

Withdrawals

- Interest out first
- Income tax on interest
- 10% penalty on interest if younger than 59 ½
  - Penalty waived for disability, death, or annuitization

10.3.5.4 Annuity Payments

There are two phases to an annuity: accumulation "Pay-In" and annuitization "Pay-Out." If the owner withdraws money from an annuity in a lump sum, they face severe tax penalties on their savings. The most likely method is to receive periodic or monthly payments.

The *exclusion ratio* is used to determine the nontaxable portion of each monthly payment. The formula is applied to each annuity payment to find the portion that is excludable from gross income. The remainder is taxable at ordinary income rates.

 EXAMPLE

> The annuity owner paid $12,000 into the contract and it's now worth$19,200. The exclusion ratio is $12,000/$19,200, or 62.5%. If the monthly payment received is $100, the portion that can be excluded from gross income is $62.50 or 62.5% of $100. The $37.50 balance of each $100 monthly payment is ordinary income.

The exclusion ratio applies until the entire investment portion in the contract has been paid out. The balance is taxable.

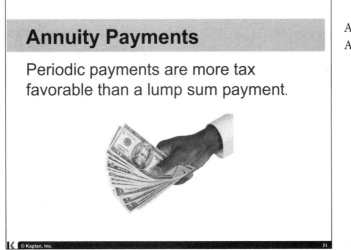

Annuity Payments After
Annuitization

- Taxed according to the exclusion
  ratio

- Premiums paid in ÷ TOTAL
  of expected payments over
  annuitants life expectancy =
  Percent of payment NOT taxed

- If annuitant lives beyond life
  expectancy, 100% of payment
  becomes taxable

10.3.5.5 Distributions at Death

At death of the annuity owner, the beneficiary has a number of options for receiving the annuity's value.

- **Lump sum**   The beneficiary can take the proceeds all at once. The gain (total value minus cost basis) is taxable.

- **Five-year withdrawal period**   The beneficiary must withdraw all proceeds within five years. These withdrawals are taxed the same as withdrawals during the owner's life. That is, the gain is taxable and all the gain must be taken out before any non-taxable cost basis is withdrawn.

- **Annuity payout**   The beneficiary may take the proceeds under an annuity payout option. This option must be selected within one year from the date of the owner's death. The payments are taxed as annuity payments – part taxable gain and part non-taxable cost-basis, with the non-taxable amount determined using the exclusion ratio.

- **Spousal option**   If the beneficiary is the owner's spouse, ownership may be transferred to the spouse without any tax consequences.

If death occurs during the annuity period, tax treatment of any continuing payments depends on whether those payments are being made to a:

- survivor annuitant, or
- beneficiary.

If payments are made to a *survivor annuitant* under a joint-and survivor annuity, they continue to be taxed as they were when made to both annuitants. If the entire cost basis has not yet been paid out, the same exclusion ratio percentage is used to determine the amount excludable from taxable income even if the payment to the survivor annuitant is reduced, such as under a joint-and-two-thirds-survivor annuity. Payments become fully taxable when the entire cost basis has been paid out.

If payments are made to a *beneficiary* under an annuity payout option that guarantees a certain payout, the entire payment becomes non-taxable until the entire cost basis has been paid out (including the portion of cost basis that was paid to the annuitant). At that point, any remaining guaranteed payments are fully taxable. If the entire cost basis was paid out to the annuitant, any guaranteed payments made to the beneficiary are fully taxable from the start.

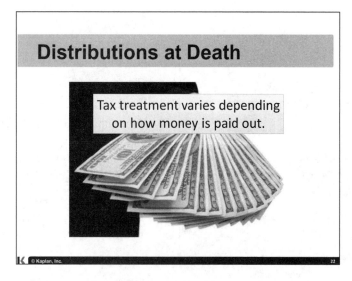

Distributions at Death to a Beneficiary

- Lump sum—all of gain is taxable
- Five year withdrawal—interest out first—no 10% penalty
- Annuity payments—taxed according to the exclusion ratio
- If spouse is beneficiary—transfer ownership to spouse with no tax consequences

10.3.6 Section 1035 Exchanges

Gain in an annuity or life insurance contract is taxable when the policy is surrendered. Under this general rule, individuals would always have to pay income tax on their gains when they surrender a life insurance policy or annuity.

Section 1035 of the tax code allows individuals to move cash values from one contract to another without having any gain taxed at that time. To qualify, the old and the new life insurance policies must have the same policyowner and the same insured. In the case of an annuity, the old and new annuity contracts must have the same contract owner and same annuitant.

Section 1035 exchange applies to:

1. life insurance, and
2. annuities.

The following movement of cash values qualifies under section 1035 with no taxable consequence:

- life insurance policy to another life insurance policy;
- annuity contract to another annuity contract; and
- life insurance policy to annuity contract.

The surrender of an annuity to move the cash values to a life insurance policy does not qualify as a 1035 exchange. The gain in the contract becomes taxable upon the surrender of the annuity.

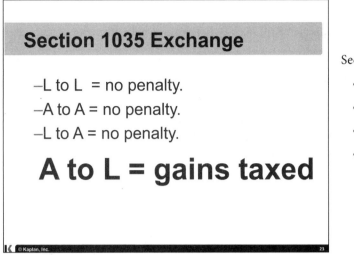

Section 1035 Exchange

- Life to life—not taxable
- Annuity to annuity—not taxable
- Life to annuity—not taxable
- Annuity to life does not qualify (A to L)
    - Annuity gains are taxable

10.4   ESTATE TAX TREATMENT

10.4.1 Life Insurance Proceeds

Estate taxes are owed if an estate's value exceeds a certain value at the time of the individual's death. The taxes are a percentage of the estate's value.

Life insurance death benefits are counted as a value in a deceased insured's estate if:

- they are payable to the estate;
- the deceased possessed any *incidents of ownership* in the policy at the time of death—the right to name or change the beneficiary, the right to access cash values, the right to assign ownership of the policy to another party, etc.; or
- the deceased assigned or transferred ownership of the policy to another person within three years of death.

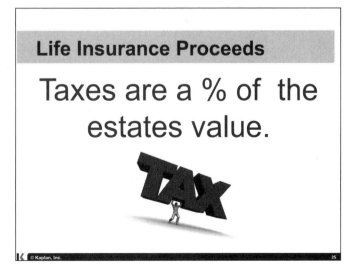

Estate Taxes

- Taxes due on transfer of wealth
- Life insurance death benefits are included as insured's gross estate if
    - Payable to the insureds estate
    - Insured owns the policy at time of death
    - Insured transferred ownership within three years of death

10.4.2 Annuities

The estate tax treatment of annuities depends on whether death occurs during the accumulation period or during the annuity period.

- If death occurs during the accumulation period, the entire value of the annuity—not just the gain, but also the cost basis—is included in the estate.

- If death occurs during the annuity period, the *present value* of any payments that will continue to a beneficiary or survivor annuitant is included in the estate.

Annuities

Tax treatment depends on when death occurs.

© Kaplan, Inc.   26

Annuities are included in gross estate if

- Death occurs during accumulation—entire value including cost is included

- Death occurs during annuitization—present value of future payments is included

QUICK QUIZ 10.B

1. None of the following premiums are tax deductible for a business EXCEPT
   A. premiums paid for an executive bonus plan
   B. key person life insurance policy premiums
   C. premiums paid in a buy-sell agreement
   D. premiums paid for life insurance that ends up reimbursing the company

2. All of the following statements regarding taxation of annuities are correct EXCEPT
   A. annuity premiums are not tax deductible, unless the annuity is held in a qualified retirement plan
   B. interest earning credited to annuities are not taxable as long as they stay in the policy
   C. if death occurs during the accumulation period, proceeds paid in a lump sum to the beneficiary are never taxable
   D. gain in an annuity or life insurance contract is taxable when a policy is surrendered

Answers can be found at the end of Unit 10.

UNIT 10 CRAM SHEET

Taxation Individual Life Insurance

- Premiums are not tax deductible
- Interest earned on cash values tax deferred
    - Not taxed while in the policy
- Full surrenders—any gain is taxable
- Cash value loans
    - Not taxed while policy is in force
    - Taxed if policy is surrendered and there is a gain
- Withdrawals
    - Taxed only if withdrawal exceeds premiums paid
    - Only the gain(if any) is taxed
- Dividends
    - Not taxed
    - Interest earned is taxed
- Death benefits
    - Not taxed if paid in a lump sum
    - Interest is taxable
    - If paid over time, part of the payment is not taxed and part is taxed
- Accelerated benefits
    - Not taxed
    - Certified terminally ill or
    - Permanently confined to a nursing home

Taxation of Business Life Policies

- Premiums not tax deductible except for executive bonus
- Death benefits not taxable
- Premiums for executive bonus policies are taxable income to the employee

Taxation of Group Life Insurance

- Premiums paid by employer are tax deductible
- Premiums paid by employee are NOT tax deductible
- Death benefits are not taxable
- Premiums paid by employer for insurance above $50,000 is taxable income to the employee

Modified Endowment Contract (MEC)

- Too much premium paid in first seven years of the policy
  - Flexible premium universal life
  - Single premium whole life
- Interest on cash values not taxed while in the policy
- Withdrawals or loans are taxed
  - Interest out first
  - 10% penalty on interest if withdrawn before age 59 ½ unless insured is disabled

Once a MEC, always a MEC

Taxation of Annuities

- Premiums not tax deductible
- Interest during accumulation not taxed in the contract
- Withdrawals
  - Interest out first
  - Income tax on interest
  - 10% penalty on interest if younger than 59 ½
    - No penalty if withdrawal due to disability or death or annuitization
- Annuity payments after annuitization
  - Taxed according to the exclusion ratio
  - Premiums paid in ÷ TOTAL of expected payments over annuitants life expectancy = Percent of payment NOT taxed
  - If annuitant lives beyond life expectancy, 100% of payment becomes taxable
- Distributions at death to a beneficiary
  - Lump sum—all of gain is taxable
  - 5 year withdrawal—interest out first—no 10% penalty
  - Annuity payments—taxed according to the exclusion ratio
  - If spouse is beneficiary—transfer ownership to spouse with no tax consequences

Section 1035 Exchange

- Life to life
- Annuity to annuity
- Life to annuity
- Annuity to life does not qualify (A to L)
  - Gain becomes taxable

Estate Taxes

- Taxes due on transfer of wealth
- Life insurance death benefits are included as insured's gross estate if
    - Payable to the insured's estate
    - Insured owns the policy at time of death
    - Insured transferred ownership within three years of death
- Annuities are included in gross estate if
    - Death occurs during accumulation—entire value including cost is included
    - Death occurs during annuitization—present value of future payments is included

UNIT 10 QUIZ

In order to measure your success, we recommend that you answer the following 10 questions correctly.

1. Which of the following would NOT qualify as a 1035 exchange?
    A. A cash value life insurance policy to another cash value life insurance policy
    B. A life insurance policy to an annuity contract
    C. An annuity contract to a life insurance policy
    D. An annuity contract to another annuity contract

2. The penalties assessed against MECs primarily affect
    A. the cost basis of the policy
    B. money put into the policy
    C. money taken out of the policy
    D. the death benefits of the policy

3. As a general rule, for federal tax purposes
    A. neither life insurance nor annuity premiums is tax deductible
    B. life insurance premiums are tax deductible but annuity premiums are not
    C. annuity premiums are tax deductible but life insurance premiums are not
    D. both life insurance and annuity premiums are tax deductible

4. Billy is receiving the proceeds of a life insurance policy as an income stream over a period of several years. What part of the money will be subject to tax?
    A. None of it; it is life insurance proceeds
    B. All of it; it is being paid out in an income stream
    C. Only the part that represents income earned on the original death benefit
    D. Only the part that represents the original death benefit and not the income earned on the original death benefit

5. For accelerated death benefits to receive the same tax treatment as regular death benefits the insured must be certified to have an illness or physical condition that can reasonably be expected to result in death within
    A. 9 months
    B. 12 months
    C. 24 months
    D. 36 months

6. All of the following statements regarding tax treatment of group life insurance are true EXCEPT
    A. group life insurance premiums paid by the employer are not tax-deductible as a business expense
    B. if a group plan is contributory, the portion paid by the employee is not tax-deductible
    C. premiums for any additional coverage above $50,000 are taxable as income to an employee
    D. premiums for the first $50,000 of coverage is not taxable to the employee

7. An individual choose to receive money from their annuity during the accumulation period. What is the penalty tax that must be paid in addition to regular taxes due on the taxable amount received?

    A. 3%

    B. 5%

    C. 6%

    D. 10%

8. What is the name of the test that is done on a life insurance policy to see if it premiums exceed those needed to fully pay up a death benefit with seven level annual payments?

    A. Accumulation test

    B. Annuitization test

    C. Endowment test

    D. Seven-pay test

9. All of the following statements regarding a modified endowment contract (MEC) are true EXCEPT

    A. withdrawals are taxed on a last-in-first-out basis

    B. withdrawals are taxed on a first-in-first-out basis

    C. policy loans and dividends are taxed the same as withdrawals

    D. once a policy is an MEC, it will always be an MEC

10. The amount of an annuity payout option or a life insurance settlement option that is taxable gain is determined by using the

    A. exclusion ratio

    B. investment in the contract ratio

    C. cost basis ratio

    D. expected return ratio

ANSWER KEY

QUICK QUIZZES

QUICK QUIZ 10.A

1. **B.** premiums are tax deductible

2. **A.** Dividends

QUICK QUIZ 10.B

1. **A.** premiums paid for an executive bonus plan

2. **C.** if death occurs during the accumulation period, proceeds paid in a lump sum to the beneficiary are never taxable

UNIT QUIZ

1. **C.** The gain in the contract become taxable upon the surrender of the annuity.

2. **C.** The penalties assessed against MECs primarily affect money taken out of the policy

3. **A.** As a general rule, for federal tax purposes, neither life insurance nor annuity premium is tax deductible.

4. **C.** If death benefits are paid out over a period of time instead of in one lump sum, the original death benefit is not taxable. The interest earned is taxable as it is received by the beneficiary.

5. **C.** Accelerated death benefits receive this same tax treatment only if they are qualified to have an illness that will result in death within 24 months or permanence in a nursing home due to a catastrophic condition. Only a doctor can qualify a person to be terminally ill.

6. **A.** Premiums paid by the employer are tax-deductible to the business.

7. **D.** Tax treatment on money received before it enters the annuity period gets similar tax treatment as a modified endowment contract.

8. **D.** If a policy fails the seven-pay test it is considered a modified endowment contract.

9. **B.** In a MEC, withdrawals are taxed on a last-in-first-out basis. Meaning that the entire taxable portion of the cash value is considered to be withdrawn before the non-taxable cost basis.

10. **A.** To calculate the exclusion ratio, divide the cost basis by the expected return.

UNIT 11 Retirement Plans

11.1 INTRODUCTION

According to a leading expert on the economic impact of retirement, over half of U.S. workers will not be able to maintain their standard of living when they retire. In fact, a large percentage will be either at or near the Federal Poverty Level. Accountability may be equally shared between employers who offer fewer sponsored plans for workers and workers who are not saving for retirement.

It's been said that people don't plan to fail, but they fail to plan; this is case with many Americans. While many savings vehicles exist, people are either unfamiliar with or unaware of their existence.

Insurance agents/producers who are familiar with the details and options available in retirement planning assist people of all ages to plan for the future. This unit provides foundational knowledge of several employer-sponsored and individual retirement plans.

⊙ 11.2   LEARNING OBJECTIVES

After successfully completing this unit, you should be able to:

◻ identify individual retirement accounts (IRAs) and the contribution limits, tax deductibility, funding vehicles, premature withdrawals, rollovers and transfers, required distributions, taxations of distributions, and distributions at death;

◻ explain Roth IRAs and how they are different from traditional IRAs;

◻ identify the tax advantages, taxation of distributions of employee sponsored retirement plans;

◻ identify the five general requirements for employer sponsored retirement plans to receive favorable tax treatment: participation, non-discrimination, vesting, reporting and disclosure, and fiduciary duty;

◻ describe the seven employer-sponsored qualified plans: Pension plans (defined benefit or defined contribution), Profit-sharing plans, Keogh plans, 401k plans, 403(b) plans, simplified employee pension plans, savings incentive match plans for employees (SIMPLEs);

◻ explain ERISA (Employee Retirement Income Security Act); and

◻ explain non-qualified plans and how they are different from qualified plans.

11.3   INDIVIDUAL RETIREMENT ACCOUNTS (IRAS)

To be eligible to set up a traditional individual retirement account (IRA), the individual must have earned income from a salary, wages, commissions, bonuses, or tips or money from a divorce decree.

NOTE: Passive income from rental properties—interest, dividends, pensions, annuities—cannot be used for eligibility.

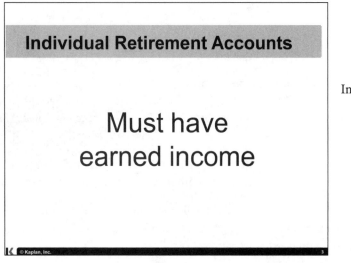

Individual Retirement Accounts

- Must have earned income
- Non-working spouse can make contributions based upon earned income of spouse (spousal IRA)

11.3.1 Contributions

11.3.1.1 Limits

Annual IRA contributions are capped at the *lesser* of:

- 100% of earned income; or
- a flat dollar amount—the tax law places limits on IRAs contributions, the amount is adjusted annually for cost-of-living adjustments.

The flat dollar limit also applies to spousal IRAs.

Individuals age 50 or over have a *catch-up* provision available to increase the flat dollar amount.

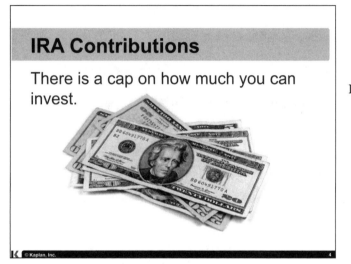

IRA Contributions
- Up to 100% of earned income
- Subject to annual maximums
- Extra contributions—age 50 or over

11.3.1.2 Deductibility

Individuals may deduct IRA contributions from taxable income if:

- the individual or spouse is not covered by an employer-sponsored retirement plan; or
- the adjusted gross income (AGI) is under a certain limit.

IRA contributions can be deducted (partially or full) on a federal income tax return and the income limit ranges are adjusted annually.

The entire contribution is deductible for incomes below the range.

A portion of the contribution is deductible for incomes between the ranges.

No portion of a contribution is deductible for incomes above the range.

A full annual limit contribution is allowed whether it will or will not be deducted from federal income taxes.

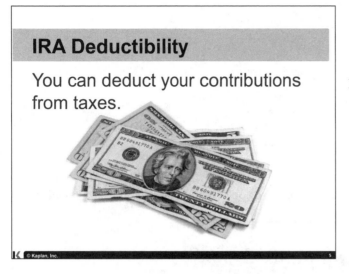

IRA Deductibility of Contributions

- Phase out of deduction based upon adjusted gross income (AGI)

- No deduction if income above maximum AGI

11.3.2 Funding Vehicles

There are some restrictions on the types of products in which IRA funds may be invested. The following are *not* allowed:

- life insurance;
- collectibles—such as artwork, antiques, stamps, coin collections; and
- hard assets—precious gems and precious metals in bullion form, but US-minted gold and silver coins are allowed.

Products that may be used include:

- flexible premium annuities,
- bank accounts,
- brokerage accounts, and
- mutual funds.

IRA Funding

- Investment can't be put in
  - Life insurance
  - Artwork, antiques, stamps or coin collections
  - Gold or silver bullion
    - US minted coins okay

11.3.3 Premature Withdrawals

Earnings on IRA contributions are tax-deferred—income tax is not due until the earnings are withdrawn. A *premature withdrawal*—withdrawal taken before age 59½—may incur a 10% penalty tax in addition to income tax due on the amount withdrawn. The 10% penalty is waived for the following reasons.

- Periodic payments made over the owner's life expectancy
- Certain medical expenses
- Payment of health insurance premiums while unemployed
- Certain higher education expenses
- Down payment for a first time home purchase ($10,000 maximum)
- Birth and adoption expenses ($5,000 maximum)
- Distributions made under a divorce decree to an ex-spouse or dependent child
- Correcting an excess contribution

Withdrawals

Common examples of withdrawals that may avoid a tax penalty:
- down payment of first home
- college education
- health insurance if unemployed

© Kaplan, Inc.

Premature Withdrawals

- Withdrawals taken before 59½ may have a penalty tax and income tax applied
- There are ways penalty can be waived

11.3.4 Rollovers and Transfers

There are two ways to move IRA accounts from one company to another or from an employer-sponsored plan to an individual IRA:

- **rollovers**: the money from the original IRA or qualified plan is distributed to the owner and they deposit it to the new IRA carrier; and
- **transfers**: called *direct transfers*—the money from the original IRA or qualified plan is distributed directly to the new IRA carrier without coming into the owner's possession.

Three rules for rollovers:

- *the money must be deposited within 60 days of its receipt by the owner*, or it becomes taxable. And if the owner is under age 59½, it will also incur a 10% penalty tax unless an exception applies;
- *if the rollover is coming from an employer-sponsored plan it is subject to withholding tax rate of 20%.* For example, the owner will only receive $80,000 of a $100,000 employer-sponsored plan rollover. Twenty-thousand dollars (20%) will be sent to the IRS. The owner will get the $20,000

withholding back at tax filing time if the owner deposits $100,000 with the new IRA custodian. If the owner only deposits $80,000, the $20,000 is taxable and subject to 10% tax penalty if under age 59½; and

- *an IRA may be rolled over only once in any 12-month period.*

These rules do not apply to transfers from one plan to another.

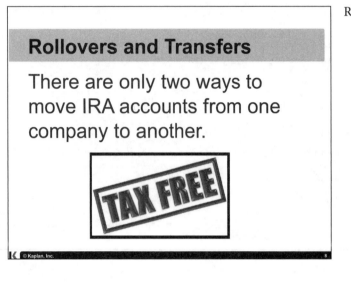

Rollovers and Transfers

- Rollover—money is withdrawn and sent to the owner
  - Owner has 60 days after receipt to put money in IRA
  - If money is coming from an employer sponsored plan
    - 20% withheld and sent to the IRS
  - Limited to one rollover every 12 months
- Transfer—money sent directly from one plan to another
  - No limit on the number of transfers
  - No money withheld and sent to the IRS

11.3.5 Required Minimum Distributions (RMDs)

Required Minimum Distributions (RMDs) of IRA must begin when the owner turns age 72. The first distribution may be delayed until April 1 of the following year and each future distribution must be happen by December 31. The amount of the RMD is based on the owner's life expectancy. Failure to take the RMD results in a tax penalty equal to 50% of the amount that should have been received by the owner.

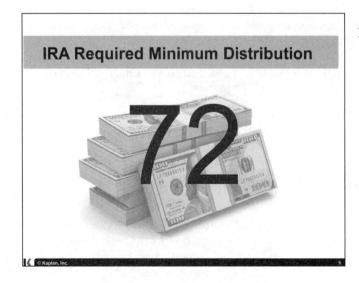

IRA Required Minimum Distribution

- Must start making with minimum withdrawals at age 72
- First minimum withdrawal can be delayed until April 1 of the year following the year the owner turns 72
- 50% penalty on taxes owed if minimum distributions not taken
- Annual minimum withdrawals are based upon the owners life expectancy

11.3.6 Taxation of Distributions

Deductible IRA contributions and earnings are taxed at distribution. Nondeductible contributions are distributed tax free.

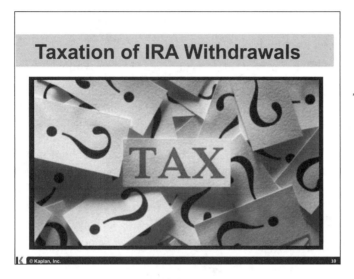

Taxation of IRA Withdrawals

- Fully taxed if all money in the IRA has not already been taxed

- Nondeductible contributions are distributed tax free

11.3.7 Distributions at Death

If the owner of an IRA dies, the requirements for distributions vary depending on the beneficiary.

- Spouses may choose to treat the IRA as their own or they may choose a lump-sum distribution.
- Non-spouse beneficiaries may take a lump-sum distribution or distributions over the 10 years following the owner's death.

The entire value of the IRA is includable in the deceased owner's estate.

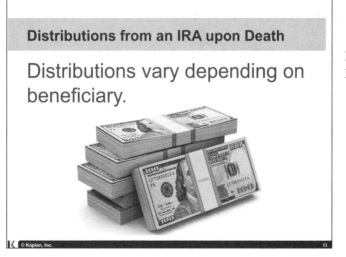

Distributions from an IRA upon Death

- Transfer to a spouse is not taxable

- The entire value of the IRA is includable in the deceased owner's estate for estate tax purposes

11.3.8 Roth IRAs

Roth IRAs were introduced in 1997. They follow rules similar to *traditional* IRAs except:

- contributions are never deductible; and
- qualified distributions are tax-free if they meet these two requirements
    1. the Roth IRA has been set up at for least five years, and
    2. distribution is after age 59½, or due to death, disability, or being a first-time homebuyer; first-time homebuyer is subject to a $10,000 limit.

Roth IRAs have no minimum distribution requirements (RMDs) and individuals may contribute to a Roth IRA regardless of their age.

Individuals may have both a Roth IRA and a traditional IRA, but the total annual contribution to both may not exceed the maximum limit for one IRA. Contributions to Roth IRAs are phased out for higher-income taxpayers.

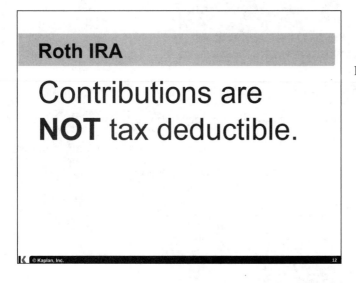

Roth IRA

- Contributions not tax deductible
- Contribution limits same as traditional IRA
- Withdrawals tax free
    - Account open for five years
    - Not before age 59 1/2

 QUICK QUIZ 11.A

1. All of the following individuals meet eligibility requirements for setting up an IRA EXCEPT
    A. Jan is 55 and works full time at a restaurant earning wages in tips
    B. Sal is 21 and just started a full time commissioned position as a sales representative
    C. Michelle works 10 hours a week at a book store and is paid hourly
    D. Mitch is unemployed but does receive rental income of $2,000 a month

2. Which of the following products cannot be used to fund an IRA?
    A. Life insurance
    B. Bank accounts
    C. Mutual funds
    D. Flexible premium annuities

3. Which of the following early withdrawals from an IRA would be subject to a 10% penalty?

   A. Payment of higher education expenses

   B. $10,000 down payment of a first home

   C. Premature withdrawal at age 55 in order to pay off a credit card

   D. Payment of health insurance premiums while unemployed

Answers can be found at the end of Unit 11.

11.4 EMPLOYER-SPONSORED QUALIFIED PLANS

11.4.1 Tax Advantages

All employer-sponsored qualified plans have the following tax advantages.

- Employer contributions are tax-deductible to the business.

- Employee contributions are tax-deductible to the employee.

- Neither employer nor employee contributions are taxable as current income to employees.

- All (except for the Roth 401(k) feature) earnings grow tax-deferred.

11.4.2 Taxation of Distributions

All (except for the Roth 401(k) feature) distributions from employer-sponsored qualified plans are taxable, because they come from deductible contributions and tax-deferred earnings.

Tax rules for distributions from employer-sponsored qualified plans are similar to traditional IRAs.

- Withdrawals taken before age 59½ are considered premature, unless there is an exception, a 10% penalty tax applies in addition to any ordinary income tax.

- Required minimum distributions must begin the year the individual turns age 72, the first payment may be delayed until April 1 of the following year.

11.4.3 General Requirements

All employer-sponsored qualified plans must be approved by the IRS to qualify for favorable tax treatment. The Employee Retirement Income Security Act of 1974 (ERISA) established the following requirements for retirement plans.

- *Participation*—plans must benefit all regular employees, not just a few selected ones. Generally, participation must be open to any employee age 21 or over with one year of service.

- *Non-discrimination*—plans may not provide benefits to executives and other highly paid individuals that are out of proportion to those provided to rank-and-file employees. Plans may not discriminate on the basis of sex.

- *Vesting*—determines when employees own the money in their plan. Employees are always immediately 100% vested in their own contributions. As for employer contributions, employees generally must become 100% vested after six years.

- *Reporting and disclosure*—each participant must receive in writing, when they enroll, a summary plan description, notification of any significant changes, and an annual report.

- *Fiduciary* —anyone with control over the plan or its assets are fiduciaries. They must manage the plan solely in the best interest of its participants using the "prudent person rule."

Employer Sponsored Retirement Plans

Tax advantages to employer and/or employer depending on how plan is funded.

17

Employer Sponsored Retirement Plans

- Regulated by ERISA (Employee Retirement Income Security Act of 1974)
- Employer contributions tax deductible
- Employee contributions tax deductible
- Interest earnings grow tax deferred
- General requirements
- Participation—plans must benefit all regular employees, not just a few selected ones
- Non-discrimination—plans may not provide benefits to executives and other highly paid individuals that are out of proportion to other employees
- Vesting
  - Determines when an employee owns the money in a retirement plan
  - Employees are always 100% vested in their own contributions
  - Employer contributions— employees must become vested in at least six years
- Reporting and disclosure— each participant must receive, in writing, a summary plan description, notification of any significant changes, and an annual report
- Fiduciary duty—anyone with control over the plan or its assets are fiduciaries. They must manage the plan solely in the best interest of its participants

11.4.4 Types of Employer-Sponsored Qualified Plans

11.4.4.1 Pension Plans

Pension plans may be either defined benefit or defined contribution plans. Pension plans require employers to make funding contributions to the plan every year.

Defined benefit pension plans are designed to provide a specific benefit to an employee upon retirement. The employee payout at retirement typically depends on how long they worked and their salary. The can choose a lump-sum payout or a monthly "annuity" payment.

Defined contribution pension plans do not specify what an employee will receive at retirement; it only specifies how much money the employee and employer can contribute.

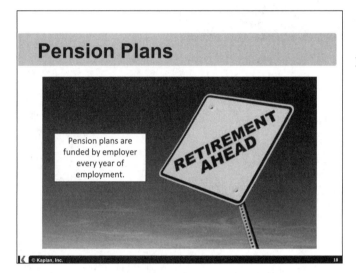

Pension Plans

- Defined benefit
  - Retirement benefit specified in the plan
- Defined contribution
  - Retirement benefit NOT specified
  - Contribution is specified

11.4.4.2 Profit-Sharing Plans

A **profit-sharing plan** is a defined contribution plan that does not require an employer to make a funding contribution every year. Rather, the amount and timing of contributions is at the employer's discretion. Contributions are dependent on the company making a profit.

The maximum amount that an employer may contribute to a profit-sharing plan as a whole is limited to 25% of the company's payroll for all employees.

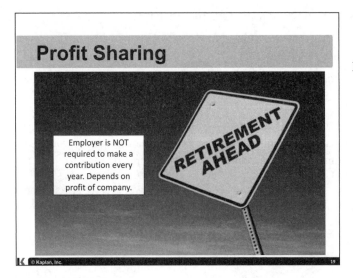

Profit Sharing

- Contributions made by employer
- Based on company profits
- Contributions not made every year
- Maximum contribution is 25% of total employee payroll

11.4.4.3 Keogh Plans

Keogh plans (*HR-10 plans*) are qualified retirement plans set up by self-employed persons and non-incorporated businesses such as sole proprietorships (individuals) and partnerships. Keogh plans may be defined benefit or defined contribution.

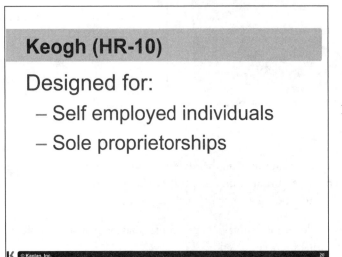

Keogh (HR-10)

- Individual sole proprietors
- Partnerships

11.4.4.4 401(k) Plans

401(k) Plans allow taxpayers a break on taxes on their deferred income. Employees can save and invest a piece of their paycheck before taxes are taken out. They won't be taxed on that money until it's withdrawn.

Employers may make matching contributions up to a certain dollar amount or percentage of the employee's contributions. The plan has annual contribution limits that are considerably higher than the limit on annual IRA contributions.

401(k)

- Employee may make contributions—salary (elective) deferral
- Employers may match contributions up to a specified percentage

11.4.4.5 403(b) Plans

403(b) Plans (also known as tax-sheltered accounts) work much like 401(k) plans, but they are for employees of non-profit organizations such as public school systems, churches, and hospitals. Employee and employer contribution limits are generally the same as those for 401(k) plans.

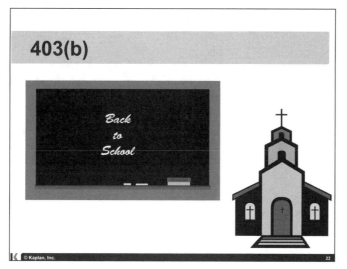

403(b)

- School employees
- Employees of nonprofit organizations

11.4.4.6 Simplified Employee Pension (SEP) Plans

Simplified Employee Pension (SEP) plans have significantly less paperwork and easier administration than qualified retirement plans. Essentially, each employee sets up an IRA and the employer makes contributions to them on the employees' behalf. Employer contribution limits for SEP-IRAs are much higher than the usual IRA limits. Annual employer contributions may not exceed 25% of the employee's compensation up to a specified maximum contribution amount.

Employees must be immediately 100% vested in employer contributions made under a SEP plan.

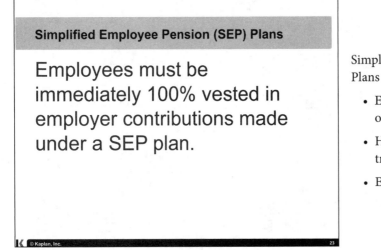

Simplified Employee Pension (SEP) Plans

- Employer makes contribution on employee's behalf
- Higher contribution limits than traditional IRA
- Employees must be 100% vested

11.4.4.7 Savings Incentive Match Plans for Employees (SIMPLEs)

Savings Incentive Match Plans for Employees (SIMPLEs) are a simplified retirement plan for small employers with 100 or fewer employees and no other type of retirement plan. A SIMPLE may be structured as an IRA or a 401(k) plan. SIMPLE plans allow employees to defer a portion of their compensation into the plan and employers are required to match those contributions dollar-for-dollar for at least 1% up to 3% of each employee's compensation. The dollar limit for employee contributions is somewhat less than the amount that applies to 401(k) and 403(b) plans. All employees earning at least $5,000 annually must be allowed to participate in the plan.

Employees are 100% vested in employer contributions made under a SIMPLE plan. A 25% penalty tax on premature distributions applies during the first two years and the standard 10% penalty applies thereafter.

Savings Incentive Match Plans for Employees (SIMPLE)

- Employers with 100 employees or less
- Employees can contribute
- 100 % immediate vesting for employer contributions
- All employees earning $5,000 or more per year must be allowed to participate
- 25% early withdrawal penalty for first two years of participation

11.5 EMPLOYEE RETIREMENT INCOME SECURITY ACT (ERISA)

ERISA was enacted to protect the interests of participants in employee benefit plans as well as the interests of the participants' beneficiaries. Much of the law deals with qualified pension plans, but some sections also apply to group insurance plans.

11.5.1 Fiduciary Responsibility

ERISA mandates very detailed standards for fiduciaries and other parties-in-interest of employee welfare benefit plans, including group insurance plans. This means that anyone with control over plan management or plan assets of any kind must discharge that fiduciary duty solely in the interests of the plan participants and their beneficiaries. Strict penalties are imposed on those who do not fulfill this responsibility.

Reporting and Disclosure ERISA requires that certain information concerning any employee welfare benefit plan, including group insurance plans, be made available to plan participants, their beneficiaries, the Department of Labor, and the IRS. Examples of the types of information that must be distributed include:

- a summary plan description to each plan participant and the Department of Labor;
- a summary of material modifications that details changes in any plan description to each plan participant and the Department of Labor;
- an annual return or report (Form 5500 or one of its variations) submitted to the IRS;
- a summary annual report to each plan participant; and
- any terminal report to the IRS.

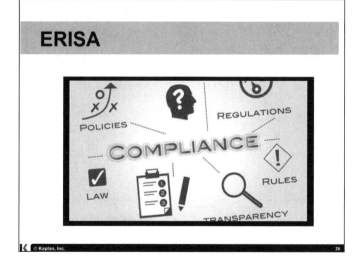

ERISA (Employee Retirement Income Security Act)

- Protects employee and beneficiaries
- Applies to qualified pensions and also group insurance.
- ERISA requires that certain information be made available to plan participants, beneficiaries, and the Department of Labor

11.6 NON-QUALIFIED PLANS

Employers who want to provide a benefit for select employees can use a non-qualified plan, a bonus plan, or a deferred compensation plan. These plans do not get the favorable tax treatment given to qualified plans. They do not need to meet the participation, non-discrimination, and other general requirements of qualified plans. Employers can design these plans in any way they wish.

Non-Qualified Plans

Employers can design these plans in any way that they want.

© Kaplan, Inc.   28

Non-Qualified Plans

- Not regulated by ERISA
- Can discriminate in favor of higher paid employees
- Contributions usually not tax deductible

QUICK QUIZ 11.B

1. Which of the following requirements of all employer-sponsored qualified retirement plans states that plans must benefit all regular employees, not just a select few?

    A. Participation

    B. Non-discrimination

    C. Vesting

    D. Fiduciary duty

2. Which of the following employer sponsored retirement plans does not require the employer to make a funding contribution every year?

    A. Pension plans

    B. Profit-sharing plans

    C. Defined contribution plans

    D. Defined benefit plans

Answers can be found at the end of Unit 11.

 # UNIT 11 CRAM SHEET

Individual retirement Accounts

- Must have earned income
- Non-working spouse can make contributions based upon earned income of spouse (spousal IRA)

IRA Contributions

- Up to 100% of earned income
- Subject to annual maximums
- Extra contributions—age 50 and over

IRA Deductibility of Contributions

- Phase out of deduction based upon adjusted gross income (AGI)
- No deduction if income above maximum AGI

IRA Funding

- Investment can't be put in
  - Life insurance
  - Artwork, antiques, stamps or coin collections
  - Gold or silver bullion

Rollovers and Transfers

- Rollover—money is withdrawn and sent to the owner
  - Owner has 60 days after receipt to put money in IRA
  - If money is coming from an employer sponsored plan
    - 20% withheld and sent to the IRS
  - Limited to one rollover every 12 months
- Transfer—money sent directly from one plan to another
  - No limit on the number of transfers
  - No money withheld and sent to the IRS

IRA Required Minimum Distribution

- Must start making with minimum withdrawals at age 72
- First minimum withdrawal can be delayed until April 1 of the year following the year the owner turns 72
- 50% tax penalty owed if minimum distributions not taken
- Annual minimum withdrawals are based upon the owners life expectancy

Distributions from an IRA upon Death

- Transfer to a spouse is not taxable
- The entire value of the IRA is includable in the deceased owner's estate for estate tax purposes

Roth IRA

- Contributions not tax deductible
- Contribution limits same as traditional IRA
- Qualified distributions are tax free
  - Account has been open for at least five years
  - Age 59½, death, disability, or first-time homebuyer

Employer Sponsored Retirement Plans

- Regulated by ERISA (Employee Retirement Income Security Act of 1974)
- Employer contributions tax deductible
- Employee contributions tax deductible
- Interest earnings grow tax deferred
- General requirements
    - Participation—plans must benefit all regular employees, not just a few selected ones
    - Non-discrimination—plans may not provide benefits to executives and other highly paid individuals that are out of proportion to other employees
    - Vesting
        - Determines when an employee owns the money in a retirement plan
        - Employees are always 100% vested in their own contributions
        - Employer contributions—employees must become vested in at least six years
    - Reporting and disclosure—each participant must receive, in writing, a summary plan description, notification of any significant changes, and an annual report
    - Fiduciary Duty—anyone with control over the plan or its assets are fiduciaries. They must manage the plan solely in the best interest of its participants

Defined benefit

- Retirement benefit specified in the plan

Defined Contribution

- Retirement benefit NOT specified
- Contribution is specified

Profit Sharing

- Contributions made by employer
- Based on company profits
- Contributions not made every year
- Maximum contribution is 25% of total employee payroll

Keogh (HR-10)

- Individual sole proprietors
- Partnerships

401(k)

- Employee may make contributions—salary (elective) deferral
- Employers may match contributions up to a specified percentage

403(b)

- School employees
- Employees of nonprofit organizations

Simplified Employee Pension (SEP) Plans

- Employer makes contribution on employee's behalf
- Higher contribution limits than traditional IRA
- Employees must be 100% vested

Savings Incentive Match Plans for Employees (SIMPLE)

- Employers with 100 employees or less
- Employees can contribute
- 100 % immediate vesting for employer contributions
- All employees earning $5,000 or more per year must be allowed to participate
- 25% early withdrawal penalty for first two years of employment

ERISA (Employee Retirement Income Security Act)

- Protects employee and beneficiaries
- Plan applies to qualified pensions and also group insurance
- ERISA requires that certain information be made available to plan participants, beneficiaries, and the Department of Labor

Non-Qualified Plans

- Not regulated by ERISA
- Can discriminate in favor of higher paid employees
- Contributions usually not tax deductible

UNIT 11 QUIZ

In order to measure your success, we recommend that you answer the following 10 questions correctly.

1. Curtis knows that when he retires after age 65, he will receive 80% of his salary as a pension. This is an example of
   A. a defined-benefit plan
   B. a defined-contribution plan
   C. a profit-sharing plan
   D. a money purchase plan

2. All of the following statements about profit-sharing plans are correct EXCEPT
   A. employers are not required to make a funding contribution every year
   B. the amount of annual contributions is set by employee
   C. the maximum amount that an employer may contribute is limited to 25% of the company's payroll for all employees
   D. plan contributions are dependent on the company making a profit

3. At what age can people begin making catch-up contributions to their individual retirement plans?
   A. 50
   B. 55
   C. 60
   D. 65

4. Premature distribution from a qualified plan or an IRA can result in the amount being taxed as income plus a penalty tax of
   A. 5%
   B. 10%
   C. 15%
   D. 25%

5. A rollover from one IRA to another or from a qualified plan to an IRA must be accomplished within how many days if the owner is to avoid an income tax liability on the amount rolled over?
   A. 10
   B. 30
   C. 60
   D. 90

6. At what age is an individual no longer subject to early withdrawal penalties under an IRA?
   A. 55
   B. 55½
   C. 59
   D. 59½

7. Which of the following organizations would be eligible to offer a 403(b) arrangement?
   A. Police department
   B. Public school system
   C. Any small business
   D. Any corporation

8. Carmen owns a business with 200 employees that provides a retirement plan whereby the business makes contributions on the employee's behalf. Carmen's plan is most likely
   A. a 401(k)
   B. a Keogh plan
   C. a 403(b) plan
   D. an SEP

9. Delbert is self-employed and sets up a
    retirement plan for himself. Delbert most likely
    sets up
    A. a SIMPLE plan
    B. a Keogh plan
    C. a 403(b) plan
    D. a 401(k) plan

10. Kim is required to take a $2,000 minimum
    annual distribution from her IRA. She fails to
    comply and only takes a $1,000 distribution.
    Because of this failure, Kim will be subject to
    A. a 10% penalty tax
    B. a 25% penalty tax
    C. a $500 fine
    D. a 50% penalty tax

ANSWER KEY

QUICK QUIZZES

QUICK QUIZ 11.A

1. **D.** Mitch is unemployed but does receive rental income of $2,000 a month

2. **A.** Life insurance

3. **C.** Premature withdrawal at age 55 in order to pay off a credit card

QUICK QUIZ 11.B

1. **A.** Participation

2. **B.** Profit-sharing plans

UNIT QUIZ

1. **A.** This is a defined benefit plan because it is designed to provide a specific benefit amount at retirement.

2. **B.** Under a defined contribution plan, the amount of any annual contributions is left to the employer's discretion.

3. **A.** People age 50 and up can make additional catch-up contributions.

4. **B.** Premature distribution from a qualified plan or an IRA can result in the amount being taxed as income plus a penalty tax of 10%.

5. **C.** A rollover from one IRA to another or from a qualified plan to an IRA must be accomplished within 60 days to avoid an income tax liability on the amount rolled over.

6. **D.** At age 59½, an individual is no longer subject to early withdrawal penalties under an IRA.

7. **B.** Any non-profit organizations such as public school systems, churches, and hospitals are eligible to offer a 403(b) arrangement.

8. **D.** Employees must be immediately 100% vested in employer contributions under a SEP plan.

9. **B.** Self-employed individuals and non-incorporated businesses can set up Keogh plans.

10. **D.** Individuals who take no distribution or anything less than the required minimum amount must pay a 50% penalty tax on the shortfall.

UNIT 12 Introduction to Health Insurance

12.1 INTRODUCTION

How could our society function and prosper without access to quality medical care? Who would help doctors and hospitals finance viable practices that provide care and advance medical innovation?

When health insurance became a reality a century ago it began to answer those questions. It's a simple concept with enormous benefits and having health insurance is often the difference between living one's life with a feeling of security versus tempting fate on a daily basis.

Health insurance is a cornerstone of a family's economic stability and this unit introduces the types of coverage available and the important terms, principles, and definitions.

12.2 LEARNING OBJECTIVES

After successfully completing this unit, you should be able to:

◻ define the two perils that health insurance is designed to cover: accident and sickness;

◻ identify health insurance covered benefits including hospital/medical expense coverage, disability income insurance, dental expense insurance, and long-term care (LTC) insurance;

◻ compare and contrast the different classes of health insurance policies: individual versus group, private vs. government, and limited vs. comprehensive;

◻ identify the limited benefit plans: limited perils, limited benefits, notice to proposed insured;

◻ describe the eight types of limited policies: Accident-only, Specified (dread) disease/critical illness, Hospital income (indemnity) insurance, credit disability insurance, blanket coverage, prescription drug coverage, vision care, and hearing; and

◻ list the common health insurance exclusions.

12.3 DEFINITIONS OF PERILS

Health insurance is designed to cover two perils:

- *accident*: unintentional bodily injury caused by an unforeseen event; and

- *sickness*: a need for medical care due to a cause other than an accident.

A pre-existing condition is an illness or disease that existed before an individual's health insurance went in to effect. The federal Affordable Care Act (ACA) eliminated pre-existing condition exclusions for medical expense policies affected by ACA. However, it is important to note that pre-existing condition exclusions are still allowed for disability policies, long-term care insurance, Medicare supplements, and limited benefit policies.

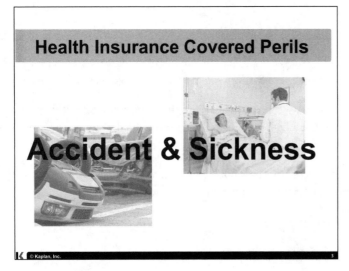

Health Insurance Covered Perils

- Sickness
  - Medical care not caused by an accident

12.4 POLICY TYPES AND COVERAGE

There are various health insurance policies that provide coverage for specific medical conditions and for this reason some individuals purchase multiple policies.

- *Hospital/medical expense coverage* helps pay doctor and hospital bills. It includes coverage for diagnostic and treatment-related expenses such as lab tests, x-rays, and medical supplies. Many medical expense plans also cover the cost of prescription drugs.

- *Disability income insurance* pays a stated amount of income to the insured when an accident or sickness leaves them unable to work for an extended period. While medical expense coverage pays doctor and hospital bills, disability income insurance provides money to pay other bills. Disability income insurance is frequently referred to as income replacement or loss-of-time coverage.

- *Dental expense insurance* is similar to medical expense coverage in the respect that it helps to pay dental bills. Coverage is generally provided for routine dental care such as cleanings, fillings, crowns, root canals, and braces.

- *Long-term care (LTC) insurance* provides coverage for medical and non-medical care for individuals with:

  - chronic illnesses;

  - cognitive impairment; or

  - difficulty performing *activities of daily living* (ADLs) such as bathing, dressing, eating, toileting, transferring, or continence.

Health Insurance Covered Benefits

Individuals may purchase various types of health insurance products.

© Kaplan, Inc.   5

Health Insurance Covered Benefits

- Hospital and medical bills
- Loss of income—disability
- Dental bills
- Long-term care—medical and non-medical expenses

12.5 CLASSES OF HEALTH INSURANCE POLICIES

12.5.1 Individual vs. Group Insurance

The major differences between individual and group health coverage are depicted in this chart.

Comparison of Individual and Group Plans

Individual	Group
Anyone can apply for coverage.	Only group members may be covered. Group must meet size and purpose definitions.
Each person has a policy.	There is one master contract. Individuals are given certificates as evidence of coverage.
Individual can choose coverage from whatever is available in the health insurance market.	Benefits are essentially the same for all group members. Individuals may be able to choose among a limited number of pre-established packages.
Individual's health is evaluated. A medical exam may be required.	Group as a whole is evaluated; usually no individual underwriting. No evidence of insurability required if individual enrolls within a given time after becoming eligible.
Coverage renewable at option of the insured, sometimes insurer.	Group sponsor may change coverage. Coverage stops when insured leaves the group.
All accidents are covered regardless of when or where they occur.	Only off-the-job accidents are generally covered. (On-the-job accidents are covered by workers' compensation, a state-mandated program.)

12.5.2 Private vs. Government Insurers

Commercial insurers compete for business in the private sector. Government insurers provide benefits to eligible individuals mandated by the law. Most government programs are partially or wholly paid for by tax dollars.

These are the Federal health insurance programs:

- TRICARE—for active duty and retired military personnel
- Veterans Benefits—for discharged military service members
- Medicare—healthcare primarily for senior citizens & recipients of Social Security disability
- Medicaid—healthcare for individuals and families who are or become poor
- Social Security disability—for eligible individuals who become totally and permanently disabled

Certain state governments act as the insurer for workers' compensation benefits and some states have established programs for disability benefits.

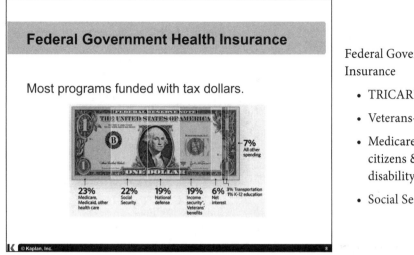

Federal Government Health Insurance

Most programs funded with tax dollars.

Federal Government Health Insurance

- TRICARE—military
- Veterans—former military
- Medicare—primarily for senior citizens & Social Security disability
- Social Security disability

12.5.3 Limited vs. Comprehensive Coverage

Comprehensive policies offer broad coverage for health care services. Limited policies provide benefits for only a particular type of loss and there are a number of special health insurance policies that provide limited coverage.

12.6 LIMITED PLANS

Limited benefit plans are characterized by the following:

- *limited perils*—while medical expense plans cover losses that arise from almost any cause with just a few exceptions, limited benefit plans cover losses that arise only from one peril or one type of peril, or which occur relative to a specific situation or location;

- *limited benefits*—while medical expense plans have moved quickly toward providing very high or unlimited benefits, the amounts paid by limited benefit plans are typically much smaller and often restricted to stated amounts; and

- *notice to proposed insured*—to assure that insureds understand the limited nature of the coverage they are buying, states require these policies to contain a prominent notice on their first page stating that the coverage provides only limited benefits.

Limited Plans

- Cover very specific types of losses
- Not comprehensive

© Kaplan, Inc.   10

Limited Plans

- Limited benefits
- Limited perils—such as cancer or vision
- Notice—insured must be informed of the limited benefits

 QUICK QUIZ 12.A

1. Which of the following types of health insurance covers the cost of providing non-medical custodial care to individuals with cognitive problems?

   A. Disability income insurance

   B. Long-term care insurance

   C. Hospital expense coverage

   D. Medical expense coverage

2. All of the following are characteristics of a group health insurance plan EXCEPT

   A. only group members may be covered

   B. there is one master contract

   C. each person has a policy

   D. benefits are essentially the same for all group members

Answers can be found at the end of Unit 12.

12.7 TYPES OF LIMITED POLICIES

12.7.1 Accident-Only

Accident-only policies only cover accidents as a peril, and exclude any type of sickness or disease. Consequently, the premiums are smaller than policies that cover both illness and injury. Accident-only policies may also pay a benefit if an accident results in dismemberment, disability, or death.

12.7.2 Specified (Dread) Disease/Critical Illness

Specified or **dread disease** policies were originally developed to cover one, or one type, of catastrophic illness specified in the policy such as cancer or heart disease. Today these policies may cover a number of life-threatening diseases or serious conditions including stroke, coma, liver failure, kidney failure, and paralysis as well as the need for organ or bone marrow transplants. Some contain a health screening benefit to help with early diagnosis of catastrophic illnesses. These wider-ranging policies are sometimes called **critical illness** plans. But one thing they all have in common is that, whether they cover one disease or many, benefits are strictly limited to those diseases specifically named in the policy.

These policies cover illnesses that are unlikely to affect everyone but are very expensive for those diagnosed with the condition. These specified policies are fairly inexpensive compared to comprehensive medical expense coverage.

Most policies may not pay the full cost of every treatment. There may be no coverage for transportation or reimbursement for hospital room-and-board expenses may be limited to certain dollar amounts. Some of these policies simply pay a lump sum benefit upon diagnosis of a specified disease.

12.7.3 Hospital Income (Indemnity) Insurance

A **hospital income**, or **hospital indemnity**, plan pays a flat dollar amount as a daily benefit for each day that the insured is hospitalized as an inpatient. The payment is made directly to the insured, not to the hospital. These plans are not designed to reimburse the insured for the expenses of hospitalization but to provide income that the insured can use in any way he or she wants. Individuals may use this kind of policy to meet the deductible and coinsurance payments on their medical expense policies or to pay their other bills while they are in the hospital and unable to work.

12.7.4 Credit Disability Insurance

When retailers or lenders extend credit for a large purchase, they often require the consumer to have **credit disability insurance** to secure the loan. If the consumer (*debtor*) becomes disabled, the policy's benefit is paid to the creditor (lender) to pay off the loan.

The credit disability policy is a group policy with the retailer as master policyowner and the debtors are the group members. Retailers offer to include it as part of the credit/purchase transaction. Group credit disability policies have the following features.

- As group insurance, no individual underwriting is done, so no evidence of insurability is required.

- The amount of coverage under the policy cannot be more than the amount of indebtedness remaining under the credit contract at any time, so the disability benefit may not exceed the monthly credit installment payment, or if the insurance coverage calls for a lump sum benefit, the amount of coverage will decrease over time as installment payments are made on the debt.

- Consumers must be clearly notified that they are buying credit insurance coverage as part of the credit/purchase transaction; the coverage cannot be included in the transaction without the consumer's knowledge and agreement.

While retailers or lenders can require a consumer to have insurance to secure credit, they cannot require that the consumer obtain the coverage through them. Debtors may obtain their own individual coverage or assign the benefit of an existing policy to secure the loan.

12.7.5 Blanket Coverage

Blanket coverage is a type of group insurance where the group members are identified as all the persons engaged in a similar activity, such as employees at a company picnic, passengers on an airplane, players or spectators at a sporting event, or students while they are on school grounds. Members are automatically covered when they are part of the group, and coverage automatically ceases when the person is no longer part of the group. Because group membership can change so quickly with people coming and going, the individual members are not named, and there is no application for insurance or certificate of coverage.

12.7.6 Prescription Drugs

Prescription drug coverage can be included in a medical expense plan, added as a supplement to a medical expense plan, or issued as stand-alone coverage. Usually, insureds must use a specific network of pharmacies in order to receive benefits. Prescription drug plans generally work in one of two ways:

- Insureds are reimbursed for their prescription drug expenses using standard claim forms; or,
- Insureds are given a prescription drug card to present to a participating pharmacy, and they make a relatively small co-payment to the pharmacy directly for each prescription refill. Co-payments are generally $5 or $10 for generic drugs, and $15 or more for name brand drugs.

Prescription drug plans generally do not cover every drug. The list of drugs the plan covers is called its *formulary*. A plan's formulary is required to include at least one drug in every non-elective therapeutic category.

12.7.7 Vision Care

Medical expense policies cover disease and injury to the eyes, but not routine eye care and vision correction. This coverage gap can be filled with a vision care plan, which covers:

- eye examinations;
- cost of lenses and frames;
- cost of contact lenses; and
- other corrective items.

Typically, vision care plans operate within a network of optometrists and eyeglass providers. The insured must use this network to receive benefits. Co-payments and certain limitations may apply. For example, the plan may pay for only one eye exam and one set of lenses every two years, and there may be a limit on the amount the plan will pay toward frames or prescription sunglasses.

12.7.8 Hearing Insurance

Most comprehensive health insurance policies do not cover costs related to hearing loss. These limited plans may provide coverage for hearing exams and some or all of the cost for hearing aids.

12.7.9 Short-Term Medical Expense Plans

A short-term medical policy is sold as a means of temporary health insurance coverage. For example, a person may be in the waiting period for their group insurance and need temporary coverage. The length of coverage is typically 90 days, 6 months, or 12 months. These policies are not renewable and must be qualified for. The insured may only apply for one additional policy, which can be refused by the insurer if claims were filed under the previous short-term policy. These plans offer short-term limited benefits at a low cost.

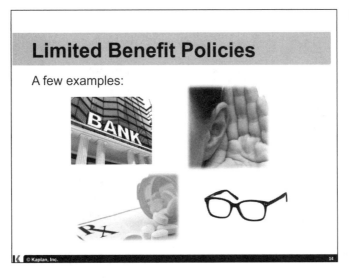

Limited Benefit Policies

- Accident only
- Dread disease
- Critical illness
- Hospital indemnity
- Credit disability
- Blanket coverage
- Prescription drugs
- Vision
- Hearing
- Short-term medical expense plans

12.8 COMMON HEALTH INSURANCE EXCLUSIONS

12.8.1 Intentional Self-Inflicted Injuries

Health insurance is designed to cover unforeseen accidents or sickness not intentional injury or illness.

12.8.2 War or Act of War

Excluded regardless of service in the military.

12.8.3 Elective Cosmetic Surgery

Cosmetic surgery is not considered to be health related and is typically excluded. However, if treatment is required due to accident or birth defect, the coverage may apply.

12.8.4 Workers Compensation

Injury or illness that is worked related is normally not covered by health insurance but is covered by workers compensation.

12.8.5 Commission or Attempted Felony

This exclusion is similar to the intentional loss exclusion.

Health Insurance Common Exclusions

- Intentional
- War or act of war
- Elective cosmetic surgery
- Workers compensation
- Felony

 QUICK QUIZ 12.B

1. All of the following are common exclusions in health insurance policies EXCEPT
   A. war or act of war
   B. felonious act
   C. intentional injury
   D. injury in a natural disaster

2. With a hospital income plan, the flat dollar payment is made directly to the
   A. hospital
   B. insurer
   C. insured
   D. doctors

Answers can be found at the end of Unit 12.

 UNIT 12 CRAM SHEET

Health Insurance Covered perils

- Accident
  - Unintentional injury
  - Unforeseen
- Sickness
  - Medical care not caused by an accident

Health Insurance Covered Benefits

- Hospital and medical bills
- Loss of income—disability
- Dental bills
- Long-term care—medical and non-medical expenses

Federal Government Health Insurance

- TRICARE—active military
- Veterans—former military
- Medicare—primarily for senior citizens & Social Security disability
- Social Security disability

Limited Plans

- Limited benefits
- Limited perils—such as cancer or vision
- Notice—insured must be informed of the limited benefits

Limited Benefit Policies

- Accident only
- Dread disease
- Critical illness
- Hospital indemnity
- Credit disability
- Blanket coverage
- Prescription drugs
- Vision
- Hearing

Health Insurance Common Exclusions

- Intentional
- War or act of war
- Elective cosmetic surgery
- Workers compensation
- Felony

UNIT 12 QUIZ

In order to measure your success, we recommend that you answer the following 10 questions correctly.

1. Julia has a policy that excludes any type of sickness or disease and covers only accidents as a peril. Julia probably has
   A. a blanket policy
   B. a medical expense insurance policy
   C. an accident-only policy
   D. a critical illness policy

2. George's brother, Jerry, has a policy that will provide him an income if he is disabled from illness or injury, but only if he is confined to a hospital. George's brother probably has
   A. a disability income policy
   B. a medical expense insurance policy
   C. a long-term care policy
   D. a hospital income insurance policy

3. Dread disease policies
   A. have extremely high premiums compared to comprehensive medical expense coverage
   B. cover any disease defined by the ADA as a dread disease
   C. cover only specific diseases as named in the policy, such as heart disease, kidney failure, or cancer
   D. are a good replacement for general health insurance

4. Sin Lan has a hospital income policy that will pay $50 a day. If Sin Lan is hospitalized, to whom will the insurer make payments?
   A. The hospital
   B. Sin Lan
   C. The doctor
   D. The beneficiary

5. Credit disability (health) insurance covers
   A. a creditor
   B. a debtor
   C. either a creditor or a debtor
   D. the lender

6. All of the following apply to individual health insurance policies EXCEPT
   A. anyone can apply for coverage
   B. individual's health is evaluated
   C. all accidents are covered regardless of when they occur
   D. insureds are given certificates of insurance instead of a policy

7. An unintentional bodily injury caused by an unforeseen event is known as
   A. an accident
   B. a sickness
   C. a peril
   D. a loss

8. A need for medical care due to a cause other than an accident is known as
   A. an accident
   B. a sickness
   C. a peril
   D. a loss

9. Melissa was involved in an accident that left her unable to work for an extended period of time. She has a policy that will pay her a stated amount of income on a regular basis while she is off work. Melissa most likely has

    A. hospital/medical expense insurance

    B. disability income insurance

    C. hospital income insurance

    D. long-term care (LTC) insurance

10. A type of group insurance where the group members are identified as all the persons engaged in a similar activity is known as

    A. an accident-only plan

    B. a critical illness plan

    C. blanket coverage

    D. workers compensation

ANSWER KEY

QUICK QUIZZES

QUICK QUIZ 12.A

1. **B.** Long-term care insurance

2. **C.** each person has a policy

QUICK QUIZ 12.B

1. **D.** injury in a natural disaster

2. **C.** insured

UNIT QUIZ

1. **C.** These are for individuals who practice a healthy lifestyle and feel that they are not likely to get sick, but know that accidents can happen to anybody. Premiums are typically lower for accident-only policies.

2. **D.** A hospital income insurance policy provides income to an individual who is disabled by illness or injury and confined to a hospital.

3. **C.** These wider-ranging policies are sometimes called critical illness plans. But one thing they all have in common is that, whether they cover one disease or many, benefits are strictly limited to those diseases specifically named in the policy.

4. **B.** A hospital income policy will pay the insured.

5. **B.** If the consumer (often referred to as the debtor) becomes disabled, the policy's benefit is paid to the creditor (or lender) to pay off the loan.

6. **D.** In a group plan the individuals are given a certificate of insurance. In an individual plan, each individual has a policy.

7. **A.** Accident is an injury caused by an unforeseen event.

8. **B.** Sickness is need for medical care due to a cause other than an accident.

9. **B.** Disability income insurance is also called income replacement insurance or loss-of-time coverage.

10. **C.** Members are automatically covered when they are part of a group, such as students while on school grounds, a basketball team, a company picnic, or spectators at a sporting event.

UNIT 13 Affordable Care Act

13.1 INTRODUCTION

The Affordable Care Act was passed by Congress and signed into law by President Obama on March 23, 2010. On June 28, 2012, the Supreme Court made the decision to uphold the law. The health care law includes reforms to the affordability, quality, and availability of health insurance, and regulations for both public and private health insurance companies.

In this unit, you will learn the federal Affordable Care Act (ACA) details. It is important to know that some state insurance laws are more generous than the Affordable Care Act (ACA). Please read the Kaplan state law supplement and reference your state exam content outline for insurance law and regulation exam material that is specific to your state.

13.2 LEARNING OBJECTIVES

After successfully completing this lesson, you should be able to:

◻ explain the purpose of the Affordable Care Act;

◻ list the insurance reforms that began due to the Affordable Care Act;

◻ understand grandfathered and nongrandfathered plans;

◻ explain what the individual mandate means to U.S citizens and legal residents;

◻ identify the nine essential health benefits that health insurance exchanges must cover;

◻ understand the role of the required health insurance exchange; and

◻ explain employer responsibilities related to the Affordable Care Act.

13.3 AFFORDABLE CARE ACT (ACA)

Note: Some state insurance laws are more generous than the Affordable Care Act (ACA). Please read the Kaplan state law supplement for insurance law and regulation exam material that is specific to your state.

The Affordable Care Act (ACA) was signed into law by President Obama in 2010. The law has also been referred to as Patient Protection and Affordable Care Act (PPACA), Obamacare, or Health Care Reform. Some ACA provisions were implemented in 2010, while others happened later. Health insurance reforms that began in 2010 are:

- no lifetime dollar limits or annual dollar limits on essential health benefits (EHBs);

- no rescissions (cancellations), except for fraud;

- specific preventive services are covered free of charge to insured;

- dependent coverage until a child's 26th birthday; and

- pre-existing conditions must be covered for children under age 19.

Health insurance reforms that began January 1, 2014, are:

- pre-existing conditions must be covered for all eligible individuals (not just children);

- guaranteed issue of health insurance policies;

- no discrimination based on gender and health status, or due to pre-existing conditions;

- community rating rules for premiums;

- health insurance exchanges or marketplaces;

- qualified health plans (QHPs);

- essential health benefits (EHBs);

- premium tax credits and cost-sharing subsidy; and

- the creation of navigators.

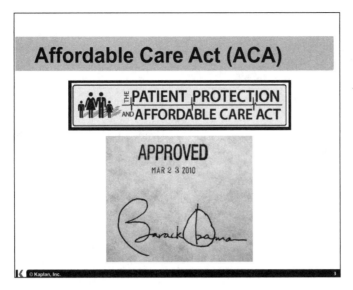

ACA

- Also known as PPACA, Obamacare, and Heath Care Reform
- Signed in 2010 with some reforms
- Additional reforms began January 2014

13.3.1 Grandfathered and Nongrandfathered Plans

A **grandfathered health policy** is one that existed prior to the Affordable Care Act. Costs cannot be increased and benefits may not be reduced on these policies. A grandfathered plan is not required to comply with some of the consumer protections of the ACA that apply to other health plans. **Nongrandfathered plans** must comply with all rules and laws of the ACA.

The following consumer protections apply to all plans (grandfathered and nongrandfathered):

- Lifetime dollar limits cannot be applied to essential health benefits.
- A policy cannot be canceled solely because of an honest mistake on an application.
- Dependent coverage must be extended to adult children until age 26.

Group plans and grandfathered plans are NOT required to:

- provide certain recommended preventive services for free;
- offer new protections when an insured is appealing claims and coverage denials; or
- allow any choice of health care providers access to emergency care.

Grandfathered individual health plans are NOT required to:

- phase out annual dollar limits on essential health benefits (dollar limits can remain); or
- eliminate pre-existing condition exclusions for children under 19 years old (pre-existing conditions can be excluded).

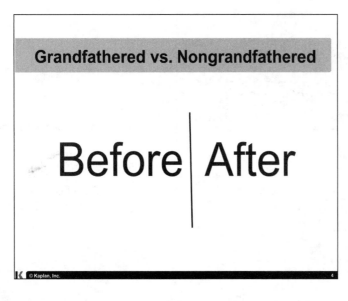

Grandfathered—existed before ACA

Nongrandfathered—existed after ACA

 QUICK QUIZ 13.A

1. All of the following statements are true regarding grandfathered plans EXCEPT
   A. a grandfathered health policy existed before ACA
   B. a grandfathered plan is required to comply with all of the consumer protections of the ACA
   C. grandfathered plans are not required to provide certain recommended preventative services for free
   D. grandfathered individual plans are not required to eliminate pre-existing condition exclusions for children under 19 years old

2. Which of the following is NOT a common name for the Affordable Care Act?
   A. Health Care Reform
   B. Obamacare
   C. Patient Protection and Affordable Care Act (PPACA)
   D. Social Insurance Program

Answers can be found at the end of Unit 13.

13.3.2 Individual Mandate

U.S. citizens and legal residents are required to have qualifying health care coverage (*minimum essential coverage*). Insurance provided by employers satisfies this universal health insurance mandate. Individuals who lose or choose not to purchase qualifying coverage must pay a tax penalty. The Tax Cuts and Jobs Act of 2017 (TCJA) did not repeal the individual mandate. The individual mandate is still law. However, starting in 2019, the TCJA reduced the penalty to $0 and 0%, meaning that there is no monetary penalty if an individual does not comply with the mandate.

Exemptions to the individual mandate may be granted for financial hardship, religious objections, American Indians, those without coverage for less than three months, undocumented immigrants, incarcerated (imprisoned) individuals, those for whom the lowest cost plan option exceeds 8% of an individual's income, and those with incomes below the tax-filing threshold.

13.3.2.1 Minimum Essential Coverage

Minimum essential coverage means coverage from any of the following:

- Government-sponsored programs (e.g., Medicare, Medicaid, CHIP, TRICARE, COBRA)
- Employer-sponsored plans (small or large group market)
- Plans in the individual market
- Grandfathered health plans
- Other coverage (e.g., state health benefits risk pool)

Minimum essential coverage does not include *excepted benefits*. *Excepted benefits* means benefits under one or more (or any combination) of the following:

- Accident only or disability income insurance
- Liability and supplemental liability insurance
- Workers' compensation or similar insurance
- Automobile medical payment insurance
- Credit-only insurance
- On-site medical clinics
- Other similar insurance coverage under which benefits for medical care are secondary or incidental to other insurance benefits
- The following, if provided in a separate policy:
    - Limited scope dental or vision benefits
    - Long-term care insurance
    - Coverage only for a specified disease or illness
    - Hospital indemnity or other fixed indemnity insurance
    - Medicare supplements

Individual Mandate

Health insurance is
REQUIRED!

© Kaplan, Inc.

Individual Mandate

- U.S. citizens and legal residents are required to have qualifying health care coverage.
- There is a tax penalty if they do not have coverage (with some exemptions).

13.3.3 Benefits

13.3.3.1 Essential Health Benefits (EHBs)

Health plans offered in the individual and small group markets must be qualified according to ACA standards. *Qualified health plans (QHPs),* Medicaid state plans, and insurance policies in health insurance exchanges must cover (or offer) the following *essential health benefits:*

- Ambulatory patient services
- Emergency services
- Hospitalization
- Maternity and newborn care
- Mental health and substance use disorder services
    - Must be treated with parity; deductibles, co-pays, and coinsurance must not differ from patients with physical conditions.
- Prescription drugs
- Rehabilitative services and devices
- Laboratory services
- Preventive and wellness services and chronic disease management
- Pediatric services, including oral and vision care

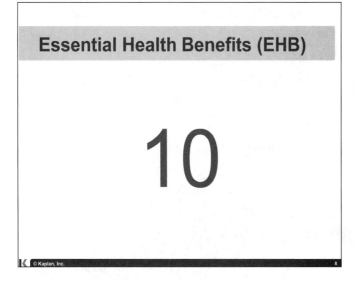

EHB

- Health plans must be qualified to fit ACA standards.
- QHPs, Medicaid state plans, and insurance on the health exchange must meet requirements.

13.3.3.2 Emergency Medical Services

The ACA provides that emergency services are essential health benefits (EHBs). When an emergency occurs, no pre-authorization may be demanded by insurers, whether the insured seeks help in-network or out-of-network. Out-of-network providers who provide emergency services must comply with normal cost-sharing requirements and may not impose administrative requirements or coverage limits that are more restrictive than emergency services provided in-network.

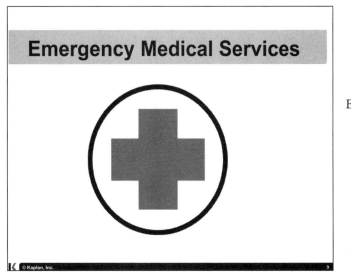

Emergency Medical Services

- No pre-authorization required
- In-network or out-of-network
- Normal cost-sharing requirements

13.3.3.3   Primary Care Provider Designation

Every subscriber and dependent must designate a participating primary care provider (PCP) who will serve as his usual source of medical care.

Primary Care Provider

- Every insured and dependent must have a PCP.

13.3.3.4   Prohibition on Lifetime and Annual Limits

Individual and group plan carriers (unless they receive a waiver from the Secretary of the U.S. Department of Health and Human Services) are prohibited from putting annual and lifetime dollar limits on *essential health benefits (EHBs)*.

- Plans are allowed to place annual dollar limits and lifetime dollar limits on health care services that are not essential health benefits.

- Grandfathered individual health plans are allowed to have annual dollar limits on *essential health benefits*.

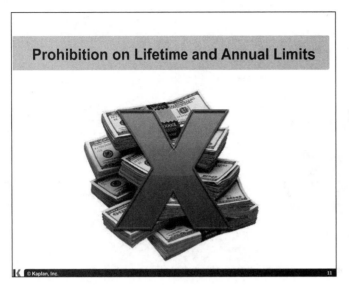

Prohibition on Lifetime/Annual Limit

- On all EHBs (except for grandfathered plans)Limits allowed on non-EHBs

13.3.3.5 Metal Tiers (Categories)

The ACA standardized the types of benefits and cost sharing allowed in health plans offered through the *Health Insurance Marketplace* into four levels of coverage. Each plan level must cover the same minimum *essential health benefits*. Individual and small group health plans categorize plans into one of four different metal tiers. The tiers represent the average portion of expected costs a plan will cover for an average population (a.k.a. actuarial value). The following are the percentages the plans will spend, on average:

- Bronze plan—60%
- Silver plan—70%
- Gold plan—80%
- Platinum plan—90%

The higher the amount of coverage, the higher the premium will be for the insured.

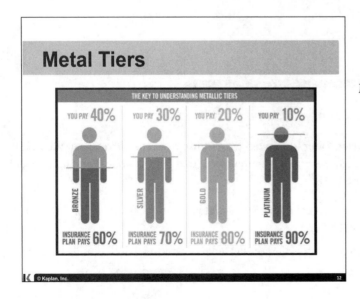

Metal Tiers

- Four levels of coverage; each must cover minimum EHBs.
- Tiers represent average portion of expected costs.
- Percentages represent how much plan will pay.

13.3.3.6 Free Preventive Care

The ACA focuses on prevention and primary care to help people stay healthy and manage chronic medical conditions before they become more complex and costly to treat.

Free Preventative Care

- Take care of yourself now to prevent costly, future, chronic conditions.

13.3.3.7 Pre-Existing Conditions

"Pre-existing condition exclusion" means a limitation or exclusion of benefits based on a physical or mental condition that was present before the effective date of coverage.

Except for grandfathered individual health insurance policies, health plans may no longer limit or exclude coverage for any individual (any age) by using pre-existing condition exclusions.

Pre-Existing Conditions

Physical or mental conditions present before effective date may no longer be excluded.

Pre-Existing Conditions

- Health plans can no longer exclude pre-existing conditions (except for grandfathered plans).

13.3.3.8 Coverage of Children to Age 26

Group health plans and health insurance issuers offering group or individual health insurance coverage that provide dependent coverage to children of the insured must make coverage available for adult children **up to age 26**. There is no requirement to cover the child or spouse of a dependent child. Grandchildren may be covered if the grandparent is the legal guardian or adoptive parent of the child to be insured.

- Children can join or remain on the parent's plan even if they are:
  - married;
  - not living with the parents;
  - attending school;
  - not financially dependent on their parent(s); or
  - eligible to enroll in their employer's plan.
- An unmarried child (of any age) who has a physical or mental impairment and is financially dependent on the parents may stay on a parent's health insurance past age 26 with proper verification of dependency.

Coverage of Children to Age 26

- Up to, not including, age 26
- Children can remain if:
  - married;
  - not living with parents;
  - attending school;
  - not finanically dependent; or
  - eligible to enroll in employer's plan
- Past age 26 if unmarried, financially dependent, and have physical or mental impairment

13.3.3.9 Eligibility

Depending on a person's income, employment status, and whether health insurance coverage is available through his employer, a person may be eligible for health insurance coverage through Medicaid, health insurance exchanges, group insurance, or individual coverage.

- Individual tax credits and cost-sharing subsidies are only available through the health insurance exchange plans.

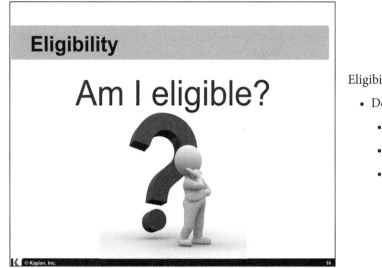

Eligibility

- Depends on:
    - Income
    - Employment status
    - If you have coverage through employer

13.3.3.10 Guaranteed Issue

This is a requirement that health plans permit you to enroll, regardless of health status, age, gender, or other factors that might predict the use of health services.

Subject to rules regarding enrollment periods, network plans, and insurer financial capacity, a health insurance issuer that offers health insurance coverage in the individual, small group, or large group market must offer to any individual or employer in the state all products that are approved for sale in the applicable market, and must accept any individual or employer that applies for any of those products.

Guaranteed Issue

- Must be offered to any individual or employer in the state
- Subject to rules

QUICK QUIZ 13.B

1. Group health plans and health insurance issuers offering group or individual health insurance coverage that provide dependent coverage to children of the insured must make coverage available for adult children

   A. up to age 26

   B. up to age 21

   C. up to age 18

   D. up to age 25

2. A limitation or exclusion of benefits based on a physical or mental condition that was present before the effective date of coverage is also known as

   A. a grandfathered exclusion

   B. a pre-existing condition

   C. a conditional exclusion

   D. a preventative limitation

Answers can be found at the end of Unit 13.

13.3.4 Health Benefit Exchanges/Marketplaces

ACA requires states to have a health insurance exchange operated by either the state or the federal government. Individuals, families, and small businesses can access, view, and sign up for health insurance plans using the federal government's *Health Insurance Marketplace* at www.healthcare.gov.

Initial enrollment in the plans available through the exchange began before the ACA was enacted. Individuals and families have an annual open enrollment each year. Special enrollment periods are available following certain *qualifying events* including:

- Marriage
- Birth or adoption of a child
- Permanently moving to an area that offers different health plans
- Loss of health coverage due to divorce, job loss, or loss of eligibility for coverage

Health Benefit Exchanges/Marketplaces

- Required
- Operated by state or federal government
- Annual open enrollment and special enrollment depending on qualifying events

Qualified health plans (QHP) are insurance plans sold on the health insurance exchange. QHPs provide essential health benefits, follow established limits on cost-sharing (like deductibles, co-payments, and out-of-pocket maximum amounts), and meet other requirements.

- QHPs are only available on the health insurance exchange and are the only plans that provide premium tax credits and cost-sharing reductions for eligible individuals.

QHPs

- Provide EHBs
- Only available on the exchange
- Only plan that provides tax credits and cost sharing

13.3.4.1   Small Business Health Options Program (SHOP)

The SHOP marketplace provides an online application where small employers can shop and compare a variety of health insurance plans. The employer must have 50 or fewer full-time employees.

SHOP

- Online application to compare health plans
- 50 or less full-time employees

13.3.4.2 Subsidies

To help defray the cost of health care purchased via the exchanges, the law offers subsidies that vary based on an individual or family's household income. The subsidy could be in the form of *advanced premium tax credits (APTCs)* that may be applied to lower the insured's monthly premiums or cost-sharing reductions such as lower co-payment, coinsurance, and out-of-pocket limits. The cost-sharing reduction is only available through a health plan from the silver metal tier plan category. When the insured applies through an exchange, their identity and income is verified and compared to federal poverty level incomes. The exchange calculates what subsidies are available (if any).

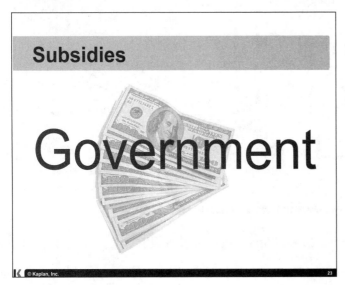

Subsidies

- A sum of money given by the federal government
- Advanced premium tax credits (APTC)
- Cost-sharing (only available in Silver tier)

13.3.4.3 Navigators

Navigators are funded by the federal government to help individuals determine their eligibility for public assistance programs using the health insurance exchange/marketplace website. Navigators cannot legally provide advice to consumers about which health insurance plan to choose and are not permitted to sell insurance.

Marketplaces are required to have a navigator program available for consumers to assist with eligibility, enrollment, and coverage questions related to the Affordable Care Act. Federally funded grants train navigators to educate consumers and refer consumers to health insurance consumer assistance programs.

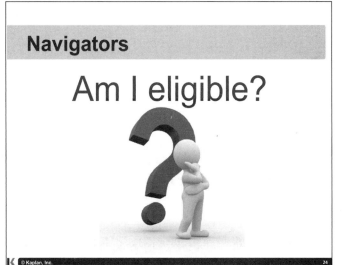

Navigators

- Funded by government through federal grants

- CANNOT sell insurance or provide advice

- Help determine eligibility for public assistance

13.3.5 Employer Responsibilities

13.3.5.1 Employer Notification Responsibilities

Employers are required to inform employees about their rights to affordable coverage and possible subsidies. Access to coverage can be either via plans offered through employment or through the health exchange individually. A Department of Labor notice entitled "New Health Insurance Marketplace Coverage: Options and Your Health Coverage" should be distributed in the workplace.

13.3.5.2 Employer Mandate – Employer Shared Responsibility

Employers with 50 or more full-time employees (FTE) or full-time equivalents must pay a $2,000 penalty per full-time employee if the employer does not offer health coverage and at least one full-time employee receives a federal premium subsidy for coverage purchased through a health insurance exchange.

Employers with 50 or more full-time employees that offer coverage but have at least one full-time employee receiving a premium subsidy will pay the lesser of $3,000 for each employee receiving a premium subsidy, or $2,000 for each full-time employee (excluding the first 30 employees).

Employers with less than 50 full-time employees are exempt from the above penalties.

Employer Responsibilities

- Employer notification responsibilities
  - Required to let employees know their rights to affordable coverage
- Employer mandate—employer shared responsibility
  - For employers with 50 or more employees
  - Penalty if not followed
  - Exempt if less than 50 employees

13.3.5.3 Health Care Tax Credit for Small Employers

Small employers and small tax-exempt organizations can get tax credits to help offset the cost of the company's health plan premium contribution. The maximum credit is 50% of premiums paid for small business employers and 35% of premiums paid for small tax-exempt employers.

To be eligible for the credit, a small employer must pay premiums on behalf of employees enrolled in a qualified health plan offered through the Small Business Health Options Program (SHOP) Marketplace or qualify for an exception to this requirement. The credit is available to eligible employers for two consecutive taxable years.

The credit is targeted to help employers with low and moderate income workers afford to offer employees health insurance coverage. The eligibility formula is based on the number of full-time equivalent employees, not the total number of employees. Employers must have less than 25 FTE employees and cover at least 50% of the cost of employee-only (not family or dependent) health care coverage for each employee.

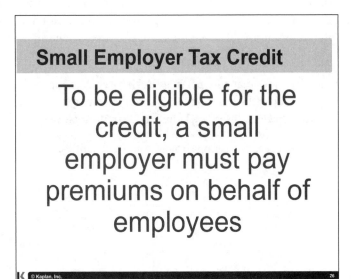

- Health care tax credit for small employers
  - Maximum credit
    - 50% of premiums paid for small business employers
    - 35% of premiums paid for small tax-exempt employers.
  - Eligible for two years

QUICK QUIZ 13.C

1. 1. All of the following statements about navigators are correct EXCEPT

   A. navigators are funded by the federal government

   B. navigators are not permitted to sell insurance

   C. navigators can legally provide advice to consumers about which health plan to choose

   D. navigators can help individuals determine their eligibility for public assistance programs

2. What is the penalty for an employer that does NOT offer health coverages and has 50 or more full-time employees?

   A. $2,000 per full-time employee

   B. $2,000 per year

   C. $5,000 per full-time employee

   D. $10,000 per year

Answers can be found at the end of Unit 13.

 UNIT 13 CRAM SHEET

ACA

- Also known as PPACA, Obamacare, and Heath Care Reform
- Signed in 2010 with some reforms
- Additional reforms began January 2014

Grandfathered—existed before ACA

Nongrandfathered—existed after ACA

Individual Mandate

- U.S. citizens and legal residents are required to have qualifying health care coverage.
- There is a tax penalty if they do not have coverage (with some exceptions).

EHB

- Health plans must be qualified to fit ACA standards.
- QHPs, Medicaid state plans, and insurance on the health exchange must meet requirements.

Emergency Medical Services

- No pre-authorization required
- In-network or out-of-network
- Normal cost-sharing requirements

Primary Care Provider

- Every insured and dependent must have a PCP.

Prohibition on Lifetime/Annual Limit

- On all EHBs (except for grandfathered plans)
- Limits allowed on non-EHBs

Metal Tiers

- Four levels of coverage; each must cover minimum EHBs.
- Tiers represent average portion of expected costs.
- Percentages represent how much plan will pay.

Free Preventative Care

- Take care of yourself now to prevent costly, future, chronic conditions.

Pre-existing conditions

- Health plans can no longer exclude pre-existing conditions (except for grandfathered plans).

Coverage of Children to Age 26

- Up to, not including, age 26
- Children can remain if:
    - married;
    - not living with parents;
    - attending school;
    - not financially dependent; or
    - eligible to enroll in employer's plan.
- Past age 26 if unmarried, financially dependent, and have physical or mental impairment

Eligibility

- Depends on:
    - Income
    - Employment status
    - If you have coverage through employer

Guaranteed Issue

- Must be offered to any individual or employer in the state
- Subject to rules

Health Benefit Exchanges/Marketplaces

- Required
- Operated by state or federal government
- Annual open enrollment and special enrollment depending on qualifying events

QHPs

- Provide EHBs
- Only available on the exchange
- Only plan that provides tax credits and cost sharing

SHOP

- Online application to compare health plans
- 50 or less full-time employees

Subsidies

- A sum of money given by the federal government
- Advanced premium tax credits (APTC)
- Cost-sharing (only available in Silver tier)

Navigators

- Funded by government through federal grants
- CANNOT sell insurance or provide advice
- Help determine eligibility for public assistance

Employer Responsibilities

- Employer notification responsibilities
  - Required to let employees know their rights to affordable coverage
- Employer mandate—employer shared responsibility
  - For employers with 50 or more employees
  - Penalty if not followed

Health Care Tax Credit for Small Employers

- Maximum credit
  - 50% of premiums paid for small business employers
  - 35% of premiums paid for small tax-exempt employers
  - Eligible for two years

UNIT 13 QUIZ

In order to measure your success, we recommend that you answer the following 10 questions correctly.

1. Which of the following is NOT a consumer protection that applies to both grandfathered and nongrandfathered plans?
    A. Lifetime dollar limits cannot be applied to essential health benefits.
    B. Dependent coverage must be extended to adult children until age 26.
    C. A policy cannot be canceled solely because of an honest mistake on an application.
    D. A policy must provide certain recommended preventive services for free.

2. Which of the following individuals is excluded from the required minimum essential coverage?
    A. Sarah, age 30, a legal resident of the U.S.
    B. Ricardo, from Mexico, a legal resident of the U.S.
    C. William, born and is raised in the U.S.
    D. Maska, age 27, an American Indian

3. Minimum essential coverage means coverage from any of the following EXCEPT
    A. on-site medical clinics
    B. grandfathered health plans
    C. government-sponsored programs
    D. employer-sponsored plans

4. Which of the following percentages represents the average portion of expected costs covered in the Gold plan?
    A. 90%
    B. 80%
    C. 70%
    D. 60%

5. All of the following statements regarding the essential health benefit of 'coverage of children to age 26' are correct EXCEPT
    A. children can join or remain on the parent's plan even if they are married
    B. grandchildren may be covered if the grandparent is the legal guardian of the child to be insured
    C. grandchildren may be covered if the grandparent is the adoptive parent of the child to be insured
    D. there is a requirement to cover the child of a dependent child

6. Jodi missed the deadline for the annual open enrollment. Which of the following qualifying events would NOT allow her to have a special enrollment?
    A. Marriage
    B. Birth or adoption of a child
    C. Moving to a new state with same health plans
    D. Loss of health coverage due to divorce

7. Which of the following percentages represents that average portion of expected costs covered in Platinum plan?
    A. 70%
    B. 80%
    C. 90%
    D. 100%

8. ABC Printing, a small tax nonexempt company, can get tax credits to help offset the cost of the company's health plan premium contribution for its employees. The maximum credit is

A. 75% of premiums paid

B. 50% of premiums paid

C. 25% of premiums paid

D. 10% of premiums paid

9. How many full-time employees (FTEs) must a company have to be eligible for the Health Care Tax Credit for Small Employers?

A. Less than 2

B. Less than 10

C. Less than 20

D. Less than 25

10. Advanced premium tax credits (APTC) may be applied to lower the insured's monthly premiums. The cost-sharing reduction is only available through a health plan from which tier?

A. Bronze

B. Silver

C. Gold

D. Platinum

ANSWER KEY

QUIZ QUIZZES

QUICK QUIZ 13.A

1. **B.** a grandfathered plan is required to comply with all of the consumer protections of the ACA

2. **D.** Social Insurance Program

QUICK QUIZ 13.B

1. **A.** up to age 26

2. **B.** a pre-existing condition

QUICK QUIZ 13.C

1. **C.** navigators can legally provide advice to consumers about which health plan to choose

2. **A** $2,000 per full-time employee

UNIT QUIZ

1. **D.** Group plans and grandfathered plans are not required to provide certain recommended preventative services for free. Nongrandfathered plans do have this requirement.

2. **D.** Exemptions to the individual mandate may be granted for financial hardship, religious objections, American Indians, those without coverage for less than three months, undocumented immigrants, incarcerated (imprisoned) individuals, those for whom the lowest cost plan option exceeds 8% of an individual's income, and those with incomes below the tax-filing threshold.

3. **A.** Minimum essential coverage does not include on-site medical clinics. On-site medical clinics are considered an excepted benefit.

4. **B.** The percentages the plans will spend, on average, are: Bronze plan 60%, Silver plan 70%, Gold plan 80%, and Platinum plan 90%.

5. **D.** There is no requirement to cover the spouse or child of a dependent child.

6. **C.** Jodi would have to be permanently moving to an area that offers different health plans in order to be eligible for a special enrollment. If she does not have a qualifying event, she will have to wait until the annual enrollment period.

7. **C.** The percentages the plans will spend, on average, are: Bronze plan 60%, Silver plan 70%, Gold plan 80%, and Platinum plan 90%.

8. **B.** The maximum credit is 50% of premiums paid for small business employers and 35% of premiums paid for small tax-exempt employers.

9. **D.** The eligibility formula is based on the number of full-time equivalent employees, not the total number of employees. Employers must have less than 25 FTE employees and cover at least 50% of the coverage cost of employee-only.

10. **B.** The cost-sharing reduction is only available through a health plan from the Silver plan.

UNIT 14 Health Insurance Policy Provisions

14.1 INTRODUCTION

As you learned in earlier units, policies are legal documents that are written to protect the interests of both the insurance company and consumers. In the past, this was especially true regarding health insurance policies.

The Uniform Individual Accident and Sickness Policy Provisions Law standardized contract language in individual accident and health policies. By providing consistent information written using understandable terms, consumers can more easily understand the health products they seek to purchase.

This unit introduces required, optional, and other provisions found in health insurance policies such as required time frames for insureds and insurers to provide proof of loss notices, claims notices, grace periods, and reinstatement provisions.

14.2   LEARNING OBJECTIVES

After successfully completing this unit, you should be able to:

◻ identify the 12 uniform required health insurance policy provisions;

◻ identify the 10 optional health insurance policy provisions; and

◻ identify the five other health insurance provisions.

14.3 UNIFORM POLICY PROVISIONS—HEALTH INSURANCE

The following 12 standard provisions are **MANDATORY** in every insurance contract as directed by the Uniform Health Insurance Policy Provision. Insurance companies are not required to use the exact wording of these provisions, they are allowed to reword them as long as the wording is not **less favorable to the insured.**

14.3.1 Entire Contract; Changes

This provision states that the insurance policy represents a contract between the insurer and the insured and consists of:

- application—copy of the application, if attached to the policy;
- insurance policy—the actual insurance contract itself; and
- riders (endorsements), any other papers or amendments attached to the policy.

In order for something to be included in the contract, it must be in writing, and it must be attached to the policy.

An agent or producer may not change a policy or waive any of its provisions. For a change to be made, it must be approved in writing by an executive officer of the insurance company and attached to the policy in the form of an amendment.

Entire Contract

- Application
- Insurance Policy
- Riders

14.3.2 Time Limit on Certain Defenses (Incontestability Clause)

This provision states that after two years from the date of policy issue, no misstatements, except for fraudulent misstatements made by the applicant in the application for the policy, shall be used to void the policy or deny a claim for loss after this time period. Fraudulent statements are grounds to contest a policy at any time. In addition, the policy cannot deny a claim or reduce benefits on the grounds that an illness or a condition was pre-existing after the policy has been in force for two years. This does not prevent an insurer from specifically excluding coverage for a certain condition, but to be excluded, the condition must be named or specifically described in the policy when it is written and is referred to as an impairment waiver or rider.

NOTE: The federal Affordable Care Act (ACA) eliminated pre-existing condition exclusions for medical expense policies affected by ACA. However, it is important to note that pre-existing condition exclusions are still allowed for disability policies, long-term care insurance, Medicare supplements, and limited-benefit policies.

Time Limit on Contesting Application Information

- Two years after application
- Fraud in the application can void the policy when discovered

14.3.3 Grace Period

A grace period is a specified time following the due date of a premium payment in which the premium has not been paid. A loss that occurs during the grace period would be covered minus the premium that was due.

The grace periods are as follows:

- 7 days—weekly premium policies;
- 10 days—monthly premium policies; or
- 31 days—all other policies (annually, semiannually, or quarterly).

Grace period following due date of premium

- 7 days if premium paid weekly
- 10 days if premium paid monthly
- 31 days if premium paid annual, semi-annual or quarterly
- Insurance still in force during grace period
- Unpaid premiums deducted from a claim

14.3.4 Reinstatement

If the premium on the health policy is not paid by the end of the grace period, the policy will lapse and coverage will terminate. The policy is reinstated when the delinquent payment is accepted by the insurer or its agent. If the insurer requires a reinstatement application to be submitted, a conditional receipt will be issued for the premium and reinstatement is effective on approval of the application. Coverage is automatically reinstated 45 days after the application is submitted if the insurer has not disapproved the application and notified the applicant by that time. The premium may be applied to a previous period of unpaid coverage, but that unpaid period may not be more than 60 days before the date of reinstatement.

Once a policy is reinstated, there is a **10-day** probationary period for sickness coverage. There is no probationary period for accident coverage.

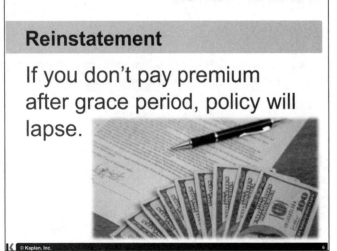

Reinstatement

- Application and receipt
- Must deny within 45 days after application or policy is in effect
- Accident claims covers immediately
- Sickness claims covered 10 days after reinstatement

14.3.5 Notice of Claim

Written notice of claim must be given to the insurer within **20 days** after occurrence or commencement of any loss covered by the policy or as soon thereafter as is reasonably possible.

If the insured suffers loss of time on account of disability for which indemnity may be payable for at least **two years,** the insured shall give notice to the insurer once every **six months** of the continuance of the disability except in the case of legal incapacity.

Notice of Claim

- 20 days after loss
- If continuing disability can only be required to provide proof every six months

14.3.6 Claim Forms

Insurers must provide a claim form within 15 days upon receipt of the insured's notice of a claim. If the forms are not furnished within 15 days, the insured shall be deemed to have complied with the proof of loss requirement upon submitting written proof that describes the occurrence and the character and extent of the loss.

Claim Forms

Insur<u>ers</u> provide the claim form to the insur<u>ed</u>.

Claim Forms

- Must be furnished to insured within 15 days of notice of loss

14.3.7 Proof of Loss

Written proof of loss must be provided to the insurer within 90 days of the date of loss. If it is not reasonably possible to furnish proof within 90 days, it does not invalidate nor reduce any claim. Proof of loss may be filed up to one year after the date of loss unless the insured has a legal incapacity.

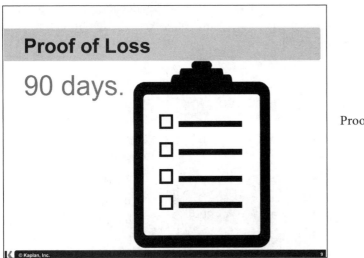

Proof of Loss

- Within 90 days

14.3.8 Time of Payment of Claims

Insurers must pay lump sum claims immediately after receiving proof of loss. For claims involving periodic payments such as disability income, payments must be made at least monthly.

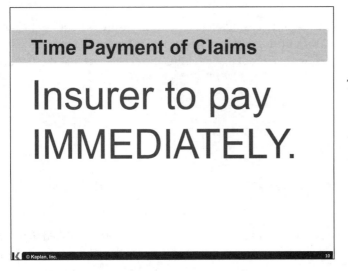

Time Payment of Claims

- Immediately
- At least monthly if a periodic claim such as a long term disability policy or long term care policy

14.3.9 Payment of Claims

This provision states how and to whom payments are to be made. All benefits are payable to the insured while they are alive unless the policy designates a different payee. Death benefits will be paid to either:

- the named beneficiary, or
- the insured's estate if no beneficiary is named or the beneficiary is deceased.

If the insured was receiving monthly benefits and some accrued benefits remain after the insured's death, they will be paid to the beneficiary or the insured's estate.

Policies may also include an optional provision allowing payment of up to $1,000 in benefits to any relative of the insured or beneficiary by blood or marriage that appears to be entitled to them. A second optional provision can allow the payment of benefits directly to a medical provider.

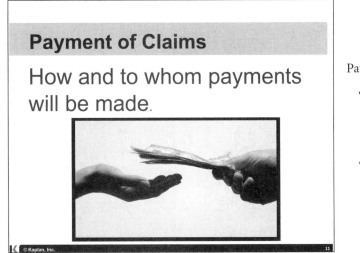

Payment of Claims
- Any death benefits
  - Beneficiary
  - Insured's estate
- Facility of payment
  - $1,000 to a family member

14.3.10   Physical Examination and Autopsy

Insurers may require insureds to submit to a physical examination. Insurers may also require an autopsy to be performed on a deceased insured. The insurer pays the cost of the physical exam and autopsy.

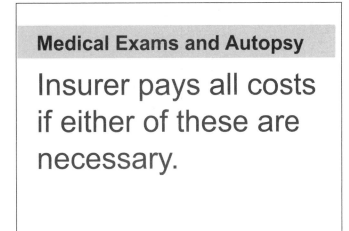

Medical Exams and Autopsy
- If company requires and state law allows

14.3.11   Legal Actions

No action at law can be brought to recover on the policy:

- prior to 60 days after filing a written proof of loss, or
- after the expiration of 3 years after filing a written proof of loss.

Legal Action Against Insurer

- Earliest 60 days after proof of loss
- Maximum three years after proof of loss

14.3.12   Change of Beneficiary

The right to change beneficiaries is up to policyowner. If the beneficiary is designated as irrevocable, changes may not be made to the policy without the beneficiary's permission.

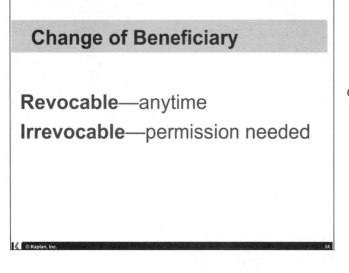

Change of Beneficiary

- Any time by owner if revocable
- Permission of beneficiary needed if irrevocable

 QUICK QUIZ 14.A

1. Marcus pays his insurance premium monthly and has a grace period of

   A. 7 days

   B. 10 days

   C. 30 days

   D. 31 days

2. All of the following are mandatory health insurance provisions, EXCEPT

   A. time limit on certain defenses

   B. proof of loss

   C. payment of claims

   D. renewability

Answers can be found at the end of Unit 14.

14.4 OPTIONAL POLICY PROVISIONS

The following 10 optional provisions may or may not be included in a policy. Insurers may use any of them they choose.

14.4.1 Change of Occupation

The risk involved in an occupation affects the chances of an insured being disabled. This provision states that the insurance company may make changes to the premium rates or benefits if the insured changes occupations.

If the insured changes to a **more hazardous** occupation, the insurer will **reduce benefits** to whatever the premium would have purchased at the higher risk occupation.

If the insured changes to an occupation classified as **less hazardous**. The insurer will **reduce the premium** rate accordingly and return the excess pro rata unearned premium to the insured.

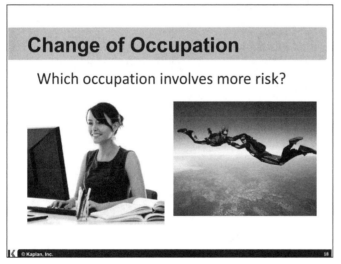

Change of Occupation
- More hazardous
  - Reduction of benefits
- Less hazardous
  - Refund of excess premiums

14.4.2 Misstatement of Age

If an insured's age is misstated on the application, all amounts payable shall be adjusted to the amount the premium paid would have purchased at the correct age. The insurer will adjust benefits based on the correct information.

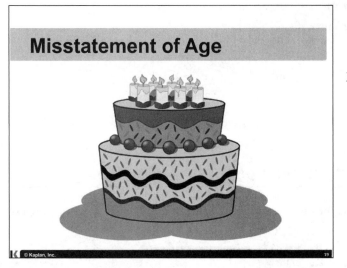

Misstatement of Age

- Younger than stated in application
  - Benefits increased
- Older than stated in application
  - Benefits reduced

14.4.3 Other Insurance with This Insurer

If an insured has more than one policy of a similar type with an insurance company, the insurer can limit the amount of benefits that will be paid under all contracts. Insurance over a specified amount is considered to be void and the premium paid for these benefits will be returned to the insured or their estate.

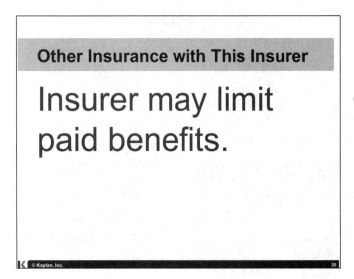

Other Insurance with This Insurer

- Total of all polices exceeds maximum
  - Benefits reduced
  - Excess premiums refunded

14.4.4 Insurance with Other Insurers

If an insured has coverage with another insurer providing benefits for the same loss, the amount paid by the two insurers will be prorated. Any excess premium will be refunded to the policyowner.

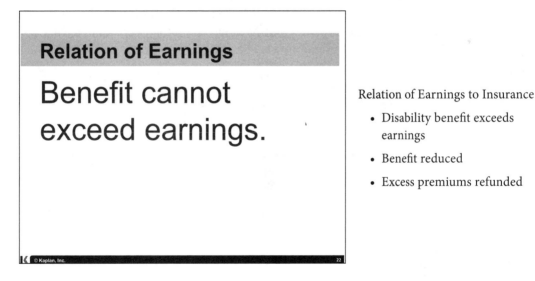

Insurance with Other Insurer

- Each company pays a proportionate share
- Excess premiums are refunded

14.4.5 Relation of Earnings to Insurance (Average Earnings)

If an insured's total disability income benefit exceeds the greater of the insured's earnings at the time of disability or the insured's average monthly earnings for the past two years, the benefit payable is reduced accordingly and the premium paid for the excess coverage is refunded to the insured.

Relation of Earnings to Insurance

- Disability benefit exceeds earnings
- Benefit reduced
- Excess premiums refunded

14.4.6 Unpaid Premium

If a premium is due at the time a claim is made under a policy, the amount of the premium will be deducted from the benefit payable under the claim.

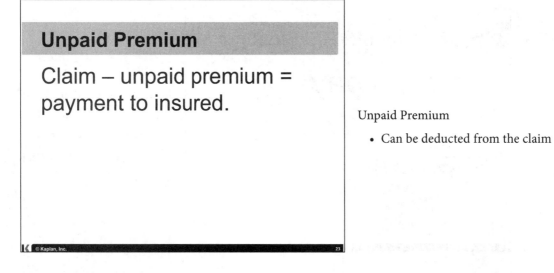

Unpaid Premium

- Can be deducted from the claim

14.4.7 Cancellation

The insurer may cancel a policy at any time by giving the insured five days written notice. If an insured cancels a policy, cancellation is effective when written notice is received by the insurer. In either case, cancellation does not affect any pending claim.

If the insurer cancelled the policy, unearned premium will be returned to the insured on a *pro rata* basis. If the insured cancelled the policy, the insurer is allowed to calculate the unearned premium on a *short rate* basis, unearned premium minus company expenses will be returned to the policyowner.

Cancellation

- Company must give at least a five day notice
- Unearned premium must be refunded pro rata
- Insured cancels short rate penalty will apply

14.4.8 Conformity with State Statutes

This provision automatically amends any policy provision to conform to the minimum requirements of the insured's state of residence.

Conformity with the State

Minimum requirements must be met.

25

Conformity with State Statutes

- Makes policy comply with laws of the insured's state of residence

14.4.9 Illegal Occupation

The insurer will not be liable for any loss that was caused by the insured's commission of or attempt to commit a felony. The insurer also is not liable for a loss caused by the insured engaging in an illegal occupation.

Illegal Occupation

26

Illegal Occupation

- No benefits
  - If committing a felony
  - Engaged in an illegal occupation

14.4.10   Narcotics

The insurer shall not be liable for any loss sustained by the insured while under the influence of alcohol or a narcotic unless it was taken under the advice of a physician.

Narcotics

- No benefits
  - Loss caused by alcohol or narcotics unless doctor's orders

QUICK QUIZ 14.B

1. All of the following are optional health insurance provisions EXCEPT
    A. change of beneficiary
    B. narcotics
    C. unpaid premium
    D. insurance with other insurer

2. How many days' notice must the insured be given if an insurer cancels a policy?
    A. 2
    B. 3
    C. 5
    D. 10

Answers can be found at the end of Unit 14.

14.5   OTHER HEALTH INSURANCE PROVISIONS

14.5.1 Right to Examine (Free Look)

When a policy is delivered to the insured, they have the right to look it over and decide whether or not to keep it. If the policy is not wanted for any reason, it may be returned for a full refund of premium. The most common health insurance free-look period is 10 days. However, long-term care insurance and Medicare supplements have 30-day free-look periods. If the policy is returned during the free look, the contract is void and the insurer is not liable for any claim.

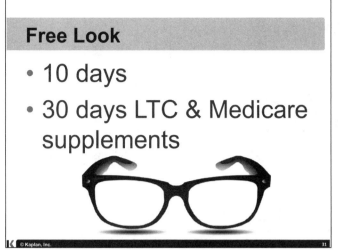

Free Look

- 10 days from receipt (30 days for senior products-Medicare Supplements, Long Term Care)
- Begins date received by policy holder
- If policy returned—complete refund of money

14.5.2 Insuring Clause

The **insuring clause** states the insurer's promise to pay under the conditions described in the policy. It also identifies the type of loss covered by the contract.

Insuring Clause

- Promise to pay
- Conditions of payment

14.5.3 Consideration Clause

Consideration is an exchange of value and is a necessary element of a legal contract. The consideration clause in a health insurance policy identifies the insurer's consideration as its promise to pay benefits and the consideration given by the insured are the statements made in the application and the premium.

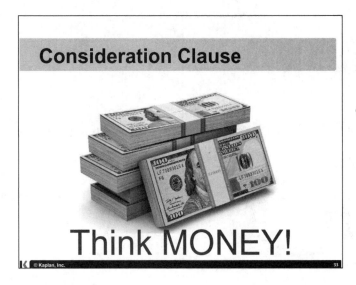

Consideration Clause

- Company promises to pay
- Applicant provides information and pays premium

14.5.4 Renewability

Health policies have to be renewed periodically. The policyowner always has the right to cancel a policy or allow it to lapse.

Whether an insurer may refuse to renew a policy depends upon the renewability provision in the policy. The more favorable the renewability provision is to the insured, the higher the premium. The less favorable the provision is to the insured, the lower the premium.

The renewability provisions can be classified into five types. They are listed from the least favorable and least expensive for the insured (cancellable) to the most favorable and most expensive for the insured (non-cancelable):

- *cancelable*; the insurer can cancel it at any time;

- *optionally renewable*; the insurer has the option to renew or not for any reason on a premium due or anniversary date. Premiums may be increased on the policy anniversary for a class of insureds;

- *conditionally renewable*; the insurer may terminate coverage but only for reasons not based on the insured's health such as reaching a certain age. Premiums may be increased on the policy anniversary for a class of insureds;

- *guaranteed renewable*; the policy cannot be canceled except for non-payment of premium, and premiums may increase on a renewal date if the insurer has raised premiums for all insureds in that coverage classification; or

- *non-cancelable*; the insurer cannot cancel coverage (except for non-payment of premium) or raise premiums.

Renewability

- Five types of provisions
- More favorable for insured = higher premium

Renewability (Extension of Policy)

- Cancelable
  - Any time
- Optionally renewable
  - Company may not renew
    - Anniversary or premium due date
- Conditionally renewable
  - Nonrenewal can occur only under certain conditions
  - Such as reaching age 65
- Guaranteed renewability
  - Insurer must renew
  - Premiums can be raised by classes
- Noncancelable
  - Insurer must renew
  - Premiums cannot be raised

14.5.5 Military Suspense Provision

Under this provision, coverage is temporarily suspended if the insured is serving in the military. Coverage is reactivated when the insured leaves military service.

Military Suspense

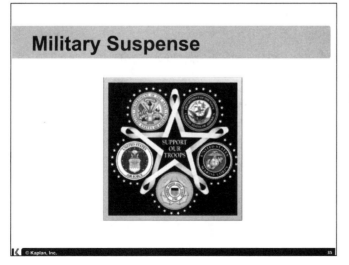

Military Suspense

- Temporary suspension while in military
- Reactivated after leaving military

QUICK QUIZ 14.C

1. Which provision allows new insureds the right to examine a policy for a specified period of time with the option to return it?

    A. Insuring clause

    B. Free look period

    C. Consideration clause

    D. Renewability

2. The exchange of something of value is known as

    A. a consideration

    B. an insuring agreement

    C. a free-look

    D. a provision

Answers can be found at the end of Unit 14

UNIT 14 CRAM SHEET

Health Policy Provisions

- Entire contract (remember "AIR")

    – Application of insurance

    – Insurance Policy

    – Riders

- Time limit on contesting application information

    – Two years after application

    – Fraud in the application can void the policy when discovered

- Grace period following due date of premium

    – Insurance still in force during grace period

    – 7 days if premium paid weekly

    – 10 days if premium paid monthly

    – 31 days if premium paid annual, semi-annual or quarterly

    – Unpaid premiums deducted from a claim

- Reinstatement

    – Application and receipt

    – Must deny within 45 days after application or policy is in effect

    – Accident claims covers immediately

    – Sickness claims covered 10 days after reinstatement, a probationary period will apply

- Notice of claim
  - 20 days after loss
  - If continuing disability can only be required to provide proof every 6 months
- Claim forms
  - Must be furnished to insured within 15 days of notice of loss
- Proof of loss
  - Within 90 days
- Time payment of claims
  - Immediately
  - At least monthly if disability or long term care insurance
- Payment of claims
  - Any death benefits
    - Beneficiary
    - Insured's estate
  - Facility of payment
  - $1,000 to a family member
- Medical exams and autopsy
  - If company requires and state law allows
  - Company pays all costs
- Legal action against insurer
  - Earliest 60 days after proof of loss
  - Maximum three years after proof of loss
- Change of beneficiary
  - Any time by owner if revocable
  - Permission of beneficiary needed if irrevocable

Optional provisions

- Change of occupation
  - More hazardous
    - Reduction of benefits
  - Less hazardous
    - Refund of excess premiums
- Misstatement of age
  - Younger than stated in application
    - Benefits increased
  - Older than stated in application
    - Benefits reduced

- Other insurance with this insurer
  - Total of all polices exceeds maximum
    - Benefits reduced
    - Excess premiums refunded
- Insurance with other insurer
  - Each company pays a proportionate share
  - Excess premiums are refunded
- Relation of earnings to insurance
  - Disability benefit exceeds earnings
  - Benefit reduced
  - Excess premiums refunded
- Unpaid premium
  - Can be deducted from the claim
- Cancellation
  - Company must give at least a five day notice
  - Unearned premium must be refunded pro rata
  - Insured cancels short rate penalty will apply
- Conformity with state statutes
  - makes policy comply with laws of the insured's state of residence
- Illegal occupation
  - No benefits
    - If committing a felony
    - Engaged in an illegal occupation
- Alcohol and narcotics
  - No benefits
    - Loss caused by alcohol and narcotics unless doctor's orders

Other Provisions

- Free look
  - 10 days from receipt (30 days for senior products-Medicare Supplements, Long Term Care Insurance)
  - Begins date received by policy holder
  - If policy returned—complete refund of money
- Insuring clause
  - Promise to pay
  - Conditions of payment

- Consideration clause
  - Company promises to pay
  - Applicant provides information and pays premium
- Renewability (extension of policy)
  - Cancelable
    - Any time
- Optionally renewable
  - Company may not renew
    - Anniversary or premium due date
- Conditionally renewable
  - Nonrenewal can occur only under certain conditions
  - Such as reaching age 65
- Guaranteed renewability
  - Insurer must renew
  - Premiums can be raised by classes
- Noncancelable
  - Insurer must renew
  - Premiums cannot be raised
- Military suspense
  - Temporary suspension while in military
  - Reactivated after leaving military

UNIT 14 QUIZ

In order to measure your success, we recommend that you answer the following 10 questions correctly.

1. According to the entire contract provision, the entire contract includes all of the following EXCEPT
   A. the insurance policy
   B. the premium payment
   C. any endorsements
   D. any attachments

2. Generally, written proofs of loss must be furnished within how many days after the loss?
   A. 15
   B. 45
   C. 60
   D. 90

3. If there is no beneficiary listed on a policy, benefits will be paid to
   A. the state
   B. the insured's estate
   C. the insured's nearest blood relative
   D. the insured's nearest relative by marriage or blood

4. The insurer may generally require an autopsy at its own expense unless
   A. the deceased requests in writing that an autopsy not be performed
   B. the deceased's relatives request that an autopsy not be performed
   C. the deceased's relatives have proven religious objections to an autopsy being performed
   D. the state has an applicable law that forbids autopsy

5. When Betty purchased her insurance policy, her age was recorded as 32 when she was actually 34. Assuming her policy includes the misstatement of age provision and the insurance company discovers this four years later, Betty's policy
   A. will be canceled for misrepresentation
   B. will be unchanged because the incontestable period has expired
   C. limits will be lowered
   D. limits will be raised

6. The optional provisions that deal with multiple insurance policies of the same type on a single insured deal with the problem of
   A. underinsurance
   B. over-insurance
   C. inappropriate insurance
   D. incorrect insurance

7. A pro rata return is one in which the insurer returns
   A. less than the proportionate amount of the unearned premium
   B. the proportionate amount of the unearned premium
   C. both earned and unearned premium
   D. neither earned nor unearned premium

8. The grace period varies according to
   A. premium payment frequency
   B. premium payment amount
   C. method of premium payment
   D. type of policy

9. Mike allows his policy to lapse, then applies for reinstatement using the company's required application. The company does not inform Mike either that the policy has been accepted or that the policy is being rejected. At what point can Mike consider the policy reinstated?

   A. Not until the insurer notifies him that it has been reinstated

   B. As soon as the application has been submitted

   C. After 45 days

   D. After 90 days

10. A reinstated policy will cover

    A. sickness immediately and accidents after 10 days

    B. both sickness and accidents after 10 days

    C. accidents after 10 days and sickness after 30 days

    D. accidents immediately and sickness after 10 days

ANSWER KEY

QUICK QUIZZES

QUICK QUIZ 14.A

1. **B.**   10 days

2. **D.**   renewability

QUICK QUIZ 14.B

1. **A.**   change of beneficiary

2. **C.**   5

QUICK QUIZ 14.C

1. **B.**   Free look period

2. **A.**   a consideration

UNIT QUIZ

1. **B.**   The entire contract clause specifies what is included in the contract and that all parts must be in writing and attached. The premium is not part of the entire contract.

2. **D.**   Proof of loss must be provided to the insurer within 90 days of the actual loss.

3. **B.**   If there is no beneficiary listed on a policy, benefits will be paid to the estate.

4. **D.**   The insurer must pay for the cost of the autopsy.

5. **C.**   Because her age was understated, her limits will be lowered.

6. **B.**   Other insurance with this insurer and insurance with others insurers address the issue of over-insurance.

7. **B.**   The proportionate amount of the unearned premium is the entire amount and must be returned if the insurer cancelled the policy.

8. **A.**   31 days for annual premium payments, 10 days for monthly premium payments, and 7 days for premiums paid weekly.

9. **C.**   Coverage is automatically reinstated 45 days after the application is submitted by the insured.

10. **D.**   When benefits are reinstated, the policy will cover accidents immediately and sickness after 10 days.

UNIT 15 Disability Income Insurance

15.1 INTRODUCTION

Most people can understand the need for health, life, and auto insurance, but what would happen to someone's income if they couldn't work due to an illness or injury. Not only would they have the stress of meeting everyday living expenses, they might have to put other goals, like saving for retirement, on hold.

This unit discusses disability income insurance, a product that provides supplementary income in the event of an illness or accident resulting in a disability that would prevent the insured from working at their regular employment.

15.2   LEARNING OBJECTIVES

After successfully completing this unit, you should be able to:

▫ identify when an individual qualifies for disability benefits;

▫ explain the differences between own occupation and any occupation when determining disability;

▫ describe pure loss of income (income replacement contracts);

▫ identify presumptive disability;

▫ explain physician care requirement;

▫ identify individual disability income insurance and the benefits, elimination period, benefit period, and waiver or premium;

▫ explain the coordination of disability insurance with Government benefits: Additional monthly benefit rider, Social insurance supplement riders, and occupational versus non-occupational;

▫ describe at-work benefits: partial disability, residual disability, and recurrent disability;

▫ identify other provisions affecting income benefits: cost-of-living adjustment rider, future increase option rider, and the relation of earning to insurance provision;

▫ explain other cash benefits including Accidental death and dismemberment, rehabilitation benefit, and medical reimbursement benefit;

▫ explain the refund provisions—return of premium and cash surrender value—and their exclusions;

▫ identify the unique aspects of disability underwriting: occupational limits, benefits limits, and policy issuance alternatives;

▫ describe group disability income insurance and the know the difference between group and individual;

▫ explain short term disability and long-term disability;

▫ identify business disability insurance including key person, business overhead expense policy, and disability buy-sell insurance;

▫ describe social security disability and the benefits available and how to qualify; and

▫ explain workers' compensation and its relationship to disability insurance.

15.3   QUALIFYING FOR DISABILITY BENEFITS

The criteria needed for an individual to qualify for disability benefits are universal for most policies with very rare exceptions.

Benefits can be paid only after meeting the requirements defined in the DI policy.

15.3.1   Inability to Perform Work Duties

Disability is defined as the inability to work.

Work can be categorized as:

- one's own occupation, or
- any occupation.

15.3.1.1 Own Occupation

Under the **own occupation** definition, disability is defined as an insured's inability to perform any or all of the duties of their occupation at the time the disability begins. Lee is a page layout specialist and loses three fingers on each hand in an accident. Under the own occupation definition, Lee is unable to use the keyboard—a primary duty of his occupation, and is disabled.

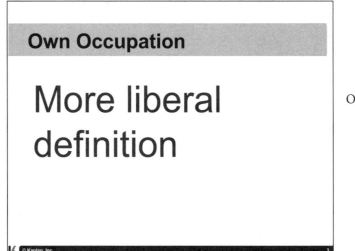

Own Occupation

- Inability to perform any or all of the duties of insured's normal occupation

15.3.1.2 Any Occupation

With the **any occupation** definition, an insured is disabled if they are unable to perform the duties of *any* occupation for which they are reasonably qualified by education, training, or experience. Lee personally could not format pages but he could teach others that skill. Using the any occupation definition Lee would not qualify for disability benefits.

Some policies use both definitions—own occupation for a few years, then any occupation for the remainder of the disability period.

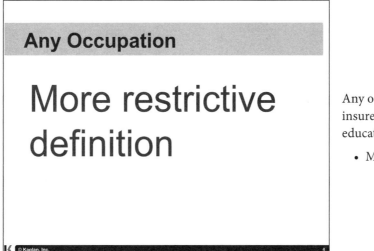

Any occupation for which the insured is qualified by training education and experience

- More difficult to qualify

15.3.2 Pure Loss of Income (Income Replacement Contracts)

An **income replacement contract** pays a benefit if the insured experiences a loss of income as a result of suffering a covered illness or injury. The benefit trigger is the amount of income the insured is receiving at the time of the claim.

Lee cannot work due to a disability and is not earning an income following his accident. He would receive the full benefit under an income replacement contract. Lee was able to use a stylus and voice-activated software to proofread documents. The proofreading job did not pay as well as his formatting job. His income replacement contract would pay part of its benefit so that the combination of Lee's earnings and the benefit would replace a specified percentage of his former earnings.

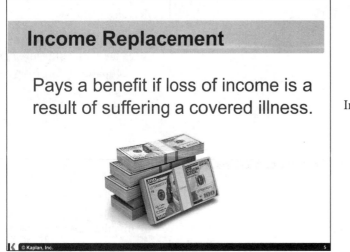

Income Replacement

- A reduction in income triggers payment

15.3.3 Presumptive Disability

Presumptive disability is a condition that automatically qualifies insureds for disability benefits whether or not they can work. Conditions generally considered to be presumptive disabilities include:

- loss of or loss of use of any two limbs;
- total and permanent blindness in both eyes;
- total loss of speech; and
- total loss of hearing in both ears.

If Lee's right arm and leg are severed in an accident; he is presumptively disabled. However, if only his left leg is lost, he is not considered disabled because only one limb is involved.

Presumptive disability may also be determined using the loss of earnings test. The insured's level of earnings before disability is compared to the level of earnings after disability. If post-disability earnings fall below pre-disability earnings by a given percentage, the insured is considered totally disabled and eligible for a full benefit even if he or she is earning some income.

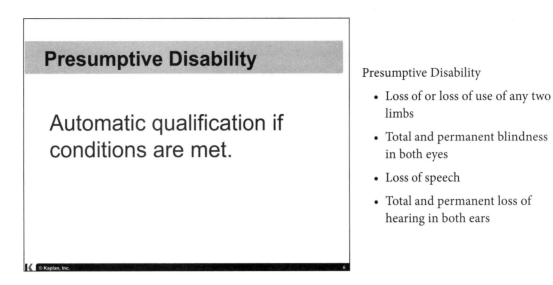

Presumptive Disability

- Loss of or loss of use of any two limbs
- Total and permanent blindness in both eyes
- Loss of speech
- Total and permanent loss of hearing in both ears

15.3.4 Physician Care Requirement

Some older policies required that the insured be confined to the house and under the treatment of a doctor. This is called a *medically defined* disability.

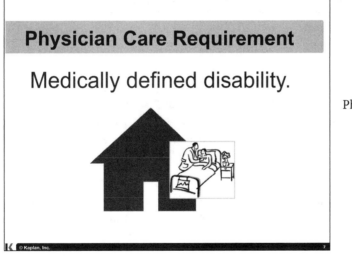

Physician Care Requirement

- House confinement and doctors care

QUICK QUIZ 15.A

1. Which of the following terms describes a condition that automatically qualifies insureds for disability benefits whether or not they can work?
   A. Own occupation
   B. Any occupation
   C. Pure loss of income
   D. Presumptive disability

2. Which type of insurance protects against loss of earned income due to sickness or injury sustained in an accident?
   A. Disability income insurance
   B. Life insurance
   C. Health insurance
   D. Accident insurance

Answers can be found at the end of Unit 15.

15.4 INDIVIDUAL DISABILITY INCOME INSURANCE

15.4.1 Basic Total Disability Plans

15.4.1.1 Benefits (Monthly Indemnity)

When an individual qualifies for benefits, disability income plans pay a monthly amount to make up for lost earnings due to the insured's inability to work. The benefit is referred to as an **indemnity**—it returns the insured to their original financial condition before the loss.

15.4.1.2 Elimination Period

The **elimination period** or **waiting period** is the time period an insured must be disabled before benefits begin. The elimination period may be thought of as a kind of deductible – a *time* deductible rather than a dollar deductible. The elimination period keeps the insurance company from paying claims for short term or temporary disabilities. When the elimination period is satisfied, benefits begin and they are not paid retroactively.

Elimination periods may be 30, 60, 90, or 180 days or longer, depending on the time period selected. A longer elimination period would reduce the insurance premium, and make the disability income policy more affordable.

15.4.1.3 Benefit Period

Benefits are paid during the disability period or until the end of a specified period of time called the **benefit period.** Typical benefit periods are one year, two years, five years, and to age 65

The longer the benefit period, the higher the policy premium.

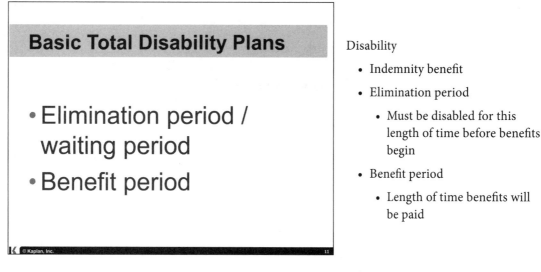

15.4.1.4 *Waiver of Premium*

The **waiver of premium** feature eliminates the need to pay premiums during any period of disability. This feature become effective after the waiting period is satisfied. The waiver premium is retroactively effective to the beginning of the waiting period and any premium paid during this period of time will be refunded once benefit payments begin.

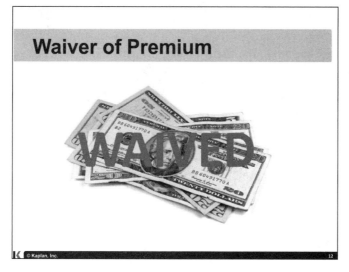

15.4.2 Coordination with Government Benefits

Disabled insureds may also receive benefits from Workers' Compensation or other government programs. During the planning process, the agent/producer must account for the possibility of an insured receiving too many benefits because this can encourage *malingering*. The other possibility is receiving benefits that do not meet the individual's income needs.

15.4.2.1 *Additional Monthly Benefit (AMB) Rider*

Government programs have long waiting periods and take a long time to process disability claims. The **Additional Monthly Benefit (AMB) rider** pays an additional benefit amount with the regular monthly benefit for a limited period of time, usually six or 12 months. This additional benefit is paid even if the insured is getting government benefits during that period of time.

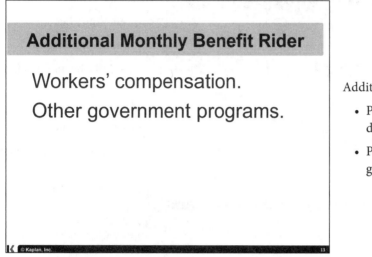

Additional Monthly Benefit Rider

- Pays an additional benefit during first six to 12 months
- Pays even if the insured receives government benefits

15.4.2.2 Social Insurance Supplements (SIS)

The **Social Insurance Supplement (SIS) rider** is a monthly benefit. For those receiving a benefit for total disability this rider pays for additional benefits, less any legislated benefits like Social Security or Workers' Compensation for the same period of time. The payment is in addition to other benefits payable under the insurance policy.

Social Insurance Supplement rider benefits continue only as long as regular policy benefits are payable:

- during the policy's benefit period, and
- while the insured remains disabled.

Social Insurance Supplement

- Pays when social benefits are not being paid
- Makes up the difference between the government benefit and the amount of the rider
- Pays only during the policy benefit period

15.4.2.3 Occupational vs. Non-occupational Coverage

Because workers' compensation covers on-the-job injuries and illnesses, some disability income insurance is **non-occupational**—covering disabilities that result from non-job-related illnesses or injuries. Most disability income insurance covers both job-related and non-job-related disabilities. Such coverage is referred to as **occupational**.

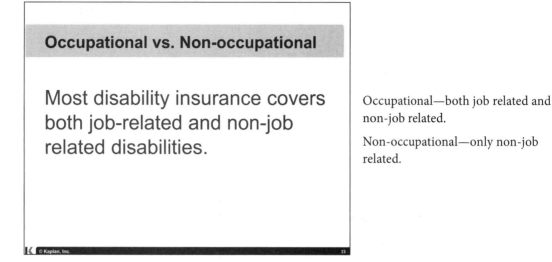

Occupational—both job related and non-job related.

Non-occupational—only non-job related.

15.4.3 At-Work Benefits

Insurers offer reduced benefits for individuals who are impaired, but not totally disabled, and return to work.

15.4.3.1 Partial Disability Benefits

Partial disability means the person can perform some, but not all, of the essential duties of his or her occupation. The partial disability benefit is 50% of the total disability benefit. Partial disability benefits are paid for a relatively short period—commonly three or six months. An individual may qualify for these benefits either as a result of suffering a partially disabling illness or injury and returns to work in a reduced capacity.

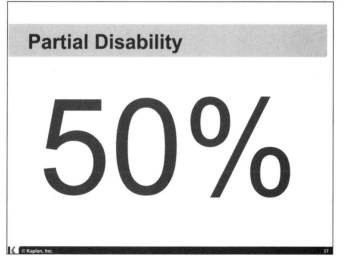

Partial Disability

- Returns to work in a reduced capacity
- Usually pays 50% of total benefit
- Usually no longer than three to six months

15.4.3.2 Residual Disability Benefits

Residual disability benefits are another alternative for partial disability. These benefits are paid when the insured cannot perform some of the duties of his or her occupation and are based on the amount of income lost rather than 50% of the total disability benefit.

To receive residual disability benefits, the insured's earnings must be reduced by a stated percentage due to the disability; example -20%. If the reduced income is less than the stated percentage, no benefit is payable.

If earnings meet or exceed the stated percentage, then the loss is multiplied by the total disability benefit to determine the benefit payment. For example, if earnings are reduced by 40% due to the disability, and the monthly disability benefit is $1,000, the insured would receive $400 each month in residual disability benefits.

Residual disability benefits can be paid whether the insured is working full-time or part-time, and are paid throughout the benefit period as long as the insured's income is reduced.

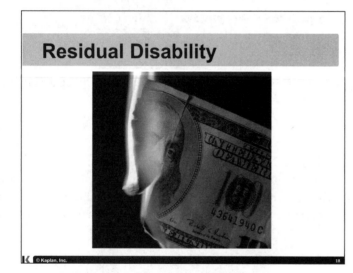

Residual Disability

- Paid whether insured is able to work full or part time

- Benefit based on reduction of income

- Pays as long as the reduction in income continues

15.4.4 Recurrent Disability

The **recurrent disability** provision protects employees who return to work, but become disabled again for the same or a related cause. If this situation occurs within a certain period of time, the insured is considered still disabled from the original disability and is not subject to a new elimination period.

This provision encourages employees to return to work without the fear of losing benefits if their disability continues.

Judy has a disability income insurance policy with a 90 day recurrent provision. She is disabled by severe back pain, receives benefits, and returns to work on February 1. On April 1, back pain again prevents Judy from working, and she begins receiving benefits immediately because of the 90-day recurrent provision.

With recurrent disability, if Judy's second period of disability had been brought on by a something other than back pain, she would have had to wait until the elimination period had passed to begin receiving benefits.

Recurrent Disability

Encourage employees to return to work.

© Kaplan, Inc.   19

Recurrent Disability

- Condition recurs after returning to work
- Doesn't have to wait to start receiving benefits
- Conditions must recur within a certain time frame after returning to work

 QUICK QUIZ 15.B

1. The amount of time an insured must be disabled before receiving benefits is known as the
   A. indemnity period
   B. elimination period
   C. benefit period
   D. grace period

2. Rachelle was injured but is still able to perform some of the essential duties of her occupation. Regardless of income lost, Rachelle will receive 50% of the benefit for total disability for six months. Rachelle most likely has a
   A. recurrent disability
   B. residual disability
   C. partial disability
   D. at-work disability

Answers can be found at the end of Unit 15

15.4.5 Other Provisions Affecting Income Benefits

15.4.5.1 Cost-of-Living Adjustment (COLA) Rider

Inflation will impact the purchasing power of disability benefits over time and for this reason most insurers offer an optional **cost-of-living adjustment (COLA) rider**. The benefit received by a disabled insured is increased automatically to match increases in the Consumer Price Index (CPI). Typically, cost-of-living adjustments are made every 12 months for as long as the insured receives disability benefits.

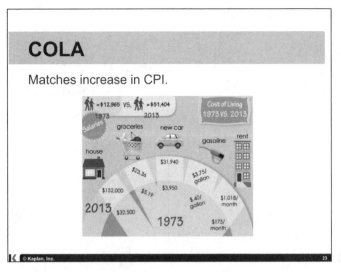

Cost of Living Rider (COLA)

- Increases benefit while receiving disability
- Based on the Consumer Price Index
- Adjustments usually made every 12 months

15.4.5.2 Future Increase Option (FIO) Rider

The future increase option (FIO) rider allows insureds to buy additional amounts of disability income insurance coverage at stated future times without having to provide proof of insurability. The rate for the additional coverage will be based on the insured's attained age at the time of purchase, not the age when the policy was originally issued.

This benefit has some limitations. To avoid over-insurance, the insured is able to buy only a predetermined amount of additional coverage at each option date. Also, the insured's earned income must have increased to the point that the additional coverage is needed.

The number of purchase option dates is also limited. Usually, the rider provides option dates every three years from ages 25 to 50.

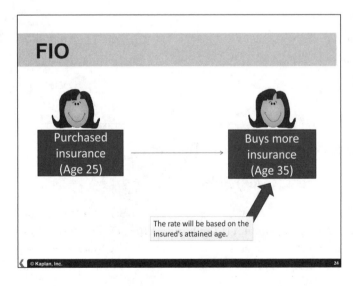

Future Increase Option (FIO)

- Allows insured to increase policy benefits
- No evidence of insurability required
- The insured's income must have increased

15.4.5.3 Relation of Earnings to Insurance

Under the **relation of earning to insurance** provision, the insurer can reduce the benefit paid to a disabled insured if the insured's income is less than when they bought the policy. The insurer will base the amount of the benefit on the insured's average income over a previous 24 month period.

Benefit reductions are made in proportion to the drop in the insured's earnings. If earnings have fallen 20% since the policy was purchased; the benefit will be reduced by 20%. The insurer will refund a portion of the insured's premium representing the decrease in coverage.

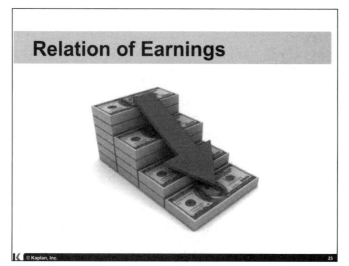

Relation of Earnings to Insurance

- Allows insurer to change policy benefit if insured's income has decreased

- Portion of the premium will be refunded

15.4.6 Other Cash Benefits

15.4.6.1 Accidental Death and Dismemberment (AD&D)

The AD&D rider pays the *principal sum,* the full benefit, if the insured dies or loses two limbs or the sight in both eyes in an accident. The *capital sum*, one-half of the principal sum, is paid if the insured loses one limb or the sight in one eye.

When attached to a disability income insurance policy, the benefit is usually expressed as a multiple of the monthly indemnity amount. For example, the death benefit might be stated as a sum equal to 48 times the monthly disability benefit.

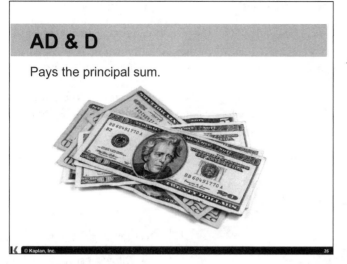

Accidental Death & Dismemberment

- Amount of the rider is the principal sum
  - Paid if accidental death – usually a multiple of the monthly disability benefit
  - Loss of sight in both eyes or loses two limbs

15.4.6.2 Rehabilitation Benefit

The rehabilitation benefit pays for vocational training to prepare insureds for a new occupation when they are totally disabled and unable to return to their normal occupation.

If the insured decides to get into an insurer-approved vocational rehabilitation program, then total disability benefits will continue as long as the insured actively participates in the program and remains disabled.

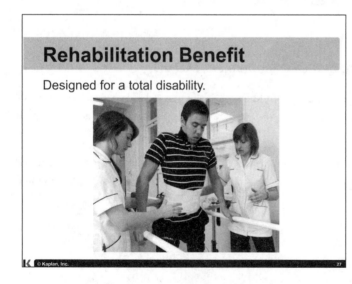

Rehabilitation Benefit

- Helps insured train for a new occupation
- Pays as long as insured is disabled and stays in the program

15.4.6.3 Medical Reimbursement Benefit (Non-Disabling Injury)

This benefit does not pay a disability benefit but instead reimburses the insured for medical expenses incurred to treat a non-disabling injury.

Medical Reimbursement

- Helps pay medical bills for a non-disabling injury

15.4.7 Provisions

15.4.7.1 Return of Premium

A **return of premium rider** provides for the return of a percentage of premiums paid (usually 80%) for a stated time period (usually every 10 years). The amount of any benefits paid during that period is subtracted from the refund amount.

The refund is made every 10 years and at age 65 or the date of death. Essentially, for an additional premium, the policyholder is guaranteed to get back 80% of his or her premium either in claims, premium refunds, or a combination of both.

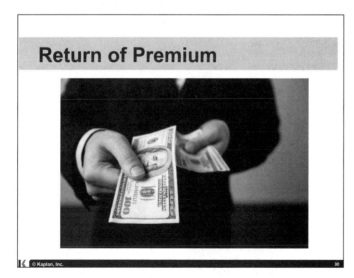

Return of Premium

- Refunds a stated percentage of the premium after a stated time
- Benefits paid are subtracted

15.4.8 Exclusions

No policy pays for every occurrence or event that can take place. The common exclusions for disability income policies are:

- war or military service,

- attempted suicide and other self-inflicted injury,
- non-commercial aviation (that is, other than a fare-paying airline passenger),
- commission of a felony, and
- living overseas.

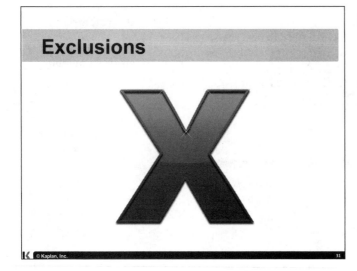

Exclusions
- Common exclusions found in disability income policies are losses arising from:
  - War or military service,
  - Suicide and other self-inflicted injury,
  - Non-commercial aviation (that is, other than a fare-paying airline passenger),
  - Commission of a felony, and
  - Living overseas.

 QUICK QUIZ 15.C

1. Which of the following allows insureds to buy additional amounts of disability income insurance coverage at stated future times without having to provide proof of insurability?
   A. Cost of living adjustment rider
   B. Future increase option rider
   C. Relation of earning to insurance provision
   D. Rehabilitation benefit provision

2. All of the following are common exclusions found in disability income policies EXCEPT for losses arising from
   A. living overseas
   B. attempted suicide
   C. military service
   D. a car accident

Answers can be found at the end of Unit 15.

15.4.9 Unique Aspects of Disability Underwriting

15.4.9.1 Occupational Considerations

The insured's occupation is the most important factor in underwriting disability income insurance. Less hazardous occupations present a much lower risk for injuries. For this reason, physicians, attorneys, and other professionals get better rates and more favorable definitions of disability than construction, warehouse, and industrial workers. Some occupations, such as firefighters, roofers, and high-rise window washers, may not be insurable at all.

15.4.9.2   Benefit Limits

Insurers are careful to limit the amount of coverage the offer to an individual. and will generally limit the amount to no more than 65% or 70% of net income, or after tax earned income. Existing coverage from another policy will be subtracted from the amount an insurer is willing to issue.

15.4.9.3   Policy Issuance Alternatives

Insurers have alternatives for individuals who are uninsurable:

- issue a rated-up policy—charge an additional premium to cover the increased risk; or
- attach an impairment rider to the policy that eliminates coverage for a particular condition that makes the individual uninsurable.

Disability Underwriting

- Occupation
- Benefit limits
- Policy issuance alternatives
  - Increased premium
  - Impairment rider

15.5   GROUP DISABILITY INCOME INSURANCE

15.5.1   Group vs. Individual Plans

A group disability policy is less expensive than an individual policy because the risk is spread over more participants. Benefits are often less in group policies, which accounts for the lower cost.

Group plans often state the benefit amount as a percentage of the employee's compensation while individual plans pay a specific dollar amount. In addition, group disability plans often provide two different types of coverage based on the benefit period: short-term disability (STD) and long-term disability (LTD).

15.5.2   Short-Term Disability (STD)

Short-term disability policies have short elimination periods—sometimes just a few days or perhaps no elimination period at all. The benefit period is normally 6 to 24 months. Benefit amounts are generally 60% or 70% of the employee's compensation.

15.5.3 Long-Term Disability (LTD)

Long-term disability plans are designed to begin paying a benefit when the short-term disability benefit ends. The elimination period of the long-term plan is usually the same as the benefit period of the short-term plan. Benefit periods are from two years up to age 65 and benefits are usually with benefit payments from workers' compensation and Social Security.

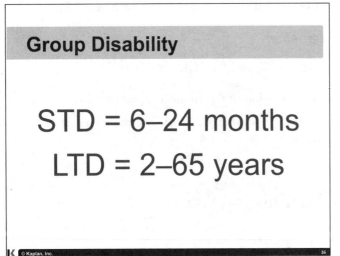

Group Disability

- Usually a percentage of pay instead of a stated benefit

- STD—Short Term Disability—6 to 24 months—very short elimination period if any

- LTD—Long Term Disability—2 years to age 65—elimination period usually the benefit period of STD

15.6 BUSINESS DISABILITY INSURANCE

15.6.1 Key Person Disability Insurance

A key person is an important member of a business and their loss due to death or extended incapacity could cause a financial loss for the company.

Key person disability income insurance pays a monthly benefit to a business to cover expenses for additional help or outside services when an essential person is disabled.

The key person's economic value to the business is determined in terms of the lost business income that would occur to replace the key person for an extended period of time. The benefit amount may be paid in a lump sum or in monthly installments. Generally, the policy's elimination period will be 30 to 90 days, and the benefit period will be one or two years.

15.6.2 Business Overhead Expense (BOE) Policy

The purpose of a Business Overhead Expense policy is to cover certain overhead expenses that continue when the business owner is disabled.

The policy will indemnify the business (not the owner) for such business expenses as rent, taxes, insurance premiums, utility bills, and employees' compensation, but not the owner's or a partner's salary. By covering these expenses the business is able to keep its doors open and continue to operate.

Generally, Business Overhead Expense policies have elimination periods of 15 or 30 days and benefit periods of one or two years. The average eligible overhead expenses of the business determine the benefit amount of the policy.

15.6.3 Disability Buy-Sell Insurance

Disability income insurance can be used to fund an agreement to buy out the interest of a business owner or partner who becomes disabled and can no longer contribute to the business. The buyout, or buy-sell, agreement will specify the value or a method of determining the value of the disabled owner's business interest. The disability insurance policy then provides the funds needed to execute the agreement.

The benefits may be paid in a lump sum or in monthly installments. If the policy provides a monthly benefit, usually the benefit period will not exceed five years.

One of the critical considerations in a disability buyout is the elimination period. At the end of the elimination period, the disability policy's funds become available and the buyout plan is put into effect. At that point, the buyout is irreversible. A business owner or partner will want to avoid having to sell his or her business interest for a short-term disability. For this reason, the elimination period for disability buyout insurance will normally be one or two years.

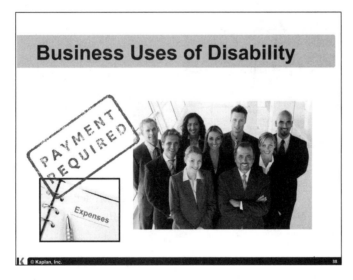

Business Uses of Disability

- Key person
- Business Overhead Expense
- Disability buy sell

15.7 SOCIAL SECURITY DISABILITY

15.7.1 Qualifying for Benefits

To qualify for Social Security disability benefits, someone must have paid Social Security payroll (FICA) taxes to earn at least 6 credits during the last 13 quarters to be *currently insured*. The number of needed credits increases with age up to age 62. **Fully insured** status is achieved when someone has paid into Social Security for 10 years, earning 40 credits.

In addition, the person must meet Social Security's definition of *totally and permanently disabled*, which means:

- the person is unable to perform the duties of any occupation; and
- the disability is expected to last for at least 12 months or end in death or total blindness.

Once a person becomes eligible for disability, there is five month (5) waiting period to receive benefits that are not paid retroactively.

15.7.2 Benefits Available

Disability benefits are based on the individual's *primary insurance amount (PIA)*, calculated using percentages of the person's income over his or her working years. Benefits are not designed to replace a worker's total earnings.

Eligible beneficiaries receive a benefit expressed as a percentage of the worker's PIA:

- a disabled worker receives a benefit equal to 100% of PIA;

- a spouse caring for the worker's unmarried child under age 16 or disabled before age 22, receives a benefit, equal to 50% of the worker's PIA; or

- each unmarried child under age 18 (19 if in high school) or disabled before age 22 receives a benefit equal to 50% of the worker's PIA.

The total family benefit is capped by a *maximum family benefit amount* based on the worker's average earnings.

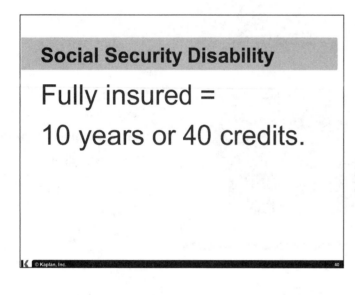

Social Security Disability

- Person must have at least 6 credits in last 13 quarters

- Number of credits required increases with age up to age 62-fully insured, earned 40 credits

- 5 month waiting period for benefits

- Not retroactive to cover first 5 months

- Disability must last 12 months

- Amount of benefit based upon the persons Primary Insurance Amount

- Spouse and children may receive benefits

15.8 WORKERS' COMPENSATION

Workers' compensation is a form of insurance providing wage replacement and medical benefits to employees injured in the course of employment in exchange for mandatory relinquishment of the employee's right to sue the employer for negligence.

The workers' compensation system is administered on a state-by-state basis, with a state governing board overseeing the system.

Benefits are payable regardless of fault—the employee does not have to prove that the employer was responsible. In return, the law considers workers' compensation benefits to be the employee's *exclusive remedy*—in most cases, employees cannot sue the employer for damages if an injury or illness occurs.

Benefits cover:

- medical treatment,
- rehabilitation,
- income lost due to disability, and
- income lost due to death.

Workers' Compensation
- Medical treatment,
- Rehabilitation,
- Income lost due to disability, and
- Income lost due to death.

 QUICK QUIZ 15.D

1. Which of the following is the most important factor in underwriting disability income insurance?
   A. The insured's occupation
   B. The insured's age
   C. The insured's home location
   D. The insured's marital status

2. All of the following statements about short-term disability are true EXCEPT
   A. short-term disability policies have short elimination periods
   B. short-term disability policies have long elimination periods
   C. short-term disability benefits are normally six to 24 months
   D. short-term disability benefit amounts are generally 60% to 70% of the employee's compensation

Answers can be found at the end of Unit 15.

🧠 UNIT 15 CRAM SHEET

Definition of Disability

- Own occupation
  - Inability to perform any or all of the duties of insured's normal occupation
  - More liberal definition for the insured
- Any occupation for which the insured is qualified by training education and experience
  - More difficult to qualify
- Income replacement
  - A reduction in income triggers payment
- Presumptive disability
  - Automatic qualification
  - Loss of or loss of use of any two limbs
  - Total and permanent blindness in both eyes
  - Loss of speech
  - Total and permanent loss of hearing in both ears
- Medically defined disability
  - House confinement and doctors care

Disability

- Indemnity benefit-fixed benefit, no offsets
- Elimination period
  - Must be disabled for this time length before payments begin
- Benefit period
  - How long will the benefits pay

Waiver of Premium

- Waives further premium payments after initial waiting period
- Refunds any premiums paid during the waiting period

Coordination with government benefits

- Additional monthly benefit rider
  - Pays an additional benefit during first 6 to 24 months
  - Pays even if the insured receives government benefits
- Social insurance supplement
  - Pays when social benefits are not being paid
  - Makes up the difference between the government benefit and the amount of the rider
  - Pays only during the policy benefit period

At Work Benefits

- Partial disability
  - Returns to work in a reduced capacity
  - Usually pays 50% of total benefit
  - Usually no longer than 3 to 6 months
- Residual disability
  - Paid whether insured is able to work full or part time
  - Benefit based on reduction of income
  - Pays as long as the reduction in income continues
- Recurrent disability
  - Condition recurs after returning to work
  - Doesn't have to wait to start receiving benefits
  - Conditions must recur within a certain time frame after returning to work

Other Provisions Affecting Benefits

- Cost of Living Rider (COLA)
  - Increases benefit while receiving disability
  - Based on the Consumer Price Index
  - Adjustments usually made every 12 months
- Future Increase Option (FIO)
  - Allows insured to increase policy benefits
  - No evidence of insurability required
  - The insured's income must have increased
- Relation of earnings to insurance
  - Allows insurer to change policy benefit if insured's income has decreased
  - Portion of the premium will be refunded

Other Cash Benefits

- Accidental death & dismemberment
  - Amount of the rider is the principal sum
    - Paid if accidental death—usually a multiple of the monthly disability benefit
    - Loss of sight in both eyes or loses two limbs
  - Smaller benefit for one limb eye etc.—capital sum
    - A percentage of the principal sum
- Rehabilitation benefit
  - Total disability
  - Helps insured train for a new occupation
  - Pays as long as insured is disabled and stays in the program

- Medical reimbursement
  - Helps pay medical bills for a non-disabling injury

Refund Provisions

- Return of premium
  - Refunds a stated percentage of the premium after a stated time
  - Benefits paid are subtracted
- Cash surrender value
  - Accumulates cash values that are ultimately equal to all premiums paid
  - If the policy is surrendered for its cash value any benefits are subtracted

Exclusions

- Common exclusions found in disability income policies are losses arising from:
  - War or military service,
  - Suicide and other self-inflicted injury,
  - Non-commercial aviation (that is, other than a fare-paying airline passenger),
  - Commission of a felony, and
  - Living overseas.

Disability Underwriting

- Occupation
- Benefit limits
- Policy issuance alternatives
  - Increased premium
  - Exclusion rider

Business Uses of Disability

- Key person
- Business overhead expense
- Disability buy sell

Social Security Disability

- Person must have at least 6 credits in last 13 quarters
- Number of credits required increases with age up to age 62
- Fully insured when 40 credits have been earned
- 5 month waiting period for benefits
- Not retroactive to cover first 5 months
- Disability must last for 12 months
- Amount of benefit based upon the persons Primary Insurance Amount
- Spouse and children may receive benefits

Workers Compensation

- Medical treatment,
- Rehabilitation,
- Income lost due to disability, and
- Income lost due to death.

UNIT 15 QUIZ

In order to measure your success, we recommend that you answer the following 10 questions correctly.

1. All of the following define a disability EXCEPT
    A. partial disability
    B. recurrent disability
    C. residual disability
    D. accidental death and dismemberment

2. The benefit that pays for the insured to learn to work in a new occupation is known as
    A. the cost-of-living benefit
    B. the rehabilitation benefit
    C. the guaranteed insurability option
    D. the lifetime benefit option

3. The rider that provides additional benefits during the first 6 to 12 months of a claim is known as
    A. the cost-of-living rider
    B. the rehabilitation rider
    C. the additional monthly benefit rider
    D. the lifetime benefit rider

4. The elimination period may be thought of as
    A. a dollar amount deductible
    B. a time deductible
    C. a dollar amount co-payment
    D. a time co-payment

5. The longer the benefit period
    A. the higher the policy's premium
    B. the lower the policy's premium
    C. the higher the policy's benefits
    D. the lower the policy's benefits

6. Which definition of total disability is more favorable to the insured?
    A. Own occupation
    B. Any occupation
    C. They are all the same in terms of benefits to the insured
    D. All occupation

7. Which of the following generally is NOT considered to be a presumptive disability?
    A. Loss of the dominant hand
    B. Loss of use of any two limbs
    C. Total and permanent blindness
    D. Loss of speech and hearing

8. Brandon injures his back working at a warehouse. Six months later, he is well enough to go back to work lifting boxes. Two weeks into working, however, he strains his back again and has to go back on bed rest. This is an example of
    A. a redundant disability
    B. a residual disability
    C. a recurrent disability
    D. a reduced disability

9. Which of the following organizations would be most likely to be eligible for business overhead expense insurance?
    A. A law firm with 25 partners
    B. A doctor's office
    C. A major multinational corporation
    D. A public library

10. To protect the business owner, the elimination period for disability buy-sell insurance normally is

A.   1 to 2 weeks

B.   3 to 6 months

C.   6 months to 1 year

D.   1 to 2 years

ANSWER KEY

QUICK QUIZZES

QUICK QUIZ 15.A

1. **D.** Presumptive disability

2. **A.** Disability income insurance

QUICK QUIZ 15.B

1. **B.** elimination period

2. **C.** partial disability

QUICK QUIZ 15.C

1. **B.** Future increase option rider

2. **D.** a car accident

QUICK QUIZ 15.D

1. **A.** The insured's occupation

2. **B.** short-term disability policies have long elimination periods

UNIT QUIZ

1. **D.** Accidental death and dismemberment is a rider that can provide additional benefits, but it does not define a disability.

2. **B.** The rehabilitation benefit pays for vocational training so that the insured can learn a new occupation.

3. **C.** This rider is paid on top of any government benefits during that same time.

4. **B.** The elimination period is the time period before the benefits will pay after a disability occurs.

5. **A.** The longer the benefit period, the higher the policy's premium.

6. **A.** The own occupation definition of total disability is more favorable to the insured. Own occupation is any or all of the duties that the insured had at the time the disability began.

7. **A.** Loss of the dominant hand is not considered to be a presumptive disability.

8. **C.** A recurrent disability is when a second period of disability arises from the same or a related cause of a prior disability.

9. **B.** Business overhead expense insurance typically covers a small business.

10. **D.** The benefits may be paid in a lump sum or in monthly installments.

UNIT 16 Medical Expense Plans

16.1 INTRODUCTION

Medical expense insurance is any program that helps pay for medical expenses, whether through privately purchased insurance, social insurance or a social welfare program funded by the government.

Medical expense plans vary widely in coverage, benefits, and the methods used for claim payments.

This unit will explore the different types of medical insurance plans and provide a general description of the benefits and available options.

16.2   LEARNING OBJECTIVES

After successfully completing this unit, you should be able to:

◻ explain the purpose of medical expense insurance;

◻ describe fee-for-service versus prepaid plans;

◻ compare specified coverages versus comprehensive care;

◻ compare benefit schedule versus usual/customary/reasonable charges;

◻ compare any provider versus limited choice providers;

◻ compare insureds versus subscribers/participants;

◻ compare and contrast basic and major medical expense policies; and

◻ identify the purpose of covered expenses, deductibles, coinsurance, stop-loss limits, and maximum out of pocket in major medical insurance.

16.3 GENERAL CONCEPTS

16.3.1 Fee-for-Service vs. Prepaid

Traditionally, physicians and hospitals provided care on a **fee-for-service** basis—that is, each time they provided a service, they were paid a fee in return. One of the new ideas that health maintenance organizations (HMOs) brought to health care was providing service on a **prepaid** basis—that is, individuals would pay the HMO a specified amount, and in return the HMO would agree to provide whatever care the individual needed during the year. If a particular individual needed very little care during the year, no money would be refunded. At the same time, if an individual needed a great deal of care, no additional money would be charged.

16.3.2 Specified Coverages vs. Comprehensive Care

Comprehensive medical expense plans cover all those types of care in one plan. The most comprehensive types of medical expense plans will cover preventive care and immunizations as well as necessary medical treatment. HMOs were among the first health care providers to cover preventive care.

16.3.3 Benefit Schedule vs. Usual/Customary/Reasonable Charges

Some medical expense policies pay providers for their services according to a **benefit schedule**. Each type of service is listed with the amount of payment. If a provider bills more for a service than is shown in the schedule, the patient must pay the difference.

Other medical expense policies pay providers according to what amount is **usual, customary, and reasonable** to charge for that service in that geographic area. As long as the provider's charge is in line with the amount other providers in the area are charging for that service, the policy will pay the full amount. However, if the provider's charge is more than the usual, customary, and reasonable amount, the patient may be billed for the difference.

16.3.4 Any Provider vs. Limited Choice of Providers

Under older health insurance plans, the insured could use any provider. Under modern managed care plans, the choice of providers is limited to those participating in the managed care plan. For example, HMOs only pay providers who are members of the HMO. The insured could use a non-HMO provider, but they must pay for those visits.

Preferred provider organization (PPO) plans have a panel of physicians and hospitals under contract to provide health care services and generally cover 80%–100% of the cost. Individuals who choose to use other providers are covered for a smaller percentage of the visits, such as 60%.

16.3.5 Insureds vs. Subscribers/Participants

Customers can be the **insured**, **subscriber** or **participant** depending on the type of plan:

- traditional *fee-for-service* plans, refer to customers as *insureds* because these plans are issued by insurance companies; and

- *prepaid* plans refer to their customers as *subscribers/participants*, these plans are offered by entities consisting of the providers themselves, such as HMOs.

Medical Plans General Concepts

May be written on an individual or group basis.

© Kaplan, Inc.

Medical Plans General Concepts

- Fee for service—provider is paid as services are provided—customers called insureds

- Prepaid—provider is paid a set fee in advance—customers called subscribers/participants

- Specified coverage—covers only specific services

- Comprehensive care—covers broad range of services

- Benefit schedule—pays only a specified amount regardless of the actual charge

- Usual, customary, reasonable (UCR)—pays full charge if reasonable and customary in the same geographical area

- Any provider—any provider the insured chooses

- Limited choice—limited to contracted providers

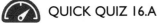 QUICK QUIZ 16.A

1. Traditional fee for service plans refer to their customers as
   A. insureds
   B. subscribers
   C. participants
   D. plan members

2. Which of the following terms describes a medical expense policy that pays a provider a set fee for their services regardless of the charge?
   A. Fee for service
   B. Benefit schedule
   C. Usual, reasonable, and customary
   D. Specified coverages

Answers can be found at the end of Unit 16.

16.4 TYPES OF MEDICAL EXPENSE PLANS

Choosing a health care plan comes down to cost and to comparing the monthly premium with the amount of coverage available. Major medical insurance is designed to cover everything from routine check-ups to catastrophic events. Basic health insurance, by contrast, is a cash reimbursement plan that can pay for some, but not all types of medical services.

16.4.1 Basic Hospital, Medical, and Surgical Policies

Basic hospital, medical, and surgical policies were the original medical expense plans. They were developed before today's highly technical equipment and expensive treatments existed. Basic hospital, medical, and surgical policies are characterized by:

- low coverage limits, and
- first-dollar coverage (no deductible).

Coverage and payment limits for basic hospital, medical, and surgical plans were listed individually for in-hospital benefits, miscellaneous hospital benefits, surgical, physician, and nursing services. If a procedure or service was not on that list it was not covered. If expenses exceeded the scheduled payment limit the insured paid the difference.

The good news with this coverage was the insured did not have immediate "out of pocket" expenses; deductibles, co-pays, and co-insurance were not included in these plans. However the limit of coverage was low and the bad news was the insured frequently paid "out of pocket" on the back end.

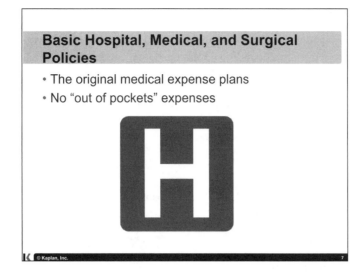

Basic Hospital, Medical, and Surgical Policies

- Low coverage amounts
- No deductibles

16.4.2 Major Medical Insurance

Major medical insurance covers a much broader range of medical expenses with fewer gaps and provides higher maximum limits. These more expensive policies are divided into two general groups.

- **Supplemental major medical insurance** is used to back-up or enhance a basic policy. The basic plan will pay covered expenses with no deductible, up to the policy limits, then the supplemental plan kicks-in. When leaving the basic plan, because the limits are reached, the insured must pay a *corridor deductible* to begin using the supplemental plan coverage.

- **Comprehensive major medical insurance** is a stand-alone plan and benefits are available after the *deductible* is satisfied. Another feature is the concept of *coinsurance,* which is the sharing between the insurer and insured of covered expenses that exceed the deductible amount. The sharing ends when the *stop-loss limit (maximum out-of-pocket limit)* is reached.

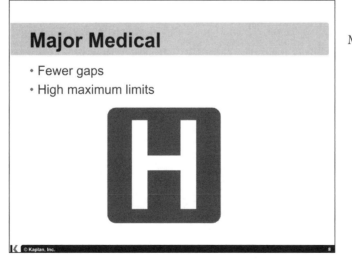

Major Medical

- Broader coverage
  - Supplemental major medical
    - Insured has a basic policy
    - Major medical pays when basic ends
  - Comprehensive major medical
    - Stand alone policy

16.4.2.1 Covered Expenses

Major medical insurance, whether supplemental or comprehensive, covers a wide range of medical expenses. Though covered expenses can vary depending on the particular policy, they typically include the following:

- hospital inpatient room and board, including intensive and cardiac care,
- hospital medical and surgical services and supplies,
- physicians' diagnostic, medical, and surgical services,
- other medical practitioners' services,
- nursing services, including private-duty service outside a hospital,
- anesthesia and anesthetist services,
- outpatient services,
- ambulance service to and from a hospital,
- first aid and emergency room care,
- x-rays and other diagnostic and laboratory tests,
- radiological and other types of therapy,
- prescription drugs administered in the hospital,
- blood and blood plasma,
- oxygen and its administration,
- dental services resulting from injury to natural teeth,
- convalescent or rehabilitative facility care,
- home health care services,
- prosthetic devices when initially purchased,
- casts, splints, trusses, braces, and crutches,
- rental of durable equipment such as hospital-type beds and wheelchairs, and
- hospice care—terminal illness care that includes pain relief, symptom management, and counseling but no curative treatment.

Major Medical Covered Expenses

- Both supplemental and comprehensive include a range of medical expenses

© Kaplan, Inc.

Major Medical Covered Expenses

- Hospital inpatient room and board, including intensive and cardiac care
- Hospital medical and surgical services and supplies
- Physicians' diagnostic, medical, and surgical services
- Other medical practitioners' services
- Nursing services, including private-duty service outside a hospital
- Anesthesia and anesthetist services
- Outpatient services
- Ambulance service to and from a hospital
- First aid and emergency room care
- X-rays and other diagnostic and laboratory tests
- Radiological and other types of therapy
- Prescription drugs administered in the hospital
- Blood and blood plasma
- Oxygen and its administration
- Dental services resulting from injury to natural teeth
- Convalescent or rehabilitative facility care
- Home health care services
- Prosthetic devices when initially purchased
- Casts, splints, trusses, braces, and crutches
- Rental of durable equipment such as hospital-type beds and wheelchairs
- Hospice care—terminal illness care that includes pain relief, symptom management, and counseling but no curative treatment

16.4.2.2 Deductibles

Deductibles are one way major medical expense insurance shares costs with insureds to keep premiums for coverage affordable.

The deductible requires the insured to pay a certain amount of their medical expenses each calendar year before coverage begins. For example, if an insured had a $500 deductible and the cost of medical treatment received totaled $750, they would pay $500. The remaining $250 would be eligible for payment by the insurer.

Policies that cover entire families usually have a *family deductible* rather than an individual deductible. For example, the individual deductible is $500, and the family deductible is $1,000. A family of six would pay no more than $1,000, not $3,000 that would apply if each individual paid a $500 deductible.

With supplemental major medical insurance, the deductible kicks in after the basic policy limits are reached. The *corridor deductible* applies to begin using the supplemental plan and another deductible would apply.

For example, Ray has a basic medical policy with a $1,000 limit and supplemental major medical insurance with a $500 deductible. Ray exceeds the $1,000 medical expense plan limit, pays a corridor deductible and any expenses that exceed $1,000 will be picked up by the supplemental major medical policy after its deductible has been satisfied.

16.4.2.3 Coinsurance

Coinsurance is a cost-sharing feature that keeps major medical insurance affordable. The insured pays a certain percentage of medical expenses after the deductible has been satisfied. Different coinsurance arrangements are available, the most common is 80-20, the insurer pays 80% and the insured pays 20% during the time the sharing arrangement applies.

Dick has major medical insurance with a $500 deductible and an 80/20 coinsurance clause. He has a $1,200 medical expense and pays the $500 deductible, plus his 20% coinsurance of the remaining $700 ($140). Dick's total medical expense is $640 and the insurer pays the remaining $560.

16.4.2.4 Stop-Loss Limits

Major medical policies often include a **stop-loss limit,** the insured is no longer required to pay coinsurance when medical expenses exceed this amount.

If Dick had a stop-loss limit of $5,000, he would no longer be required to pay coinsurance after medical expenses totaled $5,500. At that point, he would have paid $1,000 in coinsurance ($5,000 x 20%) plus the $500 deductible.

16.4.2.5 Maximum Out of Pocket

Major medical policies include a **maximum out of pocket**; the deductible plus the insured's coinsurance percentage times the stop loss limit. Using the above example, Dick's maximum out of pocket limit would be $1,500: the $500 deductible + the $1,000 (5,000 × 20%) coinsurance amount.

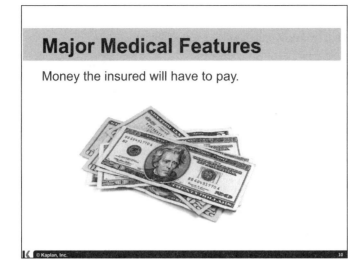

Major Medical Features

- Deductible
    - Paid by insured before policy pays
    - Calendar year
- Coinsurance
    - Insured continues to pay part of the bill after the deductible
    - Insurance company starts paying
    - Usually 80% insurance company and 20% insured
- Stop Loss
    - Insured no longer shares in the cost when total medical bills above the deductible exceed this number
- Insured maximum out of pocket
    - Deductible plus coinsurance

16.4.2.6 Limitations

Medical expense policies often place limits on coverage or benefits for certain types of treatment. The most common limitations are for the following:

- rehabilitation and skilled nursing care facility care,
- home health care,
- hospice care,
- ambulance services,
- outpatient treatment,
- durable medical equipment, such as hospital beds,
- infertility treatment,
- maternity care,
- mental illness or substance abuse treatment,
- organ transplants, and
- reimbursement for chiropractic or other non-physician services.

16.4.2.7 Exclusions

The following are typically excluded from coverage under medical expense plans:

- self-inflicted injuries,
- injury resulting from war or acts of war, whether or not war is officially declared,
- illness or injury suffered during active military duty,
- injury resulting from air travel unless the insured is a paying passenger,
- injury suffered while committing a felony,
- experimental procedures,
- care covered by workers' compensation,
- care received in a government facility,
- elective cosmetic surgery (restoration required because of a covered illness or injury is covered),
- hearing aids, and
- custodial care.

Limitations & Exclusions

- Self-inflicted injuries
- Injury resulting from war or acts of war, whether or not war is officially declared
- Illness or injury suffered during active military duty
- Injury resulting from air travel unless the insured is a paying passenger
- Injury suffered while committing a felony
- Experimental procedures
- Care covered by workers' compensation
- Care received in a government facility
- Elective cosmetic surgery (restoration required because of a covered illness or injury is covered)
- Hearing aids
- Custodial care

QUICK QUIZ 16.B

1. Major medical benefits usually begin after the insured has incurred an initial annual amount of out-of-pocket expense called a

   A. stop loss limit

   B. coinsurance limit

   C. deductible

   D. maximum out of pocket limit

2. All of the following are typically excluded from medical expense plans EXCEPT

   A. self-inflicted injuries

   B. cosmetic surgery

   C. care covered by workers' compensation

   D. mental illness treatment

Answers can be found at the end of Unit 16.

UNIT 16 CRAM SHEET

Medical Plans General Concepts

- Fee for service—provider is paid as services are provided—customers called insureds
- Prepaid—provider is paid a set fee in advance—customers called subscribers/participants
- Specified coverage—covers only specific services
- Comprehensive care—covers broad range of services
- Benefit schedule—pays only a specified amount regardless of the actual charge
- Usual, Customary, Reasonable (UCR)—pays full charge if reasonable and customary in the same geographical area
- Any provider—any provider the insured chooses
- Limited choice—limited to contracted providers

Basic Hospital, Medical, and Surgical Policies

- Low coverage amounts
- No deductibles

Major Medical

- Broader coverage
  - Supplemental major medical
    - Insured has a basic policy
    - Major medical pays when basic ends
  - Comprehensive major medical
    - Stand alone policy

Major Medical Covered Expenses

- Hospital inpatient room and board, including intensive and cardiac care
- Hospital medical and surgical services and supplies
- Physicians' diagnostic, medical, and surgical services
- Other medical practitioners' services
- Nursing services, including private-duty service outside a hospital
- Anesthesia and anesthetist services
- Outpatient services
- Ambulance service to and from a hospital
- First aid and emergency room care
- X-rays and other diagnostic and laboratory tests
- Radiological and other types of therapy
- Prescription drugs administered in the hospital
- Blood and blood plasma
- Oxygen and its administration
- Dental services resulting from injury to natural teeth
- Convalescent or rehabilitative facility care
- Home health care services
- Prosthetic devices when initially purchased
- Casts, splints, trusses, braces, and crutches
- Rental of durable equipment such as hospital-type beds and wheelchairs
- Hospice care—terminal illness care that includes pain relief, symptom management, and counseling but no curative treatment

Major Medical Features

- Deductible
  - Paid by insured before ;policy pays
  - Calendar year
- Coinsurance
  - Insured continues to pay part of the bill after the deductible
  - Insurance company starts paying
  - Usually 80% insurance company and 20% insured
- Stop Loss
  - Insured no longer shares in the cost when total medical bills above the deductible exceed this number
- Insured Maximum Out of Pocket
  - Deductible plus coinsurance

Exclusions

- Self-inflicted injuries
- Injury resulting from war or acts of war, whether or not war is officially declared
- Illness or injury suffered during active military duty
- Injury resulting from air travel unless the insured is a paying passenger
- Injury suffered while committing a felony
- Experimental procedures
- Care covered by workers' compensation
- Care received in a government facility
- Elective cosmetic surgery (restoration required because of a covered illness or injury is covered)
- Hearing aids
- Custodial care

UNIT 16 QUIZ

In order to measure your success, we recommend that you answer the following 10 questions correctly.

1. The out-of-pocket limit is also known as the
   A. deductible
   B. co-payment
   C. stop-loss limit
   D. maximum benefit

2. Which of the following is least likely to be covered by a major medical expense?
   A. Outpatient services
   B. Dental care
   C. Prescription drugs administered in a hospital
   D. Blood and blood plasma

3. A type of health insurance that provides a much broader range of medical expenses and higher benefit amounts is a
   A. basic medical expense policy
   B. major medical expense policy
   C. simple medical expense policy
   D. prepaid medical expense policy

4. Hospice care is used to
   A. treat diseases only, not accident-related medical issues
   B. control pain and suffering as well as to treat illness
   C. alleviate pain and suffering for terminally ill patients, but does not attempt to cure
   D. cure mental illness

5. The dollar limit beyond which the insured is no longer required to pay coinsurance the
   A. deductible
   B. coinsurance
   C. stop-loss limit
   D. maximum benefit

6. The sharing of expenses between the insured and the insurer is an example of the
   A. deductible
   B. coinsurance
   C. stop-loss limit
   D. maximum benefit

7. A deductible that falls between two periods where the insurance company pays is known as a
   A. stop-loss deductible
   B. capitated deductible
   C. corridor deductible
   D. limited deductible

8. Prepaid medical expense plans refer to their customers as
   A. insureds
   B. subscribers/participants
   C. members
   D. policyholders

9. Sarah has a $200 deductible and a 20% coinsurance for her medical expense plan. Her first medical bill of the year is $1200. Sarah will pay the $200 deductible. How much money will Sarah still need to pay?

    A. $200

    B. $240

    C. $800

    D. $1000

10. Which of the following terms describes the limits that a person will have to pay in any calendar year for covered medical expenses?

    A. Coinsurance

    B. Stop-loss limit

    C. Maximum out of pocket

    D. Deductible

ANSWER KEY

QUICK QUIZZES

QUICK QUIZ 16.A

1. **A.** insureds

2. **B.** Benefit schedule

QUICK QUIZ 16.B.

1. **C.** deductible

2. **D.** mental illness treatment

UNIT QUIZ

1. **C.** The out-of-pocket limit is also known as the stop-loss limit and once the insured hits this amount they are no longer required to pay coinsurance.

2. **B.** There is a large list of what is covered under a major medical expense plan. Dental care is typically excluded from coverage.

3. **B.** A major medical expense policy provides high maximum coverage for medical care and is available as supplemental major medical insurance and comprehensive major medical insurance.

4. **C.** This includes pain relief, symptom management, and counseling for the family.

5. **C.** The stop-loss limit is the dollar limit beyond which the insured no longer participates in payment of expenses.

6. **B.** The sharing of expenses between the insured and the insurer is an example of coinsurance. A common split between insurer and insured is 80/20.

7. **C.** A corridor deductible runs between the first dollar coverage of a basic policy and the comprehensive coverage of a supplemental policy.

8. **B.** These plans are not offered by insurance companies but by the providers themselves.

9. **A.** Her first bill of the year is $1,200. She pays her $200 deductible and will still owe 20% of the $1000 left over after deductible is subtracted. $1200-$200 (deductible) = $1000 x 20% coinsurance = $200.

10. **C.** The maximum out of pocket is the insured's deductible plus the insured's share of the coinsurance equals the stop loss limit.

UNIT 17 Other Health Plans

17.1 INTRODUCTION

The Health Maintenance Organization Act of 1973, which began as an experiment, changed the landscape of the health care delivery system permanently. The act was introduced as an alternative to the existing fee-for-service method of payment for health services. In the following decades, other forms of managed care emerged, such as Preferred Provider Organizations (PPOs) and Point-of-Service (POS) plans.

This unit discusses the various plans, their range of services, and the various types of providers.

🎯 17.2   LEARNING OBJECTIVES

After successfully completing this unit, you should be able to:

- explain the general characteristics of Health maintenance organizations (HMOs): combined health care delivery and financing, prepayment of heath care services, co-payments, gatekeeper concept, limited choice of provider, and limited service area;

- identify the categories of care that are a part of a health maintenance organization (HMOs) including preventative care, emergency care, hospital services, and other services;

- explain preferred provider organizations (PPOs) and how they are different from health maintenance organizations (HMOs);

- describe open panel vs. closed panel;

- explain the relationship between the PPOs and its providers and list the parties to a provider contract;

- identify Point-of-Service Plans;

- describe indemnity (traditional insurance) plans;

- explain heath care cost containment (managed care) and the cost saving measures; and

- identify utilization management, prospective review, concurrent review, and retrospective.

17.3 HEALTH MAINTENANCE ORGANIZATIONS

17.3.1 General Characteristics

Health maintenance organizations (HMOs) are managed care entities. They departed from the traditional health care delivery and payment system in several key respects. HMOs provide both the health care service and the health care financing, while traditional health care insurance companies provide only the financing.

17.3.1.1 Combined Health Care Delivery and Financing

In the traditional system, the insurance company acts as financing entity, collecting premiums and either paying the bulk of the patients' medical bills or reimbursing their medical expenses. Insurers assumed a certain amount of risk by hoping premiums would be sufficient to pay for provided medical care.

Health maintenance organizations changed this procedure by combining both the provision and the financing of health care into one entity. HMOs are made up of an array of physicians, hospitals, and other medical providers who offer a full range of health care services. Individuals pay for services directly to the HMO, and it agrees to provide needed medical care. The HMO is a financing entity and assumes that the cost of medical care will not exceed the subscription fees.

17.3.1.2 Prepayment for Health Care Services

HMOs are considered prepaid plans because the consumer (subscriber) pays a subscription fee in advance for health care services they may need in the future. In addition to a co-payment paid by the subscriber, the HMO pays a capitation fee to a health care provider. The capitation fee is a fixed monthly fee paid to the healthcare provider based on the number of HMO members, not per HMO subscriber visit or service.

17.3.1.3 Co-payments (Co-pays)

HMOs introduced the concept of **co-payments**, or *co-pays* instead of deductibles or coinsurance. A co-pay is a relatively small, flat dollar amount that subscribers must pay for each doctor visit.

17.3.1.4 Gatekeeper Concept (Primary Care Physician)

Another way HMOs control overutilization of their services by subscribers is with the **gatekeeper concept**. When subscribers join an HMO, they must choose a doctor with a general medical practice as their **primary care physician** (PCP) and they must always see them first (except in emergencies) when seeking medical care from the HMO.

Subscribers cannot see specialists without a referral from a primary care physician.

17.3.1.5 Limited Choice of Provider

HMO subscribers must choose a provider/physician under contract with the HMO. If a new subscriber's current physician is not under contract with the HMO, they must choose a doctor from the HMO. In some cases, the individual's current doctor may be able to join the HMO.

17.3.1.6 Limited Service Area

HMOs operate within a specific geographic area or *designated service area* such as a certain county or within the surrounding area. Individual must live within the designated service area to subscribe to the HMO.

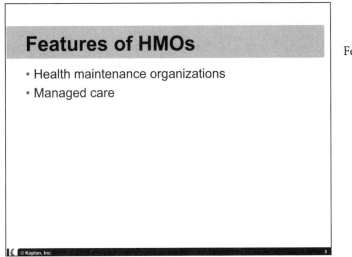

Features of HMOs

- Health maintenance organizations
- Managed care

© Kaplan, Inc.

Features of HMOs

- Managed care
- Prepaid services
- Co-pays
- Gatekeeper (Primary Care Physician)
- Limited choice of providers
- Limited service area

17.3.2 Categories of Care

17.3.2.1 Preventive Care

A major difference between HMOs and the traditional health care system is the emphasis on *preventive care*. Traditional health insurance pays for the medical treatment of existing illnesses or other conditions. HMOs seek to reduce the need for medical treatment by detecting conditions early before they require more extensive treatment. Routine physicals, well-child care, immunizations, and diagnostic screening are all included in the HMO subscription fee.

17.3.2.1.1 Emergency Care

HMOs must provide emergency care, including ambulance service, available 24-hours a day, and 365 days a year, within its designated service area. In addition, HMOs must reimburse subscribers for emergency care obtained outside of the HMO's designated service area from non-HMO providers.

17.3.2.2 Hospital Services

Inpatient hospital and physician care must be provided for a period per calendar year for treatment of illness or injury. Hospital services must include the following:

- room and board,
- maternity care,
- general nursing care,
- use of operating room and facilities,
- use of intensive care unit,
- x-rays, laboratory, and other diagnostic tests,
- drugs, medications, and anesthesia, and
- physical, radiation, and inhalation therapy.

17.3.2.3 Other Services

HMOs must also provide for other basic office-based care provided by physicians and other medical professionals such as diagnostic services, treatment services, short-term physical therapy and rehabilitation services, laboratory and x-ray services, and outpatient surgery.

HMOs may include certain supplemental health care services or provide them for an additional fee, such as:

- prescription drugs,
- vision care,
- dental care,
- home health care,
- nursing services,
- long-term care, and
- substance abuse treatment.

HMO Services

- Major emphasis on **preventative care**
- Goal: detect conditions early before before they require more treatment

© Kaplan, Inc.   4

HMO Services

- Preventive care
- Emergency care—in or out of the service area
- Hospital services
- Office based care and outpatient services

 QUICK QUIZ 17.A

1. What is an HMO known for?
   A. Extravagant fees
   B. Cosmetic surgeries
   C. Fee-for-service plan
   D. Preventative care

2. All of the following are features of HMO's EXCEPT
   A. medical services are provided first, and then they are billed and paid for
   B. medical services are prepaid before treatment
   C. HMO's do not have deductibles or coinsurance, but instead co-payments
   D. HMO subscribers are not free to choose any provider that they wish

Answers can be found at the end of Unit 17.

17.4 PREFERRED PROVIDER ORGANIZATIONS

Preferred provider organizations (PPOs) are another managed care entity. PPOs contract with a network of hospitals, physicians, laboratories, and other medical practitioners to provide medical services for a fee that is somewhat lower than the usual rate for that area. Individuals sign up to receive their medical care through the PPO in order to take advantage of those lower fees. The providers agree to accept a lower fee in order to have access to the PPO's subscribers.

PPOs operate on a fee-for-service rather than a prepaid basis like an HMO. PPO subscribers pay an insurance premium when they enroll in the PPO. The premium is generally less than an HMO fee, but PPO plans also have deductibles, coinsurance, and also co-pays. Out-of-pocket costs depend on the amount of care provided.

17.4.1 Open Panel vs. Closed Panel

HMOs are typically **closed-panel,** or *closed network,* entities subscribers must seek care only from providers/physicians that belong to the HMO (except in out-of-network emergencies).

PPOs are typically **open panel**, or *open network,* entities and subscribers are not strictly limited to the plans providers. The reimbursement percentage on care received from out-of-network providers however is usually considerably lower (50% to 60% than that for in-network providers (80% to 90%)

17.4.2 Parties to the Provider Contract

A PPO is a risk-bearing entity separate from the providers of health care services. The relationship between the PPO and its providers is contractual.

However, a PPO can be organized by a number of different types of organizations, including:

- insurance companies;
- Blue Cross/Blue Shield;
- a hospital or a group of hospitals;
- a group of physicians;
- an HMO;
- a large employer or group of employers; and
- a trade union.

PPO

- Preferred provider organizations
- Managed care
- Fee for service rather than prepaid like HMOs

Preferred Provider Organization

- Managed care
- Fee for service
- Pre-negotiated rates
- Insured pays less in network of PPO providers

17.5 POINT-OF-SERVICE PLANS

A *Point Of Service* plan is a type of HMO that allows subscribers to obtain care from providers who do not belong to the HMO as well as those who do. The name of the plan highlights the fact that subscribers can choose their point of service.

If subscribers choose to access care within the HMO, they choose a primary care physician who acts as a gatekeeper to the HMO's network of providers. For this reason, POS plans are sometimes referred to as *gatekeeper PPOs*. In-network care is covered by the subscriber's prepaid fee. No billing is done and no claim forms need to be completed.

If subscribers choose to access care outside of the HMO, the plan operates like a PPO or traditional insurance plan:

- there is no primary care physician who acts as a gatekeeper;

- providers bill the individual a fee for services rendered, and the individual must submit a claim form to the HMO for reimbursement; and

- subscribers are not reimbursed for 100% of their expenses but rather for only a percentage such as 60% or 80%, like a coinsurance requirement.

Because subscribers are not limited to selecting only providers which belong to the HMO, POS plans are sometimes called *open-ended HMOs.*

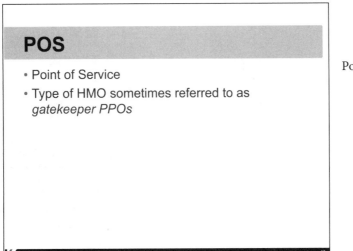

Point of Service

- HMO allows subscribers to use providers outside of the HMO

- No gate keeper for out of network services

- Subscribers pay more of the cost

- Called open-ended HMO

17.6 INDEMNITY (TRADITIONAL INSURANCE) PLANS

Traditional indemnity plans are still offered by commercial insurers. They are characterized by the following:

- provision of care on a fee-for-service basis;

- billing and submission of claim forms;

- deductibles and coinsurance requirements;

- complete freedom on choice of provider; and

- ability to access to specialists without a referral.

Some traditional insurance plans employ certain cost containment methods such as preauthorization, second surgical opinion, or utilization management. Some do not.

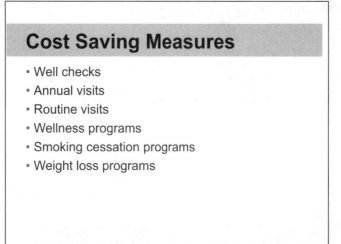

QUICK QUIZ 17.B

1. PPO subscribers are not strictly limited to using providers that have contracts with the PPO. PPO's are
   A. closed-panel entities
   B. open-panel entities
   C. closed network entities
   D. free to choose entities

2. A type of HMO that does not have a gatekeeper and allows subscribers to obtain care from either providers that do or not belong to the HMO is called a
   A. point-of-service plan
   B. traditional insurance plan
   C. preferred provider plan
   D. cost containment plan

Answers can be found at the end of Unit 17.

17.7 HEALTH CARE COST CONTAINMENT (MANAGED CARE)

Traditionally, controlling health care costs was not thought to be an area of responsibility for insurers. But as health care costs began to rise dramatically, insurers responded by implementing a number of measures to make the delivery of health care more efficient and cost-effective. These measures came to be known as **managed care.**

17.7.1 Cost Saving Measures

17.7.1.1 Preventive Care

One of the cost saving measures insurers implemented was to encourage preventive care. It is much cheaper to prevent illnesses or to find and treat them in their early stages. Insurers began providing coverage for regular physical exams, health screenings, and smoking cessation programs, and wellness programs to provide access to experts in nutrition and exercise.

Cost Saving Measures

- Well checks
- Annual visits
- Routine visits
- Wellness programs
- Smoking cessation programs
- Weight loss programs

© Kaplan, Inc.   15

Cost Containment—Managed Care

- Preventive care
- Reducing hospital care costs

17.7.1.2 Reducing Hospital Care Costs

Insurers also implemented measures designed to reduce the amount spent on inpatient hospitalization, which is the most costly type of medical care.

- **Outpatient Benefits**   Many procedures can be performed safely and effectively without the patient staying in the hospital overnight. Insurers began encouraging use of a hospital's outpatient facilities by providing relatively higher levels of reimbursement for treatment received on an outpatient rather than an in-patient basis. In addition, insurers began approving payment for treatment received in ambulatory care centers other than hospital outpatient departments such as surgicenters and urgent care centers.

- **Second Surgical Opinion**   Doctors do not always agree on whether surgery is needed to treat a particular condition. Second surgical opinion allows or requires consultation with a doctor other than their attending physician to see if an alternative method of treatment would be desirable.

- **Preauthorization**   If treatment requiring hospitalization is recommended, *precertification* is required prior to obtaining the treatment.

- **Limits on Lengths of Stay**   In consultation with medical experts, insurers determined the appropriate number of days for various types of treatment. They limited payment to a certain number of days for a given procedure, assuming no complications.

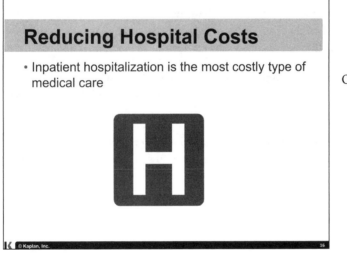

- **Alternatives to Hospital Care** Facilities other than a hospital may provide a more appropriate— and cost-effective—level of care for some patients.

  - *Skilled nursing facilities* provide round-the-clock care for patients who need inpatient supervision by a registered nurse, but who do not require the acute level of care provided by a hospital.

  - *Intermediate nursing facilities* provide intermittent nursing care for patients who do not need 24-hour supervision.

  - *Rehabilitative facilities* provide a limited amount of medical care along with the personal care necessary for patients to recover from major surgeries or serious injuries or illnesses.

  - *Home health care* is provided by agencies that employ a staff of nurses that make visits to a patient's home on a regular basis. It is used when patients need some sort of ongoing medical care but do not need supervision.

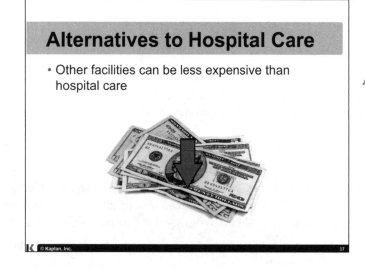

Alternatives to Hospital Care

- Skilled nursing facilities
- Intermediate nursing facilities
- Rehabilitative facilities
- Home health care

17.7.2 Utilization Management

Utilization management places oversight on the provision of medical care to make sure it is appropriate and effective. This oversight can occur at any or all of the following points in the process.

Prospective review occurs before an expensive test or treatment recommended by a physician is actually provided, requires a second opinion, or both. Information on the case is reviewed to determine necessity and cost-effectiveness. This review process is referred to as *precertification* or *preauthorization*.

Concurrent review takes place while treatment is being provided. The insured's hospital stay is monitored to assure that everything is proceeding according to schedule and that the insured will be released from the hospital as planned.

Retrospective review is done after treatment is complete. The outcome is evaluated to see if treatment was effective and if anything could be changed to produce a better or most cost-effective outcome in the future.

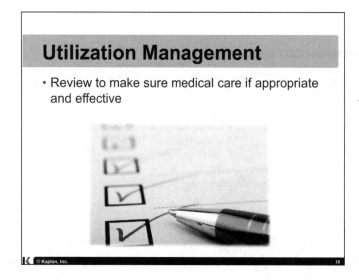

Utilization Management

- Prospective review
- Concurrent review
- Retrospective review

QUICK QUIZ 17.C

1. Which of the following cost saving measures allows or requires insureds to consult a doctor other than their attending physician to see if an alternative method of treatment would be desirable?

   A. Preauthorization

   B. Alternatives to hospital care

   C. Second surgical opinion

   D. Utilization management

2. All of the following are alternatives to hospital care EXCEPT

   A. skilled nursing facilities

   B. home health care

   C. utilization management

   D. rehabilitative facilities

Answers can be found at the end of Unit 17.

UNIT 17 CRAM SHEET

Features of HMOs

- Managed care
- Prepaid services
- Co-pays
- Gatekeeper (Primary Care Physician)
- Limited choice of providers
- Limited service area

Preferred Provider Organization

- Managed care
- Fee for service
- Pre-negotiated rates
- Insured pays less in network of PPO providers

Point of Service

- HMO allows subscribers to use providers outside of the HMO
- No gate keeper for out of network services
- Subscribers pay more of the cost
- Called open-ended HMO

Cost Containment—Managed Care

- Preventive Care

- Reducing Hospital Care Costs
  - Outpatient Benefits
    - Second Surgical Opinion
    - Preauthorization—*precertification*
    - Limits on Lengths of Stay
- Alternatives to Hospital Care
  - Skilled nursing facilities
  - Intermediate nursing facilities
  - Rehabilitative facilities
  - Home health care
- Utilization Management
  - Prospective review
  - Concurrent review
  - Retrospective review

UNIT 17 QUIZ

In order to measure your success, we recommend that you answer the following 10 questions correctly.

1. The main difference between traditional health insurance arrangements and HMOs is that
   A. traditional health insurance companies provide both the health care service and the health care financing, but HMOs provide only the health care financing
   B. traditional health care insurance companies provide both the health care service and the health care financing, but HMOs provide only the health care service
   C. HMOs provide both the health care service and the health care financing, but traditional health care insurance companies provide only the financing
   D. HMOs provide both the health care service and the health care financing, but traditional health care insurance companies provide only the service

2. Gwyneth's HMO requires that she receive health care services from a specified, limited number of health care providers chosen by the HMO. Gwyneth's HMO is
   A. open panel
   B. closed panel
   C. choice panel
   D. guarded panel

3. David has a PPO that does not limit him to use only providers that have contracts with the PPO. David's PPO is
   A. open panel
   B. closed panel
   C. choice panel
   D. guarded panel

4. All of the following are examples of managed care plans EXCEPT
   A. health maintenance organizations
   B. preferred provider organizations
   C. indemnity arrangements
   D. point-of-service plans

5. All of the following are characteristics of a PPO EXCEPT
   A. PPO's operate on a fee-for-service
   B. PPO's operate on a prepaid basis
   C. PPO's are typically open panel entities
   D. the relationship between a PPO and its providers is contractual

6. If treatment requiring hospitalization is recommended, the physician of the insured may have to get the expense approved prior to obtaining the treatment. This is known as
   A. limits on lengths of stay
   B. preauthorization
   C. referral service
   D. outpatient benefits

7. All of the following are points in the process of utilization management EXCEPT
   A. prospective review
   B. concurrent review
   C. retrospective review
   D. alternative review

8. Which utilization management review is done after the treatment is complete?
    A. Prospective review
    B. Concurrent review
    C. Retrospective review
    D. Complete review

9. Which of the following alternatives to hospital care provides intermittent nursing care for patients who do not need 24 hour supervision?
    A. Skilled nursing facility
    B. Intermediate nursing facility
    C. Rehabilitative facility
    D. Home health care

10. All of the following statements about an HMO are correct EXCEPT
    A. HMO's control overutilization of their services by subscribers with the gatekeeper concept
    B. HMO subscribers are not free to choose any subscriber that they wish
    C. HMO's are managed care entities
    D. HMO's operate on a fee for service plan

 ANSWER KEY

QUICK QUIZZES

QUICK QUIZ 17.A

1. **D.** Preventative care

2. **A.** medical services are provided first, and then they are billed and paid for

QUICK QUIZ 17.B

1. **B.** open-panel entities

2. **A.** point-of-service plan

QUICK QUIZ 17.C

1. **C.** Second surgical opinion

2. **C.** utilization management

UNIT QUIZ

1. **C.** HMOs provide both the health care service and the health care financing, but traditional health care insurance companies provide only the financing.

2. **B.** A closed-panel, or closed network, HMO specifies a limited number of health care providers from which its subscribers may receive services.

3. **A.** An open panel, or open network, allows subscribers to choose who they wish as a provider.

4. **C.** Indemnity arrangements are not managed care plans.

5. **B.** PPO's operate on a fee-for-service basis rather than a prepaid basis like an HMO.

6. **B.** This is also known as precertification.

7. **D.** Utilization management can occur at a prospective review, concurrent review, and a retrospective review.

8. **C.** The outcome is evaluated to see if treatment was effective and if anything could be changed to product a better or most cost effective outcome in the future.

9. **B.** All of these are facilities other than a hospital that may provide a more appropriate and cost effective level of care for some patients.

10. **D.** HMO's operate on a prepaid basis. Subscribers to the HMO pay their fee in advance.

UNIT 18 Group Health Insurance

18.1 INTRODUCTION

Employment-based health insurance programs have existed in the United States for more than 100 years and have been used to attract the best available talent to a company and also keep employees from leaving.

All group plans; life, health, disability, and the like have similar characteristics; enrollment eligibility, low cost coverage, no proof of insurability to enroll, and convertibility options when exiting the plan.

This unit covers the unique aspects of group health insurance and introduces you to the terms, provisions, and characteristics related to this area of insurance.

🎯 18.2 LEARNING OBJECTIVES

After successfully completing this unit, you should be able to:

- identify the characteristics of group insurance including group coverage, certificates of coverage, and experience rating versus community rating;

- describe the types of eligible groups and what makes them eligible for group life insurance;

- explain the underwriting criteria for employer group health insurance;

- describe employee eligibility, dependent eligibility, probationary period, eligibility period, and open enrollment;

- identify the coordination of benefits provision;

- explain marketing considerations including advertising, regulatory jurisdiction;

- identify change of insurance and loss of coverage including topics such as coinsurance and deductible carryover, no loss, no gain, and events that terminate coverage,; and

- explain the extension of benefits, continuation of benefits, COBRA qualifying events, qualified beneficiaries, notification statements, duration of coverage.

18.3 CHARACTERISTICS OF GROUP INSURANCE

18.3.1 Group Contract

While individual insurance policies insure one person, group insurance policies cover many people under one contract. That reduces the plan cost and lowers premiums. Group insurance premiums are less than individual coverage.

The two parties in a group insurance contract are the insurer and the sponsoring group. The policyholder/owner is the sponsoring group and it controls the master policy.

18.3.2 Certificate of Coverage

The individual members covered by the group plan are not parties to the group insurance contract and have no authority to make decisions regarding the plan. Members receive a **certificate of coverage** that provides evidence of coverage, who is covered by the plan, and summarizes the benefits.

18.3.3 Experience Rating vs. Community Rating

In general, the premium cost for group insurance is based on **experience rating**, a method of establishing the premium on the group's previous claims experience. The larger and more homogenous (similar) the group, the closer it comes to reflecting standard mortality and morbidity rates.

In contrast, **community rating** sets premium costs by using the same rate structure for all subscribers to a medical expense plan, no matter what their past loss experience has been.

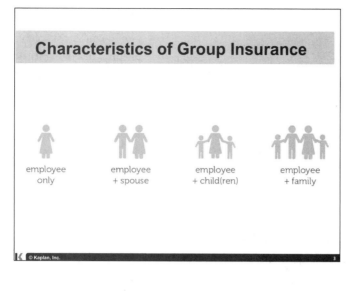

Characteristics of Group Insurance

- Insures many people in one contract
- Usually less expensive than individual insurance
- Sponsor receives the master contract
- Participants receive a certificate of insurance
- Premium
  - Experience rating—based on claims history of the individual group
  - Community rating—based on pooling groups (also used in rating individual insurance)

18.4 TYPES OF ELIGIBLE GROUPS

The general eligibility rule is; a group must have been formed for a purpose other than obtaining insurance for its members. This defines a **natural group**. The insurance plan must be *incidental to the group* rather than its primary reason for being.

Group insurance eligibility is limited to only the following types of groups.

- An employer may sponsor a group insurance plan for its employees. These are known as *employer group plans*. They are sometimes referred to as *employee* group plans.

- A *multiple employer trust* (MET) is a group of small employers in the same industry who either form together in order to purchase group insurance as one entity or self-fund a plan.

- Multiple Employment Welfare Arrangements (MEWAs) provide health and welfare benefits to two or more unrelated employers. The purpose is to provide affordable health coverage to small employers.

- A labor union may sponsor a group insurance plan for its members, or two or more labor unions may join together to provide group insurance for their collective members. Labor union plans are sponsored under a *Taft-Hartley trust*.

- A trade, professional, or other type of association may sponsor a group plan for its members. These are known as *association group plans*.

- A lender, or creditor, may sponsor a group health (disability) insurance plan for its group of debtors. This is known as *group credit disability insurance*. Two features separate group credit insurance from other types of group insurance:

  - while other types of group insurance may not be made payable to the sponsoring group, group credit insurance can be; and

  - the amount of coverage under a group credit insurance plan is limited to the amount of the insured's debt.

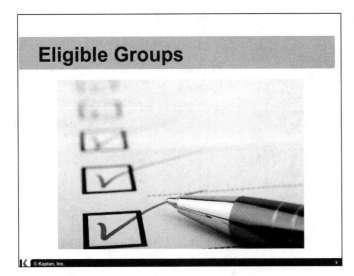

Eligible Groups

- Group can't exist solely for the purpose of buying insurance
- Employer sponsored
- Multiple employers combined
    - Multiple employer trust (MET)
    - Multiple Employer Welfare Arrangement (MEWA)
- Labor unions
    - Taft Hartley Trust
- Trade or professional association
- Lender group
    - Lender is paid
    - Amount insurance no greater than the debt

 QUICK QUIZ 18.A

1. What do the individual members of a group receive as evidence that they are covered by a group health insurance policy?
    A. A master policy
    B. A contract
    C. A certificate of coverage
    D. A document of insurability

2. All of the following are characteristics of group health insurance EXCEPT
    A. it insures more people under one contract
    B. it is more expensive than individual insurance
    C. it is less expensive than individual insurance
    D. participants receive a certificate of insurance

Answers can be found at the end of Unit 18.

18.5 EMPLOYER GROUP HEALTH INSURANCE

18.5.1 Underwriting Criteria

Group insurance underwriters do not evaluate the risk represented by each individual. They look at the risk presented by the characteristics of the group and the plan as a whole. Once the group plan is in force, premiums are based on the experience of the group and can change at each renewal.

Group underwriting means that individuals can enroll in a group insurance plan without providing evidence of insurability. Rather than submitting an application that asks for medical information, each individual submits an enrollment card with basic identifying information.

Group underwriting criteria includes the following.

- **Size of the group**: larger groups can more likely avoid adverse selection. Small group = 2 to 50 lives, Large group = 51 or more lives.

- **Composition of the group**: ages, sex, and income of the members of the group will affect the potential benefits that will be paid.

- **Flow of members through the group**: individuals joining and leaving the group on a regular basis reduces the risk of adverse selection.

- **Plan design**: what will be covered, and for how much.

- **Contributory or noncontributory**: employees pay part of the cost in *contributory* plans, and at least 75% of those eligible must participate in the plan; the employer pays the entire cost in a *noncontributory* plan, and 100% of eligible employees must participate.

- **Persistency**: When employers keep their group coverage with the same insurer year after year, the insurer's expenses are reduced.

- **Administrative capability**: large employers can lower group premium costs by helping administer the plan and use the insurer for stop-loss coverage and/or claims processing.

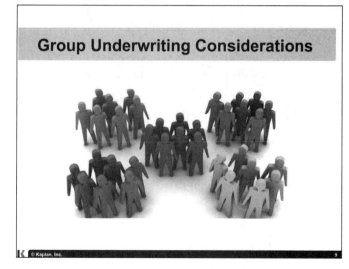

Group Underwriting Considerations

- Size of the group
- Composition of the group
- Flow of members through the group
- Plan design
- Contributory or noncontributory:
  - Contributory—employees pay part or all of the cost
    - Minimum 75% participation
  - Non-contributory—employer pays entire cost
    - 100% participation
- Persistency
- Administrative capability

18.5.2 Eligibility for Coverage

18.5.2.1 Employee Eligibility

Employers cannot discriminate with group benefits. All employees that are eligible can enroll regardless of their age, handicaps, or sex. Pregnancy and maternity must be treated like any other covered condition.

Employers can establish basic employment criteria. The employee must be:

- full-time, and
- actively at work—that is, not on disability leave or other inactive status.

Employers may also exclude union workers as a class, since their compensation and benefits are covered by a collective bargaining agreement.

18.5.2.2 Dependent Eligibility

Coverage must also be made available to a participating employee's spouse or children up to age 26. This includes step-children and adopted children, and it applies whether or not the child is married or a student. Coverage may also be made available to a participating employee's dependent parents.

Many states require that children older than age 26 be covered by a plan if they are mentally or physically disabled and unable to support themselves.

18.5.2.3 Probationary, or Waiting, Period

During a **probationary period** new employees must wait before they can enroll in an employer's group health insurance plan. Probationary periods typically range from one to six months.

18.5.2.4 Eligibility Period and Open Enrollment

When the probationary period ends, new employees can enroll in the group health insurance plan during the *eligibility or enrollment period*, which is typically 30 or 31 days.

Most states require insurers to also offer an **open enrollment** period every year. Individuals who declined coverage during the initial eligibility period can enroll in the health plan during this period without providing evidence of insurability.

Late enrollees—individuals who want to enroll for coverage at any time other than the initial eligibility period or an annual open enrollment period may be required to provide evidence of insurability.

Eligibility

- Employee
  - Full time
  - Actively at work
  - Completed probationary period (if required)
- Dependents
  - Spouse
  - Children younger than age 26
  - Disabled child regardless of age
- Enrollment
  - Follows probationary period
  - Usually no medical questions
- Open enrollment
  - Usually once a year
  - No medical questions
- Late enrollment
  - Medical questions

18.5.3 Coordination of Benefits

Many working couples are covered as employees under their own employer's plan, and each is also covered as a dependent under their spouse's plan. This type of double coverage can result in individuals being **over insured**—which means the individual is able to collect benefits in excess of the amount of the loss.

To avoid this situation, group health insurance policies contain a **coordination of benefits** provision which says that if a loss is payable under two group health insurance plans, one plan will be considered *primary* and the other will be considered *secondary*. The primary plan pays benefits up to its limit first, the secondary insurance plan will pay up to its limit for costs not covered by the primary plan. The provision describes how to determine which plan is primary and which is secondary.

With a married couple, the primary plan is the individual's employer plan, and the secondary plan is the spouse's employer plan. For example, Philip and Kendra are married and have group coverage at work. Both are covered under each person's group plan. Under the coordination of benefits provision, Phillip's employer-sponsored plan is his primary coverage, and Kendra's employer-sponsored plan is his secondary coverage. Kendra's employer-sponsored plan is her primary coverage, and Philip's employer-sponsored plan is her secondary coverage.

A different rule called the "birthday rule" is used for determining the primary plan if a married couple has children. The parent whose birthday comes earliest during the year will use their plan as primary coverage for their children. If Philip's birthday was March 4 and Kendra's was May 8, Philip's plan would be the primary payer for their children's covered medical expenses.

If parents are separated or divorced, the plan of the parent with custody is primary, barring any other legal arrangements.

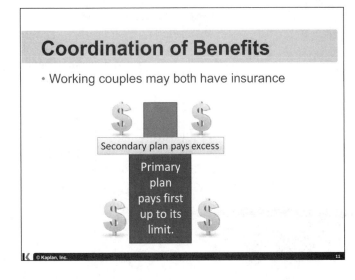

Coordination of Benefits

- Applies when a person is covered by two group policies
- One plan is primary—pays first
- Other plan is secondary—pays only if loss is greater than primary coverage
- Employee plan is primary
- Children—primary plan is parent whose birthday comes first in the calendar year (not the oldest)
  - Custody may determine primary

QUICK QUIZ 18.B

1. Dependent coverage for employees must be made available to a participating employee's spouse or children who are under age

   A. 18

   B. 21

   C. 25

   D. 26

2. Insurers usually allow a period of 30 or 31 days for employees to sign up for health insurance without having to prove evidence of insurability. This period of time is known as the

   A. enrollment period

   B. waiting period

   C. benefits period

   D. coordination of benefits

Answers can be found at the end of Unit 18.

18.6   MARKETING CONSIDERATIONS

18.6.1 Advertising

States regulate the marketing and advertising of accident and health insurance policies to ensure truthful and full disclosure of pertinent information when selling these policies. As a rule, the insurer is held responsible for the content of advertisements of its policies. Advertisements must:

- not be misleading or obscure; and

- clearly outline all policy exclusions or limitations on coverage as well as policy benefits.

18.6.2 Regulatory Jurisdiction

There are no regulatory jurisdiction issues when an employer purchases a group insurance plan from an insurer domiciled in the employer' home state.. Many insurers and employers however do business in multiple states and for this reason the insurance regulator in each state involved would oversee these transactions.

A group health insurance policy is regulated by the state in which it is delivered, assuming that state is also where the employer has its principal business office.

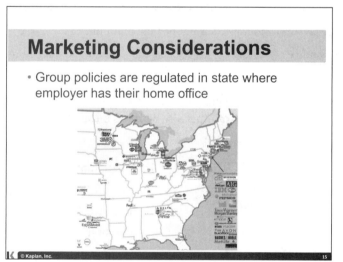

Marketing Considerations for Group Insurance

- Advertising may not be misleading

- Group policy is regulated in the state where employer has office

18.7   CHANGE OF INSURERS AND LOSS OF COVERAGE

18.7.1 Coinsurance and Deductible Carryover

When a group health insurance policy is replaced by another plan, the new insurers will allow coinsurance and deductibles paid under the old plan to count toward the new plans requirements. This eases the transition to the new plan for covered employees.

18.7.2 No Loss, No Gain

Many states have **no loss, no gain** statutes that require benefits for ongoing (disability) claims that started under an old plan to continue without imposing the new plan's eligibility requirements.

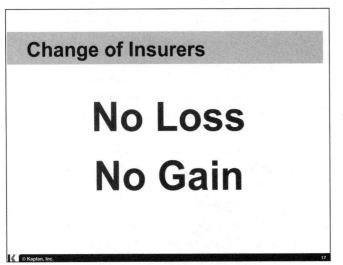

Change of Insurers

- No loss or gain in benefits for current claim

18.7.3 Events That Terminate Coverage

Coverage under a group health insurance plan may be terminated when any of the following occur.

- The employer discontinues the plan or discontinues coverage for a certain class of employees.
- The group policy lapses because the employer did not pay the premium.
- The employee or their dependent's coverage lapses because they did not pay the premium.
- A covered employee quits, is laid off, or they lose their full-time employment status.
- A spouse and children lose connection to the plan due to a divorce from the insured employee or the employee dies, terminates employment, or otherwise becomes ineligible for coverage.
- A non-disabled dependent child reaches age 26.

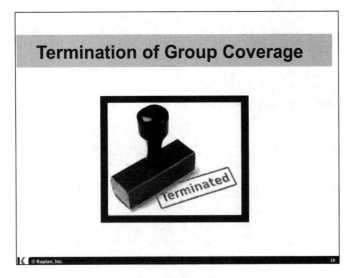

Termination of Group Coverage

- Employer terminates the plan
- Employer didn't pay the premium
- Employee
  - Quits
  - Laid off
  - Reduction in hours
- Dependents
  - Divorce
  - Employee dies
  - Employee employment terminated
  - Too old

18.7.4 Extension of Benefits

Extension of benefits requires, by state laws, that benefits paid by an in-force policy continue after the policy is terminated. Some states require an extension of benefits to a totally disabled member at the time of policy discontinuance.

18.7.5 Continuation of Benefits

The **Consolidated Omnibus Budget Reconciliation Act (COBRA)** is a federal law that requires employers with 20 or more employees to allow former employees and their dependents to continue the benefits provided by the employer's group health insurance plan. Coverage may be continued for 18 to 36 months. Employees or dependents must pay the entire premium for the coverage. COBRA specifies rates, coverage, qualifying events, qualifying beneficiaries, notification procedures, and time of payment requirements for the continued insurance.

18.7.5.1 Qualifying Events

A qualifying event occurs when an employee, spouse, or dependent child lose coverage under the group insurance contract. Qualifying events include:

- death of a covered employee;
- termination of a covered employee, **except** for gross misconduct;
- reduction of work hours of a covered employee;
- Medicare eligibility for a covered employee;
- divorce or legal separation of a covered employee from the covered employee's spouse;
- termination of a child's dependent status; and
- bankruptcy of the employer.

18.7.5.2 Qualified Beneficiary

A **qualified beneficiary** is any individual covered under an employer-maintained group health plan on the day before a qualifying event. Usually this includes:

- covered employees,
- spouse of covered employees, and
- dependent children of covered employees, including children born or adopted during the first 18 months of a benefit continuation period.

18.7.5.3 Notification Statements

Employers must provide notification statements to individuals eligible for COBRA continuation within 14 days. This notification must be provided when:

- a plan becomes subject to COBRA;
- an employee is covered by a plan subject to COBRA; and
- a qualifying event occurs.

The company must notify new employees of their rights under COBRA when they are informed of other employee benefits. Notification of an employee's spouse or other dependents must be made in writing and sent to the last known address of the spouse or dependent.

The option to elect continuation expires 60 days after an individual receives the notification.

18.7.5.4 Duration of Coverage

The maximum period of coverage continuation for termination of employment or a reduction in hours of employment is 18 months. For all other qualifying events, the maximum period of coverage continuation is 36 months.

Certain disqualifying events can result in a termination of coverage before the specified time periods. These disqualifying events and their dates are as follows:

- the first day a premium is overdue;
- the date the employer ceases to maintain any group health plan;
- the date on which the individual is covered by another group plan (even if coverage is less); and
- the date the individual becomes eligible for Medicare.

The coverage must be the same the insured had while employed. The premium must also be the same, except now the terminated employee must pay the entire premium, including any portion previously paid by the employer. The terminated individual may also have to pay an additional amount each month not exceeding 2% of the premium to cover the employer's administrative expenses.

Continuation applies only to health benefits under COBRA.

18.8 OMNIBUS BUDGET RECONCILIATION ACT OF 1989 (OBRA)

OBRA extended the minimum COBRA continuation of coverage period to 29 months for qualified beneficiaries disabled at the time of termination. The disability must meet the Social Security definition of disability. The plan can charge qualified beneficiaries an increased premium, up to 150% of the group premium, during the 11-month disability extension (months 19 to 29).

COBRA– Consolidated Omnibus Budget Reconciliation ACT

- Federal law
- Applies to employers who regularly employ 20 or more people
- Employers must allow employee or dependents to remain on the group plan
- Applies to medical and dental– not life insurance
- Extends coverage for 18 months if
    - Employees employment is terminated
    - Reduction in hours
- Extends coverage for 36 months if dependents no longer qualify due to
    - Divorce
    - Too old
    - Death of employee
- Premium is 102% of regular group premium
    - Employer does not contribute
- COBRA automatically ends
    - Premium not paid
    - Employer stops the group plan
    - Individual becomes covered by another plan
    - Individual becomes eligible for Medicare
- OBRA
    - 29 months if disabled at time of termination

18.9 FEDERAL LAWS AND REGULATIONS FOR GROUP HEALTH INSURANCE

18.9.1 Health Insurance Portability and Accountability Act (HIPAA)

1. The state insurance exam content outline may still show HIPAA as an exam topic. It is important for students to know HIPAA for the exam. But, it is also important to understand that current federal law due to the Affordable Care Act (ACA) changed the preexisting conditions portion of HIPAA. ACA is discussed in Unit 12.

2. HIPAA took effect July 1, 1997. It ensured portability of group insurance coverage and included various mandated benefits that affect small employers, the self-employed, pregnant women, and the mentally ill.

3. **Preexisting conditions** A group health plan may not define a preexisting condition more restrictively than: A *condition in which medical advice, diagnosis, care, or treatment was recommended or received during the six months prior to the enrollment date in the plan.*

   a. A preexisting condition can be excluded for up to 12 months (18 months for a late enrollee).

4. **Creditable coverage** includes most health coverage, including coverage under a group health plan, an HMO, an individual health insurance policy, Medicaid, or Medicare. As long as there is not a break in creditable coverage of 63 or more days, an individual's prior creditable coverage reduces the maximum preexisting condition exclusion period that the new group health plan can apply to that individual. This means if an individual had prior creditable coverage of 12 months or more (18 months if a late enrollee), and there was not a gap of 63 or more days between coverage on the prior plan and the new plan then the new plan would not be allowed to apply a preexisting condition exclusion.

5. **Mandated Benefits** HIPAA guarantees coverage for a 48-hour hospital stay for new mothers and their babies after a regular delivery (96 hours for a cesarean section birth). Also, it expands coverage for mental illness by requiring similar coverage for treatment of mental and physical conditions. The law eliminates insurance policy limits that apply only to mental health coverage. *Small employers* cannot be denied group health insurance coverage because one or more employees are in poor health.

6. **Privacy Disclosures** HIPAA imposes specific requirements on health care providers, insurers, and producers with respect to the privacy of the insureds' health and medical information.

   a. The applicant must be given notice of the following

      - the insurer's privacy practices;
      - the applicant's rights to maintain privacy; and
      - the applicant's opportunity to opt-out.

   b. The producer must provide the applicant with the *Notice of Insurance Information Practices.*

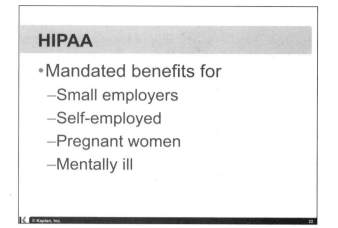

HIPAA

- Preexisting conditions
- Includes most health coverage
- Guaranteed 48 hour hospital stay for new mothers after regular delivery and 96 hours for C-section
- Small employers cannot be denied

18.10 EMPLOYEE RETIREMENT INCOME SECURITY ACT (ERISA)

ERISA was enacted to protect the interests of participants in employee benefit plans as well as the interests of the participants' beneficiaries. Much of the law deals with qualified pension plans, but some sections also apply to group insurance plans.

18.10.1   Fiduciary Responsibility

ERISA mandates very detailed standards for fiduciaries and other parties-in-interest of employee welfare benefit plans, including group insurance plans. This means that anyone with control over plan management or plan assets of any kind must discharge that fiduciary duty solely in the interests of the plan participants and their beneficiaries. Strict penalties are imposed on those who do not fulfill this responsibility.

Reporting and Disclosure   ERISA requires that certain information concerning any employee welfare benefit plan, including group insurance plans, be made available to plan participants, their beneficiaries, the Department of Labor, and the IRS. Examples of the types of information that must be distributed include:

- a summary plan description to each plan participant and the Department of Labor;
- a summary of material modifications that details changes in any plan description to each plan participant and the Department of Labor;
- an annual return or report (Form 5500 or one of its variations) submitted to the IRS;
- a summary annual report to each plan participant; and
- any terminal report to the IRS.

ERISA (Employee Retirement Income Security Act)

- Protects employee and beneficiaries
- Plan deals with qualified pensions and also group insurance
- ERISA requires that certain information be able to plan participants, beneficiaries, and the Department of Labor

 QUICK QUIZ 18.C

1. A state law that requires benefits that began to be paid while a health insurance policy was in force to continue to be paid after the policy is terminated is known as

   A. continuation of benefits

   B. extension of benefits

   C. qualified benefits

   D. COBRA

2. All of the following are events that terminate coverage EXCEPT

   A. a non-disabled dependent child reaches age 25

   B. the employer discontinues the coverage for a certain class of employees

   C. a covered employee quits

   D. a covered employee is laid off

Answers can be found at the end of Unit 18.

UNIT 18 CRAM SHEET

Characteristics of Group Insurance

- Insures many people in one contract
- Usually less expensive than individual insurance
- Sponsor receives master contract
- Participants receive a certificate of insurance
- Premium
    - Experience rating—based on claims history of the individual group
    - Community rating—based on pooling groups (also used in rating individual insurance)

Eligible Groups

- Group can't exist solely for the purpose of buying insurance
- Employer sponsored
- Multiple employers combined
    - Multiple employer trust (MET)
    - Multiple Employer Welfare Arrangement (MEWA)
- Labor unions
    - Taft Hartley Trust
- Trade or professional association
- Lender group
    - Lender is paid
    - Amount insurance no greater than the debt

Group Underwriting Considerations

- Size of the group-small group, 2-50 lives, large group, 51 or more lives
- Composition of the group
- Flow of members through the group
- Plan design
- Contributory or noncontributory:
    - Contributory—employees pay part or all of the cost
        - Minimum 75% participation
    - Non-contributory—employer pays entire cost
        - 100% participation
- Persistency
- Administrative capability

Eligibility

- Employee
- Full time
- Actively at work
- Completed probationary period (if required)
- Dependents
    - Spouse
    - Children younger than age 26
    - Disabled child regardless of age
- Enrollment
    - Follows probationary period
    - Usually no medical questions

- Open enrollment
  - Usually once a year
  - No medical questions
- Late enrollment
  - Medical questions

Coordination of Benefits

- Applies when a person is covered by two group policies
- One plan is primary—pays first
- Other plan is secondary—pays only if loss is greater than primary coverage
- Employee plan is primary
- Children—primary plan is parent whose birthday comes first in the year (not the oldest)
  - Custody may determine primary

Change of insurers

- No loss or gain in benefits for current claim

Termination of Group Coverage

- Employer terminates the plan
- Employer didn't pay the premium
- Employee
  - Quits
  - Laid off
  - Reduction in hours
- Dependents
  - Divorce
  - Employee dies
  - Employee employment terminated
  - Too old

COBRA—Consolidated Omnibus Budget Reconciliation ACT

- Federal law
- Applies to employers who regularly employ 20 or more people
- Employers must allow employee or dependents to remain on the group plan
- Applies to medical and dental—not life insurance
- Extends coverage for 18 months if
  - Employees employment is terminated
  - Reduction in hours
- Extends coverage for 36 months if dependents no longer qualify due to
  - Divorce

- – Too old

- – Death of employee

- Premium is 102% of regular group premium

  - – Employer does not contribute

- COBRA automatically ends

  - – Premium not paid

  - – Employer stops the group plan

  - – Individual becomes covered by another plan

  - – Individual becomes eligible for Medicare

- OBRA

  - – 29 months if disabled at time of termination

HIPAA (Health Insurance Portability and Accountability Act)

- Preexisting conditions

- Includes most health coverage

- Guaranteed 48 hour hospital stay for new mothers after regular delivery and 96 hours for C-section

- Small employers cannot be denied

UNIT 18 QUIZ

In order to measure your success, we recommend that you answer the following 10 questions correctly.

1. All of the following could be considered dependents except the insured's
    A. adopted children
    B. parents
    C. 26–year–old child
    D. 26-year-old child who is disabled

2. The coordination of benefits provision provides that when a person is covered under more than one plan the
    A. primary plan pays up to its limits first and then the secondary plan pays the rest
    B. primary plan and secondary plan split the cost
    C. secondary plan pays up to its limits first and then the primary plan pays the rest
    D. secondary play does not have to pay anything

3. When both parents have employer-provided group coverage, which plan would be the primary payer that their children would be covered under?
    A. The father's plan
    B. The mother's plan
    C. The plan of the parent whose birthday falls closest to the child's birthday
    D. The plan of the parent whose birthday falls earliest in a calendar year

4. Which federal law requires employers with more than 20 employees to include in their group insurance plan a continuation of benefits provision for all eligible employees?
    A. COBRA
    B. OBRA
    C. ERISA
    D. TEFRA

5. The option to elect continuation of benefits after an employee's group plan is terminated expires
    A. 30 days after the individual receives notification
    B. 45 days after the group plan is terminated
    C. 60 days after the individual receives notification
    D. 90 days after the individual receives notification

6. A lender, or creditor may sponsor a group health insurance plan for its group of debtors. This is known as
    A. multiple employer welfare arrangements
    B. group credit disability insurance
    C. association group plans
    D. credit life insurance

7. A health insurance plan where the employees pay part of the cost and at least 75% of those eligible must participate in is known as
    A. a contributory plan
    B. a noncontributory plan
    C. an association plan
    D. an administrative plan

8. An insurer requirement that new employees must wait for a certain period of time before they can enroll in an employer's group health plan is called a(n)
    A. eligibility period
    B. enrollment period
    C. new hire period
    D. probationary period

9. Under COBRA, the maximum period of coverage for termination of employment or a reduction in hours is
    A. 12 months
    B. 18 months
    C. 24 months
    D. 36 months

10. A method of establishing the premium of a group based on the group's previous claim experience is known as
    A. community rating
    B. experience rating
    C. premium rating
    D. group rating

ANSWER KEY

QUICK QUIZZES

QUICK QUIZ 18.A

1. **C.** A certificate of coverage

2. **B.** it is more expensive than individual insurance

QUICK QUIZ 18.B

3. **D.** 26

4. **A.** enrollment period

QUICK QUIZ 18.C

1. **B.** extension of benefits

2. **A.** a non-disabled dependent child reaches age 25

UNIT QUIZ

1. **C.**   Age 26 is the cutoff for children as dependents unless the child is disabled.

2. **A.** The coordination of benefits provision provides that when a person is covered under more than one plan, the total benefits cannot exceed the total medical expenses or loss of wages.

3. **D.** When a married couple has children, the parents' birthdays are used to determine whose insurance is primary payer.

4. **A.** COBRA requires employers with more than 20 employees to include in their group insurance plan a continuation of benefits provision for all eligible employees. Coverage may be continued for 18-36 months.

5. **C.** The company must notify employees, and dependents in writing of their rights under COBRA.

6. **B.** The amount of coverage available under a group credit insurance plan is limited to the insured's debt.

7. **A.** At least 75% of eligible employees must participate in a contributory plan. In a noncontributory plan, 100% must participate.

8. **D.** Probationary periods, also known as waiting periods, range from one to six months.

9. **B.** For all other qualifying events, besides termination of employment or a reduction in hours, the maximum period of coverage is 36 months.

10. **B.** Experience rating is based on claims history of the individual group while community rating is based on pooling of groups.

UNIT 19 Dental Insurance

19.1 INTRODUCTION

Unlike health insurance, which is more or less mandatory in many parts of the country, dental insurance is still considered an optional insurance. However, just like the ever-increasing cost of medical care, dental costs are increasing as well. Dental insurance generally covers a percentage of costs for basic and major services.

This unit covers the various types of treatments and features of dental insurance and provides an overview of group dental coverage.

19.2   LEARNING OBJECTIVES

After successfully completing this unit, you should be able to:

▫ identify the seven types of dental expense plans: diagnostic and preventative, restorative, oral surgery, endodontics, periodontics, prosthodontics, and orthodontics;

▫ explain the coverage features of dental insurance including choice of provider, scheduled versus nonscheduled plans, combination of plans, deductibles, coinsurance, and limits, exclusions, and predetermination of benefits;

▫ describe employer group dental expense plans including integrated deductible vs. standalone; and

▫ explain how to minimize adverse selection in a dental plan.

19.3   DENTAL EXPENSE PLANS

19.3.1 Types of Dental Treatment

Dental expense plans usually provide coverage for the following types of dental treatment:

- diagnostic and preventive—routine exams and x-rays, regular cleanings, fluoride treatments;

- restorative—repairing or restoring teeth that have been damaged, usually by tooth decay; fillings and crowns are restorative treatments;

- oral surgery—surgery performed in the oral cavity, for example, the removal of wisdom teeth;

- endodontics—treatment of the pulp (the soft tissue substance located in the center of each tooth); root canals are an endodontic treatment;

- periodontics—treatment of the supporting structures of the teeth – that is, the gums;

- prosthodontics—artificial replacements, such as bridges and dental implants; and

- orthodontics—correction of irregular alignment of the teeth; most commonly, braces.

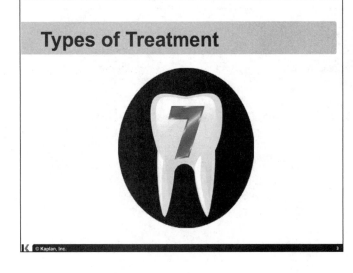

Types of Treatment

- Diagnostic and preventive
- Restorative
- Oral surgery
- Endodontics
- Periodontics
- Prosthodontics
- Orthodontics

19.3.2 Coverage Features

19.3.2.1 Choice of Provider

Dental expense coverage may be offered under a traditional indemnity plan which places no limits on the insured's choice of dentist. Many dental expense plans are offered through preferred provider organizations (PPOs) which have contracted with particular dentists to provide services for pre-arranged fees. In order to get the highest reimbursement rates (80% to 100%) on the treatment the insured must choose a dentist that belongs to the PPO network. The insured may go outside the network, but reimbursement rates will be much lower (50% to 60%).

19.3.2.2 Scheduled vs. Nonscheduled Plans

Some dental expense plans are scheduled; benefits are limited to a specified maximum per procedure, with first dollar coverage, much like basic hospital, medical, and surgical plans. Most, however, are nonscheduled plans that pay on a usual, customary, and reasonable (UCR) basis like comprehensive medical expense coverage.

19.3.2.3 Combination Plans

Some dental expense plans combine features of both the scheduled (basic) and nonscheduled (comprehensive) plans. They typically cover diagnostic and preventive treatment on a usual, customary, and reasonable basis but use a fee schedule for other dental services.

19.3.2.4 Deductibles, Coinsurance, and Limits for Various Benefit Categories

Deductibles, coinsurance, and limits often apply differently to various levels of treatment.

- *Diagnostic/preventive services* are usually covered without deductibles or coinsurance to encourage preventive dental care. However, routine exams and cleanings are generally limited to twice a year and diagnostic x-rays to once every two or three years.

- *Basic services* such as fillings, crowns, and local anesthesia may be subject to a deductible and 20% coinsurance or a limit per service in excess of which the insured must pay. There may also be an overall annual limit on benefits for all basic services.

- *Major services* such as oral surgery, root canals, periodontics, bridges, and implants may be subject to a higher coinsurance rate, such as 50%, as well as per-service limits. Replacement of dentures may be limited to once every five years. Orthodontia usually has its own separate deductible, higher coinsurance rate, and annual limit.

19.3.2.5 Predetermination of Benefits

Most dental expense plans recommend, and a few require, that dentists provide patients with a written treatment plan showing the estimated charge for each service to be performed, along with a breakdown of how much of the cost is expected to be paid by the dental plan, and how much will remain for the insured to pay. Often the recommendation or requirement applies only to treatment that will exceed a certain amount, such as $200 or $300. These plans help the insured to evaluate their treatment options and budget for their upcoming treatment.

Features of Dental Insurance

- Choice of provider
- Scheduled vs. nonscheduled
- Combination
- Deductibles/coinsurance/limits
- Predetermination of benefits

© Kaplan, Inc.   4

Features of Dental Insurance

- Any provider versus PPO
- Scheduled versus non-scheduled benefits
- Diagnostic and preventative—usually covered 100%
- Basic services—fillings, crowns, anesthesia—coinsurance usually 80/20—subject to annual limit
- Major services—root canals, oral surgery, gum treatment etc., coinsurance usually 50/50 subject to annual limit
- Predetermination of benefits often required

19.3.2.6 Exclusions

The following are typically excluded from coverage under dental expense plans:

- cosmetic treatment, such as teeth whitening, and elective treatment beyond what is needed to restore or maintain dental health;
- oral hygiene instruction;
- replacement of teeth missing at the time coverage became effective;
- completion of services begun before coverage became effective;
- replacement of lost dentures, duplicate dentures;
- occupational injuries covered by workers' compensation; and
- treatment received in government facilities.

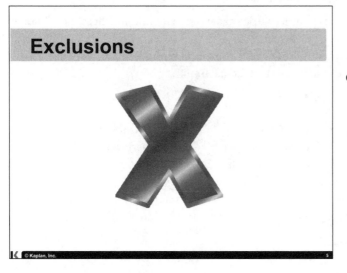

Exclusions

© Kaplan, Inc.   5

Common Exclusions:

- Cosmetic treatment
- Replacement of teeth missing before coverage
- Loss of dentures
- Occupational injuries

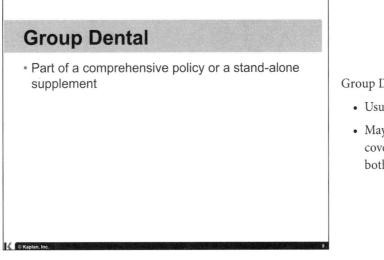

QUICK QUIZ 19.A

1. Which of the following dental expense plans covers the removal of wisdom teeth?
   A. Diagnostic and preventative
   B. Restorative
   C. Oral surgery
   D. Endodontics

2. A dental plan that has benefits limited to specified maximums per procedure with first dollar coverage is considered to be
   A. scheduled
   B. nonscheduled
   C. combined
   D. predetermined

Answers can be found at the end of Unit 19.

19.3.3 Employer Group Dental Expense Plans

19.3.3.1 Integrated Deductible vs. Stand-Alone Plan

In regard to employer group coverage, dental expense coverage may be integrated within a comprehensive health plan or provided as a stand-alone supplement along with a health plan. When integrated into a comprehensive health plan, the dental expense coverage will not have a separate deductible – only the health plan deductible needs to be satisfied. More often, dental expense coverage is offered as a stand-alone supplement with its own deductible and coinsurance requirements.

Group Dental

• Part of a comprehensive policy or a stand-alone supplement

© Kaplan, Inc.   9

Group Dental

- Usually a separate policy
- May be integrated with medical coverage—one deductible for both

19.3.3.2 Minimizing Adverse Selection

Dental expense coverage differs from medical coverage in significant ways.

- Patients' choices in treatment options often represent a big difference in costs. For instance, a patient can choose bridgework that is fixed or removable and inlays that are made of gold or a less expensive but equally durable material.

- Needed dental work can often be postponed longer than necessary medical treatment. Employees who need dental work may be able to wait until a dental expense plan becomes effective, causing the insurer to be liable for larger benefits than it would otherwise expect to pay.

Insurers often implement the following restrictions to minimize the increased potential for adverse selection in dental expense plans.

- Probationary periods (a period of time after the employee becomes eligible to join the group plan before dental expense coverage is effective).

- Limitations on benefits for late enrollees (those that want to sign up for coverage after the end of the 30-day enrollment period that follows the eligibility period).

- Reduced benefit limits during the first year of coverage.

- No conversion privilege to convert the dental expense coverage to an individual plan if the group coverage terminates (however, dental expense coverage is subject to COBRA continuation rules).

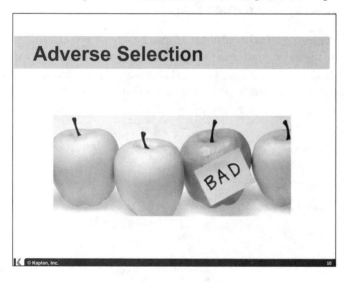

Adverse Selection

- Probationary periods
- Limitations on benefits for late enrollees
- Reduced benefit limits during the first year of coverage

🧠 UNIT 19 CRAM SHEET

Types of Treatment

- Diagnostic and preventive—routine exams and x-rays, regular cleanings, fluoride treatments;
- Restorative—repairing or restoring teeth that have been damaged, usually by tooth decay
- Oral surgery—surgery performed in the oral cavity
- Endodontics—treatment of the pulp (the soft tissue substance located in the center of each tooth)
- Periodontics—treatment of the supporting structures of the teeth—that is, the gums

- Prosthodontics—artificial replacements, such as bridges and dental implants
- Orthodontics—correction of irregular alignment of the teeth

Features of Dental Insurance

- Any provider versus PPO
- Scheduled versus non-scheduled benefits
- Diagnostic and preventative—usually covered 100%
- Basic services—fillings, crowns, anesthesia—coinsurance usually 80/20—subject to annual limit
- Major services—root canals, oral surgery, gum treatment etc. Coinsurance usually 50/50 subject to annual limit
- Predetermination of benefits often required

Group Dental

- Usually a separate policy
- May be integrated with medical coverage—one deductible for both

Adverse Selection

- Probationary periods
- Limitations on benefits for late enrollees
- Reduced benefit limits during the first year of coverage

UNIT 19 QUIZ

In order to measure your success, we recommend that you answer the following 10 questions correctly.

1. All of the following are common exclusions in a dental policy EXCEPT
    A. replacement of lost dentures
    B. teeth that are knocked out in an accident
    C. oral hygiene instructions and plaque control programs are often limited or excluded
    D. cosmetic treatment such as teeth whitening

2. The ability of an individual to wait until covered by dental insurance before seeking treatment for dental issues is an example of
    A. improper insurance
    B. improper selection
    C. adverse selection
    D. adverse insurance

3. A root canal is an example of which of the following types of dental treatment?
    A. Periodontics
    B. Oral surgery
    C. Restorative
    D. Endodontics

4. Today, most dental plans are offered through
    A. PPOs
    B. HMOs
    C. self-insurance
    D. government insurance

5. A dental plan that pays on a usual, customary, and reasonable basis (UCR) is also known as a
    A. scheduled plan
    B. nonscheduled plan
    C. maximum plan
    D. first dollar coverage plan

6. All of the following statements regarding deductibles that apply to various levels of dental treatment EXCEPT
    A. preventative services are usually covered without deductibles to encourage preventative dental care
    B. routine exams are limited to twice a year
    C. diagnostic X-ray exams are limited to every 2 or 3 years
    D. basic services such as fillings and crowns are covered without deductibles and coinsurance

7. A written treatment plan provided to patients showing the estimated charge for each service to be performed, along with a breakdown or how much of the cost is expected to be paid by the dental plan is known as a
    A. predetermination of benefits
    B. combination plan
    C. scheduled benefit
    D. nonscheduled benefit

8. All of the following statements regarding group dental expense plans are correct EXCEPT
    A. with a group plan that integrates a comprehensive plan and a dental plan, the dental plan will not have a separate deductible
    B. a stand-alone supplement has its own deductible and coinsurance requirements
    C. most dental expense coverage is integrated into a comprehensive health plan
    D. most dental expense coverage is offered as a stand-alone supplement

9. Fillings, crowns, and restoring teeth that have been damaged by tooth decay is an example of
    A. diagnostic and preventative dental treatment
    B. restorative dental treatment
    C. oral surgery
    D. endodontics

10. All of the following are examples of major dental services EXCEPT
    A. orthodontia
    B. local anesthesia
    C. oral surgery
    D. root canals

ANSWER KEY

QUICK QUIZZES

QUICK QUIZ 19.A

1. **C.** Oral surgery

2. **A.** scheduled

UNIT QUIZ

1. **B.** Teeth knocked out in an accident will be covered unless that accident happened while the insured was driving a car for work. In that case, workers compensation would cover the expense.

2. **C.** Employees who need dental work may wait until their dental expense plan becomes effective and this causes insurer to be liable for larger benefits.

3. **D.** Endodontics is treatment of the soft tissue substance located in the center of each tooth (pulp).

4. **A.** Most dental expense plans are offered through preferred provider organizations (PPOs) which have contracted with particular dentists to provide services for agreed-upon fees.

5. **B.** Most dental plans pay on a usual, reasonable, and customary basis like comprehensive medical expense coverage.

6. **D.** Basics services are subject to a deductible and 20% coinsurance or a limit per service in excess of which the insured must pay.

7. **A.** These plans help insured evaluate their treatment options and budget for upcoming treatment.

8. **C.** Most often dental expense insurance is offered as a stand-alone supplement.

9. **B.** Restorative dental treatment is repairing or restoring teeth that have been damaged.

10. **B.** Local anesthesia is a basic service along with fillings and crowns. Major services include oral surgery, root canals, periodontia, bridges, and implants.

UNIT 20 Medicare and Medicaid

20.1 INTRODUCTION

Medicare and Medicaid are two governmental programs that provide medical and health-related services to specific groups of people. Although the two programs are very different, they are both managed by the Centers for Medicare and Medicaid Services, a division of the U.S. Department of Health and Human Services.

When an individual turns age 65 and has obtained fully insured status with Social Security, Medicare becomes either their primary or secondary health insurance plan.

Medicaid, on the other hand, is not an entitlement. It's a means-tested health and medical services program for families and individuals with low incomes and few resources.

This unit will look at these government sponsored programs:

- Medicare,
- Medicare supplement insurance, a commercial coverage designed specifically to work with Medicare, and
- Medicaid

⊙ 20.2   LEARNING OBJECTIVES

After successfully completing this unit, you should be able to:

- identify the government sponsored health insurance programs: Medicare, Medicare supplement insurance, and Medicaid;

- describe Medicare and the benefits provided under Medicare Part A, B, C, and D;

- explain enrollment and eligibility for Medicare Part A, available coverage, and exclusions with inpatient hospital coverage, skilled nursing facility, home health care, and hospice care;

- explain enrollment and eligibility for Medicare Part B, available coverage, and cost sharing amounts;

- explain the claims process and terminology;

- list Medicare exclusions;

- describe Part C: Medicare Advantage, its distinctions from Medicare A and B, and the four types of plans available;

- explain Medicare Part D: Prescription drug coverage;

- explain coordination of coverage between Medicare and employer group health coverage;

- identify Medicare supplement insurance (Medigap) and the 10 standard Medigap plans;

- explain disclosure, sales and marketing, required provisions, and replacement regulations with Medicare;

- define Medicare SELECT; and

- identify Medicaid and eligibility requirements.

20.3   MEDICARE

20.3.1 Nature, Financing, and Administration

Medicare pays a large portion of the health care bill for persons who:

- are age 65 or over;

- have end-stage renal disease (kidney failure); or

- have been receiving Social Security disability benefits for at least 24 months.

In order to be covered by Medicare, an individual must be "fully insured" according to Social Security. Qualification requires accumulating at least 40 credits, which are earned by generating a minimum amount of work-related income over at least the past 10 years and paying Social Security (FICA) taxes.

Medicare is federally funded by The Centers for Medicare & Medicaid Services (CMS), which is a branch of the Department of Health and Human Services (HHS). Private healthcare insurance companies process medical claims for Medicare and are known as Medicare Administrative Contractors (MAC).

The initial enrollment for Medicare is a seven-month period that begins three months before the month an individual turns 65, includes the month they turn 65, and ends three months after the month they turn 65.

Medicare coverage is divided into four parts.

- Part A covers hospital, skilled nursing facility, hospice, and home health care.
- Part B covers medical care provided by physicians and other medical services.
- Part C covers health care delivered by managed care plans.
- Part D covers prescription drugs,

Eligibility for Medicare Coverage

- Age 65 and over or
- Kidney failure (end-stage renal disease) or
- Received Social Security disability for at least 24 months

20.3.2 Medicare Part A

20.3.2.1 Enrollment

For people age 65 and covered by Social Security, enrollment in Medicare Part A is automatic on the first day of the month that they reach age 65 and is free. People not covered by Social Security may obtain Part A coverage under certain circumstances by paying a premium.

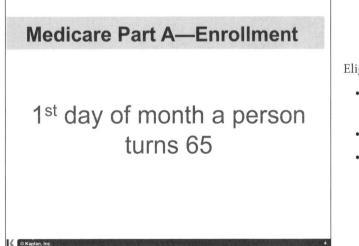

Eligibility

- Automatic for persons age 65 and eligible for Social Security
- Supported by payroll taxes
- Premium charge for those not fully qualified for Social Security

20.3.2.2 Inpatient Hospital Coverage

Medicare Part A's **inpatient hospital coverage** is for a semi-private room and the other usual charges for necessary hospital care: meals, supplies, medical services, drugs taken as an inpatient, and so on.

It does *not* cover:

- physician or surgeon charges;
- private duty nursing;
- the first three pints of blood (the *blood deductible*—this is the total combined deductible that must be met, including any blood received under Part B); or
- charges for a phone, a TV, or other non-medical services.

Part A inpatient hospital coverage is based on *benefit periods* rather than the calendar year. A benefit period begins when someone is admitted to the hospital and ends 60 days after discharge. If the person is re-admitted within 60 days of discharge, it does not start a new benefit period but is a continuation of the initial one.

For each benefit period, inpatient hospital coverage and cost-sharing amounts are as follows:

- the patient pays a deductible, which changes annually (but remember that the deductible applies per benefit period, not per calendar year);
- days 1 through 60—fully paid by Medicare (after the deductible); and
- days 61 through 90—Medicare pays most of the cost, and the patient pays a daily co-pay amount which changes each year.

For a stay over 90 days, the patient may draw upon 60 lifetime reserve days. The daily co-pay for lifetime reserve days is double that of days 61 through 90. This co-pay amount also changes each year.

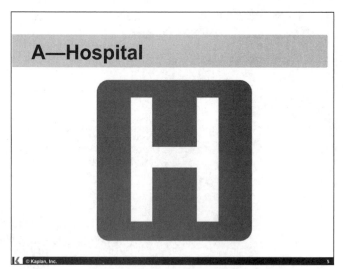

Hospital

- 90 days per benefit period
- New benefit period starts 60 days after discharge
- Additional 60 lifetime reserve days
- Deductible per benefit period–after deductible Medicare pays 100% of first 60 days
- Patient pays co-pay per day for days 61-90
- Patient pays a higher daily co-pay for lifetime reserve days

20.3.2.3 Skilled Nursing Facility (SNF) Care

A **skilled nursing facility (SNF)** is for people that need round-the-clock medical care provided by licensed nurses, but does not need the acute care provided by a hospital. A facility that provides only intermediate (less than round-the-clock) medical care or custodial care (help with the activities of daily living—ADLs—such as eating, bathing, and so on) is not a skilled nursing facility. **Intermediate Care and Custodial Care are not covered by Medicare.**

Medicare covers skilled nursing facility care if:

- it is a Medicare-approved facility; and
- the SNF stay begins immediately after release from a hospital stay of at least three days.

If those conditions are met, Medicare coverage and cost-sharing amounts for a skilled nursing facility stay are as follows:

- day 1 through 20—fully paid by Medicare; and
- days 21 through 100 —Medicare pays most of the cost and the patient pays a daily co-pay amount which changes each year.

After day 100, Medicare pays nothing.

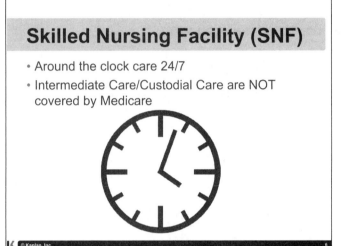

Skilled Nursing Facility (SNF)

- Medical treatment
- Following a hospital stay of at least three days
- 100 days of coverage
  - Day 1–20—100% paid by Medicare
  - Days 21–100—daily co-pay paid by patient

20.3.2.4 Home Health Care

If a patient is confined at home, Medicare Part A's **home health care** benefit covers:

- visits (not round-the-clock care) by a home health aide to provide medical services such as part-time nursing care and physical, occupational, or speech therapy; and
- 80% of the cost of durable medical equipment such as hospital beds or wheelchairs.

The home health care benefit does not pay for:

- meals; or
- homemaker services such as shopping, cleaning, and laundry.

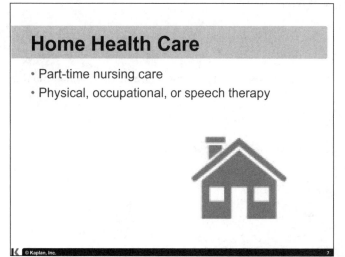

Home Health

- Skilled care provided in the home
- Not sitting services
- 100% paid by Medicare
- Medicare pays 80% of durable medical equipment in the home

20.3.2.5 Hospice Care

Hospice care is for terminally ill patients and their families. It includes counseling, pain relief, and symptom management.

It may also include *respite care*, which is care provided temporarily in a hospice facility for a patient who is normally cared for in the home. The respite is for the usual caregivers.

- Hospice
  - Comfort care for terminally ill and family
  - Can be provided in the home or an approved facility

20.3.2.6 Exclusions

Medicare Part A does not cover:

- first three pints of blood,
- private duty nursing,
- non-medical services,
- intermediate care, or
- custodial care.

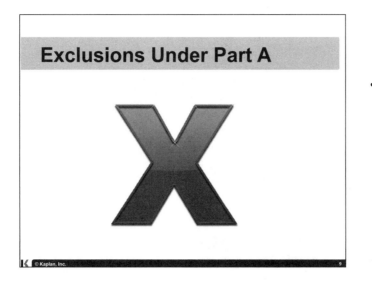

- Excluded Under Part A
  - First three pints of blood
  - Private duty nursing
  - Non-medical services
  - Intermediate care
  - Custodial care

 QUICK QUIZ 20.A

1. All of the following are exclusions under Medicare Part A EXCEPT
   A. first 3 pints of blood
   B. custodial care
   C. hospice care
   D. private duty nursing

2. Which of the following Medicare Part A coverages is for individuals that need round-the-clock medical care provided by licensed nurses, but do not need the acute care provided by a hospital?
   A. Inpatient hospital coverage
   B. Skilled nursing facility
   C. Home health care
   D. Hospice care

Answers can be found at the end of Unit 20.

20.3.3 Medicare Part B

20.3.3.1 Enrollment

Individuals who enroll in Part A are automatically enrolled in Part B unless they request otherwise. Part B is optional and requires a monthly Part B premium. The Part B monthly premium is tied to an individual's income level and is deducted from the Social Security monthly benefit check.

If Part B enrollment occurs before the month an individual reaches age 65, coverage begins on the first day of that month (same as Part A coverage). If an individual initially declines Part B enrollment, they can enroll during the *general enrollment period* that occurs each year from January 1 through March 31 and coverage begins on the following July 1.

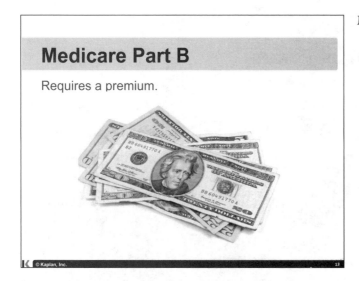

Medicare Part B

- Monthly premium that increases with income level
- Not required—can have Part A only
- Initial enrollment period
  - 3 months before age 65
  - Month of age 65
  - 3 months after age 65
- Annual open enrollment
  - January 1 through March 31 each year
  - Coverage effective July 1

20.3.3.2 Coverage

Medicare Part B provides coverage for three general kinds of medical services: inpatient and outpatient physician services, home health care (if not covered by Part A), and outpatient medical services and supplies. Also covered are physical, occupational, and speech therapy, medically necessary ambulance service, prosthetics, and drugs that cannot be self-administered.

Some preventive care is included under Medicare Part B:

- an initial routine physical examination within the first six months of enrollment;
- screening tests for cholesterol, diabetes, and colorectal cancer;
- annual mammograms (age 40 and over), pap tests, pelvic examinations, and clinical breast exams for women;
- annual prostate cancer screenings for men age 50 and over;
- glaucoma testing once every 12 months;
- bone mass measurements for qualified individuals and
- flu shots.

20.3.3.3 Cost-Sharing Amounts

Medicare Part B has an annual deductible that changes each year and also a 20% coinsurance. Any part of the three-pint blood deductible that has not been met under Part A must be met under Part B.

- Coverage
  - Doctor
  - Outpatient services—tests etc.
  - Home health (if not covered by Part A)
- Calendar year deductible
- 80/20 coinsurance after deductible
- No stop loss

20.3.4 Claims Process

Medicare determines what the reasonable charge is for a particular service, and the patient must pay the difference if the actual charge is more, unless the doctor or supplier agrees to accept *assignment*. This means that the doctor or supplier will accept Medicare's approved amounts as full payment and cannot legally bill the patient for anything above that amount. Doctors and suppliers are not required to accept assignment.

If Medicare decides that an expense is medically unnecessary, the patient must pay the entire cost.

If a doctor has not accepted a Medicare assignment, the bill is sent directly to the patient. They must fill out a Medicare claim form with the itemized bills including the date and place of treatment, description of treatment, and the doctor's name. The form and accompanying documents are sent to the Medicare carrier for the patient's area. Upon receiving the claim, the carrier sends the patient a form called *Explanation of Medicare Benefits* that itemizes the services covered and the approved payment for each service.

20.3.5 Exclusions

Medicare Part B does not cover:

- routine foot, vision, dental, or hearing care;
- most immunizations;
- most outpatient prescription drugs;
- physician charges above Medicare's approved amount;
- private-duty nursing;
- cosmetic surgery (unless needed to repair an accidental injury);
- most care received outside the US; and
- expenses incurred as a result of war or act of war.

Medicare Part B Exclusions

- Routine physical exams beyond the initial one described previously;

- Routine foot, vision, dental, or hearing care;

- Most immunizations;

- Most outpatient prescription drugs;

- Physician charges above Medicare's approved amount;

- Private-duty nursing;

- Cosmetic surgery (unless needed to repair an accidental injury);

- Most care received outside the US; and

- Expenses incurred as a result of war or act of war.

 QUICK QUIZ 20.B

1. All of the following are covered under Medicare EXCEPT
   A. annual prostate cancer screenings for men age 50 and over
   B. screening tests for cholesterol and diabetes
   C. flu shots
   D. routine foot, vision, dental, or hearing care

2. The initial enrollment period for Medicare Part B begins
   A. on the day a person turns 65
   B. 3 months before the month a person turns 65
   C. every year on January 1
   D. the first day of the month a person turns 65

Answers can be found at the end of Unit 20.

20.3.6 Medicare Part C: Medicare Advantage

20.3.6.1 Distinction from Parts A and B

Medicare Parts A and B were signed into law in 1965 and are referred to as the *Original Medicare*; both parts operate on a fee-for-service basis.

In the 1990s, a new option, Medicare Part C – called Medicare Advantage – was enacted. Private companies contract with Medicare to provide Medicare beneficiaries with their Part A and Part B coverage, and some additional benefits, for usually an additional cost. Many Medicare Advantage plans include prescription drug coverage.

Medicare beneficiaries can choose to receive their benefits from a Medicare Advantage plan but they still must enroll in Part A and B, pay the Part B premium, and pay the Medicare Advantage plan premium.

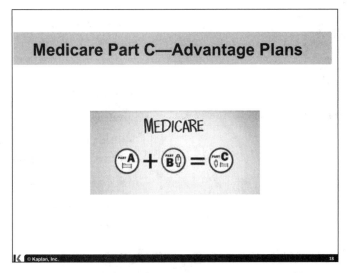

Medicare Part C—Advantage Plans

- Medicare contracts with and pays private companies
- Enrollees medical expenses paid by the private plan
- Enrollee must be enrolled in Medicare Part A & B
- Private company may charge the enrollee a fee
- May provide outpatient drug coverage

20.3.6.2 Types of Medicare Advantage Plans

There are four types of Medicare Advantage plans.

- **Medicare managed care plans**—these operate like health maintenance organization (HMO) or point-of-service (POS) plans. Care must be obtained from the plan's network of providers under the direction of a primary care physician who acts as a gatekeeper. Enrollees may have to pay a small co-payment per doctor visit, but they do not have to pay Medicare deductibles and coinsurance amounts. These plans often cover services not covered by original Medicare, such as routine physical exams, prescription drugs, vision care, and dental care.

- **Medicare preferred provider organization (PPO) plans**—these plans have a network of providers, but no gatekeeper. Enrollees pay more of their costs if they go outside the plan's network.

- **Medicare private fee-for-service (PFFS) plans**—these plans operate on a fee-for-service basis like original Medicare, but rather than using the fees established by Medicare, a private company negotiates the fees that providers will be paid.

- **Medicare specialty plans**—these plans focus on the particular needs of defined groups of patients, such as those who are eligible for both Medicare and Medicaid, or those with a certain medical condition like kidney failure or diabetes.

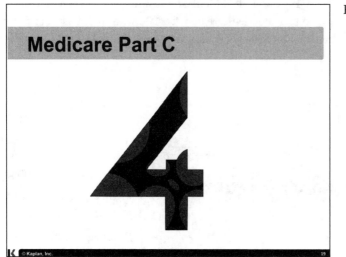

Four types of Medicare Advantage Plans

- Medicare managed care plans
    - HMO or POS
    - Gatekeeper
    - Care must be obtained from the plan's network of providers
    - Enrollees may have to pay a co-payment per doctor visit
- PPO
    - No gate keeper
    - More cost if outside of network
- Private fee-for-service (PFFS) plans
    - Plan negotiates the fees that providers will be paid
- Medicare specialty plans
    - Special needs such as kidney failure

20.3.7 Medicare Part D: Prescription Drug Coverage

Medicare Part D makes prescription drug coverage available to people covered by Medicare. Individuals with Part A and B can obtain this coverage by signing up with a stand-alone prescription drug plan (PDP) and beneficiaries pay the following cost:

- a monthly premium—high-income beneficiaries may pay a relatively higher premium;
- an annual deductible with a maximum amount—not all PDPs have a deductible, or charge the maximum deductible; and
- 25% coinsurance—until total expenditures reach the threshold amount for the *coverage gap*.

When Medicare Part D started, there was a coverage gap commonly referred to as the *donut hole*. In this gap, the insured paid 100% of the cost of prescription drugs. Under the PPACA of 2010, the donut hole coverage gap was gradually reduced through a combination of measures, including brand-name and generic drug discounts and a gradual decrease in the catastrophic coverage threshold.

Beginning in 2020, once the insured reaches the coverage gap, they will pay no more than 25% of the cost for the plan's covered brand-name prescription drugs and generic prescription drugs. Again, prior to the Affordable Care Act, the insured paid 100% of the cost in the coverage gap.

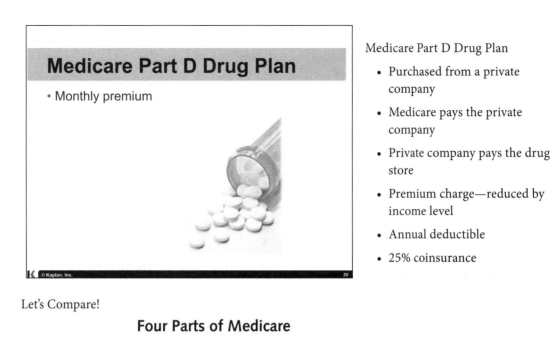

Medicare Part D Drug Plan

- Purchased from a private company
- Medicare pays the private company
- Private company pays the drug store
- Premium charge—reduced by income level
- Annual deductible
- 25% coinsurance

Let's Compare!

Four Parts of Medicare

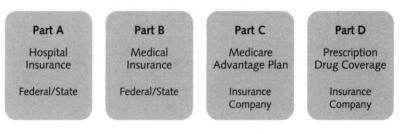

Part A	Part B	Part C	Part D
Hospital Insurance	Medical Insurance	Medicare Advantage Plan	Prescription Drug Coverage
Federal/State	Federal/State	Insurance Company	Insurance Company

20.3.8 Medicare and Employer Group Health Coverage

An individual age 65 or over may be covered by a group health plan and Medicare. Which plan is primary depends on the size of the employer and whether the individual is still an employee or is retired. If the employer has less than 20 employees, Medicare is primary. If the employer has 20 or more employees and the individual is still an employee, the group health plan is primary and Medicare is secondary. If the employer has 20 or more employees and the individual is retired, Medicare is primary and the group plan is secondary. Regardless of employer size, a Medicare-eligible person could choose to reject the group health coverage, in which case Medicare becomes the primary payer for Medicare-covered health services.

For individuals under age 65 and on Medicare because of a disability or end-stage renal disease, the employer plan will be primary if it is a large group health plan covering at least 100 employees. Medicare would be primary if the group is not a large group health plan.

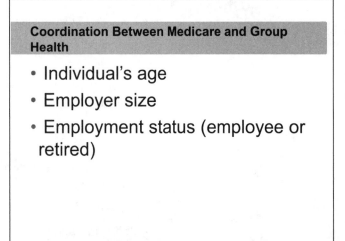

20.4 MEDICARE SUPPLEMENT INSURANCE

A **Medicare supplement insurance** (*Medigap*) policy, sold by private companies, can help pay some of health care cost that Original Medicare doesn't cover, like co-payments, coinsurance, and deductibles. A Medicare supplement policy is designed to fill the "gaps" in original Medicare and Parts A and B. It is illegal for anyone to sell a Medicare supplement policy to a person who is in a Medicare Advantage plan (Medicare Part C).

20.4.1 Standard Plans

Medicare supplements have been standardized by the Centers for Medicare and Medicaid Services (CMS) into 10 different plans, labeled A through N and sold by private companies. Each plan offers a different combination of benefits and the premium cost is proportional to the coverage provided.

The rules governing the sale and offerings of Medigap policies vary from state to state. Some states such as Massachusetts, Minnesota, and Wisconsin require Medicare supplements to provide additional coverage than what is defined in the standardized plans.

This section has a table that shows the benefits provided by each of the 10 standard Medigap plans. Certain standard plans have been dropped and others added over the years, so letters do not run consecutively.

- All standard Medigap plans must include certain basic, or core, benefits:
    - 100% of the Part A hospital coinsurance plus the full cost of 365 additional days after all Part A hospital benefits are exhausted;
    - Part B coinsurance or co-payment after the annual deductible is met—100% for all plans except K (50%) and L (75%); and
    - the cost of the first three pints of blood each year—100% for all plans except K (50%) and L (75%).
- Plan A covers only the basic benefits. Insurers do not have to offer every Medigap plan, but if they offer any, they must offer Plan A.

- All the other Medigap plans include various combinations of other benefits in addition to the basic benefits.

- Plans K and L offer some unique benefits compared to the other plans – they also have lower premiums than those plans. But plans K and L require higher out-of-pocket costs because these plans were designed to give beneficiaries an incentive to control costs. Plans K and L are similar, but differ in the percentage of coverage for claims and in the maximum amount of out-of-pocket costs.

Figure 1:   10 Standard Medigap Plans

Benefits	A	B	C*	D	F*	G*	K	L	M	N
Part A coinsurance and hospital costs up to an additional 365 days after Medicare benefits are used up	Yes	Yes	Yes	Yes	Yes	Yes	Yes	Yes	Yes	Yes
Part B coinsurance or co-payment	Yes	Yes	Yes	Yes	Yes	Yes	50%	75%	Yes	Yes***
Blood (first 3 pints)	Yes	Yes	Yes	Yes	Yes	Yes	50%	75%	Yes	Yes
Part A hospice care coinsurance or co-payment	Yes	Yes	Yes	Yes	Yes	Yes	50%	75%	Yes	Yes
Skilled nursing facility care coinsurance	No	No	Yes	Yes	Yes	Yes	50%	75%	Yes	Yes
Part A deductible	No	Yes	Yes	Yes	Yes	Yes	50%	75%	50%	Yes
Part B deductible	No	No	Yes	No	Yes	No	No	No	No	No
Part B excess charges	No	No	No	No	Yes	Yes	No	No	No	No
Foreign travel	No	No	Yes	Yes	Yes	Yes	No	No	Yes	Yes
Out-of-pocket limit**	N/A	N/A	N/A	N/A	N/A	N/A	$4,940	$2,470	N/A	N/A

* Only applicants first eligible for Medicare before 2020 may purchase Plans C, F, and high-deductible F. Also, it is important to note that Plans F and G also have a high-deductible option, which requires first paying a plan deductible before the plan begins to pay. Once the plan deductible is met, the plan pays 100% of covered services for the rest of the calendar year. High-deductible Plan G does not cover the Medicare Part B deductible. However, high-deductible Plans F and G count payment of the Medicare Part B deductible toward meeting the plan deductible.

** After meeting the out-of-pocket yearly limit and the yearly Part B deductible, the Medigap plan pays 100% of covered services for the rest of the calendar year.

*** Plan N pays 100% of the Part B coinsurance, except for a co-payment of up to $20 for some office visits and up to a $50 co-payment for emergency room visits that don't result in inpatient admission.

Medicare Supplement Plans (Medigap)

- 10 standard plans
- Can help pay:
  - copayments
  - coinsurance
  - deductibles

© Kaplan, Inc.   24

Medicare Supplement Plans (Medigap)

- Private insurance plan
- Premiums not subsidized by Medicare
- Cannot be sold to an enrollee in a Medicare Advantage plan
- Core benefit Plan A
  - Must cover hospital co-pays for days 61-90 and lifetime days
  - Adds an additional 365 days of coverage to a benefit period— covered at 100%
  - Covers Medicare Part B coinsurance
  - Must be offered if company sells any Medicare supplement plans
  - Doesn't cover Part A & B deductibles

QUICK QUIZ 20.C

1. Medicare Part A and Part B are often referred to as
   A. original Medicare
   B. the 65 and over plan
   C. Medicare advantage plans
   D. hospital plans

2. Which of the following types of Medicare Advantage plans focus on the particular needs of a defined group of patients such as those with a certain medical condition?
   A. Medicare managed care plans
   B. Medicare PPO plans
   C. Medicare PFFS plans
   D. Medicare specialty plans

3. Which of the following is a commercial coverage designed to pay some of the medical expenses that the original Medicare leaves to the beneficiary?
   A. Medicare and employer group coverage
   B. Medicare Part C
   C. Medicare Part D
   D. Medicare supplement insurance

Answers can be found at the end of Unit 20.

20.5 REGULATIONS

20.5.1 *Disclosure*

A buyer's guide, such as the one developed by the NAIC entitled *A Guide to Health Insurance for People with Medicare,* must be given to all applicants for a Medicare Supplement policy at the time of application or the upon delivery of the policy.

Applicants must also be given an Outline of Coverage that describes the policy's principal coverage and benefits, premium, renewal provisions.

The first page of the policy must contain:

- the words *Notice to Buyer—this policy may not cover all of your medical expenses;*
- prominent notice of the 30-day free look period; and
- the policy's renewal provision including a description of any premium increases that may be involved.

20.5.2 *Sales and Marketing*

During the *open enrollment* period, insurers must guarantee issue the Medigap policy if the applicant is both 65 or older and has enrolled in Medicare Part B within the last six months. Pre-existing conditions can be excluded for the first six months of coverage but only if the condition was treated in the six months immediately preceding the effective date of the policy.

Producers must determine the suitability for a Medigap policy sale and if the plan is appropriate for the circumstances and discover if the applicant already owns a policy.

Producers may not engage is twisting, high-pressure tactics, cold lead advertising (not disclosing that the purpose is to solicit insurance), or any other deceptive sales practice.

First year sales compensation—including bonuses, gifts, awards, or finder's fees—may not exceed 200% of compensation paid for the second year's renewal. Renewal compensation must be level for years two through five.

First year compensation may not exceed the amount of renewal compensation when a replacement policy is sold.

If a group Medigap policy is replaced, the new policy must cover everyone that was covered under the old policy, and no pre-existing condition limitations may be imposed that would not have applied under the old policy.

If a group Medigap policy is terminated, all group members must be offered individual coverage.

If an individual leaves the group Medicare plan and continuation of benefits is not available, they must be offered individual coverage.

20.5.3 *Required Provisions*

Medigap policies must be at least guaranteed renewable.

Medigap policy benefits must be automatically adjusted for changes in Medicare.

Medigap policies may not duplicate benefits provided by Medicare.

Medigap policies must have a 30-day free look period.

Pre-existing conditions limitations may not last longer than six months from the date of issue.

20.5.4 *Replacement*

The applicant must sign a *Notice to Applicant Regarding Replacement of Medicare Supplement Insurance*, when a Medigap policy is replaced. One copy of the signed notice is retained by the applicant, and another copy by the insurer.

If a Medigap policy is replaced, the applicant must be given:

- a refund of unearned premium on the replaced policy; and
- credit under the new policy for any time elapsed under the pre-existing condition provision of the replaced policy.

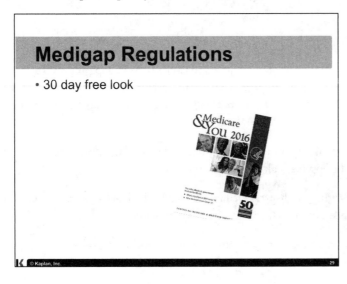

Medigap Regulations

- Must be given an NAIC buyers Guide
- 30 day free look
- Guaranteed renewal
- Guaranteed acceptance if bought within six months of enrollment in Medicare Part B
- Cold lead advertising not allowed
- Sales commissions cannot exceed 200% of renewal commissions
- Renewal commissions must be level in years 2–5
- Replacement sales commissions cannot be greater than the new policies renewal commission
- If allowed, preexisting conditions cannot be excluded for more than six months

20.5.5 *Medicare SELECT*

Medicare SELECT is coverage offered through a restricted provider network, like a managed care plan. Insurers may not sell Medicare SELECT policies to individuals outside the network service area. Medicare SELECT policyholder must have the option to switch to a Medigap policy without a restricted provider network.

Medicare SELECT

- Similar to a managed care plan

20.6 MEDICAID

Medicaid is a government insurance program for persons of all ages whose income and resources are insufficient to pay for health care. It is a means-tested program that is jointly funded by the state and federal government, managed by the state, and the state establishes eligibility guidelines.

Medicaid recipients must be U.S. citizens or legal permanent residents, and may include low-income adults, their children, and people with certain disabilities. Poverty alone does not necessarily qualify someone for Medicaid.

To receive Medicaid, a person must qualify for either:

- Temporary Assistance for Needy Families (TANF—generally called welfare); or
- Supplemental Security Income (SSI), assistance program for people living at or near the poverty line who are age 65 or over, blind, or disabled.

For those who qualify, Medicaid covers most health care costs, including hospital and doctor bills and custodial care in a nursing home. Medicaid is also required by law to pay Medicare premiums, deductibles, and coinsurance for Medicare-eligible Medicaid patients.

Medicaid

- Insurance program for low income & disabled people
- Funded by state and the government
- Managed by the state

© Kaplan, Inc.   32

Medicaid

- Health coverage for the poor
- Regardless of age
- A person can be covered by Medicare and Medicaid
- Funded by state and federal government

 QUICK QUIZ 20.D

1. A coverage offered through a restricted provider network, like a managed care plan is known as
   A. Medicaid
   B. Medicare SELECT
   C. Medicare Part C
   D. Medicare Part B

2. All of the following statements regarding Medigap required provisions are true EXCEPT
   A. Medigap policies must have a 30 day free look period
   B. Medigap policies are not guaranteed renewable
   C. Medigap policy benefits must be automatically adjusted for changes in Medicare
   D. pre-existing conditions limitations may not last longer than 6 months from the date of issue

Answers can be found at the end of Unit 20.

UNIT 20 CRAM SHEET

Eligibility for Medicare Coverage

- Age 65 and over or
- Kidney failure (end-stage renal disease) or
- Received Social Security disability for at least 24 months

Medicare Part A

- Eligibility
   - Automatic for persons age 65 and eligible for Social Security

- Supported by payroll taxes
- Premium charge for those not fully qualified for Social Security
- Coverages
  - Hospital
    - 90 days per benefit period
    - New benefit period starts 60 days after discharge
    - Additional 60 lifetime days
    - Deductible per benefit period—after deductible Medicare pays 100% of first 60 days
    - Patient pays co-pay per day for days 61-90
    - Patient pays a higher daily co-pay for lifetime reserve days
  - Skilled Nursing Facility (SNF)
    - Medical treatment
    - Following a hospital stay of at least three days
    - 100 days of coverage
      - Days 1–20— 100% paid by Medicare
      - Days 21 – 100—daily co-pay paid by patient
  - Home Health
    - Health care provided in the home
    - Not sitting services
    - 100% paid by Medicare
    - Medicare pays 80% of durable medical equipment in the home
  - Hospice
    - Comfort care for terminally ill and family
    - Can be provided in the home or an approved facility
  - Excluded
    - First three pints of blood
    - Private duty nursing
    - Non-medical services
    - Intermediate care
    - Custodial care

Medicare Part B

- Monthly premium that increases with income level
- Not required—can have Part A only
- Initial enrollment period
  - Three months before age 65
  - Month of age 65
  - Three months after age 65

- Annual open enrollment period (AEP)
  - January 1 through March 31 each year
  - Coverage effective July 1
- Coverages
  - Doctor
  - Outpatient services—tests etc.
  - Home health (if not covered by Part A)
- Calendar year deductible
- 80/20 coinsurance after deductible
- No stop loss

Medicare Exclusions

- Routine physical exams beyond the initial one described previously;
- Routine foot, vision, dental, or hearing care;
- Most immunizations;
- Most outpatient prescription drugs;
- Physician charges above Medicare's approved amount;
- Private-duty nursing;
- Cosmetic surgery (unless needed to repair an accidental injury);
- Most care received outside the US; and
- Expenses incurred as a result of war or act of war.

Medicare Part C—Advantage Plans

- Medicare contracts with and pays private companies
- Enrollees medical expenses paid by the private plan
- Enrollee must be enrolled in Medicare Part A & B
- Private company may charge the enrollee a fee
- May provide outpatient drug coverage
- Four types of Medicare Advantage plans:
  - Medicare managed care plans
    - HMO or POS
    - Gatekeeper
    - Care must be obtained from the plan's network of providers
    - Enrollees may have to pay a co-payment per doctor visit
  - PPO
    - No gate keeper
    - More cost if outside of network
  - Private fee-for-service (PFFS) plans
    - Plan negotiates the fees that providers will be paid.

– Medicare specialty plans

▪ Special needs such as kidney failure

Medicare Part D Drug Plan

- Purchased from a private company

- Medicare pays the private company

- Private company pays the drug store

- Premium charge—reduced by income level

- Annual deductible

- 25% co-pay until gap

- Payment by policy stops—donut hole

    – Discounts on drug costs in donut hole

- 5% co-pay after donut hole

- Gap—donut hole—ends in 2020

Group Health/Medicare

- Employers with less than 20 employees

    – Medicare is primary

- Employers with 20 or more employees

    – Group plan is primary for employees

    – Medicare is primary for retirees

- Medicare eligible individuals under age 65

    – Group plan is primary if a large group plan

Medicare Supplement Plans (Medigap)

- Private insurance plan

- Premiums not subsidized by Medicare

- Cannot be sold to an enrollee in a Medicare Advantage plan

- Core benefit Plan A

    – Must cover hospital co-pays for days 61-90 and lifetime days

    – Adds an additional 365 days of coverage to a benefit period—covered at 100%

    – Covers Medicare Part B coinsurance

    – Must be offered if company sells any Medicare supplement plans

    – Doesn't cover Part A & B deductibles

Medigap Regulations

- Must be given an NAIC buyers Guide

- 30 day free look

- Guaranteed renewal

- Guaranteed acceptance if bought within six months of enrollment in Medicare Part B

- Cold lead advertising not allowed
- Sales commissions cannot exceed 200% of renewal commissions
- Renewal commissions must be level in years 2–5
- Replacement sales commissions cannot be greater than the new policies renewal commission
- If allowed, preexisting conditions cannot be excluded for more than six months
- Some states, premiums are community rated

Medicaid

- Health coverage for the poor
- Regardless of age
- A person can be covered by Medicare and Medicaid
- Funded by state and federal government

UNIT 20 QUIZ

In order to measure your success, we recommend that you answer the following 10 questions correctly.

1. Under Medicare Part B, individuals pay a deductible each
    A. benefit period
    B. week
    C. month
    D. year

2. Doctors and suppliers who agree to accept the amount Medicare will pay are said to have agreed to
    A. payment
    B. assignment
    C. assessment
    D. capitation

3. Which of the following outpatient services is excluded from Part B coverage?
    A. Annual mammograms (age 40 and over)
    B. Screening tests for colorectal cancer
    C. Glaucoma testing once every twelve months
    D. Hearing exams

4. The Original Medicare Plan consists of
    A. Medicare Part A
    B. Medicare Part B
    C. Medicare Parts A and B
    D. Medicare Parts C and D

5. Michelle is 65 and starting to receive Social Security benefits. To receive Medicare Part A, she needs to
    A. fill out an enrollment form at her local Social Security office
    B. pay a monthly premium
    C. prove eligibility
    D. do nothing, she is automatically enrolled for free

6. What part of Medicare covers only prescription drugs outside the hospital?
    A. Part A
    B. Part B
    C. Part C
    D. Part D

7. The annual general enrollment period for Medicare Part B begins on
    A. January 1
    B. March 1
    C. March 31
    D. July 1

8. Medicare supplement policies are also known as
    A. Medicare policies
    B. Medigap policies
    C. Medicaid policies
    D. Medichoice policies

9. All of the following statements about Medigap insurance are correct EXCEPT
   A. all standard Medigap plans exclude the cost of the first 3 pints of blood
   B. Medigap policies are sold by private insurance companies
   C. Medigap policies were standardized by the NAIC
   D. someone with a Medicare Advantage Plan does not need Medigap

10. Which of the following individuals is NOT likely to be eligible for Medicaid?
   A. Pam, a single mom who relies on Aid to Families with Dependent Children to help feed her family
   B. Darrell, who has been unable to work since becoming blind 2 years ago
   C. Carmen, who has not been able to work since losing both legs in an accident
   D. Ginny, who is over 65 and working as a manager of a retail outlet

🔑 ANSWER KEY

QUICK QUIZZES

QUICK QUIZ 20.A

1. **C.** hospice care

2. **B.** Skilled nursing facility

QUICK QUIZ 20.B

1. **D.** routine foot, vision, dental, or hearing care

2. **B.** 3 months before the month a person turns 65

QUICK QUIZ 20.C

1. **A.** original Medicare

2. **D.** Medicare specialty plans

3. **D.** Medicare supplement insurance

QUICK QUIZ 20.D

1. **B.** Medicare SELECT

2. **B.** Medigap policies are not guaranteed renewable

UNIT QUIZ

1. **D.** Part B deductibles are annual and they change each year.

2. **B.** Doctors and suppliers who agree to accept the amount Medicare will pay are said to have agreed to assignment. If they agree to this they cannot legally bill the patient for anything above that amount.

3. **D.** Routine foot care, vision, dental, and hearing exams are excluded from Part B coverage.

4. **C.** Part A and B made up the Original Medicare Plan.

5. **D.** For people age 65 and covered by Social Security, enrollment in Medicare Part A is automatic.

6. **D.** Part D of Medicare covers prescription drugs filled outside the hospital.

7. **A.** The annual general enrollment period for Medicare Part B begins on January 1.

8. **B.** Medicare supplement is also known as Medigap.

9. **A.** All standard Medigap plans must include the cost of the first 3 pints of blood.

10. **D.** Medicaid is not age or injury related; it is lack of income related.

UNIT 21) Long-Term Care

21.1 INTRODUCTION

Long-term care insurance is usually purchased as a means to pay for some or all of the services that can stem from a long or chronic illness, disability, or cognitive impairment like Alzheimer's disease. Often, the services that are most needed are those that assist with the *Activities of Daily Living* (ADLs) which include bathing, dressing, eating, transferring, using the toilet, and caring for incontinence.

Long-term care and health care focus on sometimes overlapping issues: health care provides ways to improve a person's health, while long-term care provides services based on the condition as it stands currently. While the average life span has increased to 84 years, so have the costs for nursing homes, assisted living, skilled care, and other care associated with the aging process. Assisted living facilities can range from the mid-five figures, at a minimum, to hundreds of thousands of dollars annually, depending on the type of facility and care needed. Premiums for long-term care insurance can be expensive. They are based on the applicant's age, health, and the level of benefits, coverage, and options chosen.

In this unit, you will learn about the structure of the long-term care policy, how and why it is carefully regulated and monitored, and the protection it provides for millions of senior citizens.

🎯 21.2   LEARNING OBJECTIVES

After successfully completing this unit, you should be able to:

- explain the purpose of long-term care (LTC) insurance;

- identify Medicare's and Medicaid's LTC insurance coverage, and LTC insurance coverage;

- explain who is eligible for LTC insurance and benefit triggers such as activities of daily living and cognitive impairment;

- memorize the activities of daily living (ADLs);

- describe the different care levels covered under LTC policies;

- identify the policy provisions of LTC insurance including benefit periods, benefit amount, elimination period, and optional benefits;

- list the exclusions in LTC policies;

- describe qualified LTC insurance plans;

- identify the state LTC Partnership programs;

- describe underwriting considerations for LTC insurance; and

- identify regulation of LTC policies including marketing standards, and minimum benefit standards.

21.3   MEDICARE, MEDICAID, AND LONG-TERM CARE

21.3.1 Medicare's Long-Term Care Coverage

One of the largest costs involved in long-term care services is custodial care, which includes assistance with personal care or supervision. Medicare does not pay for these costs except under specific circumstances.

Medicare assistance is available for short-term stays in a skilled nursing facility, for hospice care, and for home health care as long as the insured has recently been in the hospital at least three days and has been admitted to a Medicare-certified nursing facility within 30 days after the hospital and skilled nursing, physical therapy, or other skilled care is needed.

As discussed in a previous unit, costs for skilled care in a nursing home are covered for up to 100 days. The first 20 days are covered 100% by Medicare. However, the insured is responsible for a daily co-payment for days 21 through 100, and there is no Medicare coverage after 100 days. Hospice care, other than grief counseling, is covered if the insured has a terminal illness and is not expected to live more than six months.

Medicare also provides some home and other care services as long as they are medically necessary to treat an injury or illness. As long as a doctor, every 60 days, determines this care is medically necessary, there is no time limit on how long the care may be received.

Medicare supplement insurance plans also do not cover long-term care needs such as custodial care, adult day care, care for those with Alzheimer's disease, or assisted living.

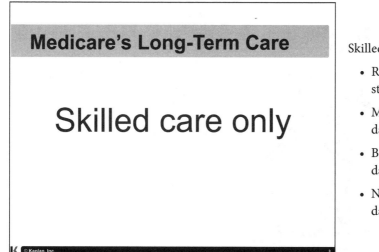

Skilled care in nursing home

- Requires prior 3-day hospital stay
- Medicare pays 100% for first 20 days
- Beneficiary has a daily co-pay days 21–100
- No Medicare coverage after 100 days

21.3.2 Medicaid's Long-Term Care Coverage

Medicaid covers the type of long-term care most people need, but only if they are impoverished. This is in keeping with Medicaid's purpose of providing a safety net for the poor. Many of the elderly Americans whose long-term care costs are paid by Medicaid did not start out poor. They spent themselves into poverty paying for their own long-term care. Once they are on Medicaid, all of their income except for a small monthly allowance must go to help pay for their care. After a Medicaid beneficiary dies, Medicaid has the right to recover the amount of benefits it paid on that person's behalf from assets in the deceased beneficiary's estate.

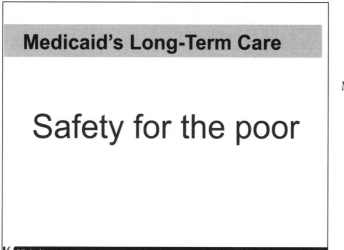

Medicaid's Long-Term Care

- Only for the poor
- Income paid to Medicaid
- May take assets from the person's estate upon death

21.3.3 Long-Term Care Insurance Coverage

With a long-term care policy individuals can plan for their future needs. They can select the long-term care they will receive by choosing the amount and type of policy benefits; they can maintain financial independence and preserve assets for their heirs.

Long-Term Care Insurance
- Bought from an insurance company
- Insured chooses type and amounts of coverage
- Protects assets upon death

21.4   BENEFIT ELIGIBILITY (BENEFIT TRIGGERS)

21.4.1 Activities of Daily Living (ADLs)

Activities of daily living (ADLs) are used as measurements to determine someone's ability to live independently. The ADLs have been standardized and are listed from the least to the most impaired person:

- bathing—in a tub, shower, or by sponge bath;
- dressing;
- toileting;
- transferring—getting out of bed and into a chair, moving about the house;
- continence—bladder and bowel control; and
- eating.

Insureds become eligible for benefits under a long-term care insurance policy if they are unable to perform some number of the ADLs by themselves. Generally, the number is two, but policies can vary.

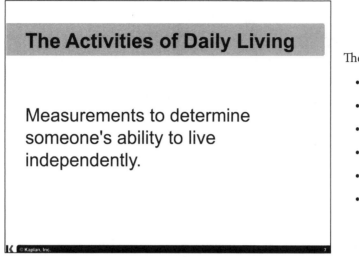

The Activities of Daily Living

- Bathing
- Dressing
- Toileting
- Transferring
- Continence
- Eating

21.4.2 Cognitive Impairment

An individual may be eligible for long-term care insurance benefits if they are **cognitively impaired**. Tests administered by medical practitioners or social workers can measure an individual's ability to perceive, reason, or remember. Benefits are triggered when the cognitive impairment requires someone to be supervised for their own safety or the safety of others.

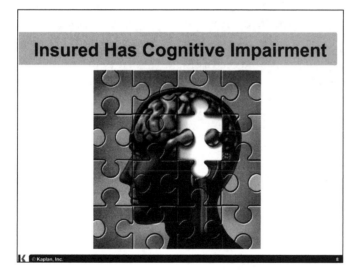

Insured has cognitive impairment

- Ability to perceive, reason, or remember
- Safety concerns

21.5 LEVELS OF CARE

There are three levels of long-term care and they vary depending on the intensity of the services provided.

- **Skilled nursing care (24/7)** is provided on a round-the-clock basis and can be performed only by licensed nurses under a doctor's orders.
- **Intermediate care (only 7)** is intermittent (less than round-the-clock) care performed by licensed nurses nursing under a doctor's orders.
- **Custodial care** is help in performing ADLs and can be performed by someone without medical training.

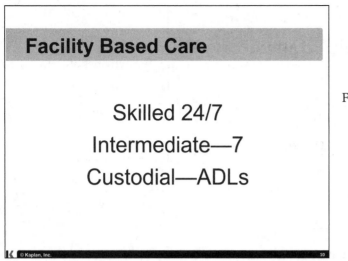

Facility Based Care

- Skilled nursing care
- Intermediate care.
- Custodial care

Types of care are defined in long-term care insurance policies.

- **Home health care** refers to skilled medical and therapy services performed in the individual's home by visiting home health aides.

- **Adult day care** provides company, supervision, along with social and recreational support for people whose grown children care for them at home but need to work during the day.

- **Respite care** is similar to that provided in connection with hospice care; professionals care for someone temporarily in order to give a few days rest to the family member or friend who usually provides the care.

- **Assisted living facilities** are for people who need assistance from time to time, but can live more independently than people who need custodial care. Assisted living facilities provide housing, meals, and help with personal care; some offer more extensive services such as social programs and medical care.

Other Types:

- Home health care
- Adult day care
- Respite care
- Assisted living facilities

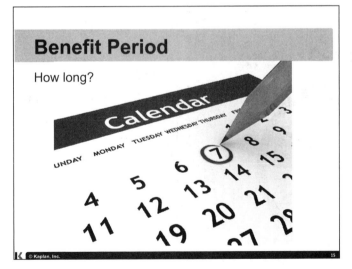

QUICK QUIZ 21.A

1. The type of care that provides assistance with the activities of daily living performed by unskilled helpers is known as

    A. home health care

    B. adult day care

    C. custodial care

    D. intermediate care

2. All of the following are activities of daily living EXCEPT

    A. working

    B. eating

    C. dressing

    D. toileting

Answers can be found at the end of Unit 21.

21.6   POLICY PROVISIONS

21.6.1   Benefit Periods

Long-term care insurance policies provide coverage for at least 12 months. Most policies allow applicants to choose among benefit periods of from two to five years; the longer the benefit period, the higher the premium. Some policies offer lifetime benefit periods with a lifetime maximum benefit amount. The benefit period would end when the limit has been reached.

Benefit Period

How long?

Calendar

© Kaplan, Inc.   15

Benefit Period—How Long

- Minimum 12 months

- Usually two to five years

- May choose lifetime

- Subject to lifetime maximum amount

- Longer the benefit period— higher the premium

21.6.2   Benefit Amount

Benefit amounts are usually expressed as dollars per day. Most applicants choose a benefit amount that is close to the average daily cost of facility-based care in their area. Naturally, higher daily benefits mean higher annual premiums. For indemnity policies, the daily benefit amount is the most the policy will pay regardless of the actual cost of care. Long-term care coverage can also be issued on a reimbursement basis, which pays the lesser of the cost of care or the daily benefit.

If the policy is *comprehensive*—that is, it provides coverage for both facility-based and home-based care – the home care amount is usually stated as 50% of the daily facility-based care benefit.

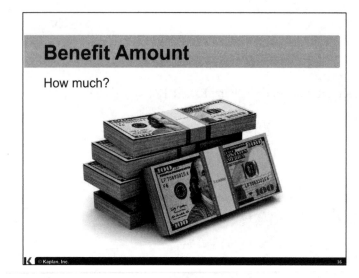

Benefit Amount—How Much

- Indemnity-Stated dollar amount per day
- Reimbursement-lesser of actual expense or daily benefit
- Home care—if covered usually 50% of facility amount
- Policy may have a lifetime maximum
- Higher the benefit, higher the premium

21.6.3 Elimination Period

Similar to disability income policies, long-term care insurance policies usually contain an **elimination period**. The insured must receive care for a stated number of days before the policy begins to pay.

Insureds may select a longer elimination period to make a policy more affordable – the longer the elimination period, the lower the premium.

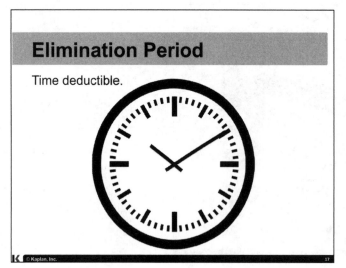

Elimination period

- Insured qualifies for benefits
- Benefits not paid until end of period
- Time deductible
- Longer the elimination period, lower the premium

21.6.4 Optional Benefits

Insureds may have the option of adding the following benefits to their policy:

- **guaranteed insurability**—allows the insured to buy additional coverage at specified future times using their attained age and without providing evidence of insurability;

- **nonforfeiture benefits**—provides for a growing cash value or for a guaranteed return of some percentage of the premium, minus any paid benefits if the policy is lapsed or surrendered; and

- **inflation protection**—provides for automatic annual benefit increases based on a Cost of Living Adjustment (COLA).

Optional Benefits

- Guaranteed insurability
  - Allows insured to raise daily benefit
  - No medical questions
  - Uses insured's attained age
  - Not currently receiving benefits
- Nonforfeiture
  - Cash value or return of percentage of premiums
  - Minus claims paid
  - Policy has been surrendered or has lapsed for nonpayment of premiums
- Inflation protection
  - Yearly increase in benefit coverage by a stated percentage
  - Simple
  - Compound

21.7 EXCLUSIONS

Long-term care insurance policies have the same exclusions common to all health insurance policies:

- war or acts of war;

- alcohol or drug abuse;

- self-inflicted injuries;

- treatment provided without cost to the insured (such as that received in a veteran's hospital); and

- mental illness and nervous disorders without a demonstrable organic cause—note, however, that this does not exclude Alzheimer's disease, dementia, and other organic-based mental illnesses, which are covered.

Exclusions

- War or acts of war
- Alcohol or drug abuse
- Self-inflicted injuries
- Treatment provided without cost to the insured
- Mental illness and nervous disorders without a demonstrable organic cause
  - Dementia or Alzheimer's is covered

 QUICK QUIZ 21.B

1. An insured must receive care for a stated number of days before a long term care policy can pay benefits. This time deductible is known as the
   A. elimination period
   B. waiting period
   C. benefit period
   D. enrollment period

2. All of the following are exclusions in long term care insurance policies EXCEPT
   A. drug abuse
   B. self-inflicted injuries
   C. mental illness
   D. Alzheimer's

Answers can be found at the end of Unit 21.

21.8 QUALIFIED LONG-TERM CARE INSURANCE PLANS

The Health Insurance Portability and Accountability Act of 1996 (HIPAA) set forth some rules for income taxation of long-term care insurance policies and spells out the requirements that must be met in order for a policy to be considered "Qualified."

- Must be unable to perform two out of six ADLs
- Must be certified by a health professional as having a chronic illness that will last for a minimum of 90 days
- Must have a severe cognitive impairment requiring substantial supervision
- Guaranteed renewability
- Coverage of only long-term care expenses
- No benefits for expenses reimbursable under Medicare
- No cash surrender value
- Any dividends or refunds of premiums must be used to offset future premiums or increase benefits
- Conforms to specified consumer protection marketing and benefit standards (these standards actually apply to all long-term care insurance policies and are covered later in this unit)

Benefits are received income-tax free up to a specified amount that is indexed for inflation (for indemnity policies) or the actual amount of expenses incurred (for reimbursement policies).

Premiums paid by self-employed people are tax-deductible up to an age-based limit that is indexed for inflation. Individuals, other than the self-employed, may include their long-term care insurance premiums, up to the age-based limit, in their itemized medical expenses which are deductible to the extent they exceed a certain percentage of the person's gross income.

Employers who pay long-term care insurance premiums on behalf of employees may deduct them as a business expense. Employer-paid premiums are not taxable income to the employees.

HIPAA does not prohibit the sale of nonqualified long-term care insurance policies. In fact, since nonqualified policies do not have to meet HIPAA's requirements, they may offer benefits that are more attractive than qualified policies. But nonqualified policies do not receive favorable tax treatment. Premiums are not deductible and benefits are taxable as income.

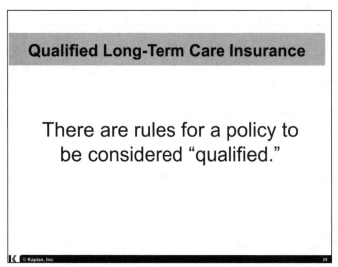

Qualified Long Term Care Insurance

- Receives favorable tax treatment
  - Benefits are paid tax free
  - Premiums may be tax deductible
- Requirements to be a qualified policy
  - Benefit triggers: inability to perform at least two ADLs for at least 90 days or cognitive impairment requiring substantial supervision, certified by a physician
  - Guaranteed renewability
  - Coverage of only long-term care expenses
  - No benefits for expenses reimbursable under Medicare
  - No cash surrender value
  - Any dividends or refunds of premiums must be used to offset future premiums or increase benefits
  - Conforms to specified consumer protection marketing and benefit standards

21.9 STATE LONG-TERM CARE PARTNERSHIP PROGRAMS

Many middle-class families have too much money to qualify for Medicaid but can't afford to self-insure the potential catastrophic costs of long-term care. In an effort to encourage more people to purchase long-term care insurance, the Deficit Reduction Act of 2005 (DRA) created the Qualified State Long Term Care Partnership program.

State long-term care insurance partnership programs are a joint effort of:

- commercial insurers, who develop, market, and issue the policies and pay their benefits;
- a state's insurance department, which regulates the companies and producers who sell the policies; and
- the state Medicaid agency that provides the policy with unique *asset protection* features.

A partnership program works this way: An individual purchases a LTCI partnership policy meeting the requirements for that state. If benefits are needed the LTCI policy will pay and the state Medicaid program does not have to cover the cost. If the policy benefits are exhausted due to a long time need for care and the insured needs to apply to Medicaid, they are not obligated to spend down all their assets to qualify. Under what is called the *dollar-for-dollar approach,* this person may keep assets equal in amount of the benefits received under the partnership policy and the assets are exempt from Medicaid estate recovery and so are preserved for their heirs.

State Long-Term Care Partnership Programs

- Joint effort between state and insurance companies
- Asset protection

© Kaplan, Inc.   26

State Long Term Care Partnership Programs

- Joint effort
  - Insurance companies
  - State insurance department
  - State's Medicaid agency
- Benefits
  - Dollar-for-dollar asset protection

21.10 INDIVIDUAL VS. GROUP LTC CONTRACTS

The advantages and disadvantages of individual versus group long-term care insurance are the same as those for individual versus group insurance generally. Group insurance offers lower rates and people can get coverage without providing evidence of insurability. Group insurance plans however, are not tailored to meet individual needs because the employer chooses the plan coverage for all the participants.

21.11 UNDERWRITING CONSIDERATIONS

Underwriting factors for long-term care insurance differ from those used for other health insurance plans. For example, people with heart disease or diabetes would be rated as substandard risks under a health insurance plan. But because long-term care insurance policies focus on aging people, a different underwriting classification would be used for this condition.

The main issue for long-term care policies is whether an individual can perform the activities of daily living (ADLs) and to what degree of proficiency. If heart disease condition does not interfere with one's ability to perform the ADLs, they would be rated as a standard risk for a long-term care policy. Conversely, a person in otherwise great health who walks with the use of a cane may not be eligible for long-term care insurance.

21.12 REGULATION

21.12.1   Marketing Standards

Marketing standards for long-term care insurance are basically the same as those for Medicare supplement insurance:

- provide applicants with a shopper's guide and outline of coverage;

- consider whether the purchase is suitable for the applicant's needs, objectives, and circumstances;

- determine whether the sale will involve replacement, and if so, have the applicant sign a *Notice Regarding Replacement*;

- provide a 30-day free-look period;

- assure that advertising is not misleading; and

- describe the policy's renewal conditions on its first page.(Guaranteed Renewable).

21.12.2   Minimum Benefit Standards

A long-term care insurance policy's provisions must meet the following requirements:

- the policy must be at least guaranteed renewable- the only way the policy can be cancelled is for nonpayments of premium, insurer can raise premium for all those who have the same policy;

- a sale must include an offer of inflation protection (option to raise the limits of coverage due to inflation);

- a pre-existing condition may not be defined more restrictively than a condition for which medical advice or treatment was sought within six months before the policy's effective date;

- long-term care policies cannot condition payment of benefit on a prior hospital stay;

- group long-term care insurance policies must give insureds the opportunity to continue benefits if membership in the group ceases or to convert to individual coverage if coverage terminates; and

- insureds must be protected against unintentional lapse by giving the insurer the name of another individual to whom a premium due notice will be sent if the policy enters its grace period.

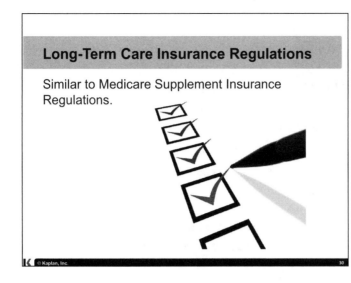

Long-Term Care Insurance Regulations

Similar to Medicare Supplement Insurance Regulations.

© Kaplan, Inc.   30

Long Term Care Insurance Regulations

- Marketing
  - Provide applicants with a shopper's guide and outline of coverage
  - Consider whether the purchase is suitable for the applicant's needs, objectives, and circumstances
  - Determine whether the sale will involve replacement
    - Notice Regarding Replacement
  - 30-day free-look period
  - Advertising is not misleading
  - Describe the policy's renewal conditions on its first page.
- Standards
  - The policy must be at least guaranteed renewable
  - A sale must include an offer of inflation protection
  - A pre-existing condition may not be defined more restrictively than a condition for which medical advice or treatment was sought within six months before the policy's effective date
  - Long-term care policies cannot condition payment of benefit on a prior hospital stay
  - Group long-term care insurance policies must give insureds the opportunity to continue benefits if membership in the group ceases or to convert to individual coverage if coverage terminates
  - Insureds must be protected against unintentional lapse by giving the insurer the name of another individual to whom a premium due notice will be sent if the policy enters its grace period

QUICK QUIZ 21.C

1. All of the following statements regarding tax treatment of long-term care insurance are true EXCEPT
   A. premiums paid by self-employed people are tax deductible up to an age-based limit
   B. employers who pay long-term care insurance premiums on behalf of their employees may deduct them as a business expense
   C. employer paid premiums are tax deductible to employees
   D. benefits received from a qualified long term care insurance plan are received income tax free up to a certain amount

2. Marketing standards for long-term care policies require a free look period of?
   A. 15 days
   B. 30 days
   C. 45 days
   D. 60 days

Answers can be found at the end of Unit 21.

UNIT 21 CRAM SHEET

Long-Term Care

- Assistance with living
- Not medical treatment
- Usually not covered by Medicare
- Skilled care in nursing home
    - Requires prior 3-day hospital stay
    - Medicare pays 100% for first 20 days
    - Beneficiary has a daily co-pay days 21–100
    - No Medicare coverage after 100 days
- Long-term care insurance
    - Bought from an insurance company
    - Insured chooses type and amounts of coverage
    - Protects assets upon death

Long-Term Care Benefit Triggers

- Insured unable to perform activities of daily living
    - Eating
    - Dressing
    - Toileting

- Continence—bladder and bowel control

- Bathing—in a tub, shower, or by sponge bath

- Transferring—getting out of bed and into a chair or moving about the house

■ Insured has cognitive impairment

- Ability to perceive, reason, or remember

- Safety concerns

Types of Long-Term Care

■ Facility based care

- Skilled nursing care—performed only by licensed nurses under a doctor's orders.

- Intermediate care—intermittent care performed by licensed nurses nursing under a doctor's orders.

- Custodial **care**—help in performing ADLs, informal caregiver.

■ Home health care—skilled medical and therapy services performed in the insured's home.

■ Adult day care—company, supervision, along with social and recreational support for the insured during the day.

■ Respite care—professionals care for someone temporarily to give a few days rest to the family member or friend who usually provides the care.

■ Assisted living facilities—for insureds who need assistance from time to time, but can live more independently than people who need custodial care.

Long-Term Care Policy Provisions

■ Benefit amount—how much

- Indemnity-Stated dollar amount per day

- Reimbursement-Actual expense or stated dollar amount per day, whichever is less

- Home care—if covered usually 50% of facility amount

- Policy may have a lifetime maximum

- Higher the benefit—higher the premium

■ Benefit period—how long

- Minimum 12 months

- Usually 2 to 5 years

- May choose lifetime

- Subject to lifetime maximum amount

- Longer the benefit period—higher the premium

■ Elimination period

- Insured qualifies for benefits

- Benefits not paid until end of period

- Time deductible

- Longer the elimination period—lower the premium

- Optional benefits
  - Guaranteed insurability
    - Allows insured to raise daily benefit
    - Uses attained age
    - No medical questions
    - Not currently receiving benefits
  - Nonforfeiture
    - Cash value or return of percentage of premiums
    - Minus claims paid
    - Policy has been surrendered or has lapsed for nonpayment of premiums
  - Inflation protection
    - Yearly increase in benefit coverage by a stated percentage
      - Simple
      - Compound

Exclusions

- War or acts of war
- Alcohol or drug abuse
- Self-inflicted injuries
- Treatment provided without cost to the insured
- Mental illness and nervous disorders without a demonstrable organic cause
  - Dementia or Alzheimer's is covered

Qualified Long-Term Care Insurance

- Receives favorable tax treatment
  - Benefits are paid tax free
  - Premiums may be deducted
- Requirements to be a qualified policy
  - Benefit triggers: inability to perform at least two ADLs for at least 90 days or cognitive impairment requiring substantial supervision, certified by a physician
  - Guaranteed renewability
  - Coverage of only long-term care expenses
  - No benefits for expenses reimbursable under Medicare
  - No cash surrender value
  - Any dividends or refunds of premiums must be used to offset future premiums or increase benefits
  - Conforms to specified consumer protection marketing and benefit standards

State Long-Term Care Partnership Programs

- Joint effort
  - Insurance companies
  - State insurance department
  - State's Medicaid agency
- Benefits
  - Dollar-for-dollar asset protection

Long-Term Care Insurance Regulations

- Marketing
  - Provide applicants with a shopper's guide and outline of coverage
  - Consider whether the purchase is suitable for the applicant's needs, objectives, and circumstances
  - Determine whether the sale will involve replacement
    - *Notice Regarding Replacement*
  - 30-day free-look period
  - Advertising is not misleading
  - Describe the policy's renewal conditions on its first page
- Standards
  - The policy must be at least guaranteed renewable
  - A sale must include an offer of inflation protection
  - A pre-existing condition may not be defined more restrictively than a condition for which medical advice or treatment was sought within six months before the policy's effective date
  - Long-term care policies cannot condition payment of benefit on a prior hospital stay
    - Group long-term care insurance policies must give insureds the opportunity to continue benefits if membership in the group ceases or to convert to individual coverage if coverage terminates
    - Insureds must be protected against unintentional lapse by giving the insurer the name of another individual to whom a premium due notice will be sent if the policy enters its grace period

UNIT 21 QUIZ

In order to measure your success, we recommend that you answer the following 10 questions correctly.

1. The elimination period may be thought of as a
   A. dollar amount deductible
   B. time deductible
   C. dollar amount co-payment
   D. time co-payment

2. Which of the following is NOT considered an activity of daily living?
   A. Transferring
   B. Dressing
   C. Bathing
   D. Driving

3. All of the following are levels of facility based long-term care EXCEPT
   A. skilled nursing care
   B. intermediate care
   C. custodial care
   D. adult day care

4. Benefit amounts in a long-term care policy are usually expressed as
   A. dollars per day
   B. dollars per month
   C. dollars per quarter
   D. dollars per year

5. All of the following are optional benefits in a long-term care insurance policy EXCEPT
   A. inflation protection
   B. nonforfeiture benefits
   C. elimination period
   D. guaranteed insurability

6. Which of the following is excluded in a long-term care insurance policy?
   A. Alzheimer's disease
   B. Dementia
   C. Nervous disorder without organic cause
   D. Mental illness with organic cause

7. All of the following statements about a nonqualified long-term care insurance policy are true EXCEPT
   A. they do not receive favorable tax treatment
   B. premiums are not deductible
   C. benefits are taxed as income
   D. HIPPA prohibits the sale of these policies

8. Medical or rehabilitative care performed on an intermittent basis is known as
   A. home health care
   B. intermediate care
   C. custodial care
   D. adult day care

9. Individuals that need assistance from time to time but can live more independently than people who need custodial care may need
   A. assisted living care
   B. respite care
   C. home health care
   D. intermediate care

10. In regards to underwriting considerations of long-term care policies, the key decision is based on
    A. family and personal health history
    B. whether an individual can perform the activities of daily living
    C. current occupation
    D. marital status

⚷ ANSWER KEY

QUICK QUIZZES

QUICK QUIZ 21.A

1. **C.** custodial care

2. **A.** working

QUICK QUIZ 21.B

1. **A.** elimination period

2. **D.** Alzheimer's

QUICK QUIZ 21.C

1. **C.** employer paid premiums are tax deductible to employees

2. **B.** 30 days

UNIT QUIZ

1. **B.** The elimination period may be thought of as a time deductible.

2. **D.** Driving is not an activity of daily living. Eating, dressing, bathing, toileting, continence, bathing, and transferring are activities of daily living.

3. **D.** Adult day care is not considered facility based long-term care.

4. **A.** Most applicants choose a benefit amount that is close to the average daily cost of facility-based care in their area.

5. **C.** Long-term care policies have an elimination period, or time deductible. The longer the elimination period, the lower the premium will be.

6. **C.** Organic based mental illnesses and nervous disorders are covered under a long-term care policy.

7. **D.** Nonqualified policies do not have to meet HIPPAs requirements and may offer more attractive benefits than qualified policies.

8. **B.** Intermediate care is intermittent care performed by licensed nurses nursing under a doctor's orders.

9. **A.** Assisted living facilities provide housing, meals, and help with personal care.

10. **B.** Long term care insurance policies have a focus on age.

UNIT 22) Taxation of Health Insurance

22.1 INTRODUCTION

When the need arises throughout the year, health insurance coverage comes in handy and it's a rather simple process—pay the deductible and the insurance company kicks in the rest.

Simple however can become complex at tax filing time. Are premiums for health insurance a tax-deduction? How does the tax law handle co-pays and prescription drug payments? If an individual does an E-Z file tax return can they deduct out-of-pocket medical bills?

Although insurance agents are not CPA's, they do need to know basic taxation issues regarding health insurance plans and premiums and that is the focus of this unit.

22.2 LEARNING OBJECTIVES

After successfully completing this unit, you should be able to:

- explain tax treatment of personally owned, employer paid, and employee paid health insurance plans premiums and benefits;

- identify tax treatment of medical expense coverage of sole proprietors and partnerships;

◻ explain the tax treatment of the three types of business disability insurance;

◻ describe health savings accounts (HSAs), eligibility, and their tax treatment;

◻ define a high deductible health plan (HDHPs); and

◻ identify how Health savings accounts (HSAs), Health reimbursement accounts (HRAs) and Flexible spending arrangements (FSA) are taxed.

22.3 PERSONALLY OWNED AND GROUP HEALTH PLANS

The tax treatment of an individual or group health plan depends on:

- who is paying the premiums; and
- the type of plan.

The following table summarizes this topic.

Tax Treatment of Personally Owned and Group Health Insurance

	Personally Owned	Employer Paid Group	Employee Paid Group
Medical/Dental Expense			
Premiums	Included with other itemized medical expenses; amount of total that exceeds a percentage of gross income is deductible	Deductible to employer; not taxable to employee	Not deductible
Benefits	Tax free	Tax free	Tax free
Disability Income			
Premiums	Not deductible	Deductible to employer; not taxable to employee	Not deductible
Benefits	Tax free	Income taxable; also, for first 6 months, subject to FICA tax	Tax free; but, for first 6 months, subject to FICA tax
Qualified Long-Term Care			
Premiums	Includible with other itemized medical expenses up to age-based limit; amount of total that exceeds a percentage of gross income is deductible	Deductible to employer; not taxable to employee	Includible with other itemized medical expenses up to age-based limit; amount of total that exceeds a percentage of gross income is deductible
Benefits	Tax free (up to specified, inflation-indexed limits for indemnity plans)	Tax free (up to specified, inflation-indexed limits for indemnity plans)	Tax free (up to specified, inflation-indexed limits for indemnity plans)
Accidental Death & Dismemberment			
Premiums	Not deductible	Deductible to employer; not taxable to employee	Not deductible
Benefits	Tax free	Tax free	Tax free

22.4 MEDICAL EXPENSE COVERAGE FOR SOLE PROPRIETORS AND PARTNERSHIPS

Self-employed persons are allowed to deduct 100% of what they pay for health insurance (including qualified long-term care insurance) from their gross income. To claim this deduction, however, the self-employed:

- must show a net profit for the year; and
- cannot claim the deduction for any month in which they were eligible to participate in a health plan subsidized by another employer, if they are also self-employed, or by the employer of their spouse.

Premiums paid by a partnership on an accident and health insurance policy are generally deductible by the partnership. The amount of the premium is included in the partner's gross income, and is deductible on the same basis as for self-employed persons.

Benefits are considered a reimbursement of expenses and are not taxable.

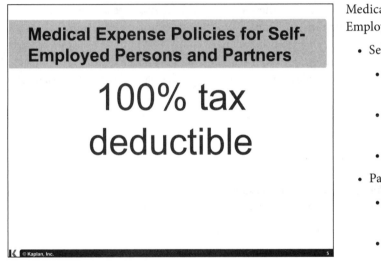

Medical Expense Policies for Self Employed Persons and Partners

- Self Employed
    - Deduct premiums if have a net profit from business
    - Not covered by a group policy
    - Benefits not taxable
- Partnerships
    - Premiums deductible for partnership
    - Premiums are income to partners
    - Benefits not taxable

22.5 BUSINESS DISABILITY INSURANCE

There are three types of business disability insurance plans:

- buy-sell,
- key person, and
- business overhead expense (BOE).

The following table summarizes the tax treatment of these plans.

	Premiums	Benefits
Buy-Sell	Not deductible	Tax free
Key Person	Not deductible	Tax free
Business Overhead Expense	Deductible	Taxable

22.6 HEALTH SAVINGS ACCOUNTS

A **Health Savings Account (HSA)** is a tax-advantaged medical savings account available to taxpayers enrolled in a high-deductible health plan (HDHP):

- contributions to an HSA are tax-deductible;
- earnings in the HSA grow tax-deferred; and
- HSA distributions are tax-free when used to pay qualified medical expenses.

Individuals do not need IRS authorization the set up an HSA. They can establish an account with a bank, insurance company, or investment company which will act as a trustee, similar to an individual retirement account (IRA). Unlike a Flexible Spending Account (FSA), funds roll over and accumulate year to year if not spent. Distributions for other than qualified medical expenses are subject to income tax; a 20% penalty tax also applies unless the account beneficiary has died, become disabled, or is age 65 or older.

22.6.1 Eligibility

Individuals are eligible to establish an HSA if they:

- have no other comprehensive medical expense coverage, including Medicare (they have a limited benefit plan, disability income, or long-term care insurance);
- cannot be claimed as a dependent on another person's tax return; and
- are enrolled in a High-Deductible Health Plan (HDHP).

Health Savings Account

EMPLOYEE: Tax free withdrawals for qualified medical expenses.

© Kaplan, Inc.

Heath Savings Accounts

- Individually owned medical expense savings account
- Contributions are tax deductible
- Withdrawals are tax free
  - Used to pay qualified medical expenses
- Must have a high deductible health plan
- Account values accumulate from year to year

22.6.2 High Deductible Health Plans (HDHPs)

A high deductible health plan (HDHP) is a health plan that offers lower premiums and requires the insured to pay a high deductible when the plan is used. The amount of the deductible required changes yearly.

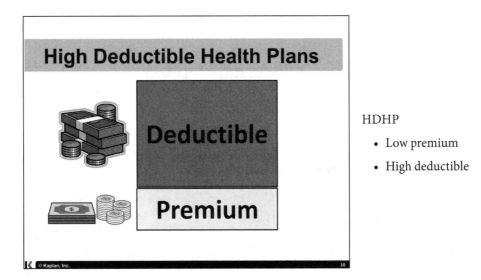

HDHP
- Low premium
- High deductible

 QUICK QUIZ 22.A

1. Employer paid group medical and dental health insurance benefits are tax free and the premiums are
   A. deductible to the employee
   B. deductible to the employer
   C. deductible to both the employee and employer
   D. not deductible

2. Self-employed persons are allowed to deduct what percentage of the amount they pay for health insurance?
   A. 25%
   B. 50%
   C. 75%
   D. 100%

Answers can be found at the end of Unit 22.

22.7 HEALTH REIMBURSEMENT ACCOUNTS

Some employers provide employees with health plans with relatively high deductibles and create a tax-favored **Health Reimbursement Account (HRA)** for each covered employee. Unlike the HSA, a high-deductible health plan (HDHP) is not required in order for the employer to establish an HRA. Similar to the HSA, the employee can obtain reimbursement from the HRA for medical expenses that are subject to deductibles, coinsurance, and co-payments. HRA contributions are pretax and made only by the employer. The employer may restrict the use of the funds in an HRA, and the funds roll over year to year.

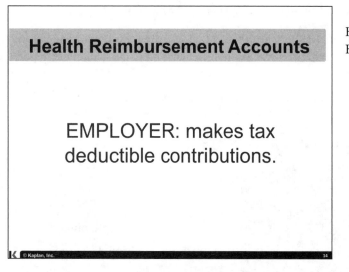

Health Reimbursement Accounts – HRA

- Established by the employer
- Employer contributions are pretax
- HDHP not required
- Employee can use money in the HRA to pay deductibles, coinsurance and co-payments
- Money rolls over from year to year

22.8 FLEXIBLE SPENDING ARRANGEMENTS

A **Flexible Spending Arrangement (FSA)** is a *cafeteria plan* benefit that is funded with employee money by means of a salary reduction. Employee contributions are made on a pre-tax basis, and as a qualified employee benefit plan, employee benefits are non-taxable. Working spouses are also covered by the employee's benefit plan and choices can be made to avoid duplicating benefits provided by their spouse's plan.

From the employer's perspective:

- the plan is funded with employee contributions, so the employer's expenses are limited to administrative costs; and
- the salary reduction method results in a reduced payroll and therefore reduced payroll taxes for the employer.

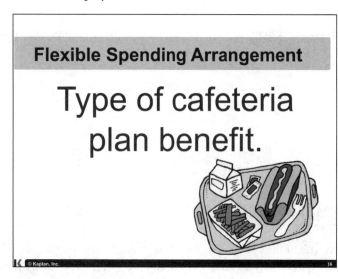

Flexible Spending Arrangement— FSA

- Employee authorizes employer to reduce employee's salary
- Employer puts the money into FSA account
- Withdrawals by employee are not taxed
  - Only certain approved benefits
- Spend it or lose it

QUICK QUIZ 22.B

1. Which of the following was created to help employees and self-employed individuals pay for their medical care expenses on a tax advantaged basis?
    A. Health savings account
    B. Medical savings account
    C. Health reimbursement account
    D. Flexible spending arrangement

2. Which of the following is a cafeteria plan benefit and is funded with employee money by means of a salary reduction?
    A. Medical savings account
    B. Individual retirement account
    C. Health reimbursement account
    D. Flexible spending arrangement

Answers can be found at the end of Unit 22.

UNIT 22 CRAM SHEET

Tax Treatment of Personally Owned and Group Health Insurance

Medical Expense Policies for Self Employed Persons and Partners

- Self Employed
    - Deduct premiums if have a net profit from business
    - Not covered by a group policy
    - Benefits not taxable
- Partnerships
    - Premiums deductible for partnership
    - Premiums are income to partners
    - Benefits not taxable

Business Disability Insurance

Health Savings Account—HSA

- Individually owned medical expense savings account
- Contributions are tax deductible
- Withdrawals are tax free
    - Used to pay qualified medical expenses
- Must have a high deductible health plan
- Account values accumulate from year to year

Medical Savings Account—MSA

- Employed by small employer
    - Less than 50
- Self employed
- Contributions deductible
- Must have high deductible health plan
- Values accumulate from year to year
- Tax free withdrawals
    - Used to pay qualified medical expenses
- New plans not allowed after 2006

Health Reimbursement Accounts—HRA

- Established by the employer
- Employer contributions are pretax
- HDHP not required
- Employee can use money in the HRA to pay deductibles, coinsurance and co-payments
- Money rolls over from year to year

Flexible Spending Arrangement—FSA

- Employee authorizes employer to reduce employee's salary
- Employer puts the money into FSA account
- Withdrawals by employee are not taxed
    - Only certain approved benefits
- Spend it or lose it

UNIT 22 QUIZ

In order to measure your success, we recommend that you answer the following 10 questions correctly. .

1. Wanda's employer pays the entire premium for her group disability coverage. If Wanda became disabled, how much of her benefits from this coverage would be subject to tax?
   A. 0%
   B. 50%
   C. 100%
   D. It depends on her tax bracket

2. If Wanda paid her entire premium for her group disability coverage, how much of her benefits from this coverage would be subject to tax?
   A. 0%
   B. 50%
   C. 100%
   D. It depends on her tax bracket

3. The XYZ Coffee Company may deduct its premiums from taxes but the benefits are taxable. The type of business disability plan that the company must have is a
   A. buy-sell
   B. key person
   C. business overhead expense
   D. medical expense

4. The premiums paid by a company for group medical for its employees are
   A. not tax deductible to either the company or the business
   B. tax deductible by the company and not considered taxable income to the employees
   C. tax deductible by the company and considered taxable income to the employees
   D. tax deductible to the employees and the company

5. Benefits paid by personally owned accident, health, disability, or long-term care policies generally are
   A. received income-tax free
   B. taxed at the end of the year
   C. received partially tax free by the taxpayer
   D. taxed upon receipt by the taxpayer

6. Qualified group long-term care coverage premiums that are paid for by the employer are
   A. deductible by both the company and the employee
   B. not deductible by either the company or the employee
   C. deductible by the company but not the employee
   D. deductible by the employee but not the company

7. Personally owned disability income insurance premiums are
    A. deductible to the insured, and the benefits are received tax free
    B. not deductible to the insured, but the benefits are received tax free
    C. deductible to the insured, but the benefits are taxed
    D. not deductible to the insured, and the benefits are taxed

8. A health plan that offers relatively low premiums but requires that the insured pay a high deductible is a
    A. health savings account
    B. health reimbursement account
    C. flexible spending account
    D. high deductible health plan

9. All of the following statements about a health savings account (HSA) are correct EXCEPT
    A. contributions to an HSA are not tax deductible
    B. inside the HSA earnings are tax-deferred
    C. HSA distributions are tax-free if used to pay for qualified medical expenses
    D. individuals are eligible for an HSA if they cannot be claimed as a dependent on another person's tax return

10. The premiums are deductible and the benefits are taxable for which of the following business disability plans?
    A. Buy-sell
    B. Key person
    C. Business overhead expense
    D. None of these

ANSWER KEY

QUICK QUIZZES

QUICK QUIZ 22.A

1. **B.** deductible to the employer

2. **D.** 100%

QUICK QUIZ 22.B

1. **A.** Health savings account

2. **D.** Flexible spending arrangement

UNIT QUIZ

1. **C.** Since Wanda's company can deduct the premiums, all of Wanda's benefits are taxable.

2. **A.** If the employee pays their own premiums, the benefit is tax free and the premiums are not deductible by the employer.

3. **C.** Business overhead expense is the only business disability plan in which the premiums are tax deductible and the benefits are taxable.

4. **B.** The premiums paid by a company for group medical for its employees are tax deductible by the company and not considered taxable income to the employees.

5. **A.** Benefits paid by individually owned accident, health, disability, or long-term care policies generally are received income-tax free by the taxpayer, provided benefits do not exceed actual expenses.

6. **C.** Group LTC premiums are tax deductible by the employer. Because the employer is paying all the premium, the premium is not deductible by the employee. Benefits are tax free to the employee.

7. **B.** Personal disability insurance premiums are not deductible to the insured, but the benefits are received tax free.

8. **D.** The amount of the deductible typically changes yearly.

9. **A.** Contributions to an HSA are tax-deductible.

10. **C.** Business overhead expense is the only business disability plan in which the premiums are tax deductible and the benefits are taxable

Glossary

A

absolute assignment Policy assignment under which the assignee (person to whom the policy is assigned) receives full control over the policy and also full rights to its benefits. Generally, when a policy is assigned to secure a debt, the owner retains all rights in the policy in excess of the debt, even though the assignment is absolute in form. (*See* assignment)

accelerated benefits rider A life insurance rider that allows for the early payment of some portion of the policy's face amount should the insured suffer from a terminal illness or injury.

acceptance (*See* offer and acceptance)

accident and health insurance Insurance under which benefits are payable in case of disease, accidental injury, or accidental death. Also called health insurance, personal health insurance, and sickness and accident insurance.

accidental bodily injury provision Disability income or accident policy provision that requires that the injury be accidental in order for benefits to be payable.

accidental death and dismemberment (AD&D) Insurance providing payment if the insured's death results from an accident or if the insured accidentally severs a limb above the wrist or ankle joints or totally and irreversibly loses eyesight.

accidental death benefit rider A life insurance policy rider providing for payment of an additional benefit when death occurs by accidental means.

accidental dismemberment Often defined as "the severance of limbs at or above the wrists or ankle joints, or the entire irreversible loss of sight." Loss of use in itself may or not be considered dismemberment.

accidental means provision Unforeseen, unexpected, unintended cause of an accident. Requirement of an accident-based policy that the cause of the mishap must be accidental for any claim to be payable.

accumulation unit Premiums an annuitant pays into a variable annuity are credited as accumulation units. At the end of the accumulation period, accumulation units are converted to annuity units.

acquired immune deficiency syndrome (AIDS) A life-threatening condition brought on by the human immunodeficiency virus; insurers must adhere to strict underwriting and claims guidelines in regard to AIDS risks and AIDS-related conditions.

acute illness A serious condition, such as pneumonia, from which the body can fully recover with proper medical attention.

adhesion An insurance policy is a "contract of adhesion" because buyers must "adhere" to the terms of the contract already in existence. They have no opportunity to negotiate terms, rates, values, and so on.

adjustable life insurance Combines features of both term and whole life coverage with the length of coverage and amount of accumulated cash value as the adjustable factors. Premiums may be increased or decreased to fit the specific needs. Such adjustments are not retroactive and apply only to the future.

administrative-services-only (ASO) plan Arrangement under which an insurance company or an independent organization, for a fee, handles the administration of claims, benefits, and other administrative functions for a self-insured group.

admitted insurer An insurance company that has met the legal and financial requirements for operation within a given state.

adult day care Type of care (usually custodial) designed for individuals who require assistance with various activities of daily living, while their primary caregivers are absent. Offered in care centers.

adverse selection Selection "against the company." Tendency of less favorable insurance risks to seek or continue insurance to a greater extent than others. Also, tendency of policyowners to take advantage of favorable options in insurance contracts.

agency Situation wherein one party (an agent) has the power to act for another (the principal) in dealing with third parties.

agent Anyone not a duly licensed broker, who solicits insurance or aids in placing risks, delivering policies, or collecting premiums on behalf of an insurance company.

agent's report The section of an insurance application where the agent reports personal observations about the applicant.

aleatory Feature of insurance contracts in that there is an element of chance for both parties and that the dollar given by the policyholder (premiums) and the insurer (benefits) may not be equal.

alien insurer Company incorporated or organized under the laws of any foreign nation, providence, or territory.

ambulatory surgery Surgery performed on an outpatient basis.

annually renewable term (ART)   A form of renewable term insurance that provides coverage for one year and allows the policyowner to renew coverage each year, without evidence of insurability. Also called yearly renewable term (YRT).

annuitant   One to whom an annuity is payable, or a person upon the continuance of whose life further payment depends.

annuity   A contract that provides a stipulated sum payable at certain regular intervals during the lifetime of one or more persons, or payable for a specified period only.

annuity unit   The number of annuity units denotes the share of the funds an annuitant will receive from a variable annuity account after the accumulation period ends and benefits begin. A formula is used to convert accumulation units to annuity units.

any occupation   A definition of total disability that requires that for disability income benefits to be payable, the insured must be unable to perform any job for which the insured is "reasonably suited by reason of education, training, or experience."

apparent authority   The authority an agent appears to have, based on the principal's (the insurer's) actions, words, deeds or because of circumstances the principal (the insurer) created.

application   Form supplied by the insurance company, usually filled in by the agent and medical examiner (if applicable) on the basis of information received from the applicant. It is signed by the applicant and is part of the insurance policy if it is issued. It gives information to the home office underwriting department so it may consider whether an insurance policy will be issued and, if so, in what classification and at what premium rate.

appointment   The authorization or certification of an agent to act for or represent an insurance company.

approval receipt   Rarely used today, a type of conditional receipt that provides that coverage is effective as of the date the application is approved (before the policy is delivered).

assessment insurance   Plan by which either the amount of insurance is variable or the number and amount of the assessments are variable. It is offered by assessment associations, either pure or advance.

assignee   Person (including corporation, partnership, or other organization) to whom a right or rights under a policy are transferred by means of an assignment.

assignment   Signed transfer of benefits of a policy by an insured to another party. The company does not guarantee the validity of an assignment.

assignment provision (health contracts)   Commercial health policy provision that allows the policyowner to assign benefit payments from the insurer directly to the health care provider.

assignor   Person (including corporation, partnership, or other organization or entity) who transfers a right or rights under an insurance policy to another by means of an assignment.

attained age   With reference to an insured, the current insurance age.

authority   The actions and deeds an agent is authorized to conduct on behalf of an insurance company, as specified in the agent's contract.

authorized company   Company duly authorized by the insurance department to operate in the state.

automatic premium loan provision   Authorizes insurer to automatically pay any premium in default at the end of the grace period and charge the amount so paid against the life insurance policy as a policy loan.

average indexed monthly earnings (AIME)   The basis used for calculating the primary insurance amount (PIA) for Social Security benefits.

aviation exclusion   Either attached by rider or included in standard policy language excepting from coverage certain deaths or disabilities due to aviation, such as "other than a fare-paying passenger."

B

backdating   The practice of making a policy effective at an earlier date than the present.

basic medical expense policy   Health insurance policy that provides "first dollar" benefits for specified (and limited) health care, such as hospitalization, surgery, or physician services. Characterized by limited benefit periods and relatively low coverage limits.

beneficiary   Person to whom the proceeds of a life or accident policy are payable when the insured dies. The various types of beneficiaries are primary beneficiaries (those first entitled to proceeds), secondary beneficiaries (those entitled to proceeds if no primary beneficiary is living when the insured dies), and tertiary beneficiaries (those entitled to proceeds if no primary or secondary beneficiaries are alive when the insured dies).

benefit   May be either money or a right to the policyowner upon the happening of the conditions set out in the policy.

benefit period   Maximum length of time that insurance benefits will be paid for any one accident, illness, or hospital stay.

binding receipt   Given by a company upon an applicant's first premium payment. The policy, if approved, becomes effective from the date of the receipt.

blackout period   Period following the death of a family breadwinner during which no Social Security benefits are available to the surviving spouse.

blanket policy Covers a number of individuals who are exposed to the same hazards, such as members of an athletic team, company officials who are passengers in the same company plane, and so on.

broker Licensed insurance representative who does not represent a specific company but places business among various companies. Legally, the broker is usually regarded as a representative of the insured rather than the company.

business continuation plan Arrangements between the business owners that provide that the shares owned by any one of them who dies or becomes disabled shall be sold to and purchased by the other co-owners or by the business.

business overhead expense insurance A form of disability income coverage designed to pay necessary business overhead expenses, such as rent, should the insured business owner become disabled.

buyer's guides Informational consumer guide books that explain insurance policies and insurance concepts; in many states, they are required to be given to applicants when certain types of coverages are being considered.

buy-sell agreement Agreement that a deceased business owner's interest will be sold and purchased at a predetermined price or at a price according to a predetermined formula.

C

cafeteria plan Employee benefit arrangements in which employees can select from a range of benefits.

cancellable contract Health insurance contract that may be terminated by the company or that is renewable at its option.

capital sum Amount provided for accidental dismemberment or loss of eyesight. Indemnities for loss of one member or sight of one eye are percentages of the capital sum.

case management The professional arrangement and coordination of health services through assessment, service plan development, and monitoring.

cash or deferred arrangements A qualified employer retirement plan under which employees can defer amounts of their salaries into a retirement plan. These amounts are not included in the employee's gross income and so are tax deferred. Also called 401(k) plans.

cash refund annuity Provides that, upon the death of an annuitant before payments totaling the purchase price have been made, the excess of the amount paid by the purchaser over the total annuity payments received will be paid in one sum to designated beneficiaries.

cash surrender option A nonforfeiture option that allows whole life insurance policyowners to receive a payout of their policy's cash values.

cash surrender value Amount available to the owner when a life insurance policy is surrendered to the company. During the early policy years, the cash value is the reserve less a "surrender charge"; in later policy years, it usually equals or closely approximates the reserve value at time of surrender.

cash value The equity amount or "savings" accumulation in a whole life policy.

churning The practice by which policy values in an existing life insurance policy or annuity contract are used to purchase another policy or contract with that same insurer for the purpose of earning additional premiums or commissions without an objectively reasonable basis for believing that the new policy will result in an actual and demonstrable benefit.

class designation A beneficiary designation. Rather than specifying one or more beneficiaries by name, the policyowner designates a class or group of beneficiaries. For example, "my children."

classification Occupational category of a risk.

close corporation A corporation owned by a small group of stockholders, each of whom usually has a voice in operating the business.

COBRA "Consolidated Omnibus Budget Reconciliation Act of 1985," extending group health coverage to terminated employees and their families for up to 18 or 36 months.

coinsurance (percentage participation) Principle under which the company insures only part of the potential loss, the policyowners paying the other part. For instance, in a major medical policy, the company may agree to pay 75% of the insured expenses, with the insured to pay the other 25%.

collateral assignment Assignment of a policy to a creditor as security for a debt. The creditor is entitled to be reimbursed out of policy proceeds for the amount owed. The beneficiary is entitled to any excess of policy proceeds over the amount due the creditor in the event of the insured's death.

commercial health insurers Insurance companies that function on the reimbursement approach, which allows policyowners to seek medical treatment then submit the charges to the insurer for reimbursement.

Commissioner Head of a state insurance department; public officer charged with supervising the insurance business in a state and administrating insurance laws. Called "superintendent" in some states, "director" in others.

Commissioner's Standard Ordinary (CSO) Table Table of mortality based on intercompany experience over a period of time, which is legally recognized as the mortality basis for computing maximum reserves on policies issued within past years. The 1980 CSO Table replaced the 1958 CSO Table.

common disaster provision Sometimes added to a policy and designed to provide an alternative beneficiary in the event that the insured as well as the original beneficiary dies as the result of a common accident.

competent parties To be enforceable, a contract must be entered into by competent parties. A competent party is one who is capable of understanding the contract being agreed to.

comprehensive major medical insurance Designed to give the protection offered by both a basic medical expense and major medical policy. It is characterized by a low deductible amount, a coinsurance clause, and high maximum benefits.

concealment Failure of the insured to disclose to the company a fact material to the acceptance of the risk at the time application is made.

conditional contract Characteristic of an insurance contract in that the payment of benefits is dependent on or a condition of the occurrence of the risk insured against.

conditionally renewable contract Health insurance policy providing that the insured may renew the contract from period to period, or continue it to a stated date or an advanced age, subject to the right of the insurer to decline renewal only under conditions defined in the contract.

conditional receipt Given to the policyowners when they pay a premium at time of application. Such receipts bind the insurance company if the risk is approved as applied for, subject to any other conditions stated on the receipt.

consideration Element of a binding contract; acceptance by the company of payment of the premium and statements made by the prospective insured in the application.

consideration clause The part of an insurance contract setting forth the amount of initial and renewal premiums and frequency of future payments.

contestable period Period during which the company may contest a claim on a policy because of misleading or incomplete information in the application.

contingent beneficiary Person(s) named to receive proceeds in case the original beneficiary is not alive. Also referred to as secondary or tertiary beneficiary.

continuing care Type of health or medical care designed to provide a benefit for elderly individuals who live in a retirement community; addresses full-time needs, both social and medical. Also known as residential care.

contract An agreement enforceable by law whereby one party binds itself to certain promises or deeds.

contract of agency A legal document containing the terms of the contract between the agent and company, signed by both parties. Also called agency agreement.

contributory plan Group insurance plan issued to an employer under which both the employer and employees contribute to the cost of the plan. Generally, 75% of the eligible employees must be insured. (*See* noncontributory plan)

conversion factor A stated dollar-per-point amount used to determine benefit amounts paid for the cost of a procedure under a health insurance plan. For example, a plan with a $5-per-point conversion factor would pay $1,000 for a 200-point-procedure.

conversion privilege Allows the policyowner, before an original insurance policy expires, to elect to have a new policy issued that will continue the insurance coverage. Conversion may be effected at attained age (premiums based on the age attained at time of conversion) or at original age (premiums based on age at time of original issue).

convertible term Contract that may be converted to a permanent form of insurance without medical examination.

coordination of benefits (COB) provision Designed to prevent duplication of group insurance benefits. Limits benefits from multiple group health insurance policies in a particular case to 100% of the expenses covered and designates the order in which the multiple carriers are to pay benefits.

corridor deductible In superimposed major medical plans, a deductible amount between the benefits paid by the basic plan and the beginning of the major medical benefits.

cost of living (COL) rider A rider available with some policies that provides for an automatic increase in benefits (typically tied to the Consumer Price Index), offsetting the effects of inflation.

credit accident and health insurance If the insured debtor becomes totally disabled due to an accident or sickness, the policy premiums are paid during the period of disability or the loan is paid off. May be individual or group policy.

credit life insurance Usually written as decreasing term on a relatively small decreasing balance installment loan that may reflect direct borrowing or a balance due for merchandise purchased. If borrower dies, benefits pay balance due. May be individual or group policy.

credit report A summary of an insurance applicant's credit history, made by an independent organization that has investigated the applicant's credit standing.

cross-purchase plan An agreement that provides that upon a business owner's death, surviving owners will purchase the deceased's interest, often with funds from life insurance policies owned by each principal on the lives of all other principals.

currently insured Under Social Security, a status of limited eligibility that provides only death benefits.

custodial care   Level of health or medical care given to meet daily personal needs, such as dressing, bathing, getting out of bed, and so on. Though it does not require medical training, it must be administered under a physician's order.

D

death rate   Proportion of persons in each age group who die within a year; usually expressed as so many deaths per thousand persons. (*See* expected mortality)

debit insurer   (*See* home service insurer)

decreasing term insurance   Term life insurance on which the face value slowly decreases in scheduled steps from the date the policy comes into force to the date the policy expires, while the premium remains level. The intervals between decreases are usually monthly or annually.

deductible   Amount of expense or loss to be paid by the insured before a health insurance policy starts paying benefits.

deferred annuity   Provides for postponement of the commencement of an annuity until after a specified period or until the annuitant attains a specified age. May be purchased either on single-premium or flexible premium basis.

deferred compensation plan   The deferral of an employee's compensation to some future age or date. These plans are frequently used to provide fringe benefits, such as retirement income, to selected personnel.

defined benefit plan   A pension plan under which benefits are determined by a specific benefit formula.

defined contribution plan   A tax-qualified retirement plan in which annual contributions are determined by a formula set forth in the plan. Benefits paid to a participant vary with the amount of contributions made on the participant's behalf and the length of service under the plan.

delayed disability provision   A disability income policy provision that allows a certain amount of time after an accident for a disability to result, and the insured remains eligible for benefits.

dental insurance   A relatively new form of health insurance coverage typically offered on a group basis, it covers the costs of normal dental maintenance as well as oral surgery and root canal therapy.

dependency period   Period following the death of the breadwinner up until the youngest child reaches maturity.

deposit term   Has modest endowment feature. Normally is sold for 10-year terms with a higher first-year premium than for subsequent years. If policy lapses, insured forfeits the "deposit" and receives no refund.

disability   Physical or mental impairment making a person incapable of performing one or more duties of his occupation.

disability buy-sell agreement   An agreement between business co-owners that provides that shares owned by any one of them who becomes disabled shall be sold to and purchased by the other co-owners or by the business using funds from disability income insurance.

disability income insurance   A type of health insurance coverage, it provides for the payment of regular, periodic income should the insured become disabled from illness or injury.

disability income rider   Typically a rider to a life insurance policy, it provides benefits in the form of income in the event the insured becomes totally disabled.

discrimination   In insurance, the act of treating certain groups of people unfairly in the sale and/or pricing of policies; treating any of a given class of risk differently from other like risks. Discrimination is expressly prohibited in most state insurance codes.

dividend   Policyowner's share in the divisible surplus of a company issuing insurance on the participating plan.

dividend options   The different ways in which the insured under a participating life insurance policy may elect to receive surplus earnings: in cash, as a reduction of premium, as additional paid-up insurance, left on deposit at interest, or as additional term insurance.

domestic insurer   Company within the state in which it is chartered and in which its home office is located.

dread disease policy   (*See* limited risk policy)

E

elimination period   Duration of time between the beginning of an insured's disability and the commencement of the period for which benefits are payable.

employee benefit plans   Plans through which employers offer employees benefits such as coverage for medical expenses, disability, retirement, and death.

employee stock ownership plan (ESOP)   A form of defined contribution profit-sharing plan, an ESOP invests primarily in the securities or stock of the employer.

endowment   Contract providing for payment of the face amount at the end of a fixed period, at a specified age of the insured, or at the insured's death before the end of the stated period.

endowment period   Period specified in an endowment policy during which, if the insured dies, the beneficiary receives a death benefit. If the insured is still living at the end of the endowment period, the insured receives the endowment as a living benefit.

enrollment period   Period during which new employees can sign up for coverage under a group insurance plan.

entire contract provision   An insurance policy provision stating that the application and policy contain all provisions and constitute the entire contract.

entity plan   An agreement in which a business assumes the obligation of purchasing a deceased owner's interest in the business, thereby proportionately increasing the interests of surviving owners.

equity indexed annuity   A fixed deferred annuity that offers the traditional guaranteed minimum interest rate and an excess interest feature that is based on the performance of an external equities market index.

errors and omissions insurance   Professional liability insurance that protects an insurance producer against claims arising from service the producer rendered or failed to render.

estate   Most commonly, the quantity of wealth or property at an individual's death.

estate tax   Federal tax imposed on the value of property transferred by an individual at the individual's death.

estoppel   Legal impediment to denying the consequences of one's actions or deeds if they lead to detrimental actions by another.

evidence of insurability   Any statement or proof regarding a person's physical condition, occupation, and so forth, affecting acceptance of the applicant for insurance.

examiner   Physician authorized by the medical director of an insurance company to make medical examinations. Also, person assigned by a state insurance company to audit the affairs of an insurance company.

excess interest   Difference between the rate of interest the company guarantees to pay on proceeds left under settlement options and the interest actually paid on such funds by the company.

exclusion ratio   A fraction used to determine the amount of annual annuity income exempt from federal income tax. The exclusion ratio is the total contribution or investment in the annuity divided by the expected ratio.

exclusion rider   Health insurance policy rider that waives insurer's liability for all future claims on a preexisting condition.

exclusions   Specified hazards listed in a policy for which benefits will not be paid.

exclusive provider organization (EPO)   A variation of the PPO concept, an EPO contracts with an extremely limited number of physicians and typically only one hospital to provide services to members; members who elect to get health care from outside the EPO receive no benefits. (*See also* preferred provider organization)

expected mortality   Number of deaths that theoretically should occur among a group of insured persons during a given period, according to the mortality table in use. Normally, a lower mortality rate is anticipated and generally experienced.

experience rating   Review of the previous year's claims experience for a group insurance contract in order to establish premiums for the next period.

express authority   The specific authority given in writing to the agent in the contract of agency.

extended term insurance   Nonforfeiture option providing for the cash surrender value of a policy to be used as a net single premium at the insured's attained age to purchase term insurance for the face amount of the policy, less indebtedness, for as long a period as possible, but no longer than the term of the original policy.

F

face amount   Commonly used to refer to the principal sum involved in the contract. The actual amount payable may be decreased by loans or increased by additional benefits payable under specified conditions or stated in a rider.

facility-of-payment provision   Clause permitted under a uniform health insurance policy provision allowing the company to pay up to $1,000 of benefits or proceeds to any relative appearing entitled to it if there is no beneficiary or if the insured or beneficiary is a minor or legally incompetent.

Fair Credit Reporting Act   Federal law requiring an individual to be informed if that individual is being investigated by an inspection company.

family plan policy   All-family plan of protection, usually with permanent insurance on the primary wage earner's life and with spouse and children automatically covered for lesser amounts of protection, usually term, all included for one premium.

FICA   Contributions made by employees and employers to fund Social Security benefits (OASDI).

fiduciary   Person in a position of special trust and confidence (e.g., in handling or supervising affairs or funds of another).

fixed-amount settlement option   A life insurance settlement option whereby the beneficiary instructs that proceeds be paid in regular installments of a fixed dollar amount. The number of payment periods is determined by the policy's face amount, the amount of each payment, and the interest earned.

fixed annuity   A type of annuity that provides a guaranteed fixed benefit amount, payable for the life of the annuitant.

fixed-period settlement option   A life insurance settlement option in which the number of payments is fixed by the payee, with the amount of each payment determined by the amount of proceeds.

flat deductible   Amount of covered expenses payable by the insured before medical benefits are payable.

foreign insurer   Company operating in a state in which it is not chartered and in which its home office is not located.

franchise insurance   Life or health insurance plan for covering groups of persons with individual policies uniform in provisions, although perhaps different in benefits. Solicitation usually takes place in an employer's business with the employer's consent. Generally written for groups too small to qualify for regular group coverage. May be called wholesale insurance when the policy is life insurance.

fraternal benefit insurer   Nonprofit benevolent organization that provides insurance to its members.

fraud   An act of deceit; misrepresentation of a material fact made knowingly, with the intention of having another person rely on that fact and consequently suffer a financial hardship.

free look   Provision required in most states whereby policyholders have either 10 or 20 days to examine their new policies at no obligation.

fully insured   A status of complete eligibility for the full range of Social Security benefits: death benefits, retirement benefits, disability benefits, and Medicare benefits.

funding   In a retirement plan, the setting aside of funds for the payment of benefits.

G

general agent   Independent agent with authority, under contract with the company, to appoint soliciting agents within a designated territory and fix their compensation.

government insurer   An organization that, as an extension of the federal or state government, provides a program of social insurance.

grace period   Period of time after the due date of a premium during which the policy remains in force without penalty.

graded premium whole life   Variation of a traditional whole life contract providing for lower than normal premium rates during the first few policy years, with premiums increasing gradually each year. After the preliminary period, premiums level off and remain constant.

gross premium   The total premium paid by the policyowner, it generally consists of the net premium plus the expense of operation minus interest.

group credit insurance   A form of group insurance issued by insurance companies to creditors to cover the lives of debtors for the amounts of their loans.

group insurance   Insurance that provides coverage for a group of persons, usually employees of a company, under one master contract.

guaranteed insurability (guaranteed issue)   Arrangement, usually provided by rider, whereby additional insurance may be purchased at various times without evidence of insurability.

guaranteed renewable contract   Health insurance contract that the insured has the right to continue in force by payment of premiums for a substantial period of time during which the insurer has no right to make unilaterally any change in any provision, other than a change in premium rate for classes of insureds.

guaranty association   Established by each state to support insurers and protect consumers in the case of insurer insolvency, guaranty associations are funded by insurers through assessments.

H

hazard   Any factor that gives rise to a peril.

health insurance   Insurance against loss through sickness or accidental bodily injury. Also called accident and health, accident and sickness, sickness and accident, or disability insurance.

health maintenance organization (HMO)   Health care management stressing preventive health care, early diagnosis, and treatment on an outpatient basis. Persons generally enroll voluntarily by paying a fixed fee periodically.

home health care   Skilled or unskilled care provided in an individual's home, usually on a part-time basis.

home service insurer   Insurer that offers relatively small policies with premiums payable on a weekly basis, collected by agents at the policyowner's home.

hospital benefits   Payable for charges incurred while the insured is confined to or treated in a hospital, as defined in a health insurance policy.

hospital expense insurance   Health insurance benefits subject to a specified daily maximum for a specified period of time while the injured is confined to a hospital, plus a limited allowance up to a specified amount for miscellaneous hospital expenses, such as operating room, anesthesia, laboratory fees, and so on. Also called hospitalization insurance. (*See* medical expense insurance)

hospital indemnity   Form of health insurance providing a stipulated daily, weekly, or monthly indemnity during hospital confinement; payable on an unallocated basis without regard to actual hospital expense.

human life value   An individual's economic worth, measured by the sum of the individual's future earnings that is devoted to the individual's family.

I

immediate annuity   Provides for payment of annuity benefit at one payment interval from date of purchase. Can only be purchased with a single payment.

implied authority   Authority not specifically granted to the agent in the contract of agency, but which common sense dictates the agent has. It enables the agent to carry out routine responsibilities.

incontestable clause Provides that, for certain reasons such as misstatements on the application, the company may void a life insurance policy after it has been in force during the insured's lifetime, usually one or two years after issue.

increasing term insurance Term life insurance in which the death benefit increases periodically over the policy's term. Usually purchased as a cost of living rider to a whole life policy. (*See* cost of living rider)

indemnity approach A method of paying health policy benefits to insureds based on a predetermined, fixed rate set for the medical services provided, regardless of the actual expenses incurred.

independent agency system A system for marketing, selling, and distributing insurance in which independent brokers are not affiliated with any one insurer but represent any number of insurers.

indexed whole life A whole life insurance policy with a death benefit that increases according to the rate of inflation. Such policies are usually tied to the Consumer Price Index (CPI).

individual insurance Policies providing protection to the policyowner, as distinct from group and blanket insurance. Also called personal insurance.

individual retirement account (IRA) A personal qualified retirement account through which eligible individuals accumulate tax-deferred income up to a certain amount each year, depending on the person's tax bracket.

industrial insurance Life insurance policy providing modest benefits and a relatively short benefit period. Premiums are collected on a weekly or monthly basis by an agent calling at insured's homes. (*See* home service insurer)

inspection receipt A receipt obtained from an insurance applicant when a policy (upon which the first premium has not been paid) is left with the applicant for further inspection. It states that the insurance is not in effect and that the policy has been delivered for inspection only.

inspection report Report of an investigator providing facts required for a proper underwriting decision on applications for new insurance and reinstatements.

installment refund annuity An annuity income option that provides for the funds remaining at the annuitant's death to be paid to the beneficiary in the form of continued annuity payments.

insurability All conditions pertaining to individuals that affect their health, susceptibility to injury, or life expectancy; an individual's risk profile.

insurability receipt A type of conditional receipt that makes coverage effective on the date the application was signed or the date of the medical exam (whichever is later), provided the applicant proves to be insurable.

insurable interest Requirement of insurance contracts that loss must be sustained by the applicant upon the death or disability of another and loss must be sufficient to warrant compensation.

insurance Social device for minimizing risk of uncertainty regarding loss by spreading the risk over a large enough number of similar exposures to predict the individual chance of loss.

insurance code The laws that govern the business of insurance in a given state.

insurer Party that provides insurance coverage, typically through a contract of insurance.

insuring clause Defines and describes the scope of the coverage provided and limits of indemnification.

integrated deductible In superimposed major medical plans, a deductible amount between the benefits paid by the basic plan and those benefits paid by the major medical. All or part of the integrated deductible may be absorbed by the basic plan.

interest adjusted net cost method A method of comparing costs of similar policies by using an index that takes into account the time value of money.

interest-only option (interest option) Mode of settlement under which all or part of the proceeds of a policy are left with the company for a definite period at a guaranteed minimum interest rate. Interest may either be added to the proceeds or paid annually, semiannually, quarterly, or monthly.

interest-sensitive whole life Whole life policy whose premiums vary depending upon the insurer's underlying death, investment, and expense assumptions.

interim term insurance Term insurance for a period of 12 months or less by special agreement of the company; it permits a permanent policy to become effective at a selected future date.

intermediate nursing care Level of health or medical care that is occasional or rehabilitative, ordered by a physician, and performed by skilled medical personnel.

irrevocable beneficiary Beneficiary whose interest cannot be revoked without the beneficiary's written consent, usually because the policyowner has made the beneficiary designation without retaining the right to revoke or change it.

J

joint and last survivor policy A variation of the joint life policy that covers two lives but pays the benefit upon the death of the second insured.

joint and survivor annuity Covers two or more lives and continues in force so long as any one of them survives.

joint life policy Covers two or more lives and provides for the payment of the proceeds at the death of the first among those insured, at which time the policy automatically terminates.

juvenile insurance   Written on the lives of children who are within specified age limits and generally under parental control.

K

Keogh plans   Designed to fund retirement of self-employed individuals; name derived from the author of the Keogh Act (HR-10), under which contributions to such plans are given favorable tax treatment.

key-person insurance   Protection of a business against financial loss caused by the death or disablement of a vital member of the company, usually individuals possessing special managerial or technical skill or expertise.

L

lapse   Termination of a policy upon the policyowner's failure to pay the premium within the grace period.

law of large numbers   Basic principle of insurance that the larger the number of individual risks combined into a group, the more certainty there is in predicting the degree or amount of loss that will be incurred in any given period.

legal purpose   In contract law, the requirement that the object of, or reason for, the contract must be legal.

legal reserve   Policy reserves are maintained according to the standard levels established through the insurance laws of the various states.

level premium funding method   The insurance plan (used by all regular life insurance companies) under which, instead of an annually increasing premium that reflects the increasing chance of death, an equivalent level premium is paid. Reserves that accumulate from more than adequate premiums paid in the early years supplement inadequate premiums in later years.

level term insurance   Term coverage on which the face value remains unchanged from the date the policy comes into force to the date the policy expires.

license   Certification issued by a state insurance department that an individual is qualified to solicit insurance applications for the period covered; usually issued for one year, renewable on application without need to repeat the original qualifying requirements.

licensed insurer   (*See* admitted insurer)

life annuity   Payable during the continued life of the annuitant. No provision is made for the guaranteed return of the unused portion of the premium.

life expectancy   Average duration of the life remaining to a number of persons of a given age, according to a given mortality table. Not to be confused with "probable lifetime," which refers to the difference between a person's present age and the age at which death is most probable (i.e., the age at which most deaths occur).

life income settlement option   A settlement option providing for life insurance or annuity proceeds to be used to buy an annuity payable to the beneficiary for life-often with a specified number of payments certain or a refund if payments don't equal or exceed premiums paid.

life insurance   Insurance against loss due to the death of a particular person (the insured) upon whose death the insurance company agrees to pay a stated sum or income to the beneficiary.

life settlement transaction   Transfer of an ownership interest in a life insurance policy to a third party for compensation less than the expected death benefit under the policy, or the sale of a life insurance policy for a dollar amount that is less than the policy's face amount.

limited pay life insurance   A form of whole life insurance characterized by premium payments only being made for a specified or limited number of years.

limited policies   Restrict benefits to specified accidents or diseases, such as travel policies, dread disease policies, ticket policies, and so forth.

limited risk policy   Provides coverage for specific kinds of accidents or illnesses, such as injuries received as a result of travel accidents or medical expenses stemming from a specified disease. (*See* special risk policy)

Lloyd's of London   An association of individuals and companies that underwrite insurance on their own accounts and provide specialized coverages.

loading   Amount added to net premiums to cover the company's operating expenses and contingencies; includes the cost of securing new business, collection expenses, and general management expenses; excess of gross premiums over net premiums.

loan value   Determinable amount that can be borrowed from the issuing company by the policyowner using the value of the life insurance policy as collateral.

long-term care   Refers to the broad range of medical and personal services for individuals (often the elderly) who need assistance with daily activities for an extended period of time.

long-term care policy   Health insurance policies that provide daily indemnity benefits for extended care confinement.

loss sharing   (*See* risk pooling)

lump sum   Payment of entire proceeds of an insurance policy in one sum. The method of settlement provided by most policies unless an alternate settlement is elected by the policyowner or beneficiary.

M

major medical expense policy   Health insurance policy that provides broad coverage and high benefits for hospitalization, surgery, and physician services. Characterized by deductibles and coinsurance cost-sharing.

managed care   A system of delivering health care and health care services, characterized by arrangements with selected providers, programs of ongoing quality control and utilization review, and financial incentives for members to use providers and procedures covered by the plan.

master contract   Issued to the employer under a group plan; contains all the insuring clauses defining employee benefits. Individual employees participating in the group plan receive individual certificates that outline highlights of the coverage. Also called master policy.

McCarran-Ferguson Act   Also know as Public Law 15, the 1945 act exempting insurance from federal antitrust laws to the extent insurance is regulated by states.

Medicaid   Provides medical care for the needy under joint federal-state participation (Kerr-Mills Act).

medical examination   Usually conducted by a licensed physician; the medical report is part of the application, becomes part of the policy contract, and is attached to the policy. A "nonmedical" is a short-form medical report filled out by the agent. Various company rules, such as amount of insurance applied for or already in force, or applicant's age, sex, past physical history and data revealed by inspection report, and so on, determine whether the examination will be "medical" or "nonmedical."

medical expense insurance   Pays benefits for nonsurgical doctors' fees commonly rendered in a hospital; sometimes pays for home and office calls.

Medical Information Bureau (MIB)   A service organization that collects medical data on life and health insurance applicants for member insurance companies.

medical report   A document completed by a physician or other approved examiner and submitted to an insurer to supply medical evidence of insurability (or lack of insurability) or in relation to a claim.

Medicare   Federally sponsored health insurance and medical program for persons age 65 or older; administered under provisions of the Social Security Act.

Medicare Part A   Compulsory hospitalization insurance that provides specified inhospital and related benefits. All workers covered by Social Security finance its operation through a portion of their FICA tax.

Medicare Part B   Voluntary program designed to provide supplementary medical insurance to cover physician services, medical services, and supplies not covered under Medicare Part A.

Medicare Part C   Medicare Part C is called Medicare Advantage. The program offers a variety of managed care plans, a private fee-for-service plan, and Medicare specialty plans. These specialty plans provide services that focus care on the management of a specific disease or condition.

Medicare Part D   A program that offers a prescription drug benefit to help Medicare beneficiaries pay for the drugs they need. The drug benefit is optional and is available to anyone who is entitled to Medicare Part A or enrolled in Part B. This benefit is available through private prescription drug plans (PDPs) or Medicare Advantage (PPO) plans.

Medicare supplement policy   Health insurance that provides coverage to fill the gaps in Medicare coverage.

minimum deposit insurance   A cash value life insurance policy having a first-year loan value that is available for borrowing immediately upon payment of the first-year premium.

miscellaneous expenses   Hospital charges, other than for room and board (e.g., x-rays, drugs, laboratory fees, and so forth) in connection with health insurance.

misrepresentation   Act of making, issuing, circulating, or causing to be issued or circulated, an estimate, illustration, circular, or statement of any kind that does not represent the correct policy terms, dividends, or share of the surplus or the name or title for any policy or class of policies that does not in fact reflect its true nature.

misstatement of age or sex provision   If the insured's age or sex is misstated in an application for insurance, the benefit payable usually is adjusted to what the premiums paid should have purchased.

modified endowment contract (MEC)   A life insurance policy under which the amount a policyowner pays in during the first years exceeds the sum of net level premiums that would have been payable to provide paid-up future benefits in seven years.

modified whole life   Whole life insurance with premium payable during the first few years, usually five years, only slightly larger than the rate for term insurance. Afterwards, the premium is higher for the remainder of life than the premium for ordinary life at the original age of issue but lower than the rate at the attained age at the time of charge.

money purchase plan   A type of qualified plan under which contributions are fixed amounts or fixed percentages of the employee's salary. An employee's benefits are provided in whatever amount the accumulated or current contributions will produce for the employee.

moral hazard   Effect of personal reputation, character, associates, personal living habits, financial responsibility, and environment, as distinguished from physical health, upon an individual's general insurability.

morale hazard   Hazard arising from indifference to loss because of the existence of insurance.

morbidity   The relative incidence of disability due to sickness or accident within a given group.

morbidity rate   Shows the incidence and extent of disability that may be expected from a given large group of persons; used in computing health insurance rates.

mortality   The relative incidence of death within a group.

mortality table   Listing of the mortality experience of individuals by age; permits an actuary to calculate, on the average, how long a male or female of a given age group may be expected to live.

mortgage insurance   A basic use of life insurance, so-called because many family heads leave insurance for specifically paying off any mortgage balance outstanding at their death. The insurance generally is made payable to a family beneficiary instead of to the mortgage holder.

multiple employer trust (MET)   Several small groups of individuals that need life and health insurance but do not qualify for true group insurance band together under state trust laws to purchase insurance at a more favorable rate.

multiple employer welfare arrangement (MEWA)   Similar to a multiple employer trust (MET) with the exception that in a MEWA, a number of employers pool their risks and self-insure.

multiple protection policy   A combination of term and whole life coverage that pays some multiple of the face amount of the basic whole life portion (such as $10 per month per $1,000) throughout the multiple protection period (such as to age 65).

mutual insurer   An insurance company characterized by having no capital stock; it is owned by its policyowners and usually issues participating insurance.

N

National Association of Health Underwriters (NAHU)   NAHU is an organization of health insurance agents that is dedicated to supporting the health insurance industry and to advancing the quality of service provided by insurance professionals.

National Association of Insurance and Financial Advisors (NAIFA)   NAIFA is an organization of life insurance agents that is dedicated to supporting the life insurance industry and to advancing the quality of service provided by insurance professionals.

National Association of Insurance Commissioners (NAIC)   Association of state insurance commissioners active in insurance regulatory problems and in forming and recommending model legislation and requirements.

natural group   A group formed for a reason other than to obtain insurance.

needs approach   A method for determining how much insurance protection a person should have by analyzing a family's or business's needs and objectives should the insured die, become disabled, or retire.

net premium   Calculated on the basis of a given mortality table and a given interest rate, without any allowance for loading.

nonadmitted insurer   An insurance company that has not been licensed to operate within a given state.

noncancellable and guaranteed renewable contract   Health insurance contract that the insured has the right to continue in force by payment of premiums set forth in the contract for a substantial period of time, during which the insurer has no right to make unilaterally any change in any contract provision.

noncontributory plan   Employee benefit plan under which the employer bears the full cost of the employees' benefits; must insure 100% of eligible employees.

nondisabling injury   Requires medical care, but does not result in loss of time from work.

nonduplication provision   Stipulates that insureds shall be ineligible to collect for charges under a group health plan if the charges are reimbursed under their own or their spouse's group plan.

nonforfeiture options   Privileges allowed under terms of a life insurance contract after cash values have been created.

nonforfeiture values   Those benefits in a life insurance policy that, by law, the policyowner does not forfeit even if the policyowner discontinues premium payments; usually cash value, loan value, paid-up insurance value, and extended term insurance value.

nonmedical insurance   Issued on a regular basis without requiring a regular medical examination. In passing on the risk, the company relies on the applicant's answers to questions regarding the applicant's own physical condition and on personal references or inspection reports.

nonparticipating   Insurance under which the insured is not entitled to share in the divisible surplus of the company.

nonqualified plan   A retirement plan that does not meet federal government requirements and is not eligible for favorable tax treatment.

notice of claims provision   Policy provision that describes the policyowner's obligation to provide notification of loss to the insurer within a reasonable period of time.

O

offer and acceptance   The offer may be made by the applicant by signing the application, paying the first premium and, if necessary, submitting to a physical examination. Policy issuance, as applied for, constitutes acceptance by the company. Or, the offer may be made by the company when no premium payment is submitted with application. Premium payment on the offered policy then constitutes acceptance by the applicant.

Old-Age, Survivors, Disability and Hospital Insurance (OASDI)   Retirement, death, disability income, and hospital insurance benefits provided under the Social Security system.

open-panel HMO   A network of physicians who work out of their own offices and participate in the HMO on a part-time basis.

optionally renewable contract   Health insurance policy in which the insurer reserves the right to terminate the coverage at any anniversary or, in some cases, at any premium due date, but does not have the right to terminate coverage between such dates.

ordinary insurance   Life insurance of commercial companies not issued on the weekly premium basis; amount of protection usually is $1,000 or more.

other insureds rider   A term rider, covering a family member other than the insured, that is attached to the base policy covering the insured.

outline of coverage   Informational material about a specific plan or policy of insurance that describes the policy's features and benefits; in many states, an outline of coverage is required to be given to consumers when certain types of coverages are being considered.

overhead insurance   Type of short-term disability insurance reimbursing the insured for specified, fixed, monthly expenses, normal and customary in operating the insured's business.

overinsurance   An excessive amount of insurance; an amount of insurance that would result in payment of more than the actual loss or more than incurred expenses.

own occupation   A definition of total disability that requires that in order to receive disability income benefits the insured must be unable to work at his or her own occupation.

P

paid-up additions   Additional life insurance purchased by policy dividends on a net single premium basis at the insured's attained insurance age at the time additions are purchased.

paid-up policy   No further premiums are to be paid and the company is held liable for the benefits provided by the contract.

parol evidence rule   Rule of contract law that brings all verbal statements into the written contract and disallows any changes or modifications to the contract by oral evidence.

partial disability   Illness or injury preventing insured from performing at least one or more, but not all, of the insured's occupational duties.

participating   Plan of insurance under which the policyowner receives shares (commonly called dividends) of the divisible surplus of the company.

participating physician   A doctor or physician who accepts Medicare's allowable or recognized charges and will not charge more than this amount.

participation standards   Rules that must be followed for determining employee eligibility for a qualified retirement plan.

partnership   A business entity that allows two or more people to strengthen their effectiveness by working together as co-owners.

payor rider   Available under certain juvenile life insurance policies, upon payment of an extra premium. Provides for the waiver of future premiums if the person responsible for paying them dies or is disabled before the policy becomes fully paid or matures as a death claim, or as an endowment, or the child reaches a specific age.

per capita rule   Death proceeds from an insurance policy are divided equally among the living primary beneficiaries.

peril   The immediate specific event causing loss and giving rise to risk.

period certain annuity   An annuity income option that guarantees a definite minimum period of payments.

permanent flat extra premium   A fixed charge added per $1,000 of insurance for substandard risks.

personal producing general agency system (PPGA)   A method of marketing, selling, and distributing insurance in which personal producing general agents (PPGAs) are compensated for business they personally sell and business sold by agents with whom they subcontract. Subcontracted agents are considered employees of the PPGA, not the insurer.

per stirpes rule   Death proceeds from an insurance policy are divided equally among the named beneficiaries. If a named beneficiary is deceased, that beneficiary's share then goes to the living descendants of that individual.

policy   In insurance, the written instrument in which a contract of insurance is set forth.

policy loan   In life insurance, a loan made by the insurance company to the policyowner, with the policy's cash value assigned as security. One of the standard nonforfeiture options.

policy provisions   The term or conditions of an insurance policy as contained in the policy clauses.

precertification   The insurer's approval of an insured's entering a hospital. Many health policies require precertification as part of an effort to control costs.

preexisting condition   An illness or medical condition that existed before a policy's effective date; usually excluded from coverage, through the policy's standard provisions or by waiver.

preferred provider organization (PPO)   Association of health care providers, such as doctors and hospitals, that agree to provide health care to members of a particular group at fees negotiated in advance.

preferred risk   A risk whose physical condition, occupation, mode of living, and other characteristics indicate a prospect for longevity for unimpaired lives of the same age.

premium   The periodic payment required to keep an insurance policy in force.

premium factors   The three primary factors considered when computing the basic premium for insurance: mortality, expense, and interest.

prescription drug coverage   Usually offered as an optional benefit to group medical expense plans, this coverage covers some or all of the cost of prescription drugs.

presumptive disability benefit   A disability income policy benefit that provides that if an insured experiences a specified disability, such as blindness, the insured is presumed to be totally disabled and entitled to the full amount payable under the policy, whether or not the insured is able to work.

primary beneficiary   In life insurance, the beneficiary designated by the insured as the first to receive policy benefits.

primary insurance amount (PIA)   Amount equal to a covered worker's full Social Security retirement benefit at age 65 or disability benefit.

principal   An insurance company that, having appointed someone as its agent, is bound to the contracts the agent completes in its behalf.

principal sum   The amount under an AD&D policy that is payable as a death benefit if death is due to an accident.

private insurer   An insurer that is not associated with federal or state government.

probationary period   Specified number of days after an insurance policy's issue date during which coverage is not afforded for sickness. Standard practice for group coverages.

proceeds   Net amount of money payable by the company at the insured's death or at policy maturity.

producer   A general term applied to an agent, broker, personal producing general agent, solicitor, or other person who sells insurance.

professional liability insurance   (*See* errors and omissions insurance)

profit-sharing plan   Any plan whereby a portion of a company's profits is set aside for distribution to employees who qualify under the plan.

proof of loss   A mandatory health insurance provision stating that the insured must provide a completed claim form to the insurer within 90 days of the date of loss.

pure endowment   Contract providing for payment only upon survival of a certain person to a certain date and not in the event of that person's prior death. This type of contract is just the opposite of a term contract, which provides for payment only in the event the injured person dies within the term period specified.

pure risk   Type of risk that involves the chance of loss only; there is no opportunity for gain; insurable.

Q

qualified plan   A retirement or employee compensation plan established and maintained by an employer that meets specific guidelines spelled out by the IRS and consequently receives favorable tax treatment.

R

rate-up in age   System of rating substandard risks that assumes the insured to be older than the insured really is and charging a correspondingly higher premium.

rating   The making of insurance also creates the premium classification given an applicant for life or health insurance.

reasonable and customary charge   Charge for health care service consistent with the going rate of charge in a given geographical area for identical or similar services.

rebating   Returning part of the commission or giving anything else of value to the insured as an inducement to buy the policy. It is illegal and cause for license revocation in most states. In some states, it is an offense by both the agent and the person receiving the rebate.

reciprocal insurer   Insurance company characterized by the fact its policyholders insure the risks of other policyholders.

recurrent disability provision   A disability income policy provision that specifies the period of time during which the reoccurrence of a disability is considered a continuation of a prior disability.

reduced paid-up insurance   A nonforfeiture option contained in most life insurance policies providing for the insured to elect to have the cash surrender value of the policy used to purchase a paid-up policy for a reduced amount of insurance.

re-entry option   An option in a renewable term life policy under which the policyowner is guaranteed, at the end of the term, to be able to renew coverage without evidence of insurability, at a premium rate specified in the policy.

refund annuity   Provides for the continuance of the annuity during the annuitant's lifetime and, in any event, until total payment equal to the purchase price has been made by the company.

reimbursement approach   Payment of health policy benefits to insured based on actual medical expenses incurred.

reinstatement   Putting a lapsed policy back in force by producing satisfactory evidence of insurability and paying any past-due premiums required.

reinsurance   Acceptance by one or more insurers, called reinsurers, of a portion of the risk underwritten by another insurer who has contracted for the entire coverage.

relative value scale   Method for determining benefits payable under a basic surgical expense policy. Points are assigned to each surgical procedure and a dollar per point amount, or conversion factor, is used to determine the benefit.

renewable option   An option that allows the policyowner to renew a term policy before its termination date without having to provide evidence of insurability.

renewable term   Some term policies prove that they may be renewed on the same plan for one or more years without medical examination, but with rates based on the insured's advanced age.

replacement   Act of replacing one life insurance policy with another; may be done legally under certain conditions. (*See* twisting)

representation   Statements made by applicants on their applications for insurance that they represent as being substantially true to the best of their knowledge and belief, but that are not warranted as exact in every detail. (*See* warranties)

reserve   Fund held by the company to help fulfill future claims.

reserve basis   Refers to mortality table and assumed interest rate used in computing rates.

residual disability benefit   A disability income payment based on the proportion of income the insured has actually lost, taking into account the fact that the insured is able to earn some income.

respite care   Type of health or medical care designed to provide a short rest period for a caregiver. Characterized by its temporary status.

results provision   (*See* accidental bodily injury provision)

revocable beneficiary   Beneficiary whose rights in a policy are subject to the policyowner's reserved right to revoke or change the beneficiary designation and the right to surrender or make a loan on the policy without the beneficiary's consent.

rider   Strictly speaking, a rider adds something to a policy. However, the term is used loosely to refer to any supplemental agreement attached to and made a part of the policy, whether the policy's conditions are expanded and additional coverages added, or a coverage of conditions is waived.

risk   Uncertainty regarding loss; the probability of loss occurring for an insured or prospect.

risk pooling   A basic principle of insurance whereby a large number contribute to cover the losses of a few. (*See* loss sharing)

risk selection   The method of a home office underwriter used to choose applicants that the insurance company will accept. The underwriter must determine whether risks are standard, substandard, or preferred and adjust the premium rates accordingly.

rollover IRA   An individual retirement account established with funds transferred from another IRA or qualified retirement plan that the owner had terminated.

S

salary continuation plan   An arrangement whereby an income, usually related to an employee's salary, is continued upon employee's retirement, death or disability.

salary reduction SEP   A qualified retirement plan limited to companies with 25 or fewer employees. It allows employees to defer part of their pretax income to the plan, lowering their taxable income. (*See* simplified employee pension plan)

savings incentive match plan for employees (SIMPLE)   A qualified employer retirement plan that allows small employers to set up tax-favored retirement savings plans for their employees.

schedule   List of specified amounts payable, usually for surgical operations, dismemberment, fractures, and so forth.

secondary beneficiary   An alternative beneficiary designated to receive payment, usually in the event the original beneficiary predeceases the insured.

Section 457 plans   Deferred compensation plans for employees of state and local governments in which amounts deferred will not be included in gross income until they are actually received or made available.

Self-Employed Individuals Retirement Act   Passed by Congress in 1962, this Act enables self-employed persons to establish qualified retirement plans similar to those available to corporations.

self-insurance   Program for providing insurance financed entirely through the means of the policyowner, in place of purchasing coverage from commercial carriers.

self-insured plan   A health insurance plan characterized by an employer (usually a large one), labor union, fraternal organization, or other group retaining the risk of covering its employees' medical expenses.

service insurers   Companies that offer prepayment plans for medical or hospital services, such as health maintenance organizations.

service provider   An organization that provides health coverage by contracting with service providers, to provide medical services to subscribers, who pay in advance through premiums. Examples of such coverages are HMOs and PPOs.

settlement options   Optional modes of settlement provided by most life insurance policies in lieu of lump-sum payment. Usual options are lump-sum cash, interest-only, fixed-period, fixed-amount, and life income.

simplified employee pension plan (SEP)   A type of qualified retirement plan under which the employer contributes to an individual retirement account set up and maintained by the employee.

single dismemberment   Loss of one hand or one foot, or the sight of one eye.

single-premium whole life insurance   Whole life insurance for which the entire premium is paid in one sum at the beginning of the contract period.

skilled nursing care   Daily nursing care ordered by a doctor; often medically necessary. It can only be performed by or under the supervision of skilled medical professionals and is available 24 hours a day.

Social Security   Programs first created by Congress in 1935 and now composed of Old-Age, Survivors and Disability Insurance (OASDI), Medicare, Medicaid, and various grants-in-aid, which provide economic security to nearly all employed people.

sole proprietorship   The simplest form of business organization whereby one individual owns and controls the entire company.

special class   Applicants who cannot qualify for standard insurance but may secure policies with riders waiving payment for losses involving certain existing health impairments.

special risk policy   Provides coverage for unusual hazards normally not covered under accident and health insurance, such as a concert pianist insuring his hands for a million dollars. (*See* limited risk policy)

specified disease insurance   (*See* limited risk policy)

speculative risk   A type of risk that involves the chance of both loss and gain; not insurable.

spendthrift provision   Stipulates that, to the extent permitted by law, policy proceeds shall not be subject to the claims of creditors of the beneficiary or policy-owner.

split-dollar life insurance   An arrangement between two parties where life insurance is written on the life of one, who names the beneficiary of the net death benefits (death benefits less cash value), and the other is assigned the cash value, with both sharing premium payments.

spousal IRA   An individual retirement account that persons eligible to set up IRAs for themselves may set up jointly with a nonworking spouse.

standard provisions   Forerunners of the Uniform Policy Provisions in health insurance policies today.

standard risk   Person who, according to a company's underwriting standards, is entitled to insurance protection without extra rating or special restrictions.

stock bonus plan   A plan under which bonuses are paid to employees in shares of stock.

stock insurer   An insurance company owned and controlled by a group of stockholders whose investment in the company provides the safety margin necessary in issuance of guaranteed, fixed premium, nonparticipating policies.

stock redemption plan   An agreement under which a close corporation purchases a deceased stockholder's interest.

stop-loss provision   Designed to stop the company's loss at a given point, as an aggregate payable under a policy, a maximum payable for any one disability or the like; also applies to individuals, placing a limit on the maximum out-of-pocket expenses an insured must pay for health care, after which the health policy covers all expenses.

straight life income annuity (straight life annuity, life annuity)   An annuity income option that pays a guaranteed income for the annuitant's lifetime, after which time payments stop.

straight whole life insurance   (*See* whole life insurance)

subscriber   Policyowner of a health care plan underwritten by a service insurer.

substandard risk   Person who is considered an under-average or impaired insurance risk because of physical condition, family or personal history of disease, occupation, residence in unhealthy climate, or dangerous habits. (*See* special class)

successor beneficiary   (*See* secondary beneficiary)

suicide provision   Most life insurance policies provide that if the insured commits suicide within a specified period, usually two years after the issue date, the company's liability will be limited to a return of premiums paid.

supplemental accident coverage   Often included as part of a group basic or major medical plan, this type of coverage is designed to cover expenses associated with accidents to the extent they are not provided under other coverages.

supplementary major medical policy   A medical expense health plan that covers expenses not included under a basic policy and expenses that exceed the limits of a basic policy.

surgical expense insurance   Provides benefits to pay for the cost of surgical operations.

surgical schedule   List of cash allowances payable for various types of surgery, with the respective maximum amounts payable based upon severity of the operations; stipulated maximum usually covers all professional fees involved (e.g., surgeon, anesthesiologist).

surrender value   (*See* cash surrender value)

T

taxable wage base   The maximum amount of earnings upon which FICA taxes must be paid.

tax-sheltered annuity   An annuity plan reserved for nonprofit organizations and their employees. Funds contributed to the annuity are excluded from current taxable income and are only taxed later, when benefits begin to be paid. Also called tax-deferred annuity and 403(b) plan.

temporary insurance agreement   (*See* binding receipt)

term insurance   Protection during limited number of years; expiring without value if the insured survives the stated period, which may be one or more years, but usually is 5 to 20 years, because such periods generally cover the needs for temporary protection.

term of policy   Period for which the policy runs. In life insurance, this is to the end of the term period for term insurance, to the maturity date for endowments and to the insured's death (or age 100) for permanent insurance. In most other kinds of insurance, it is usually the period for which a premium has been paid in advance; however, it may be for a year or more, even though the premium is paid on a semiannual or other basis.

tertiary beneficiary   In life insurance, a beneficiary designated as third in line to receive the proceeds or benefits if the primary and secondary beneficiaries do not survive the insured.

third-party administrator (TPA)   An organization outside the members of a self-insurance group which, for a fee, processes claims, completes benefits paperwork, and often analyzes claims information.

third-party applicant   A policy applicant who is not the prospective insured.

time limit on certain defenses   A provision stating that an insurance policy is incontestable after it has been in force a certain period of time. It also limits the period during which an insurer can deny a claim on the basis of a preexisting condition.

total disability   Disability preventing insureds from performing any duty of their usual occupations or any occupation for remuneration; actual definition depends on policy wording.

traditional net cost method   A method of comparing costs of similar policies that does not take into account the time value of money.

transacting insurance   The transaction of any of the following, in addition to other acts included under applicable provisions of the state code: solicitation or inducement, preliminary negotiations, effecting a contract of insurance, transacting matters subsequent to effecting a contract of insurance, and arising out of it.

travel-accident policies   Limited to indemnities for accidents while traveling, usually by common carrier.

trust   Arrangement in which property is held by a person or corporation (trustee) for the benefit of others (beneficiaries). The grantor (person transferring the property to the trustee) gives legal title to the trustee, subject to terms set forth in a trust agreement. Beneficiaries have equitable title to the trust property.

trustee   One holding legal title to property for the benefit of another; may be either an individual or a company, such as a bank and trust company.

twisting   Practice of inducing a policyowner with one company to lapse, forfeit, or surrender a life insurance policy for the purpose of taking out a policy in another company. Generally classified as a misdemeanor, subject to fine, revocation of license, and sometimes imprisonment. (*See* misrepresentation)

U

unallocated benefit   Reimbursement provision, usually for miscellaneous hospital and medical expenses, that does not specify how much will be paid for each type of treatment, examination, dressing, and so forth, but only sets a maximum that will be paid for all such treatments.

underwriter   Company receiving premiums and accepting responsibility for fulfilling the policy contract. Company employee who decides whether or not the company should assume a particular risk. The agent who sells the policy.

underwriting   Process through which an insurer determines whether, and on what basis, an insurance application will be accepted.

Unfair Trade Practices Act   A model act written by the National Association of Insurance Commissioners (NAIC) and adopted by most states empowering state insurance commissioners to investigate and issue cease and desist orders and penalties to insurers for engaging in unfair or deceptive practices, such as misrepresentation or coercion.

Uniform Individual Accident and Sickness Policy Provisions Law   NAIC model law that established uniform terms, provisions, and standards for health insurance policies covering loss "resulting from sickness or from bodily injury or death by accident or both."

Uniform Simultaneous Death Act   Model law that states when an insured and beneficiary die at the same time, it is presumed that the insured survived the beneficiary.

unilateral   Distinguishing characteristic of an insurance contract in that it is only the insurance company that pledges anything.

uninsurable risk   One not acceptable for insurance due to excessive risk.

universal life   Flexible premium, two-part contract containing renewable term insurance and a cash value account that generally earns interest at a higher rate than a traditional policy. The interest rate varies. Premiums are deposited in the cash value account after the company deducts its fee and a monthly cost for the term coverage.

utilization review   A technique used by health care providers to determine after the fact if health care was appropriate and effective.

V

valued contract A contract of insurance that pays a stated amount in the event of a loss.

variable annuity Similar to a traditional, fixed annuity in that retirement payments will be made periodically to the annuitants, usually over the remaining years of their lives. Under the variable annuity, there is no guarantee of the dollar amount of the payments; they fluctuate according to the value of an account invested primarily in common stocks.

variable life insurance Provides a guaranteed minimum death benefit. Actual benefits paid may be more, however, depending on the fluctuating market value of investments behind the contract at the insured's death. The cash surrender value also generally fluctuates with the market value of the investment portfolio.

variable universal life insurance A life insurance policy combining characteristics of universal and variable life policies. A VUL policy contains unscheduled premium payments and death benefits and a cash value that varies according to the underlying funds whose investment portfolio is managed by the policyowner.

vesting Right of employees under a retirement plan to retain part or all of the annuities purchased by the employer's contributions on their behalf or, in some plans, to receive cash payments or equivalent value, on termination of their employment, after certain qualifying conditions have been met.

viatical broker An insurance producer licensed to solicit viatical settlement agreements between providers and policyowners of life insurance contracts.

viatical provider A company that buys a life insurance policy from a policyowner who is suffering from a terminal illness or a severe chronic illness.

viatical settlement contract An agreement under which the owner of a life insurance policy sells the policy to another person in exchange for a bargained-for payment, which is generally less than the expected death benefit under the policy.

viator An individual suffering from a terminal illness or severe chronic illness who sells his life insurance policy to a viatical company. The company becomes the policyowner and assumes responsibility for paying premiums. When the insured dies, the company receives the death benefits.

vision insurance Optional coverage available with group health insurance plans, vision insurance typically pays for charges incurred during eye exams; eyeglasses and contact lenses are usually excluded.

void contract An agreement without legal effect; an invalid contract.

voidable contract A contract that can be made void at the option of one or more parties to the agreement.

voluntary group AD&D A group accidental death and dismemberment policy paid for entirely by employees, rather than an employer.

W

waiting period (*See* elimination period)

waiver Agreement waiving the company's liability for a certain type or types of risk ordinarily covered in the policy; a voluntary giving up of a legal, given right.

waiver of premium Rider or provision included in most life insurance policies and some health insurance policies exempting the insured from paying premiums after the insured has been disabled for a specified period of time, usually six months in life policies and 90 days or six months in health policies.

war clause Relieves the insurer of liability, or reduces its liability, for specified loss caused by war.

warranties Statements made on an application for insurance that are warranted to be true; that is, they are exact in every detail as opposed to representations. Statements on applications for insurance are rarely warranties, unless fraud is involved. (*See* representation)

whole life insurance Permanent level insurance protection for the "whole of life," from policy issue to the death of the insured. Characterized by level premiums, level benefits, and cash values.

wholesale insurance (*See* franchise insurance)

workers' compensation Benefits paid workers for injury, disability, or disease contracted in the course of their employment. Benefits and conditions are set by law, although in most states the insurance to provide the benefits may be purchased from regular insurance companies. A few states have monopolistic state compensation funds.

Y

yearly renewable term insurance (YRT) (*See* annually renewable term)

Index

Notes

Notes

Notes

Notes

Notes

Notes